# ANATOMY OF THE NEW SCOTLAND

*BT Scotland* **BT**

# Anatomy of the
# New Scotland

## Power, Influence and Change

## Gerry Hassan & Chris Warhurst

MAINSTREAM
PUBLISHING

EDINBURGH AND LONDON

Copyright © the contributors, 2002
All rights reserved
The moral rights of the authors have been asserted

First published in Great Britain in 2002 by
MAINSTREAM PUBLISHING (EDINBURGH) LTD
7 Albany Street
Edinburgh EH1 3UG

ISBN 1 84018 630 5

A catalogue record for this book is available from the British Library

Typeset in Caslon

Printed in Great Britain by
Creative Print and Design Wales

# CONTENTS

# FOREWORD

BT Scotland is the exclusive sponsor of *Anatomy of the New Scotland* and is proud to be associated with this important project.

The Scottish arm of the communications giant was established in June 1988 in anticipation of Scotland's first Parliament in 300 years, and it has quickly established itself as one of the most vibrant and dynamic organisations operating in the new Scotland.

Independent research shows BT Scotland's activities generate income of £387 million and support employment of almost 19,650 across Scotland.

The company is taking the lead in the delivery of a broadband Scotland, offering fixed-line ADSL to more than a third of the population and broadband delivered by satellite to more than 99 per cent of small businesses in rural areas.

BT Scotland is dedicated to the delivery of its digital vision, using technology to benefit business, health, education, government and the community. In the last financial year it invested more than £270 million in its Scottish networks – £500 every single minute – to turn e-aspirations into reality.

By building on its partnerships with the nation's businesses, enterprise companies and local authorities, the company is playing a critical role in the country's economic development and creating a more prosperous Scotland plc.

*Brendan Dick*
*General Manager, BT Scotland*

*The opinions expressed in this publication are those of individual contributors and not necessarily those of BT Scotland.*

# PREFACE

Scotland in 2002 is at a fascinating point in its history, with recent political, social and economic developments raising new questions and issues about the very nature of the country itself.

Scottish sensibilities continue to be influenced by the election victories of Labour in 1997 and 2001, which had significant and long-term implications for the shape of the UK. After decades of *ancien régime* conservatism, Labour's first term saw the UK embark upon a period of unprecedented constitutional activity, with not only Scots and Welsh devolution, but also power-sharing in Northern Ireland, regional governance in London, a Bill of Rights and proportional representation for the European Parliament. The second term has begun to see the government address the 'unfinished business' of English regionalism and reform of the House of Lords. In Scotland, we are now three years into the first term of the first democratic Scottish Parliament, and less than one year away from the second Scottish Parliamentary elections due to be held in 2003.

The constitutional question has absorbed the political class in Scotland for the last 30 years. But it has diverted us from asking two other important questions. Firstly, in terms of its people and the institutions that they have created and maintained, what sort of country is Scotland? Secondly, what sort of country do we want Scotland to become? Since the establishment of the Scottish Parliament, there has been much debate about the relationships between the new devolved institutions of Scotland – the Parliament, the Executive and commitees – and the wider lines of communication between them and Westminster, and wider Scottish society. Those involved have hailed the changes as the beginning of a transition to a 'smart, successful Scotland'. Other commentators suggest that the changes represent little more than a tinkering with the (mis-)management of the country's continuing economic decline, and demand more radical initiatives. On the evidence so far, it seems that continuity is more prevalent than change. The debate, however, has raised some important issues that will effect Scotland's future, for example: the lamentable economic growth rate; the low business birth rate; the migration of better qualified young people out of Scotland; the persistent poverty, ill-health and social exclusion; and the lack of 'can do' attitude amongst Scots more content to see others, namely government and public agencies, take responsibility. These issues need to be addressed. As do a number of other, very important issues that have emerged. Since the Parliament was established, a number of popular and sometimes bitter debates have broken out within Scotland about the country's revealed latent sectarianism, homophobia and racism. A country that marked and prided itself on its social democracy, and was beginning to be hailed as a progressive role model, was startled by its darker self.

Despite the hopes and expectations arising from devolution, there is, therefore, much that is not right about Scotland. However, we are not offering a counsel of despair and defeatism. There are positive signs. We now know the power and influence of the forces of conservatism entrenched in Scottish civil society, Labour and the SNP, and this knowledge should be used by radicals and progressives as they strive for change. Also, compared to the 1980s and early 1990s when a very monocultural Scots identity existed in opposition to Thatcherism, we are now beginning to think and articulate a more diverse, pluralist sense of Scottishness. Both of these points – recognising the power of conservative Scotland and the extent of prejudice and bigotry in Scotland – suggest that the country needs to, and is, rethinking itself.

It is less than five years from the 300th anniversary of the Treaty of Union. By 2007, will these developments have inspired Blairite New Labourites (or perhaps Brownite post-New Labourites by then) to feel confident enough in their new settlement to celebrate the new Union that they are creating, no matter how half-hearted and half-misunderstood, or will they do what they did on the 200th anniversary of the Union of Great Britain and Ireland in 2001, and let it pass without a whimper? By then we will have more conclusive answers to the age-old questions about Scotland's place in the Union, and Scotland's place within Europe and the world beyond. By 2007 we will know whether we have shifted, in James Mitchell's words, from a unitary state (which the United Kingdom has never been except in the mindset of Westminster politicians and Whitehall mandarins) to a Union state, which reflects the diversity and pluralism of the people of these isles and their different arrangements.

Over the last few years we have attempted to contribute to the Scottish debate through various books and publications. *A Different Future: A Modernisers' Guide to Scotland* (Hassan and Warhurst, 1999) was published in the shadow of the first Scottish Parliament elections and described by Iain Macwhirter as 'the most significant [political] book since *The Red Paper on Scotland* was published in 1975'. It brought together 30 essays addressing the need for a progressive policy agenda centted on the Parliament, and included contributions from politicians, commentators, academics, policy wonks and practitioners across Scottish life. Amongst its contributors were two up and coming young ministers in the Scottish Executive – Jack McConnell and Wendy Alexander – who have since experienced very different fates.

The next project – *The New Scottish Politics* (2000) – addressed the new political terrain and environment of the Scottish Parliament one year into devolution, examining the emergent political system and culture, the new institutions, relations with wider society, and issues of identity and territoriality. Our next book, *Tomorrow's Scotland* (2002a) attempted to address the extent to which devolution had and had not changed Scotland, and the possible prospects for the future, addressing the evolving landscape: its political parties, institutions, policy and identities.

This new project – *Anatomy of the New Scotland* – which is unarguably our most far-reaching publication yet, attempts to map out a comprehensive understanding of how Scotland works, to identify power and influence across every area of Scottish life, to locate the main institutions and individuals, the contours of inclusion and exclusion – the insiders and outsiders who make contemporary Scotland work.

There have been two previous books that have carried the title 'Anatomy of Scotland', one published by James McMillan in 1969 and the other edited by Magnus Linklater and Robin Denniston in 1992. McMillan's *Anatomy of Scotland* was, according to its dust jacket, 'the biography of a country', examining 'its industry, commerce, politics, its big men, its little men, its fighting men, its sportsmen, its church men' (McMillan, 1969). Written in the aftermath of Winnie Ewing's sensational by-election victory at Hamilton in 1967, the book, while not a strict Anatomy in the Anthony Sampson sense, acutely captures a sense of a Scotland on the cusp of change, of the dying old Unionist Scotland of certainty, place and deference to the old institutions, ideas and identities, which was still hesitant and nervous of what change might involve.

Twenty years later, Linklater and Denniston produced *Anatomy of Scotland*, bringing together 11 writers to analyse some of the key areas of Scottish life. Until now, this book was the nearest to a Sampsonesque account of power and influence in Scotland, but it was hamstrung by two things. Firstly, its timing: it was published in the immediate wake of the 1992 election, which nearly everyone had expected the Tories to lose, after which Scottish constitutional change would have been imminent. Secondly, Linklater in the Foreword declared: 'It would . . . be very hard to talk about a Scottish establishment [or] . . . the notion of clubland' (1992: xiv) – not exactly the right tone for a critical and trenchant analysis of those who have power and influence.

The first Anatomy caught Scotland on the threshold of the long, painful, often nervous, 30-year debate and process of change, which eventually culminated in the establishment of a Scottish Parliament in 1999; the second Anatomy illustrated a Scotland that, for all its civic consensus and the enthusiasm of the blethering classes opinion, was still in many places hesitant and unsure of embarking on far-reaching constitutional and political change, and which in some quarters – albeit a minority – still felt some allegiance towards the old Unionist system. This book comes at a very different time in Scotland's history and politics; a time when we have started to build a new political settlement and society and, having embarked on the change, are unsure of its final destination.

We hope that readers, commentators and any interested parties wandering through this book will feel we have done justice to the Scotland of this historic moment. In devising the book, we have tried, as much as we can, to reflect the balance between issues such as politics, public services and professions and the economy – the core Anthony Sampson issues – and areas such as the media, culture, other identities and new Scots issues. We hope we have reached an appropriate balance – with, for example, analysis of the new political classes, local government and the civil service sitting next to chapters on the Gaels, gender and the gay community in Scotland.

Finally, we would like to thank the numerous people who have made this book possible and without whose enthusiasm and support our original idea could not have been brought to fruition. We would like to thank in particular Bill Campbell at Mainstream Publishing, who showed enthusiasm and understanding of this project from the outset, and Ailsa Bathgate, Kirsteen Wright and Graeme Blaikie, for their patience and professionalism. We would also like to take this opportunity to thank all of our contributors who rose to the daunting challenges, questions, enquiries and deadlines we asked of them to make the book what it is. We are also very grateful to BT Scotland for their sponsorship of this project.

Numerous other people have given of their valuable time and expertise, and it would be impossible to do justice to everyone to whom we are very grateful, but if we can mention just a few: Andrew Jaspan, Douglas Fraser, Alan Taylor, Sandy Ross, Tony Spence, Denis Robertson Sullivan, Rosie Ilett, Alan Paterson, Nigel Smith, Gordon Guthrie, Tom Nairn, Douglas Chalmers, Richard Parry, Ronald McQuaid, Kevin Kane, Carol Craig, Linda Hill and Susan McPhee. To all these and many more, our deepest and sincerest thanks.

We hope that you enjoy what we have brought together between these covers, and are always happy to hear the comments, suggestions and opinions of readers.

*Gerry Hassan*
*Chris Warhurst*
*May 2002*

# 1

# ANATOMY OF THE NEW SCOTLAND: POWER, INFLUENCE AND CHANGE

## Gerry Hassan

... the new politicians [in the Scottish Parliament] will have to contend
with another part of Scotland's hidden sub-strata that devolution will
expose to daylight. This is the Scottish establishment elite which has
quietly got on with running the country while the politicians have ranted
and raved. (Peter Jones 1997: 51)

*Scottish est
elite*

It seems to me that you are bound to assume that a self-governing
Scotland is going to be immediately morally better, and I don't see it
unless there has also been a revolution. I can't see how the people who are
likely to govern Scotland under any democratic system are going to be
any different from the undoubted Scots who are in positions of local
power. (Naomi Mitchison, 23 April 1953, quoted in Harvie 1977: 283)

## INTRODUCTION

In the last century, two dominant perspectives about how to change Scotland
existed: one emphasising the primacy of economic and social policy articulated
in the labour and trade union movements, the other stressing the
constitutional question and independence, advanced by the SNP. What has
often been ignored is the degree of convergence between the two positions on
the desired ends (for a more equal, inclusive society), with disagreement
primarily on means (the politics of class versus independence). Both
perspectives have also left unexamined some of the fundamental questions
about Scottish society: who holds power, what are the key elites and
institutions, and what kinds of change can and will happen? Peter Jones
addresses prevailing fears that devolution will not change the fundamentals of

power in Scotland, whereas Naomi Mitchison questions whether even the more far-reaching independence would actually change much unless it was accompanied by wider economic and social change.

## THE ESTABLISHMENT

The phrase 'the Establishment' was first given modern meaning in an essay by the irascible A.J.P Taylor in the *New Statesman* in 1953, examining William Cobbett's notion of 'the thing'. Taylor commented:

> The Victorians spoke of the classes and the masses; and we still understand exactly what they meant. The Establishment talks with its own branded accents, eats different meals at different times; has its privileged system of education; its own religion, even, to a larger extent, its own form of football. Nowhere else in Europe can you discover a man's social position by exchanging a few words or breaking bread with him. The Establishment is enlightened, tolerant, even well meaning. It has never been exclusive, rather drawing in recruits from outside, as soon as they are ready to conform to its standards and become respectable. (Quoted in Paxman 1990: 9)

Two years later, Henry Fairlie in *The Spectator* popularised the term in the aftermath of the defection of Guy Burgess and Donald Maclean to the Soviet Union. Fairlie defined the Establishment as 'not only the centres of official power – but rather the whole matrix of official and social relations within which power is exercised' (Quoted in Paxman 1990: 10; see also Thomas 1959). Taylor later regretted using the term and viewed that he should have used Cobbett's 'the Thing' which more fully caught 'the complacency, the incompetence and the selfishness' of those who ran things (Paxman 1990: 337).

Do we have a Scottish Establishment? Anthony Sampson described the Establishment's characteristics as 'not so much in the centre of a solar system, as in a cluster of interlocking circles . . . they are not a single Establishment but a ring of Establishments' (Sampson 1962: 624; 1982). Some do not think a Scottish Establishment(s) exists: 'Scotland is a small country', according to Magnus Linklater, shaped by 'some familiar figures. Their lines of influence cross and criss-cross, and they are represented at many different levels in Scottish life.' However, it would 'be very hard to talk about a Scottish Establishment' (Linklater 1992: xiv). A decade later, reflecting on the experience of being chairman of the Scottish Arts Council, he commented: 'You don't suddenly get absorbed into a mythical establishment. People don't come and give you a strange shake of the hand and welcome you in as soon as you start at a quango' (*Sunday Times*, 1 April 2001).

*Establishment!*

Alf Young observed that the idea of 'village Scotland' is one of the 'myths' of modern Scotland:

> Scotland is a village where everyone who is anyone knows everyone else who matters. In other words, Scotland possesses a tightly knit and supremely well-networked establishment or elite, where all the key players are on first-name terms . . . (Young 2002: 154).

*interconnect
-ing
relations*

Young's vision of a cluster of 'villages' is similar to Sampson's 'interlocking circles', which, in Young's words, 'consists of a whole series of smaller aspirant elites – in politics, business, the professions, the arts, academia, the media, the public realm, the social economy – that overlap to a greater or lesser extent but seldom coincide' (Young 2002: 155).

Richard Parry categorises the leadership of the non-elected Scottish government classes as including the heads of Scottish Executive departments, local authority chief executives, heads of major public agencies, university principals, religious leaders, judges, chief constables, heads of Scottish-based clearing banks and other financial institutions (Parry 2002: 143-4). Particularly important are what Parry calls 'the interstitial figures' such as Sir Angus Grossart and the West of Scotland engineering-based leadership personified by people such as Iain Robertson, and who are now being displaced by the leading figures of the Edinburgh-based financial institutions.

## LIVING THE HIGH LIFE

At the start of the twentieth century, Scotland's elites stood at the apex of Scottish, British and international elites; they were both distinctly Scottish, based on Scottish-owned industry, and reflected the diversity of the country, with regional centres of capital in Glasgow, Edinburgh, Dundee and Aberdeen. Post-1945 saw, in the words of Michael Fry, 'the decline of the Scottish capitalist class, from the self-made local businessmen, to the dynasties of the Clyde' (Fry 1987: 193). In the 1940s, public ownership of coal, railways and steel saw Scottish companies taken into British state-owned structures, while 40 years later, privatisation of Britoil, electricity and ports further opened the Scottish economy to English and overseas investment.

*History*

Post-war Scotland became more government-controlled, with a centralist mindset and planning – John P. Mackintosh called this 'the non-democratic elite' of corporate interests and civil servants who emerged to run Scotland (Drucker 1982). This was, in Moore and Booth's analysis, a 'close-knit community where a high level of individual contact is possible' (Moore and Booth 1989: 29), where institutional Scotland developed a 'negotiated order' in between a fully fledged corporatist state and free-market capitalism (ibid.: 50); this 'negotiated order' sat within the 'negotiated autonomy' of Scotland in the Union (Paterson 1994).

The Scots image of egalitarianism has been shaped in contradistinction to perceptions of English hierarchy and inequalities – 'the democratic intellect' tradition in education has been the nearest the Scots have got to a version of 'the American dream' examined by Jane W. Denholm and Deirdre Macleod later in the book. However, this image of inclusiveness sat beside a sense of order, respect and knowing one's place that has restricted dynamism in society. The writer H.J. Hanham, writing about Scotland over 30 years ago, caught this feeling:

> To the outsider, Scotland, with its aristocracy still largely in being and the gracious living of its big town houses . . . with the workers tucked away in their tenements out of sight, often seems much more of a traditional society than does that of England. It is the sense of social hierarchy that the outsider notices, not the mature democracy. (Hanham 1969: 26-7)

Scots culture has also been shaped by a more working-class ethos and culture than England. Paterson et al. conclude: 'People in Scotland are more likely to think of themselves as working class despite their class of origin and own social class' (2001: 109). In fact, 71 per cent of Scots think of themselves as working class versus 59 per cent in England and Wales; the difference is entirely due to upwardly mobile working-class people moving into the middle class thinking of themselves as working class in bigger proportions: 80 per cent in Scotland compared to 65 per cent in England and Wales.

Social mobility in Scotland has not been that different from England (McCrone 1996), and in recent years there has been evidence that UK social mobility has diminished as middle-class downward mobility has seized up (Adonis and Pollard 1997). Middle-class families can now increase the chances of their sons and daughters remaining in the middle class, irrespective of their skills and talents (*The Economist*, 6 April 2002). There is no sign that Scotland is any different in this respect. And there is no sign of an end to social inequalities through greater meritocracy: a word constantly misused and misunderstood by our political class (Young 1958).

## THE SCOTTISH STATE

As a 'stateless nation', post-war Scotland has paradoxically had a large, expanding state with a bigger share of middle-class professional employment than the rest of the UK. Scottish public service was seen as articulating Scots traditions of citizenship and community and, during the Thatcher era, of distinctiveness and opposition to a right-wing minority agenda.

Post-1997, with the return of Labour at Westminster and since devolution, new conflicts have arisen about the public sector, including the role of private sector finance in the public sector, the attitude of trade unions, a culture of conservatism, and the need for appropriate pay levels to attract and retain staff. Much of the Scottish debate post-1997 has viewed any attempts at modernising the public sector as an attack on Scottish sensibilities; the debate on the McCrone deal, whereby teachers were offered a 21.5 per cent pay deal over three years, showed the power of vested interests. However, by the time train drivers held strikes in 2002 for a 22 per cent pay increase, even Scottish patience was beginning to weaken. This coincided with MSPs voting themselves a 13.5 per cent pay rise and a wider debate about public sector pay remuneration. While the Prime Minister of the UK is paid £171,554 and Lord Irvine, Lord Chancellor, is the highest-paid government minister on pay of £187,685, Robert Crawford, chief executive of Scottish Enterprise, is the highest-paid quangocrat in the UK, earning £201,749.32 (see Table 1).

There are also concerns about the boundaries between the quango state and the Labour Party. A recent survey showed that 32 out of 141 (23 per cent) health board members are declared Labour activists, compared to 5 Lib Dems, 4 SNP and 1 Tory (*The Scotsman*, 23 May 2002). Similar allegations have been made about independent assessors to monitor quango appointments, half of whom are Labour Party members. Against this backdrop, Alex Neil put forward his Public Appointments (Parliamentary Approval) (Scotland) Bill which was defeated because it would 'politicise' the process and, more accurately, reveal some of the networks of civic Scotland.

**Table 1: Scottish public sector pay levels**

| | |
|---|---|
| Newly Qualified Nurse | £16,000 |
| Police Officer | £17,000 |
| Teacher (Grade Two) | £18,527 |
| ScotRail train driver | £23,000 |
| MSP | £48,228 |
| MP | £55,118 |
| General Practitioner | £56,000 |
| Holyrood Minister | £83,262 |
| First Minister | £116,063 |
| Chief Executive, Scottish Enterprise | £201,749.32 |

Source: *The Herald*, 22 March 2002; *The Scotsman*, 17 April 2002

In Scotland in April 1997 there were 42,037 permanent full-time equivalent (FTE) civil service posts in government departments and a further 3,753 industrial staff – a total of 45,790. The Scottish Office then employed 4,923 FTE civil servants (11 per cent of Scots-based civil servants), while 72 per cent of civil servants were employed in UK-wide services or delivered UK services in Scotland, such as social security (9,374), the Inland Revenue (5,689) and the Ministry of Defence (9,624) (McQuaid 2000). Data from the Cabinet Office

**Table 2:** Non-Departmental Public Bodies employing more than 20 people

| NDPB | Edinburgh | Glasgow | Aberdeen | Dundee | Stirling | Inverness | | Total |
|---|---|---|---|---|---|---|---|---|
| **Executive NDPBs** | | | | | | | | |
| Community Learning Scotland (for Scotland) | 24 | | | | | | 52 | 31 |
| Crofters Commission | | | | | | 62 | | 62 |
| Hannah Research Institute | | | | | | | | 129 |
| Highland and Island Enterprise | | | | | | 385 | | 654 |
| Learning & Teaching Scotland | | 141 | | 50 | | | | 191 |
| Macaulay Land Use Research Institute | | | 212 | | | | | 235 |
| Moredun Research Institute | 138 | | | | | | | 138 |
| National Galleries of Scotland | 270 | | | | | | | 270 |
| National Library of Scotland | 278 | | | | | | | 278 |
| National Museums of Scotland | 388 | 17 | | | | | | 430 |
| Rowett Research Institute | | | 237 | | | | | 237 |
| Royal Botanic Gardens | 210 | | | | | | | 210 |
| Royal Commission on the Ancient and Historic Monuments of Scotland | 97 | | | | | | | 97 |
| Scottish Arts Council | 92 | | | | | | | 92 |
| Scottish Children's Reporter Administration | 34 | 78 | 25 | 15 | 56 | 15 | | 419 |
| Scottish Crop Research Institute | 18 | | 6 | 342 | | | | 369 |
| Scottish Enterprise | 128 | 766 | 75 | | 67 | | | 1,640 |
| Scottish Environment Protection Agency | 144 | 25 | 85 | 74 | 210 | | | 939 |
| Scottish Funding Council for Further and Higher Education | 120 | | | | | | | 120 |
| Scottish Further Education Unit | | | | | 43 | | | 43 |
| Scottish Homes | 32 | 17 | | | | 1 | | 66 |
| Scottish Legal Aid Board | 330 | | | | | | | 330 |
| Scottish National Heritage | 247 | 385 | 41 | | 18 | 51 | | 842 |
| Scottish Qualifications Authority | 227 | | | | | | | 612 |
| Scottish Screen | | 44 | | | | | | 45 |
| Sportscotland | 150 | | | | | | | 175 |
| Visitscotland | 145 | | | | | 66 | | 212 |
| **Totals** | 3,072 | 1,473 | 681 | 481 | 394 | 580 | | 8,866 |
| Scottish Water | 657 | 973 | 240 | 359 | 175 | 269 | | |
| Water Industry Commissioner for Scotland | | | | | 24 | | | |
| Water Total | | | | | | | | 5,293 |
| Overall Total | 3,729 | 2,446 | 921 | 840 | 593 | 849 | | 14,159 |

*Source: All figure are taken from each organisation's Human Resources or Personnel Departments, 6–17 May 2002; list of NDPBs provided by SPICE, April 2002. Water industry figure have been listed separately to allow comparison with 1996 figures.*

shows the uneven distribution in civil service employment, with a Scottish average of 85 FTEs per 10,000 residents; Edinburgh led Glasgow by 9,589 to 9,586, which on the basis of jobs per 10,000 people gave it a lead of 229 to 145 FTE posts, while Aberdeen had 72 and Dundee 53. Figures four years later – for 1 April 2001 – showed that Edinburgh had increased its advantage over Glasgow, with 10,879 to 9,321: 240 per 10,000 people to 153.

Post-devolution in April 2000 the Scottish Executive employed 11,180 people on a headcount basis, comprising 3,940 in the central Scottish Executive staff, as well as a further 2,900 staff in various agencies who were previously independent of the old Scottish Office – the Crown Office and Procurator Fiscal, General Register Office, National Archive for Scotland and Registers of Scotland.

In 2002, non-departmental public bodies (NDPBs) or quangos employed 8,866 people on a headcount excluding the water industry, 14,159 including   CS
water (see Table 2). The distribution of these figures show a pro-Edinburgh bias: 3,072 of the first group are employed in Edinburgh (35 per cent); Glasgow had 1,473 (17 per cent), Aberdeen 681 (8 per cent), Dundee 481 (5 per cent), Stirling 394 (4 per cent) and Inverness 580 (7 per cent). The concentration on Edinburgh (and to a lesser extent, as a regional centre, Inverness) can be seen in an analysis of the figures by 10,000 residents – Edinburgh has 68 quango posts per 10,000 residents (excluding water), up from 59 in 1996; Glasgow has a mere 24 posts with no change from 1996. This clearly illustrates that Edinburgh has gained in both absolute and relative terms. Aberdeen has 32 posts (35 in 1996), Dundee 34 (33), Stirling 46 (31), while Inverness has gained markedly from 51 to 89 (see Table 3; on 1996 figures, McQuaid 1999).

**Table 3: Quango employment per 10,000 population, 1996 and 2002**

|  | Non-departmental public bodies employment per 10,000 residents (excluding water industry) | | Non-departmental public bodies employment per 10,000 residents (including water industry) | |
|---|---|---|---|---|
|  | 1996 | 2002 | 1996 | 2002 |
| Edinburgh | 59 | 68 | 75 | 82 |
| Glasgow | 24 | 24 | 45 | 40 |
| Aberdeen | 35 | 32 | 54 | 44 |
| Dundee | 33 | 34 | 58 | 59 |
| Stirling | 31 | 46 | 58 | 70 |
| Inverness | 51 | 89 | 90 | 130 |
| Scotland | 16 | 17 | 29 | 26 |

*City population: 1996 and 2000 estimates, 1996 figures from McQuaid 1999.*

There are also 5,293 water authority jobs, and if they are added Edinburgh's dominance remains, as does Inverness's impressive position, with figures per 10,000 residents of Edinburgh 82, Glasgow 40, Aberdeen 44, Dundee 59, Stirling 70 and Inverness 130. The number of public agency posts in the six cities is dramatically above the Scottish average of 17 per 10,000 without water posts and 26 including them. The figures also underline Glasgow's poor record in attracting public agencies. On both figures it falls behind every other city in Scotland: a lamentable record for Scotland's first city in size and population.

## THE EXTENDED STATE AND THE ROLE OF BUSINESS AND TRADE UNIONS

Scotland is one of the most over-represented places in the Western world for business organisations: the Confederation of British Industry (CBI Scotland), Institute of Directors, Scottish Council for Development and Industry (SCDI), Scottish Chambers of Commerce, Scottish Financial Enterprise and Federation of Small Businesses all compete for members and influence. The first five have in recent years tried to increase their lobbying weight by organising a 'committee of the big five'. This overrepresentation is a paradox on a number of levels. First, these 'representative' bodies are not representative of Scottish businesses in an economy of over 200,000 businesses, when the CBI has approximately 400 'real' members, SCDI 1,000 and falling and Scottish Chambers, 8,000. Second, Scotland is not that successful at entrepreneurial activity, being ranked in the lowest international rankings in a Global Entrepreneurship Monitor (GEM) study (Galloway and Levie, 2002). Third, Scottish businesses' paucity of ambition is underlined by their satisfaction with the limited politics of devolution: they are impressed by the processes of access and consultation and the minimalist agenda of the Scottish Executive and Parliament.

The trade union movement has significantly declined in numbers in the last 20 years in Scotland. The STUC's membership peaked at 1,090,839 in 1980 and declined to 800,000 two decades later (Aitken 1997: 260). Its influence in the corridors of power waned with the arrival of the Thatcher government in 1979, but at the same time its status as a vehicle for articulating a national consensus grew over industrial closures and the constitutional question. Post-devolution, the STUC's public profile has diminished, but its private influence and lobbying role has increased. However, the changing representation of trade unions on health and enterprise boards has not been transformed in the positive since devolution. Driven off various bodies by Thatcher and her business friends, post-1999, trade unions have not been welcomed back under devolution, but instead have become one of the victims of the new Nolan regime and the need for greater transparency; whether the recent Memorandum of Understanding between the Scottish Executive and STUC signed by Jack McConnell develops a new relationship remains to be seen.

# A LONG REVOLUTION?

Has power shifted in Scotland since the establishment of the Parliament? Do people feel they have finally found a voice, and have more sense of power and influence? Politically this is a complex picture: in the media and the public eye, the Scottish Parliament has become Scottish politics, yet Westminster still controls the purse-strings, spends significant amounts in Scotland, and legislates as often as the Scottish Parliament in devolved areas; after reserved areas are added, it is still the primary legislative body for Scotland (Hassan and Warhurst 2002b). Polls tell us that immediately after the establishment of the Parliament people thought it the most powerful body in Scotland; since then the position has dramatically changed, with sizeable majorities believing Westminster more powerful (66:13), and equally convincing majorities (72:13) wanting the Scottish Parliament to be the most influential body (Surridge 2002: 140). In short, while formal powers were transferred from Westminster to Holyrood on 1 July 1999, real powers have yet to move northwards. The old networks of power and influence based on the Home Civil Service still carry enormous weight, a point recently underlined by Brian Wilson's unprecedented attack on the civil service north and south of the border (while still a Westminster minister), alleging that they block change by only proceeding 'at exactly the pace that the system thinks fit – based on its own priorities, bureaucracies and timescales' (*The Scotsman*, 22 May 2002).

One of the conundrums of devolution so far has been that democratic accountability and transparency has not been increased – the shift from narrow political processes of devolution to the wider goal of greater self-government has not yet occurred. At this moment in these early and crucial years, we have shifted from one kind of 'democratic deficit' to another kind of 'democratic deficit', albeit, after the Tory years, one that is more subtle but also harder to detect in most public debate.

The politics of the Labour state have also been magnified by devolution, as Iain Macwhirter maps in his analysis of the 'Officegate' scandal and fall of Henry McLeish as First Minister. In March 2001, one in three taskforces set up in the UK since 1997 were in Scotland (*The Scotsman*, 6 March 2001) and there has been, for all the rhetoric from various ministers, no 'bonfire of the quangos'. In February 2002, after an investigation by Douglas Sinclair, chief executive of Fife Council, it was revealed that one in three people of working age in Fife worked for Fife Council and one in three Fife councillors had a relative working for the council. The report talked of problems of 'cross-over' between the Labour Party, voluntary sector and council employees: a picture that could be replicated across town halls up and down Labour Scotland. Sinclair's report talked of a 'blurring and overlap between politics and friendships creating the perception – however justified or not – that not all decisions were as transparent or as objective as they should have been'.

Parts of Scotland have changed beyond recognition in the last few years. The rise of Edinburgh – economically, culturally, politically – has coincided with the establishment of the Parliament (McQuaid 2000); Edinburgh now lives and breathes as a capital city once again. It is enjoying full employment, labour shortages in several sectors, a massive property boom and population growth. Glasgow, on the other hand, faces a more mixed picture: it has experienced impressive growth in its retail sector in the city centre, but has significant unemployment levels and areas of deprivation which are disconnected to the good things happening. Neither has the city's long-term population decline been reversed, with middle-class flight outside the city boundaries one of the main drivers.

One of the differences between Edinburgh and Glasgow is the administrative boundaries and arrangements. In Edinburgh, a number of these correspond with city boundaries, or reflect the old Lothian Region and act as an aid, not a barrier, to success. In Glasgow, post-Strathclyde, a plethora of boundaries and different arrangements apply that do not make for good, effective governance (Bailey, Turok and Docherty 1999). And this relates to the cities' political cultures: as Edinburgh has enjoyed good times, its Labour-run Council has reflected the politics and priorities of the city, working in partnership with various agencies and encouraging an open, outward vision of the city. Glasgow, on the other hand, could not have been more different, post-1999, battening down the hatches under the combative leadership of Charlie Gordon. While engaging in partnership in plans for the Clyde and the housing stock transfer, this has been a politics of reluctant change and fighting last-ditch bunker battles (such as leaving COSLA). A longer-term trend here is a decline in the quality of councillors that has been accelerated by the Scottish Parliament, a trend which Edinburgh has been able to buck.

## OLD AND NEW ELITES

Old elites still have their place in the new Scotland, such as the New Club in Edinburgh. A prestigious private members' club established in 1787, with a prime location in Princes Street, an inconspicuous doorway passers-by will not notice and a swimming-pool on the roof, it has over the years been one of the main congregating spots for many of Edinburgh's finest movers and shakers: judges, senior legal figures, civil servants, industrialists, arts, literary and cultural figures and old boys (but no girls above a certain floor!) from Edinburgh's public schools. However, change is in the air even in this rarefied sanctum of old Scotland, as club culture slowly declines and up-and-coming people find new places and ways of networking. This is graphically illustrated by the recent closure of the Caledonian Club in Edinburgh. Other institutions that remain part of the old middle-class establishment map of Scotland include the

Honourable Society of Edinburgh Golfers at Muirfield Golf Club, the oldest established golf club in the world; the Scottish Rugby Union, who are also the owners of Murrayfield; and the Royal and Ancient Golf Club, St Andrews, which is the ruling body of world golf outside Canada and the US. Glasgow's most prestigious clubs include the Western Club, the alternative-minded Glasgow Art Club and the ostentatious Stefan King-owned Corinthian; they do not have the same exclusivity and mystique as their Edinburgh counterparts.

New elites are emerging, reflecting the changing nature of society, business and politics. Some of these are what George Walden has called 'anti-elite elites' or 'egalitarian elites', which invoke 'the people's name, while preserving the lion's share of the power' (Walden 2000: 43; see also Brooks 2000). These new elites are sometimes found celebrating celebrity narcissism and dumbed-down media culture, where 'access is open to all who believe in, or are willing to pay lip service to, the populist creed'. (Walden 2000: 62)

However, another variant of the new elite has seen politicians, business interests, corporate advisers and media develop into a powerful network which has become more powerful as the old traditional political hierarchies of party weaken; this, called by Colin Crouch 'post-democracy', reflects the historical fact that the immediate post-war period of 1945–70 may have witnessed the high point of capitalist democracy and that since then the social forces which created that moment have been in retreat (Crouch 2000).

One of the most significant players in this new elite in Scotland is the media company Wark Clements, established in 1990 by husband and wife Alan Clements and Kirsty Wark. Wark, a regular presenter of the BBC's *Newsnight*, is one of the most talented broadcasters in the UK. A personal friend of the late First Minister Donald Dewar, she was one of the five members of the Scottish Office-appointed Holyrood panel that chose Enric Miralles' design for the Scottish Parliament, a plan that has subsequently burgeoned from an original £50 million cost to a figure in the region of £300 million. This saga has had unintended benefits, though, for Wark Clements, who won the contract to make the official film on the construction of the Holyrood Parliament building. Because of delays, they have had to make a longer series and seek extra injections of public cash from the BBC and Scottish Arts Council: a typical example of the smallness of 'village Scotland'.

Wark Clements also hold what are, amongst movers and shakers, some of the most well-known dinner party gatherings at their home in the West End of Glasgow. Other private individuals also do this, including Angus Grossart, the banker, and Michael Shea, previously Press Secretary to the Queen, who holds prestigious discussions at Ramsay Gardens under the auspices of the Scottish Council Foundation. Numerous corporate dinner circuits exist as well. Wark Clements gatherings are not ordinary or informal parties. The evenings are opened by Alan Clements and moderated by Kirsty Wark, who keeps the discussion focused on the agreed topic of the evening. Participants are always carefully chosen to reflect the subject, whether it be transforming Scotland's economy or the future of creative industries, and attendees at recent gatherings have included Jack McConnell, Wendy Alexander (when Enterprise and Lifelong Learning Minister), John Boyle and James Boyle (both on the board of Wark Clements), Stuart Cosgrove, Robert Crawford (chief executive of Scottish Enterprise), Fred Goodwin of the Royal Bank of Scotland, various Scottish Enterprise quangocrats and numerous entrepreneurs and venture capitalists.

This has been called 'the dinner-table leadership' of Scotland, whereby obviously willing participants eat and chat for Scotland every night of the week, often meeting the same people with the only variant being the food, sponsors and seating arrangements. All of the business organisations discussed earlier hold private dinners and gatherings, too, as do the various trade and professional bodies, big companies such as BT Scotland and ScottishPower, finance houses and public agencies.

Given the smallness of 'village Scotland' and the number of people involved in the blethering classes, what happens in these circuits is threefold. First, they encourage a closing, rather than an opening of debate, whereby the only opinions circulated and listened to are those of the prevailing orthodoxies and where radical, dissenting opinions are listened to politely but marginalised, particularly after a fine three-course meal and some good whisky. Second, given the small numbers of actual decision-makers and pressures on their time, what happens at these sorts of gatherings, particularly the more 'public' ones, is that the real movers and shakers are significantly outnumbered by corporate and public affairs hangers-on; this is a fate that has befallen the once prestigious SCDI Annual Forum, usually held at Gleneagles. Third, the banality and lack of substance of many of the discussions at these events would shock many a conspiracy theorist – but what they do contribute towards is the creation and maintenance of a 'Scottish consensus', underpinned by institutional opinions and elites, that is then taken forth into public discourse as the received wisdom of establishment Scotland.

In previous decades, certainly pre-1979, this 'Scottish consensus', as Alf Young has written, was articulated by the great and good in that wonderfully inclusive, distinctive and now quaint organisation, SCDI – but that is now but one player in a crowded marketplace of organisations competing for influence and space (Young 2002: 157-61). In one respect, we are spoilt for choice, dining-wise, but on another level, given each network is competing for some of the same members and a finite number of influencers, the choice is in reality restricted to who you want to dine under the banner of, rather than the type of conversation.

# A DEMOCRATIC, ENTERPRISING SCOT?

Scottish debates in the last 50 years or more have offered a very limited prospect, politics and vision for a future Scotland. They have focused resolutely and pessimistically on the slow, tidy management of economic decline. In so doing, they have encouraged all the 'myths' of Scottish radicalism and romanticism, a culture which has been inward-looking, risk-averting, and about passivity and paternalism. A significant section of Scotland centred on the Scottish political classes and the Labour Party has gained power and importance as a result of this – and one does not need to swallow the New Right 1980s 'dependency culture' critique of Scotland to recognise there is some truth in it. For all the benign intent and well meaning of devolution, the Executive and Parliament, and the thousands of government papers, this is still the prevailing mindset of official Scotland.

Hanham, in his acute portrait of Scotland, caught this mindset, writing at the end of the 1960s:

> The ordinary Scot since the 1930s has simply sat back and waited until the good things from the south have at last reached Scotland – new shops, new social security benefits, new industries, new towns. There has been a clamour when they have not come soon enough to please him. But there has been little disposition to do anything positive to help . . .
> (Hanham 1969: 47)

We are not perhaps as passive and compliant as then, but we are still far too much like this. This *Anatomy of the New Scotland*, if it captures any kind of snapshot about contemporary Scotland, draws a picture of the contest between the establishment forces of cautious, conservative Scotland and those favouring a more radical, democratic path. It is not and never has been an equal struggle: the former has the political parties, civil service, business and most of civic Scotland on its side, but the latter has the visionaries, dreamers and innovators who will change Scotland.

The *Anatomy of the New Scotland* is not a prescription for future change, it is about mapping the realities of power, influence and change in contemporary society. It illustrates the need to shift from a politics of management and incrementalism, to a politics defined by a more radical and democratic impetus which draws from earlier pre-socialist traditions (Tawney 1931). This would be more change-orientated, open to challenge, recognise the constant reinvention of the modern world and movement in elites, national and international, and understand the shift from an institutional-based power to a 'postmodern' one seen in the style of Clinton and Blair. We have to become less hidebound to 'the Scottish consensus' long after it has passed its sell-by date, whether it be the old version of state socialism or the newer version of the consensus articulated by our governing classes: knowledge economy fads and corporate conformity.

We have to develop a politics and culture which takes on the conservatives of the old left and Labour establishment and develops new ideas on public services, governance and communities which challenge the old producer/public sector agenda, but go beyond merely replacing it with a consumer/private driven one. The Scottish debate instead should look to more radical and distinct citizen-based models. At the same time, we have to recognise the anti-business, anti-entrepreneurial culture which is prevalent in large parts of Scotland, and which openly disparages success, energy and drive, and celebrates failure and resignation. And we also need to recognise that Scotland's culture of caution has not only been anti-entrepreneurial in the economic sense, but also in the social and civic sense, as Eleanor Shaw and Jonathan Levie argue in Chapter 16: it has been about keeping people in their place and stopping them doing things.

For this to change, as Lindsay Paterson documents in Chapter 5, the limited pluralism and incestuousness of civic Scotland has to be acknowledged – that narrow, 'official' version of civil society. To begin answering the dilemmas posed by Peter Jones and Naomi Mitchison at the outset of this chapter, we have to begin to tell a new story about who the Scots are, and develop a new narrative and vision about society and politics. This is something that small, successful countries the world over – such as Ireland, Denmark, Finland and many others – have undertaken and it involves moving from the first stage of constitutional reform – setting the institutions up – to the next stage, of developing a wider political agenda. This does not necessarily end in independence, but addresses first the kind of society we want and 'the vision thing', before examining whether we are best served by independence or by remaining a part of the UK. That is not the most important issue facing the future of Scotland. It is much more crucial for the people of Scotland to take back their country from the institutions who have run it in the name of the people for so long. It is time to start living and thinking a little dangerously.

# 2

# THE NEW SCOTTISH POLITICAL CLASSES

## *Iain Macwhirter*

The course of devolution has rarely been a smooth one these three long years, but the events of November 2001 were more than just political turbulence. Something died around that date – and it was not just Henry McLeish's political career. I suspect it was the loss of innocence, the extinction of the belief that devolution could overnight create a new politics of participatory democracy. The Scottish Executive was riven by the politics of Labour's municipal elites. It was the apotheosis of cronyism.

The McLeish episode was like an X-ray, which revealed the deep structures of the Scottish body politic, which are normally invisible to the naked eye. It exposed the Labour networks of mutual self-help which extend throughout the local state and into Holyrood itself. The people who occupy the Labour benches in the Scottish Parliament are often the same Labour trustees who used to call the shots in Labour's local authority bastions.

You began to realise that this was probably what political life was like in one of the more benign Warsaw Pact countries in the twentieth century. As in Eastern Europe, politics in large areas of Scotland takes place within the party rather than between parties in competition for power. In Scotland, as in Poland or the old East Germany, membership of the party is a precondition for personal advancement in most aspects of public life – an essential career accessory. Factionalism, rather than democracy, becomes the organising principle of politics.

We all hoped that the Scottish Parliament would be free of this kind of politics, but that was naive. However, the other great hope invested in devolution – that the Scottish Parliament would open up and reform the local state – has been realised. It may have been messy, but at least we all now see the nature and extent of the problem. And Holyrood can deliver the surest antidote, proportional representation. Even though the council cadres are massing against electoral reform, they will ultimately have to succumb to political reality.

# THE LABOUR STATE

Henry McLeish's Fife constituency office became a kind of metaphor for Scottish civic culture. The ludicrous nature of the scandal which brought down the second First Minister only made things worse. The so-called 'Officegate' affair did not involve any real corruption. Even now there is no evidence that Henry McLeish, or any of the other parties involved, actually pocketed money or even used public money illegally for campaigning purposes. What the scandal revealed was the extent to which that network which we have loosely called 'civil society' is in fact a dense coagulation of Labour politicians, their clients and apparatchiks (see Paterson 1999 and Chapter 5 of this book on civil society).

The 'Officegate' affair was all about a local charity run by the election agent of an MSP who happens to be married to the head of the social work department which pays for the charity. The sub-letting of Henry McLeish's constituency office was not in itself improper. However, it emerged that the office had been let to the Labour council of which he used to be leader and had among its tenants a prominent Labour-supporting law firm (Digby Brown) which had employed, among other up-and-coming politicians, the Labour MP Douglas Alexander and MSP (and former head of Donald Dewar's policy unit) Brian Fitzpatrick.

It did not amount to a row of beans as far as town hall corruption was concerned. There were no Poulsons pulling strings or T. Dan Smiths distributing bribes. There were not even any councillors handing out free trips. But the more the press analysed the personal networks that emerged from that office, the more sinister it all appeared. Everyone from the Chancellor, Gordon Brown, to the First Minister's wife was involved.

Henry finally resigned, not because he had fiddled his expenses, but because *The Herald* newspaper found that he had failed to mention the 'sixth sublet' – the old people's charity which had briefly rented his office space in the 1990s and which had involved his social worker wife Julie. As more layers of absurdity were heaped upon this tawdry affair, what became abundantly clear was what we all knew already – that Scotland is a small, small country. Not only the disgraced former First Minister's wife, but the wife of his successor, Jack McConnell, was also involved. The Sinclair report into the Third Age charity affair revealed that one Bridget McConnell had been involved in meetings of the management group of the organisation in the mid-1990s.

It was not so much Watergate as 'All the First Minister's Wives'. In the local state in Fife, everyone seemed to be in bed with each other – often literally. The bed was owned by the Scottish Labour Party. This broad Labour association of councils, quangos and apparatchiks is so extensive, so all-encompassing, that people in the network cannot see it. It is their universe. It was so much part of Henry McLeish's world that he never seemed to wonder what people might make of all the personal/political 'crossovers', as the Sinclair report put it, which

28

locked so many of the active personnel of local government into the same political party. It was just how things were done in Scotland.

However, he became painfully aware of the power of this network when he fell foul of it. Those who live by faction die by faction, and those who live by anonymous briefing die by anonymous briefings. Henry McLeish was killed twice over. His only actual impropriety was his failure to register his various rentals with the Westminster Fees Office. Not that the Fees Office was remotely interested, since it made a point of never asking MPs what they did with their expenses cash. The office accepted that the non-declaration was 'a simple mistake' and was quite happy to negotiate a sum to repay to bring the matter to a conclusion. The Fees Office told Elizabeth Filkin, the Standards Commissioner for Parliament, that there was no case to answer.

The failure to register, even when it became public, should never in itself have lost the First Minister his job. What happened was that the Labour cronyocracy abandoned him and forced McLeish out. The support system that functions automatically when most Labour politicians get into trouble – like the former Scottish Secretary John Reid did over his expenses – did not work for Henry. He had stepped beyond the pale and McLeish had no support network any more. He even remarked in an interview with *The Sun* that the reason he fell was not that he was corrupt but that he 'wasn't a Catholic, wasn't a Protestant and hadn't gone to Glasgow University and wasn't a member of the Lanarkshire Mafia' (*The Sun*, 7 March 2002). This was a neat encapsulation of the principal factions at work in the Scottish Labour party. The Lanarkshire Mafia is the hard school of politics that made people like John Reid, Helen Liddell and one Jack McConnell, while Glasgow University had produced a generation of Labour leaders who shaped Scottish politics, such as John Smith and Donald Dewar. That remark was the final straw for the party in Scotland and led to McLeish's humiliation at the Scottish Executive in March 2002, when they refused to endorse his candidature for the 2003 Scottish elections. However, McLeish's fate was sealed almost as soon as he took over as First Minister.

Upon his investiture in November 2000, after Donald Dewar's death, McLeish turned to his party in the Scottish Parliament and said, 'I won't let you down.' It was significant that he addressed this to his own party, rather than the nation as a whole. To McLeish at that stage the two were clearly synonymous. It was the way things were. But as soon as he entered Bute House he discovered the corrosive reality of Scottish politics. In office, he was not a Labour First Minister but the leader of a coalition with the Liberal Democrats, and was not even in charge of a majority of seats in the legislature. A natural conciliator and fixer, and former chairman of the Consultative Steering Group which set the ground rules for devolution, McLeish adapted to the new reality by taking up the policies which seemed to have majority support, like free personal care for the elderly. It was a strategy that made sense to his advisers. After all, the Parliament had to be seen to be doing something – those Scottish solutions to Scottish problems.

But the Labour Party was appalled. Ministers were outraged, spin-doctors discombobulated. The cause was not so much the policies themselves as McLeish's willingness to step outside the brotherhood and side with the enemy. The fact that he had no choice, that the First Minister was condemned to promote free elderly care because the majority of the Parliament – Tories, Lib Dems and SNP – had voted for it, didn't mollify his alienated comrades. It was just not on. The party were no' huvvin' it.

Within two months of taking office, McLeish found Labour ministers had started to brief against him. The First Minister had himself been notoriously incontinent in the company of journalists, so Labour ministers felt no compunction in rubbishing him behind his back. He was, I was told, unable to cope with the job, a pushover for the Lib Dems, an impulsive politician who adopted policies without thinking them through or costing them. His dismal, inarticulate delivery in the Parliament was a further embarrassment to Labour Scotland. Surely they could do better than this, many thought. But it was not his broken-backed English, his halting delivery or his malapropisms that did for him. By the autumn of 2001, McLeish was beyond redemption. The catalogue of offences included his suggestion that the Scottish Executive should be called a government. 'They can call themselves the White Heather Club if they want,' said a Labour Westminster minister, 'but they aren't the government.' And then McLeish seriously antagonised the Northern Ireland Secretary John Reid by describing him as a 'patronising bastard' within range of a live microphone the day after the 2001 general election.

The fact that McLeish had beaten off the SNP and delivered nearly all of the promises he had made when he became leader – free care, quango cuts, SQA – was irrelevant. The Labour tribe had turned against him. The message came loud and clear from Westminster: Henry had no friends.

When the end finally came, McLeish didn't know what hit him. His sin had been to seek to represent the interests of the coalition rather than the Labour Party, the Parliament rather than the Executive. The penalty was to be hung out to dry, to be eviscerated by anonymous briefings to the press, and to have his entrails hung on the rails outside Bute House for public ridicule by the *Daily Record*.

Systematically undermined by his Labour colleagues throughout the latter half of 2001, he also saw his intellect disparaged by Westminster MPs who dubbed him 'thick'. When the 'Officegate' affair broke, not one of his former colleagues at Westminster tried to sort things out. There is a standard procedure to be followed in such emergencies, known in the business as 'fire-fighting', whereby a group of MPs would get together and mount a defence for their stricken colleague in the media. It worked for John Reid and John Maxton when they got into difficulty with the Standards Commissioner Elizabeth Filkin (see her report in the Committee on Standards and Privileges 2000, which contains a forensic examination of the internal workings of Scottish Labour). It worked for Nigel Griffiths, the Edinburgh South MP, who was revealed to be paying himself from his Westminster expenses for an office he already owned and using the proceeds to benefit a trust fund for his sister. But it did not work for Henry. No senior Westminster politician tried to save him, nor spoke up for him, and neither did any in Scotland. The Fees Office, which helpfully issued communiqués 'exonerating' Griffiths, did nothing half as helpful for the First Minister. In Scotland, not one minister or MSP dared to speak out for McLeish, with the exception of the abrasive and often counter-productive Tom McCabe.

The First Minister was left twisting in a hostile media wind and eventually expired in November 2001. The sheer power of the Labour network was demonstrated by the fate of someone who fell foul of it. As they always say in Scottish politics, 'It's not what you know but who you know'. You do not get anywhere in Labour politics unless you have a large constituency of political friends and clients. If they disown you, there is nowhere to go but out. It is the kind of parochial politics that we all hoped would not emerge in the Scottish Parliament. We were wrong. We thought that when Henry McLeish finally went, it would be the end of the nightmare. We were wrong about that too.

## THE AGE OF McCONNELLISM?

The manner in which Jack McConnell took over after the fall of Henry McLeish was an exercise in the crudest form of council factionalism. It was a Lanarkshire lock-out, the kind of politics that flourishes in the badlands of Labour local government in west central Scotland. The summary execution of five out of six of the original Labour ministerial team established by Donald Dewar was a numpty purge which cast Jack McConnell in a new paranoid light.

Why did he do it? Certainly, a few Labour ministers had been less than enthusiastic about the coming of Jack McConnell. Jackie Baillie, the social justice minister, had been muttering behind the scenes, and the finance minister Angus MacKay was known to be no great admirer of Jack McConnell (the feeling was mutual). But, in addition, the transport minister Sarah Boyack was shown the door and the health minister, Susan Deacon, went before she was pushed. In came left-wingers such as Cathy Jamieson at education, Malcolm Chisholm at health and Mike Watson at culture and sport. Capable politicians; in Malcolm Chisholm's case, more than capable. However, they all suffered from the John West syndrome: they were the ones who had been rejected and everyone knew it. The key post of finance minister went to someone directly out of Labour's municipal culture, Andy Kerr.

It was odd for a First Minister who regarded himself as a moderniser to be surrounding himself with people who manifestly were not. Jack McConnell's strategy appeared to be to go strong on loyalty irrespective of ideological disposition. His new cabinet might be more left wing on issues such as PFI and stock-transfer, but at least they owed their jobs to Jack McConnell alone. None of them had any independent power base. None of them – Wendy Alexander aside, and she didn't hang about for very long – possessed sufficient intellect or character to pose any direct threat to McConnell. Clearly, it was better the devil you know.

Jack McConnell also sacked almost the entire policy unit, from the official spokesman Peter MacMahon to the head of policy John McTernan. In their place he drafted in trusted local government men such as Mike Donnelly, a contemporary of McConnell's from Stirling council days. Andrew Baird, a civil servant, took over from the much criticised Peter MacMahon as McConnell's chief spokesman. There were to be no more spin-doctors in the Scottish Executive. In this, the First Minister was quite consciously following Westminster's recent trend away from sophisticated media presentation. It was to be replaced by back-room fixing.

So what do we make of the new political masters? It is much too early to tell, of course, but first impressions are not exactly rosy. Jack McConnell made much of his promise to 'do less, better'. The character and purpose of the policy unit changed completely. It was no longer there to act as a bridge between the media and the Scottish Executive and come up with 'Scottish solutions to Scottish problems'. It has become instead a negotiating forum for special interest groups.

Jack McConnell always had a reputation for being something of a neo-nationalist. He was a founder member of home rule grouping, Scottish Labour Action, in the 1980s. He still commands respect from home rule academics and journalists who regard him as a champion of Scottish autonomy. Friends of McConnell insist that he has not lost his home rule orientation and that once he has placed the administration on an even keel he will begin to promote more 'Scottish' policies. But so far his main objective seems to have been to mend fences with London.

Ministers in the Scotland Office were in no doubt about the change from the McLeish days. They immediately recognised that here was a First Minister who would not fight battles he could not win and who would listen to Westminster before promoting policies such as free personal care. McConnell's first act was to accept that the Department of Work and Pensions was not going to hand over the £21 million in attendance allowances which Henry McLeish had hoped to recycle to set against the cost of free care. It was a humiliating climbdown for the Scottish Executive and a calculated slight by the pensions secretary, the Scottish Labour MP Alistair Darling.

However, McConnellism is not only about the politics of capitulation. Perhaps the most strikingly different act made by the new First Minister was his opening to the green movement. McConnell delivered the first ever speech by a First Minister on environmentalism, committing himself to improving Scotland's dismal record on waste recycling, $CO_2$ emissions and insulation, and putting his full weight behind the development of renewable energy sources such as wind- and wave-power.

In the main, though, Jack McConnell's efforts amount to municipalism with green edges. There is no mistaking the odour of town hall above his administration. He has a highly instrumental attitude to politics, which is about squaring rivals, buying off friends and destroying enemies. The test will come over electoral reform, currently out for yet more consultation (after the McIntosh 1999 and Kerley 2000 reports). It will be a major challenge to McConnell to take on his own party – many of whom are bitterly opposed to PR – and win. It will be the final test of his modernising credentials and could be the making or breaking of him as a national leader.

## DEVOLUTION, PR AND WESTMINSTER

The Labour Party has always been ambivalent about devolution (see Hassan 2002). A substantial number rejected it as nationalism and were only persuaded to home rule by the threat of the SNP going one step further. Labour's council cadres were on the one hand concerned that a Scottish Parliament would draw power from their local fiefdoms – the Charlie Gordon tendency – and on the other intrigued by the potential that devolution offered for extending their careers or their patronage. The task now for the Scottish Parliament – and it is the only body which can do this – is to shine relentless scrutiny on local politics in Scotland. Jack McConnell needs to throw his full weight behind the renewal agenda. We need to know what is going on in the darker reaches of Scottish politics.

The Sinclair report called for greater transparency in local government and, in particular, in relations between the local Labour Party, council bureaucracies and charities funded by the council. The Chief Executive of Fife Council called for a register of interests for voluntary organisations, so that we can know the extent of Labour nepotism and jobs-for-the-boys. But Sinclair also warned, rightly, that this could become a human rights issue. If people have to declare their political affiliations before they get a job, there could be a risk of discrimination. A kind of inverted cronyism might replace jobs-for-the-boys. For example, a charity applying for funds might be reluctant to declare the political leanings of its employees – especially if they are different from the dominant party in the council. Nevertheless, this is just a risk that Scotland will have to take, for there seems no other way. One of the truly staggering revelations of the Sinclair inquiry was that one in every three working people in Fife are employed by Fife council. In many areas of Scotland the council is the local economy. Hardly surprising, then, that a third of Fife councillors have a relative working for the council. Nepotism is a way of life in large parts of Labour Scotland and it is going to be virtually impossible to eradicate 'crossover' without risking discriminating against some people. Perhaps the answer is to bus in workers from other council areas. But since most of them will be Labour too, that would not make much of a difference. The only antibody to the toxin is greater openness, political scrutiny by a vigorous local opposition and regulation by the Scottish Parliament. Devolution was always about political renewal and it is Holyrood's historic task to blow the lid off local sleaze. The key task will be the manner in which it passes legislation to introduce proportional representation in local elections. That, more than anything, will open up the closed Labour communities. Jack McConnell has promised to deliver it, in the teeth of opposition from his own councillors. Let us hope he is as good as his word.

In many ways, devolution happened 20 years too late. It is a great reforming agenda for an age corroded by cynicism. Things were not so bad in 1979 when the first devolution referendum was held. By 1999 disillusion had rotted civil society and hollowed out the established political parties. The Labour Party that assumed control in the Scottish Parliament was no longer a mass political movement. Labour claims 20,000 members in Scotland, but the activists can be barely a quarter of that.

The Partnership Agreement struck between Donald Dewar and Jim Wallace after the 1999 election was an honourable one, even if the actual bargaining process was inglorious. It paved the way for the abolition of tuition fees, another look at electoral reform and the introduction of free personal care – though at least one Labour leader has been destroyed by trying to implement it. The common objective – Scottish solutions to Scottish problems – was the only possible mission statement for the Scottish Executive, and the existence of the Lib Dems gave Labour the licence to depart from the Westminster Labour line without it causing rupture – except for poor Henry.

And where do the other parties sit in this equation? The Scottish Nationalists started well in the Scottish Parliament, transformed into a professional political party by their numbers and the effects of a decade of Salmond leadership (Macwhirter 2000; Mitchell 2000) but they quickly began to struggle as their tactical manoeuvrings and hounding of the Scottish Executive did not amount to anything but adversarial, opposition politics which could not hide a lack of direction. The passing of the leadership to John Swinney has magnified such issues but did not create them. Recent campaigns on 'talking independence' cannot disguise the dilemmas devolution causes for the Nationalists and their failure to develop a convincing analysis and critique of the Labour state that runs Scotland. Time and again through the first three years of devolution the SNP seem to have suggested that it is not the Labour state that is the problem in Scotland, but the Labour politicians running it, and that they, unfettered by Westminster and Old/New Labour divisions, could make a better go of it.

The Scottish Tories – after two decades of opposing devolution – have made as decent an impact as anyone, including they themselves, expected. However, for all David McLetchie's expert debating skills and point-scoring, which culminated in his hounding of Henry McLeish out of office, it has not remade

Scottish Toryism. They have spoken in a more moderate centre-right voice, but have often seemed opportunistic, in favour of higher public spending for their interest groups, well-off students and the elderly (the latter until told otherwise by Iain Duncan Smith).

The Lib Dems have curbed the worst excesses of Labour rule in the Executive and on crucial issues have been able to influence policy. But more often than not, they have portrayed themselves as not really a national party, more a gathering of idiosyncratic, highly erratic individuals. The SNP have regarded them as 'rural Labour' – a reference from the Soviet era of peoples' democracy when various puppet parties protected the ruling Communists.

A small irritant has been caused to the existing political class by the arrival of the Scottish Socialists and Tommy Sheridan, whose charisma and political acumen have made a real impact and wrong-footed Labour on numerous occasions. Whether he can break out of his Pollok citadel and Glasgow base next time round will reveal the degree of irritant he can hope to be.

The Scottish political classes thus remain, for the moment, Labour-dominated and shaped by the Labour state. Things could be worse: the Scottish Parliament, for all its importing of bumped-up councillors and numptydom, has not been totally Labour run, as some in Westminster would like it still to be. The Scottish Parliament's electoral system, with its introduction of list MSPs into Scottish political culture, has proven a shock to some of the more unreconstructed Labour politicians, the worst of whom were to be found not in Holyrood, but in town halls and Westminster. But things have to get better: the Scottish Parliament has to find its feet lest Westminster and the Labour politicians who inhabit its recesses step back into power and influence. The Scottish Labour Party has to free itself from the politics of factionalism, the biggest being the patronage and influence of the Chancellor, Gordon Brown, whose reach and say has been dented by the arrival of Jack McConnell. And it has to curb its North Korean tendencies, which see democracy as an inconvenience in running Scotland, where it knows what is best. But for that to happen the other political parties need to challenge Scottish Labour and the Labour state, and develop convincing arguments about how Scotland could be different and better run by introducing that unknown quantity into it: democracy.

The Scottish Executive currently spends £21 billion per annum, with Westminster retaining significant power and influence north of the border. However, the key to reforming the Labour state in Scotland lies within Holyrood, not Westminster. In fact, the sad state of large acres of Scottish politics, from town halls upwards, is a direct consequence of Westminster's distant and indifferent rule: Monklands, Renfrewshire, Glasgow, North Lanarkshire – all happened on Westminster's watch. Only Holyrood, if it has the will, can sort this out.

PR is a litmus test of whether the Scottish political classes can change. The current consultation on electoral reform has revealed the weakness of the forces of change in civil society. The Labour councillors and trade unions have organised themselves against PR and hope ultimately to call a special conference to block it. They will almost certainly not succeed, since the arithmetic in the Scottish Parliament, where the Liberal Democrats hold the balance of power, should ensure that ultimately electoral reform wins. But it will be a hollow victory if it does not galvanise some of that sense of civic purpose that inspired devolution in the first place. It is Jack McConnell's historic mission, should he decide to accept it, to lead the revival in the moral purpose of Scottish democracy, renew local politics and restore public confidence in the reforming potential of the Scottish Parliament. A lot will be at stake on this: the nature of Jack McConnell's administration, the character of the Scottish Parliament in relation to other forces in Scotland and, perhaps, the destination of devolution itself. Devolution was always meant to bring about greater democratisation, but Jack McConnell will have to show courage and leadership to challenge the Labour state and backroom networks in town halls up and down the land, Holyrood and Westminster alike.

3

# CITY-STATES AND LOCAL GOVERNANCE

*George Kerevan*

When the Blair government was elected in May 1997, the 32 Scottish local authorities thought the Seventh Cavalry had arrived. They were wrong. The new Secretary of State for Scotland, Donald Dewar, was preparing a revolution in their working on a scale far bigger than the Tory abolition of Regional Councils in 1996.

In England, Blair was determined to modernise the forms of governance of local authorities, not their boundaries or menu of powers as previous reorganisations had done. Managerial efficiency lay at the heart of the new strategy. Dewar was tasked with a similar reform north of the border. A spokesperson summed up his plans: 'We have a very positive agenda for change, with a best-value regime to provide services in a pragmatic way, an ethical framework and a system of modern cabinet-style committees to make councils function more efficiently.'

To everyone's surprise, Dewar proved he was serious. Two traditional Labour councils – North Lanarkshire and East Ayrshire – were the subject of a government inquiry after their Direct Labour Organisations ran up losses of £7 million. Dewar ordered the DLOs closed. To do so, he used Tory legislation even the Conservatives had been shy of implementing.

## AN INCESTUOUS ELITE?

Who were the Scottish councillors Dewar was challenging? Their composite was a 53-year-old white male who owned his own home and car (Vestri and Fitzpatrick 2000). Curiously, he would not be manual working class but have a degree or professional qualification; church membership would be probable – this was a conservative group, with a small 'c'.

More questionable characteristics were exhibited by the Labour members who dominated local government. Fully a quarter of Labour councillors with a job were employed in local government itself – much higher than for the other parties – and well over 50 per cent in the state sector as a whole. Another 10 per cent of councillors, mostly Labour, work in the voluntary sector, which is heavily dependent on local authority funding. Taking into account full-time councillors, this constitutes an incestuous elite where those governing have a direct personal interest in how they govern. It also creates huge barriers to introducing new ideas.

Low voter turn-out means this elite are not subject to proper accountability. In the 1999 local elections in Glasgow, Labour held all but five of the 79 council seats, despite having secured less than half the vote; the SNP, with 30 per cent of the vote, won two seats. In Midlothian, the SNP got 31 per cent of the vote but not one single councillor. Even in Edinburgh, Labour won an overall majority with only 32 per cent of the vote.

The person Dewar brought in to advise him on local authority reform and efficiency was Wendy Alexander, fresh from a stint in management consultancy with Booz Allen and Hamilton. Alexander became the lightning rod for local authority resistance to change. One Labour council leader commented: 'There's a view that Donald has a couple of advisers who spent a lot of time at Keir Hardie House [former Scottish Labour Party HQ in Glasgow] and saw the very negative side of local government. As far as Wendy's concerned – she has a very strong influence. I think an undue influence. There's a sense that the agenda needs to be rolled back.'

Alexander, a life-long Labour supporter and friend of Gordon Brown, was not out to destroy Labour councils (Alexander 1999) but she was too well aware that the Scottish economy consistently underperforms in the UK and that meant less resources, in her view, to help the socially excluded. Trend annual GDP growth in Scotland runs at 2.1 per cent compared to 2.4 per cent for the UK as a whole. That implies Scottish productivity – the measure of how efficiently we use economic inputs like labour and capital – must be poorer. Yet Scottish manufacturing productivity outperforms the UK average, so something else in Scotland is wasting resources in a big way. In private, Alexander would admit that major productivity failure was in the public sector. A quarter of the Scottish workforce is in the public sector, with 15 per cent in local government, the nation's largest single employer.

A 'Stop Wendy' campaign emerged among Labour's council warlords in the west of Scotland. Senior councillors blamed her specifically for Mr Dewar's decision to order the closure of the Direct Labour Organisations in North Lanarkshire and East Ayrshire. Councillors were also upset by a series of hard-hitting speeches from Calum MacDonald, the Scottish Office local government minister at Westminster. To ameliorate them, MacDonald was replaced by Henry McLeish, ex-leader of Fife Council and a man presumed by Labour's council mafia to be a safe pair of hands. Dewar also played canny by acquiescing to letting the local government committee of Labour's Scottish Executive

Committee play with designing a model of council reform. But Dewar and Alexander had other ideas.

What motivated the normally conservative Dewar? In 1994 in Monklands, Lanarkshire, the allegations of cronyism and nepotism were so severe that the party came close to losing the parliamentary seat in a by-election following the death of Dewar's close friend John Smith. Then, just before Labour's general election victory in 1997, Glasgow Labour leader Pat Lally was suspended by the party following accusations that councillors had taken foreign trips in exchange for their loyalty in crucial votes on the council (Lally and Baxter 2000). Now in charge, Dewar had had enough of such dangerous political embarrassments.

Almost as soon as he arrived at St Andrews House in 1997, Dewar paralleled the English modernisation process by initiating an independent review of local authority governance. It was headed by the former chief executive of the recently defunct Strathclyde Regional Council, Neil McIntosh, who reported in June 1999, just after the first Holyrood elections (Commission on Local Government and the Scottish Parliament 1999). The next phase of the war took place in the very first official debate of the new Scottish Parliament after its opening in July 1999. The person in charge of local government reform was none other than Dewar's key aide, Wendy Alexander, now an MSP. The modernisers had regrouped.

'No change is not an option,' proclaimed Ms Alexander as she announced she was accepting the overwhelming majority of McIntosh's recommendations. One was for an end to the old-style committee system, the main mechanism by which patronage is traded in the Labour municipal fiefdoms. McIntosh also suggested that the Scottish Executive look at a more 'appropriate' voting system for Scottish local government, a code for proportional representation. 'I recognise that councils will need, and will welcome, help from others as they reinvent themselves,' she commented.

She was wrong. A study by the Scottish Local Government Information Unit showed 52 per cent of all councillors and 72 per cent of Labour councillors were against PR (Vestri and Fitzpatrick 2000). There were also big majorities against the cabinet idea and elected mayors. Opposition to reform came strongest from the Labour fiefdoms in the west, led by Glasgow Labour leader Charles Gordon. But even as far as Labour-held Aberdeen, there was resistance. The only major support for cabinet government came from booming Edinburgh, where Labour control was still a comparatively novel experience.

Alexander, with her limited political experience, now made what in retrospect proved a fatal error. Instead of legislating for reform immediately, she set up yet another working party to deal with the hot potato of PR, which might not be supported by Labour backbench MSPs. The Kerley committee was remarkably lightweight politically, another Alexander mistake. Kerley himself was a former Edinburgh councillor who had bailed out in favour of academia and was now director of the MBA programme at the University of Edinburgh Management School.

The delay resulting from the institution of the Kerley committee now allowed Harold Macmillan's famous 'events' to intervene with a vengeance. Alexander also announced she wanted private sector advice 'about how to make change happen' in local government. To this end, she announced she was appointing some 'Champions for Change'. The first was a certain Brian Souter, the legendary bus entrepreneur. But within months, Souter would become embroiled in a very public dispute with Alexander when he financed a campaign against her attempt to repeal the Scottish equivalent of Section 28 that banned teaching about homosexual lifestyles in schools. Dewar was forced to politically sideline Alexander when the storm over Section 28 threatened to derail his first year's political agenda.

Dewar had also suffered the loss of another close ally in the reform process: Keith Geddes. When New Labour came to power in 1997, Geddes was president of the Convention of Scottish Local Authorities (COSLA), the umbrella body representing local authorities. An able leader of Lothian Regional Council and then the new single-tier Edinburgh authority, he was an influential and trusted force among Labour councillors. He was also willing to trade modernisation of local government (even PR) in return for serious Treasury cash. This was a sophisticated, defensible strategy for Labour local interests.

But Geddes was also motivated by ambitions for a parliamentary career. He was tipped for election to the Scottish Parliament, where his experience and authority were likely to make him a key linkman between Dewar and the various city chambers. Again disaster struck as Geddes unexpectedly failed to get elected to Holyrood in May 1999, as a result of the new list system. Dewar had lost an important ally. Worse, Geddes had resigned his council seat to stand for the Scottish Parliament and so was out of COSLA as well. Rather than sweep jobless Geddes into the Lords where he could be useful, Dewar compounded the loss by simply abandoning his erstwhile ally. A bitter Geddes marooned on the political sidelines did not help the chances of local government reform.

These setbacks allowed the backwoods councillors and big city council bosses to seize the agenda. In February 2000, the Scottish Parliament's Local Government Committee reported after a four-month inquiry into the McIntosh proposals. The committee came out against directly elected provosts and warned against the imposition of cabinet-style local government on the grounds it would threaten a reduction in local democracy. The committee had been manipulated. Rejecting those reforms left only PR, the most difficult change to win support to introduce.

As a result, Dewar now shied clear of putting the main McIntosh findings into law. In England, the government was mandating cabinet government and legislating to make councils hold local referenda on the introduction of elected mayors (a neat way round councillor opposition). In Scotland, the Executive meekly tried to encourage councils to reform themselves from within. It was a holding operation pending Kerley.

In July 2000 the Kerley committee reported (Kerley Committee 2000). Kerley recommended the scrapping of the present first-past-the-post system of electing councils in favour of proportional representation. But Kerley knew the strength of the opposition and produced a tactical masterpiece. How to sell PR to threatened Labour councillors? Kerley offered them cash. He suggested that remuneration for councillors should be upped, with payments for the leaders of Edinburgh and Glasgow councils set at the same salaries as for MSPs. He also suggested postponing the introduction of PR far enough into the future to protect the seats of many current councillors till they were nearing retirement. There was still everything to play for in the reform stakes – and then, in October 2000, Donald Dewar died.

## THE AGE OF McLEISHISM AND CONSERVATIVE CAUTION

In Donald Dewar's place as First Minister came Henry McLeish. Unlike the cerebral Dewar, McLeish was a prime product of the Scottish Labour local government machine and all its shortcomings – as events would soon reveal. He was further disadvantaged by the need to cultivate his political base after a narrow victory over Jack McConnell, in which the latter won a majority of the votes of Labour MSPs. That meant, whatever the public spin, that municipal PR was now dead in the water.

McLeish faced two problems: (1) how to retreat from Donald Dewar's promises of reform, and (2) how to square his pro-PR Lib Dem coalition allies. He also had to deal with the big cities, who were growing restive about the deal they were getting under Holyrood. In particular, Glasgow now scented it could win more concessions from a weakened McLeish.

Devolution inevitably meant a changed pecking order for local councils. The big Labour municipalities still weigh in as key influencers of policy but the days when Glasgow could rule the roost are now gone. The Scottish Parliament now has a greater representation from the rural areas and small towns compared to Westminster of old. And Scottish Office secrecy regarding budget allocations has given way to a more transparent arrangement for financial allocation: the smoke-filled rooms have less smoke.

Then Glasgow suffered a worse fate (Kerevan 2001). The Glasgow big beasts on the Executive – a hangover from the city's influence on the Labour contingent at Westminster – should have guaranteed the city quiet influence. However, in short order three key Glasgow MSPs disappeared from leading posts in the Executive. First was Dewar himself; then education supremo Sam Galbraith was forced out of office in disgrace after the SQA exam results fiasco; finally, former Glasgow council boss Frank McAveety was dumped by Henry McLeish for wavering over support in McLeish's contest with McConnell.

Meanwhile, a combination of the new Parliament being located in Edinburgh allied to the capital's economic boom, led Glasgow to feel it was in danger of losing out to the east on financial support. Once the Second City of the Empire, Glasgow had seen its tax base implode as middle-class suburbs gained autonomy and professional workers fled the city (Kerevan 2000). This loss of influence led Glasgow to take the unprecedented step of quitting COSLA in December 2000, vowing to use the £300,000-a-year membership fee on services for special needs children.

Significantly, Glasgow Council leader Charles Gordon blamed the decision to leave COSLA not on his fellow councils but on the new Scottish Executive, after McLeish held talks with the Convention. Gordon explained: 'All senior officers of the council feel we put more resources into COSLA than we get out of it. That was shown when the Executive came up with an inadequate funding package for Glasgow which will do nothing to achieve social justice or tackle deprivation in the city.'

This event has been largely underplayed in evaluating recent Scottish politics. But the loss of influence of COSLA, a dominating local force in the Thatcher era, represents a fundamental long-term shift of domestic political power away from the municipalities and towards Holyrood. It is symbolic of a tectonic tension between the two that will probably result in the diminution of local council powers. Anecdotally, talk to most MSPs of any party and their opinion of councillors is low, bordering on dismissive. It is a view that extends deep into the Executive and civil service.

The response of Glasgow was to go it alone: dump COSLA and make political waves that might unsettle the national Labour leadership. Under this pressure, McLeish announced at the end of 2000 that he was setting up a Cities Commission to explore how Scotland's cities should be governed. In charge of the Cities Commission was Peter Peacock MSP, formerly the leader of the Highlands and Islands Council. Another safe pair of hands, he became a semi-official 'Minister for Cities'. This was the third policy commission on Scottish local government since 1997, a new one every 18 months, and its agenda (and composition) was left suitably vague. This left the wider reform agenda still open, offered hints of more cash to the cities, gave cities such as Glasgow and Dundee facing the twin crisis of population decline and neutered boundaries distant hope of change and postponed PR into the dim future without actually saying it was dead.

McLeish did introduce one bold 'reform' in local government: he put back the next council elections, originally due in May 2002, to coincide with the Scottish Parliament contest in 2003. Originally, under the Tory reorganisation of local government, elections were to be every three years. This was a mute attempt at making local government that bit more accountable. Now elections would revert to a four-year cycle linked to the Holyrood election. That might help increase voter turn-out, but at the expense of burying local issues.

Municipal life in Scotland seemed to return to 'normal'. In Aberdeen there was a row over the £35,000 the Labour council spent in 2001 to allow the Lord Provost, Margaret Smith, to take her pal Lesley Baird on foreign trips to Brazil, Japan, Mexico, China and other areas of vital city interest. Mrs Baird lives in East Dunbartonshire. The incident, and the ruling Labour group's insouciance over it, is only significant because Aberdeen's urban problems have become critical. Booming on oil, it desperately needs new housing and roads. But the old-fashioned council machinery is creaking and vital strategic decisions have not been made, frustrating citizens and local business. Without council reform, such situations will be repeated across the country.

As a result, the voters are getting impatient. Willie Sullivan, co-ordinator of the Labour Campaign for Electoral Reform, sums up the dilemma: 'What we have seen is that voters are becoming increasingly weary of what are effectively one-party states. The result is that since 1996 we [Labour] have lost overall control of Clackmannanshire, Inverclyde, Falkirk, West Dunbartonshire, East Dunbartonshire, Stirling and Dundee Councils.'

As if mirroring this unsteady state, the McLeish era did not last long. A scandal resulting from his misuse of parliamentary expenses caused his resignation in November 2001. The 'Officegate' affair – part tragedy, part farce – was all very redolent of the incestuous nature and lack of real accountability in Scottish local government.

## A NEW ERA?

McLeish was replaced by his old rival Jack McConnell, former leader of Stirling District Council and now MSP for Motherwell and Wishaw in the Labour municipal heartland of the central belt. On becoming First Minister, McConnell made ambiguous noises about introducing proportional representation in local government, but this was largely to pacify his Liberal Democrat coalition partners. McConnell's immediate necessity was to win Labour's re-election in 2003. The first Parliament would end without local government reform – one of its biggest policy failures. And with Wendy Alexander's resignation from the Executive in May 2002, the modernisers had been sidelined.

But not finished. One major local authority did try cabinet government: Edinburgh. This voluntary experiment began in June 2000 under the city's ambitious young leader, Donald Anderson. Under the new system, a 13-strong cabinet of councillors representing various portfolios makes key decisions, with Anderson presiding. This executive is theoretically accountable to scrutiny panels covering the main council departments.

Two issues are involved here, compared to the old committee approach. Does the cabinet system promote better decision-making? And is it more accountable? The latter is still a moot point if the vagaries of the electoral system, questionable ward boundaries and low voter turn-out keep piling up big Labour majorities on minority shares of the vote. Old habits die hard in these circumstances: opposition councillors complain that important decisions which should have gone to cabinet for consideration have instead simply been made by council leader Anderson. In the end, reform may not be a menu but an indivisible package.

As to performance, a six-month internal review of the new structures in Edinburgh was released in December 2000. This claimed the system had resulted in a 70 per cent reduction in the number of reports written and circulated for consideration by councillors. However, the council officials seemed somewhat hesitant in their evaluation. Only 50 per cent of senior officials said that decision-making had improved.

Where reform failed in Edinburgh, at least against one of Donald Dewar's original benchmarks, was in its inability to bring new blood into council management. The Edinburgh cabinet contained the same faces who had run things under the old committee system. For instance, the councillor responsible for planning, Bob Cairns, had first taken over that role in 1988 and is still going strong.

At a more strategic level, Edinburgh's preoccupation with managerialism has not produced much in the way of policy solutions to the capital's urban ills (which stem mostly from the success of its economic and construction boom). The Edinburgh authorities have been aware of the potential for the city's population to grow since the late 1980s. Integral to the creation of new jobs, for instance on Edinburgh's west side and in the city centre financial district, had to be more housing and a new mass transit system.

The solution identified in the early 1990s was to extend the city to the south-east and to develop high-density housing along the north shore. These necessary developments have been very slow to arrive. The council has singularly failed to produce a mass transit system despite several much publicised schemes being touted. If anything, cabinet-style government in Edinburgh may have acted as a fig leaf to cover strategic inaction.

## A SILENT REVOLUTION?

Has modernisation succeeded anywhere in Scottish local government post-devolution? In fact, there has been a silent revolution, but not through the medium of reformed governance. The major impact has been the use of private finance initiative (PFI) projects, where councils employ privately financed outsiders to build projects to order and then lease them back to the authority. These have proliferated in Scotland despite strong trade union opposition. The basis of this opposition seems part left-wing ideology and part a fear for members' jobs. But local government is now the largest growth area for PFI in Scotland, most recently in schools due to substantial Scottish Executive support, including financial subsidy.

Under Labour Leader Charles Gordon, Glasgow has been the driving force in using PFI despite bitter union opposition. Construction has been on a massive scale, with PFI used to rebuild all of Glasgow's secondary schools. Gordon also successfully championed the transfer of Glasgow's council housing to a private association in order to unlock another £2 billion of PFI cash to renovate the city's social housing. This culminated in a historic vote by the tenants in April 2002 to approve the scheme. The days when Scotland had more municipal housing than Stalinist Poland were over forever.

Had Glasgow not succeeded in using PFI, other authorities might have caved in to union pressure. Ultimately, Glasgow had no option but to abandon ideology in return for the resources to tackle gigantic local problems. It is still the dilemma facing local government reform in Scotland. Curiously, the villain of this anti-modernisation tale, Glasgow leader Charles Gordon, may turn out to be its hero as well. Gordon has routed the modernisers and put off PR in local government which, had Dewar lived, might have been delivered in the new Parliament's first term. But Gordon's agenda was far from being business as usual – witness his support for PFI – although the temporary retreat on PR might hearten the darker recesses of Labour's municipal denizens in the central belt.

An ex-Trotskyist rather than Old Labour, Charles Gordon has been one of the few local authority figures in Scotland who has not been eclipsed by the establishment of the new Scottish Parliament (Kerevan 2002). He has been consistently critical of the Scottish Executive, saying it failed to pay enough attention to Scotland's cities. With some truth, he maintains that the debate on urban problems has been 'as rare as hen's teeth'. What he means is that the modernisation agenda introduced by Dewar and Alexander in 1997 was in many ways about the abstractions of local government; it sought a necessary managerial revolution but did not explain what the new local authorities, post-PR, were meant to do on the ground about jobs, houses or health.

In many ways, it is that missing manifesto that has allowed the reactionaries to defend the status quo so easily. However, the pressures on the McConnell administration are complex and contradictory. The Scottish Lib Dems require PR at the minimum for remaining in coalition with Labour at Holyrood post-2003. Scottish Labour's local fiefdoms want more public money, but little change to their culture of complacency. And the McConnell era has seen a swing back to the concerns of Labour's heartlands in the Scottish Executive post-Wendy Alexander: Patricia Ferguson (Business), Mike Watson (Culture, Tourism and Sport), Margaret Curran (Social Justice) and Frank McAveety, returning as a junior – all Glasgow Labour MSPs. But whatever the future pattern of events, what has been lacking so far has been a sense of vision about the role and purpose of local government and governance in contemporary Scotland. This is what is urgently needed if the caution and conservatism of the last few years are to be overcome.

# 4

# THE CIVIL SERVICE

*Margaret Ford and Peter Casebow*

At the centre of the changes that have shaped the new Scotland sits the Scottish Executive – the political and administrative heart of the new body politic. The name chosen for the new administration in Scotland – 'Scottish Executive' – itself posed some initial confusion as it related not only to the politicians, but also to the civil servants. However, in the new Scottish arrangements, Executive was deliberately intended to convey a description of ministers and civil servants alike (Parry 2000), and although there existed some confusion and uncertainty at the start of 1999, the new arrangements have settled into a familiar and managed pattern.

Indeed, for some the pattern may be too familiar and rather too managed. In 1997, the new Scottish Office was, in contrast to the pace being set by New Labour in Whitehall, accused of 'hitting the ground strolling'. The criticism subsequently levelled at the Scottish civil service is that, for all the apparent change and transformation, very little of substance has altered in the way that the civil service in Scotland conducts its business: that it is a brake on innovation and an obstacle to reform. In short, it has remained pretty untouched by the change in constitutional arrangements and political style ushered in by the advent of a democratically elected Scottish Parliament.

This criticism has been openly articulated by former Ministers such as Angus MacKay and Susan Deacon, by Brian Fitzpatrick, policy adviser in the first post-devolution administration, and echoed by academic and independent commentators. But how valid are these criticisms? Given that the civil service by its nature cannot directly answer such charges, this chapter will chart some of the changes that have taken place since 1997, and attempt to assess whether any real progress has been made.

To understand the civil service we have to do two things: define terms and understand context. In defining terms, we need to identify the core people who work on a daily basis to support the administration – the mandarins – although that term seems hopelessly outdated in twenty-first-century Scotland. There are 4,000 core civil servants principally working in Edinburgh and Glasgow in support of ministers. Also designated as civil servants are a further 8,000 people who work in Executive agencies such as Historic Scotland, Registers of Scotland, Scottish Prison Service and Communities Scotland (formerly Scottish Homes). Staff in these bodies are employed as civil servants, subject to the Civil Service Code and capable of being transferred within the civil service in Scotland to other posts (as often happens at senior levels). Such Executive agency staff are distinct from people working in Non-Departmental Public Bodies or NDPBs (quangos) such as Scottish Enterprise, who are not civil servants and who operate under a quite different employment regime.

Since 1997, and especially in the period post-referendum, there has been an increase in the number of core civil servants, reflecting the increased range of activities necessary to support the Parliament, a greatly expanded ministerial team and the infrastructure necessary to a devolved administration. Virtually all of these jobs are located in the core civil service.

Although there have been some new and distinctive functions created, such as the Cabinet Secretariat, much of the structure of the old Scottish Office remains with departments reflecting distinctive functions and topics such as education, health, development and enterprise. With each successive change in administration, the departments have been modified to reflect the redesign of ministerial portfolios. However, the core structure is robust and has remained largely unaltered from pre-1997. This is not necessarily a problem. Even novice students of organisational change understand that structural reorganisation is not a wholly reliable indicator of successful change management. Indeed structural change for its own sake can often simply be a distraction from tackling real issues such as culture, process and relationships.

At the time of devolution, some commentators (Leicester and Mackay 1998) advocated reorganising the civil service into cross-cutting departments focusing on, say, children or social inclusion. Such proposals found little support within the civil service and the prevailing thinking left the core structure and organisational philosophy largely unchanged. It is not possible to judge whether such a shift would have delivered better policy-making and administration, since no basis for comparison exists. However, in retrospect, the decision has contributed to enabling the civil service to respond effectively to the challenge of creating an infrastructure which supported the change to a devolved government, facilitated the initial relationships between Executive and Parliament and which has withstood the shock of three First Ministers and three quite different administrations in as many years.

If the structure of the Scottish Executive looks broadly similar to its Scottish Office predecessor, what about other key aspects of the civil service? In the rest of this chapter we will look at some of the key people, some of the ways of working that have emerged and some of the challenges still facing the Scottish civil service. But before we do, we ought to pause and reflect on the changing context within which the civil service has been operating. In Scotland, there are at least four dimensions worth considering:

- A changed political administration
- A change of style and pace
- The rise of the new establishment
- Challenges to modernise government.

## A CHANGED POLITICAL ADMINISTRATION

After 18 years of Conservative government, many senior civil servants had reached the top of their careers, never having experienced anything other than a Conservative administration and working frequently in a siege mentality. For the 1980s and 1990s were characterised by nothing so much as the antipathy existing between large sections of civic society and the political regime in St Andrews House. This is an essential point in understanding the changes that have occurred since 1997. Up until then, civil servants simply did not have to finesse their process skills because government was not interested in the views of many external organisations and chose not to engage (except on its own terms) with other tiers of government.

## A CHANGE OF STYLE AND PACE

A change of style and pace was required which was far more in tune with the pre-1979 style of doing business in Scotland – and it is fair to say that much of civic Scotland felt that the civil service had to learn new habits in 1997. This alteration in style and tone arguably marked the first wave of change for the civil service in Scotland. It was challenging but, in retrospect, not especially so. Ministers were still few in number and spent the majority of their time at Westminster. The personality and inclination of many ministers such as Sam Galbraith and Donald Dewar meant that the scope and pace of change ought to have been relatively measured. But the referendum campaign and subsequent timetable for delivering the Parliament was to change all that.

Impatience for constitutional change was articulated strongly in the positive referendum result. The subsequent publication of the *Scotland's Parliament* White Paper (1997) and its associated timescale proved a powerful incentive for the Scottish Office civil servants to engage with a complex process of change in very short order. And it was not simply the timetable for change that created the impetus for delivery. The way in which politicians insisted that the process was managed signalled a clear departure from the past.

# THE RISE OF THE NEW ESTABLISHMENT

Far from the days of siege mentality in St Andrews House, probably at its height around the time of the introduction of the poll tax, the process of moving to devolution was open, transparent and inclusive. The creation of the Consultative Steering Group (1999) and expert bodies such as the Financial Issues Advisory Group (FIAG) brought a different approach and challenges for the civil service. External experts, often with long established relationships with ministers, were invited to direct and shape events from inside the Scottish Office. The Scottish establishment-in-waiting, cohesive, resourced and mobilised via the Scottish Constitutional Convention, had found its time and found its voice.

And the civil service had to respond. 'It was not always comfortable for them. They did not always get the point,' said Esther Roberton, former secretary of the Convention and member of the Consultative Steering Group, who watched the process of evolution from the old Conservative regime to the new Labour government. As one of the principal players in the campaign for a Scottish Parliament, she not only supported the principles of devolution but also championed a different style – intended to be characterised by its inclusive nature, rather than the exclusiveness of previous administrations. Roberton found it 'frankly frustrating at times'. And yet the outcomes of the Consultative Steering Group, and especially the outcomes from FIAG, signalled a radical shift in the nature of Scotland's governance, bringing different imperatives for politicians and civil servants alike.

Most senior civil servants acknowledge that the nature of parliamentary committees with their 'standing' and 'select' functions, combined to provide a level of scrutiny, openness and challenge previously unthinkable in Scottish government. If proof were needed, 'the hearings into the Scottish Qualifications Authority failings provided a textbook example of how the system is intended to work', said John Elvidge, at that time head of the Scottish Executive Education Department. That kind of public, personal scrutiny cannot have left senior civil servants and the political processes unchanged.

Closer to home, other changes are beginning to make an impact too. Where previously there were four or five ministers to support, suddenly the Executive contained a ministerial team of 22. And for the first period, to some ministers and to outside observers it looked, and indeed felt, 'chaotic'. Susan Deacon, health minister from 1999–2001, was initially astonished at the lack of coherence and management that she encountered. In an article in the *Herald* newspaper (30 November 2001) she explained that her response was to try to 'micro-manage the department' herself. Many commentators believe that the Executive had been so immersed in delivering the infrastructure of devolution that little attention had been paid to the management of the Executive's business once the first elections were over. Certainly, there was a huge increase in core workload, a new breed of ambitious, impatient ministers, and a new establishment with its hopes and priorities and which expected to be involved.

## CHALLENGES TO MODERNISE GOVERNMENT

To complete the picture, there was a momentum developing, UK-wide, to address civil service reform. 'Modernising government' had become a mantra for New Labour and there was an accelerating agenda that covered everything from regional devolution to better policy-making to electronic government. The weight of initiatives was growing daily, and by early 2000 the post-devolution Scottish Executive had no shortage of work and a huge weight of expectation hanging over it. Given this context, are the criticisms of the civil service fair? What more could have been done, or should have been done?

It is a truism that, to be effective, change and organisation development programmes need to meet certain criteria. These include:

- A clear and compelling rationale for change
- A strong sense of outcomes – 'knowing what success will look like'
- Capacity to manage the change
- Coherent, aligned activities supporting the change process.

It also helps if there is a 'burning platform', in other words, an urgent set of reasons why change is absolutely necessary and a sense that turning back or procrastination is not an option. These features of change were in place for delivery of the devolution project and it is no coincidence that the political classes and civil service delivered this in record time. The management of that process, the second wave of change, was a textbook exercise (unlike in the 1970s).

But criticism persists. *Scotland on Sunday* (14 April 2002), echoing other press comment, described Muir Russell, Scottish Executive Permanent Secretary, as 'the man that modernising ministers love to hate'. The Executive has been viewed by some, such as the Scottish Council Foundation, as not being innovative – characterised by an apparent lack of vision, a perceived reluctance to engage with external stakeholders or partners, or a retreat into pre-devolution processes (Boyle et al. 2001). Other criticisms include a lack of imagination in policy and process, a preconceived notion of consultation with institutional Scotland and a willingness to allow Westminster and Whitehall to shape policy in Scotland (Hassan and Warhurst 2002b). One commentator observed: 'Scotland's civil servants have spent all their careers applying Whitehall policy. They are doing it still, only now policy is left in quarantine at the border before a kilt is pinned on it' (Nelson 2001).

In order to respond to the charges, we need to consider that the civil service in Scotland does not operate in a vacuum. It is part of the Home Civil Service and its culture, values and operating style necessarily derive from that very distinctive culture. It operates as a core part of a much larger body and its organisational development is necessarily rooted in this much wider context. In a very real sense, it faces directly towards Whitehall.

The other sense in which the civil service does not operate in a vacuum is that it is an integral part of the fabric of Scottish society. Civil servants interact on a daily basis with a very wide range of stakeholders, partners, client groups, commentators, media and other colleagues in the wider public sector. In this regard, they have to face firmly towards a post-devolution Scotland that has acquired a renewed interest in the business of government. It is a country that has an intimately connected network of relationships, and has a professional class that has an expectation of involvement and serious levels of knowledge and expertise in many areas of the Executive's work. Facing in both directions at the same time is a difficult feat to accomplish, but one at which the Executive is arguably becoming more expert.

The process by which the student tuition fees issue was resolved is an instructive example of combining traditional civil service policy management with involving a range of expert and independent stakeholders to reach consensus. Equally, the management of foot-and-mouth disease in Dumfries was a clear example of the Executive (acting wholly in concert with Whitehall) effectively mobilising its expertise and networks in south-west Scotland and engaging meaningfully with other public sector agencies and stakeholders, such as the National Farmers' Union. So there are examples of the Executive adapting its style to fit changing circumstances.

The criticism persists, though, that the Executive tends to react effectively to individual crises or special events, but has yet to learn how to focus on outcomes, develop a sense of urgency or behave inclusively as a general way of operating. Our earlier criteria for organisational development provide us with a sense of why this might be genuinely difficult to achieve. Our first criterion was to have in place a clear rationale for change. The senior civil service are part of a pluralist form of leadership. The Management Group of the Scottish Executive is both part of the Home Civil Service and the Executive part of the Scottish government. Its vision and sense of direction needs to be created within this context and it is clear that, in political terms, there has simply been no continuity since 1999. The hugely talented Donald Dewar had many gifts and abilities but his inclination was not towards the strategic: always uncomfortable with 'the vision thing', his instinct was to deal with practical, pragmatic politics, and issues of management or change rarely engaged his interest. The first set of special advisers suffered from rapid turnover of personnel (including the loss of John Rafferty and Philip Chalmers) and arguably no clear sense of purpose or place within the system. In this context it is perhaps unfair to expect the Management Group of the Scottish Executive to have developed a clear organisational philosophy or *modus operandi*.

Within 12 months the administration headed by Henry McLeish had come and gone, characterised by even less sense of clear vision or strategic direction. Whether either Donald Dewar or Henry McLeish might have developed a more coherent organisational strategy given time is debatable, but certainly the relationships between ministers, special advisers and the civil service genuinely seemed to be developing well under the thoughtful, clear direction of John McTernan, McLeish's Chief of Staff. But we will never know because Jack McConnell succeeded McLeish within 12 months, bringing with him the third Chief of Staff (Michael Donnelly) and set of policy advisers (albeit very slimmed down) in three years.

So the idea that the senior civil service could develop (off its own bat) a strategic vision for the Executive is rather unfair, given the political change within which it was working. Equally, a huge part of our 'change test' relates to having a clear sense of what success will look like. Whilst the *Partnership for Scotland* (Scottish Executive 1999a) documents provide in part for this, the very different styles of administration meant that emphases have changed and timescales and priorities have shifted. Satisfying this aspect of the 'change test' has accordingly been genuinely difficult to do.

Nevertheless, the senior civil service is not hermetically sealed nor bereft of its own initiative. There have been other imperatives and guidance and the organisation has been developing on a number of fronts. The UK agenda for civil service reform has provided a pretty clear steer about the kind of civil service that is required in the twenty-first century, and it is on this front that the Scottish civil service is arguably doing well. The kind of inclusive, evidence-based policy that is now in vogue UK-wide was presaged in part by the principles and practice developed during the devolution process (Davies, Nutley and Smith 2000). The involvement of external experts, stakeholders and partners has continued to develop in areas such as community planning and health and social work – the Joint Venture Futures Group. There is also some evidence that the civil service is prepared to recruit experts from outside into its senior ranks, for example in specialist areas such as equal opportunities. It is no longer universally the case that every senior position is home grown in the service. There is also much more inclination to use secondments to bring fresh thinking and outside expertise into the policy process, for example in social housing and in health.

It is, however, the Executive's willingness to open up its recruitment process at senior levels that marks it out even within the Home Civil Service. The Scottish Executive is the only UK government department to open up its senior recruitment (Head of Division level) to completely open competition. The 2001 recruitment process saw external candidates recruited from academia, the private sector, the voluntary sector and other government bodies. Bringing fresh blood and thinking into the system at a senior level has now been established as a core element of Scottish Executive senior recruitment.

The Management Group itself has also embraced external input. In 2001, two non-executive directors were appointed to serve on the Executive's most senior management body. This welcome step might have had more impact had the vacancies been openly advertised instead of filled by a process of headhunting. However, the precedent has been set. So there is certainly some clear evidence that the Executive is receptive to external challenge.

The final area where there are some very interesting changes is the composition of the Management Group itself. Muir Russell has almost completely changed the personnel he inherited from his predecessor in 1997. And for a man popularly caricatured as being anti-reform, Russell has sent some very clear signals about what counts in the new Executive. Out of his seven department heads he has appointed four people whose most recent experience has been to successfully tackle complex management roles. In health he appointed Trevor Jones, an NHS operational man to his fingertips, with an impressive track record of NHS management in England and Scotland. Avoiding the path taken by his predecessors, Russell deliberately appointed a local NHS manager to this post. At enterprise, Russell has appointed a highly experienced manager, Eddie Frizzell. In contrast to the troubled regime of the 1980s, Frizzell's tenure as chief executive during the 1990s marked the longest ever period of stability in the Prison Service. His determined style and clear thinking brought the SPS through a difficult period and he was aided and abetted during that period by Jim Gallagher, who spent five years as human resources director. Gallagher, appointed by Russell to head the justice department, conceived and implemented the biggest set of changes to human resources policies and practices ever seen in prisons. Gallagher also had the task of implementing the culture change necessary to deliver flexibility to the way prisons were managed. Both he and Frizzell achieved significant success during a difficult period when criminal justice was not a political policy or spending priority.

In addition to their management track record, all three of these appointees bring strong intellect and classic policy experience. They have been joined on the Management Group most recently by Mike Ewart. In addition to a widely respected intellect, he also possesses a strong recent track record in management from his time leading the Scottish Courts Service.

At a time when the civil service is being exhorted to deliver, Russell appears to have already signalled a real change in approach: to get to the top you need to have strong policy capability and a clear track record on delivery and management. A further sign of his regard for the importance of effective management lies in the current postings of the three key people who helped deliver devolution. Robert Gordon, Paul Grice and John Ewing all played core roles in the Constitution Unit that shaped the new devolved arrangements. All three are now heading demanding delivery jobs in the Crown Office, the Parliament and the Courts Administration respectively. It is difficult to see how Muir Russell could have signalled his intentions more clearly.

Why does any of this matter? It matters because it genuinely is a departure from the past. In the days of Russell's predecessors it was clear that the key requirements for the top jobs were intellect and a certain kind of background. The prevailing prejudice about management was that people found themselves in such jobs because they were 'not quite up to' the policy task. Russell's regime has changed all of that and his track record on this issue answers the charge that he is not a moderniser. He may not be a fan of management-speak or glitzy organisational initiatives, but he genuinely appears to be ushering in a new culture that respects delivery and values proven ability of successful management. In this sense he is in the vanguard of civil service reform, for his determined progress in the area of people management sets him apart from other Whitehall department heads.

Having said all that, this is not quite the stuff of revolution. After all, most organisations learned to value management and successful delivery decades ago. But we should perhaps more charitably recall the context in which the Scottish Executive operates and recognise Russell's approach for what it is: a genuine and intuitive attempt to change the culture. And cultures, especially ones as strong and distinctive as that existing in the civil service, do not change overnight.

In addition, the culture cannot now revert. The landscape in Scotland has changed forever since devolution. The civil service in Scotland sits right at the heart of those changes and, although not by any means yet a transformed organisation, there are real signs of progress and movement. The service is part of a pluralist paradigm of leadership that exists to work with ministers to progress the business of good government. Once the McConnell administration charts a coherent and sustained political direction, the civil service needs to show that it can embrace and advance change.

If we finally return to our 'change test', the conditions for successful organisational development may now almost be in place:

- There is the prospect of a clear vision and some stable sense of outcomes emanating from the McConnell regime
- The capacity for change is being built up in the service by placing experienced and effective leaders and managers in key positions of influence
- A coherent set of management activities and support is being created, specifically under the new Public Service Delivery group.

All that is required now is the burning platform, so beloved by management consultants. The 2002 Budget signalled the biggest ever sustained investment in public services throughout the UK seen in two generations. The public now expects those people leading the public sector to respond and deliver. Perhaps the Chancellor of the Exchequer has created the platform.

The Scottish civil service is a complicated entity that occupies a unique place in the machinery of government in the UK. Having maintained a very low public profile for decades, senior people now find themselves operating in a goldfish bowl of a particularly Scottish kind. Consequently, interest in, and comment on the performance of the civil service is unlikely to change over the next while. But when the history of twenty-first-century Scottish government is eventually written, it may well be that the changes now being put in hand will stand the test of time and represent the beginnings of a genuinely new way of operating.

# 5

# CIVIC DEMOCRACY

## *Lindsay Paterson*

Any essay at this time on the Scottish Parliament's relationship to the country's civic life is bound to be much too premature. When we ask how this new institution is getting on with its much older neighbours, we cannot possibly expect a satisfactory answer after just a few years. They have mostly been around for a century, some for longer than that. The civil service brings to the Parliament the long years of serving the Secretary of State. The pressure groups and voluntary organisations have a longevity that stretches at least to the founding of the Welfare State. The media in its modern form is of much the same antiquity. The system of local government could claim a democratic pedigree as the only indigenous elected bodies since 1707. And the famous Scottish professions – the guarantor of the Scottish spirit, the defenders of the nation against Thatcher – are entrenched in their networks, their venerability and their beliefs.

This was, after all, a nation without a state, not a people without a nation. There were, as has repeatedly been pointed out, all the structures of a state without a state, all the networks of pluralism without that ultimate plural forum, a native assembly, all the jealously guarded autonomy without the supreme guarantor of it against a breakdown of the implicit bargains on which the UK had been built. It should never have been surprising, then, if the new Parliament had been constrained to do nothing but the civic networks' bidding, fulfilling their decades (or centuries) old desires.

So, as has also been long foretold, for those who want a radical transformation of Scotland – especially who want that in a socialist or radical democratic form – the fight would only start when the first Parliament was elected. It begins with the establishing of the Parliament without which any debate about social democracy in Scotland got inevitably diverted into the utopian longing for a democracy that could not but seem pure because it had not yet been established (Paterson 2000a). It starts with this forum that allows the conflicts and vested interests to be exposed properly to the nation, and allows what the radical critics would see as the truly reactionary character of much of the Scottish establishment to be put on full view. But that just makes Scotland normal, faced now with the same kinds of debate about radical democratisation of social life as may be found across the democratic world.

## THE CIVIC ORIGINS OF THE PARLIAMENT

Before we get to these options, however, let us remind ourselves of what are now the quite familiar twin strands in the origins of the Parliament. On the one hand, and by far the strongest politically, was the civic. The most well-known instance of this was the Constitutional Convention, deliberating augustly for half a dozen years (1989–95) to produce the template into which Donald Dewar and his Scottish Office lawyers could readily fit the minutiae of the 1998 Scotland Act. This was civic Scotland in its most characteristic form: dour, polite, cautious, asking not insisting, above all practical, securing its ultimate goal by slow negotiation and carefully worked out compromise.

In one direction, the Convention leads us to the Consultative Steering Group, another committee of civic representatives hand-picked by ministers, the civil service and the big political parties, cautiously reforming, putting in place the consultative principles on which the Parliament is now based. As it worked on its 1999 report (Consultative Steering Group 1999), the civic organisations of which the Group was the vanguard were staffing themselves up to the new opportunities that the CSG principles would bring, employing in abundance the research officers, the parliamentary liaison people and the lobbyists that would allow them to move swiftly into the spaces which these principles created.

In the other direction, back into history, the Convention leads us to the civic resistance to Thatcher, to the Labour Party dominance of the civic networks in the most populous parts of Scotland, and to the resulting trust which people placed in these same respectable civic dignitaries as they guarded some elements of autonomy and civic decency against the free-market onslaught. Further back still, when the Labour Party was still fresh, there was the transformation of the Victorian boards and committees into the consultative process over which the Scottish Office presided with relish – the 'middle opinion' that acquired its name (in England first) in the 1930s, but that instantly seemed to sum up all that was most Scottish about Scottish civic autonomy. That then takes us right back to the apparent beginning, to 1707 and the confused but enduring guarantees of civic independence.

All this achieved a great deal. It brought democracy by the 1930s, it inaugurated and developed the Welfare State, and it really did prevent Scotland's being swamped by the New Right. It was, indeed, reasonable for people to put their trust in this civic tradition. And it is reasonable for them to do so now, and to expect their Parliament to do the same.

But there is another tradition, also well known but always, until now, of limited political influence. This is the tradition in which radical nationalism meets radical socialism, both challenging the committees of the bourgeoisie which are, in the last analysis, what civic Scotland consists of. The best-known exponent of both strands (though not usually at the same time) has been Tom Nairn. Most recently, his argument has been the radical nationalist version: that Scotland needed self-government precisely in order to challenge the civic complacency, to expose the false autonomy which the peculiar UK non-constitution did not really guarantee (Nairn 2000; 2002). But an earlier Nairn (of his 'three dreams' essay) excoriated bourgeois nationalism in the name of socialism, and invoked in his aid (as many others in this second tradition have done) the spirit of John Maclean (Nairn 1970).

The two versions of the radical challenge have never really been separate for long however, Maclean's legacy being interpreted as showing the necessity of national self-government if any socialist transformation was ever to be truly feasible. But, like Maclean, both versions of the radical critique remained utopian, and generation after generation of sober ex-radicals followed Tom Johnston into the Scottish Office or into the civic networks against which they had earlier inveighed. How could they do otherwise when caution was exactly what the people seemed to want? How could intransigent opposition be truly democratic or patriotic when the people showed by their reiterated votes and other actions that they preferred cautious but certain reform to the uncertainties of revolution? In that, too, the Scots were not only perhaps perfectly reasonable; they were also hardly unique, since, on the whole, this is exactly the same trajectory as was followed by the people of most other European nations.

## WHAT'S HAPPENING NOW?

It should not be surprising, then, that the Parliament is behaving cautiously. It inherits a national tradition of civic caution, into which it is constrained to fit by the most recent products of that tradition – the reports of the Constitutional Convention and of the Consultative Steering Group. If the parliamentarians are required to consult, as they are, and if the people with whom they consult are, inevitably, mainly the inhabitants of that same civic world as yielded this style of 'new politics', then of course the MSPs merely reflect back to the civic institutions the ways of operating that they have long espoused. It is then no wonder at all that the most positive comments on how the Parliament is currently operating may be found from these same civic institutions, as was evident in their public contributions to the debate sponsored by the Parliament's Procedures Committee in 2001–2. The details can be found by looking at the committee's web pages, but the flavour of broadly encouraging though critical comments can be had from a few selected quotations:

The Parliament's track record in consultation procedures has been very positive. (Disabled Persons Housing Service)

Whilst in general we find the Parliament to be accessible, open and responsive, we are concerned that deliberative democratic structures favour organised interest groups at the expense of the wider public. (Christian Action Research and Education)

In the first two years of the Parliament there is evidence of consistent efforts to draw in the wider civic communities of Scotland to the work of committees. (Equal Opportunities Commission)

The Parliament and the Equal Opportunities Committee in particular have shown clear progress in identifying and progressing equality matters during the first few years of devolution. (Commission for Racial Equality)

The voluntary groups and non-governmental organisations have never been as thoroughly consulted as they are being now. Many of them have been spending so much time talking to Scottish parliamentary committees and ministers that they have little time left over for Westminster debates. In this sense the Parliament, working through the principles of the Consultative Steering Group, has indeed begun to establish a public forum, a space in which social policy in Scotland is truly being debated beyond the still secretive (and still firmly British) ranks of the Scottish civil service.

This process of self-fulfilling caution is reinforced by two political factors. One is the persistence of the Labour Party in the civic networks. In some respects Scottish public life is now less pluralistic than when the Tories staffed the Scottish Office. At least Michael Forsyth enjoyed an argument, and at least there was then the perpetual tension between his associates (including, of necessity, the civil servants in public) and the Labour-dominated networks. Now, by contrast, Labour people (or, more accurately, Labour sympathisers) are everywhere – in the voluntary organisations, in local government, in the civil service, in government, even in business.

The other relevant political fact is the supreme caution of the Scottish National Party, challenging Labour only for command of the civic networks, not challenging civic Scotland's power or legitimacy. The SNP has been chasing the Scottish professional vote ever since it became evident (by the late 1980s) that Labour had captured most of it. So the SNP, like Labour, now finds itself caught by that class's inveterate caution, summed up well by Labour's own John Smith in 1980: 'There is something about the Scottish professional middle class – something which makes them take to their heels and run, whenever a real test arrives.' He was talking about the middle class's failure of nerve in the 1979 referendum, but this could also characterise their deeper and older reluctance to countenance fundamental social change. A party which respects this caution can only ever be mildly reformist. But that same cautious reformism continues to command popular trust because, over the past century, it really has brought reform. Who can really blame the SNP for wanting to follow in these ultimately successful footsteps?

## INSIDERS AND OUTSIDERS

All this then makes Scotland into a rather neat test of the thesis that has been popularised by the US political scientist Robert Putnam – the claim that 'in a community which is rich in social capital, government is "we" not "they". In this way, social capital reinforces government legitimacy' (Putnam 2001: 347). He means by social capital the networks, norms and trust which constitute civil society. His view is that the networks of civic life strengthen democracy, and where there are rich networks democratic institutions work better and are regarded as more legitimate than where social capital is weaker. According to this view a parliament that is an emanation of civil society – as the Scottish Parliament is, in its origins and attempted modes of working – will be more thoroughly democratic than one that is in antagonism with civil society.

The alternate view of this question is a general version of the radical socialist and radical nationalist critique of Scottish civic caution. Committees of the bourgeoisie, according to this view, will never revolutionise politics or society in the way that is required. Only the state, captured by radical forces and acting specifically against the vested interests of civil society, would ever be able to achieve significant and permanent redistribution of wealth, opportunity and power. In the Scottish context, the point would be that networks of civil society are precisely what ruled the nation throughout the period of the Union, which includes therefore the entire period of Scottish capitalism hitherto. So a parliament that is thirled to these very networks, ostensibly in the name of 'new politics', can do no more than renew that very old form of domination. It cannot challenge capitalism or challenge the Union at all. Only a parliament that deliberately distanced itself from civic Scotland could effect the revolutionary transformation that, according to this view, the country needs.

These issues are not ones that can be settled by debate alone: they will be dealt with by history, by the ways in which politics responds to the pressures from civic institutions, and the ways in which both parliament and civil society are acted on by popular pressure. But what we can do, at this very early stage in the Parliament's development, is investigate what form these popular pressures are likely to take. Our most thorough source of evidence on this is the annual Scottish Social Attitudes Survey. In the 2000 survey, around 1,600 people in Scotland were asked their views about the Parliament, about politics more generally, and about aspects of social reform. They were also asked about the networks to which they belonged, and about other aspects of what Putnam calls social capital. A fuller analysis is reported elsewhere (Paterson 2002), but

Tables 1, 2 and 3 summarise some of the key points in relation to one very basic measure of social capital – whether or not people were members of any national or international organisations, ranging from politically campaigning ones (such as Greenpeace or CND) to bodies such as the National Trust for Scotland. Putnam's claim (notably in his 2001 book) is that membership of such bodies strengthens faith in and support for democracy.

**Table 1: Demographic characteristics by membership of national and international organisations**

| | Membership of national or international organisations* | |
|---|---|---|
| | no membership | at least one membership |
| | % | % |
| Higher education qualification | 25 | 54 |
| No qualification | 34 | 13 |
| Salariat | 24 | 53 |
| Working class | 32 | 10 |
| Sample size | 1417 | 246 |

* *National Trust for Scotland or for England and Wales; Royal Society for the Protection of Birds; Friends of the Earth; World Wildlife Fund or Worldwide Fund for Nature; Greenpeace; Association for the Protection of Rural Scotland; other wildlife or countryside protection group; Ramblers Association; other countryside sport or recreation group; urban conservation group; Campaign for Nuclear Disarmament.*
*Don't know and not answered included in base.*
*Percentages are weighted; sample sizes are unweighted.*
*Source: Scottish Social Attitudes Survey 2000.*

## Table 2: Ideology by membership of national and international organisations

| | Membership of national or international organisations* | |
|---|---|---|
| | no membership % | at least one membership % |
| Members of Parliament lose touch[1] | 64 | 54 |
| People have a duty to vote[2] | 67 | 79 |
| There is one law for the rich and one for the poor[1] | 70 | 50 |
| Government should redistribute wealth[1] | 52 | 39 |
| Sample size | 1417 | 246 |

* See Table 1.

[1] 'Agree strongly' or 'agree'.

[2] Proportion giving 'duty to vote' as reason for voting in general elections.

Don't know and not answered included in base.

Percentages are weighted; sample sizes are unweighted.

Source: Scottish Social Attitudes Survey 2000.

## Table 3: Views about the UK, England and Scotland, by membership of national and international organisations

| | Membership of national or international organisations* | |
|---|---|---|
| | no membership % | at least one membership % |
| The UK constitution works well[1] | 32 | 40 |
| Trust UK government to work in Scotland's interests[2] | 17 | 26 |
| Trust Scottish Parliament to work in Scotland's interests[2] | 55 | 58 |
| Support devolution | 54 | 61 |
| More powers for Scottish Parliament | 71 | 49 |
| Support independence | 32 | 19 |
| Prefer no Scottish Parliament | 10 | 20 |
| Conflict Scotland/England[3] | 40 | 28 |
| England benefits disproportionately from the Union | 45 | 29 |
| Predominantly Scottish[4] | 75 | 53 |
| Sample size | 1417 | 246 |

*See Table 1.*
1 *'Works extremely well' or 'works mainly well'.*
2 *'Just about always' or 'most of the time'.*
3 *'Very serious' or 'fairly serious' conflict.*
4 *'Scottish not British' or 'Scottish more than British'.*
*Don't know and not answered included in base.*
*Percentages are weighted; sample sizes are unweighted.*
*Source: Scottish Social Attitudes Survey 2000.*

Table 1 shows that the socially engaged tend to be middle class, and tend to have a lot of education. The much larger group of disengaged tend to be working class and to have minimal education. Table 2 shows that, compared to the disengaged, the engaged also tend to be less cynical about politicians and to have more faith in voting. But the disengaged also tend to be much more left-wing in their perception of social inequality and in their belief in government action to rectify it. So the engaged are indeed trusting, and the disengaged want radical reform.

Table 3 shows that attitudes to the constitution are quite consistent with this. Compared with the disengaged, the engaged are more trusting of both the UK constitution and (by a small margin) the Scottish Parliament, and they are more in favour of devolution. But the disengaged are more in favour of extending the powers of the Parliament, even as far as independence, and are much more likely to see conflict rather than harmony in Scotland's relationship with England. Compared to the engaged, the disengaged have a smaller minority opposed to the very existence of the Parliament. The disengaged are also much more likely than the engaged to give priority to their Scottish identity over any British identity they may feel.

Although these tables are simply one illustration of a much fuller analysis, they show the general results clearly. People who are close to Scottish social networks – the engaged – are more trusting, and are less willing to reform the constitution or capitalism fundamentally.

## WHAT IS TO BE DONE?

The cynics, and those who were opposed to a Parliament in the first place, might interpret this as a democratic failure of the fledgling institution. They might claim that the Parliament is not convincing the very people who need to be engaged if democracy is to be renewed. The obvious reply to this is that to attack the Parliament on these grounds is to attack democracy itself in Scotland. If failure to have yet reached out to the socially excluded were really an argument against having political autonomy, then we would expect the disengaged, when compared to the engaged, to be less supportive of the very existence of a Parliament, less in favour of pushing the powers of the Parliament further, and more enthusiastic about Scotland's place in the Union; yet the reality is the other way round. Just as before the Parliament was set up, strengthening democracy in Scotland tends to be interpreted as strengthening Scottish political autonomy. Now that a devolved Parliament is here, more democracy is coming to mean more powers for it.

In any case, renewing democracy in Scotland was always partly about re-establishing the networks that link civic institutions to the state, and that is indeed happening. That is why people in and around the civic organisations – the campaigning groups and others – comment favourably on the committees and the consultations, even while also urging the Parliament to do more. They are being included in these processes more thoroughly than they were in the 1980s and 1990s, or than their counterparts feel they are in Whitehall and Westminster. In this sense, the Scottish Parliament is re-legitimating the Scottish state. Perhaps invisibly to the mass of the population, it is in fact finding means by which the views of a much wider range of voices than hitherto can be brought into the policy process. That is an important achievement. It will almost certainly lead to worthwhile social reform, of the gradual type that characterised politics in Scotland from about the 1920s to the 1960s. It is the modernisation of Scottish middle opinion.

But there is, alongside this, a popular politics that hopes that the Parliament will be more than a committee of civil society, that it will be a forum for radical challenge to the existing social order. In Scotland, as the survey evidence confirms, that still includes a challenge to the Union. In this sense, Nairn is correct and Putnam could hardly be more wrong. It is those who do not have social capital who have the most thoroughly democratic views, who see that to democratise society requires that the structures of power and of wealth need to be revolutionised. They continue to believe that a democracy that is not *social* democracy is a mere form. And they continue to believe that only a Scottish state with sufficient powers will be able to make the necessary radical changes.

The problem for these radicals is that, except in brief moments, and even then only ambivalently, Scots have never broken free of the safer route of cautious reform presided over by the same civic networks as are now making the Parliament work. One such moment of boldness was at the referendum in 1997, and it could very well be that if the Parliament does manage to open up debate then it might encourage a more sustained, radical programme to be represented at the heart of politics. In any case, the presence and influence of radical opinion in the Parliament – from MSPs in several parties – is itself a reminder to the cautious reformers that the option of further change will never go away.

Careful reform will be a real, long-term victory for the Parliament, and if that is all that it does over the next half-century then it will have achieved a great deal. That is the minimum timescale that will give the necessary perspective. Whether the Scottish radical traditions can link with the apparently deep belief in profound social reform among the socially disengaged is a matter that might take as long to be settled.

6

# CLOSED SCOTLAND?: LOBBYING AT HOLYROOD

*Philip Schlesinger, William Dinan and David Miller*

## INTRODUCTION

Scottish devolution has acted as a major spur to the growth of the lobbying industry in Scotland. Of course, lobbying pre-existed the creation of the Parliament and Executive in Edinburgh in 1999. The old Scottish Office was undoubtedly a focus for such activity. However, the creation of new political institutions has changed the terms on which the game is played: in certain respects it has made the role of lobbying in Scotland much more visible. Lobbying is a debatable public policy issue for the first time. The creation of the Parliament has meant that standards of political conduct are now subject to new scrutiny. And at the close of 2001, it looks as though Holyrood is now beginning to approach the question somewhat differently from Westminster. Only as recently as spring 2001, we might have predicted that the lobbyists would find themselves slipping easily into a voluntary regime of self-regulation that simply reproduced that of Westminster. But no. A limited statutory register is in fact being proposed rather than the tacit understandings of the gentlemen's club. How did we arrive here?

This chapter follows on from our book *Open Scotland?*, which analysed the interconnections between political journalism, institutional politics at Holyrood and the lobbying industry (Schlesinger, Miller and Dinan 2001). As a result of that research, we submitted evidence to the Standards Committee's inquiry into lobbying to inject public interest arguments into the debate (Dinan, Miller and Schlesinger 2000; Stirling Media Research Institute 2001; Miller, Dinan and Schlesinger 2001). What follows, therefore, reflects our experience of both researching Scottish lobbying and the response to our arguments.

# THE IMPACT OF 'LOBBYGATE'

*undercover sting*

The 'Lobbygate' inquiry by the Scottish Parliament's Standards Committee in October 1999 has had a significant impact upon the policy debate regarding lobbying of the devolved legislature. 'Lobbygate' centred on claims by lobbyists that they had privileged access to the heart of Scottish government. These claims were exposed by an undercover 'sting' by *The Observer*, and when this story became public, it threatened the credibility of the fledgling Parliament as the vehicle for a new style of open politics that marked a departure from the bad old ways of Westminster (Schlesinger et al. 2001: Ch. 12).

*Media attention coloured public's view*

The Standards Committee is charged with upholding the proper conduct of MSPs. Its investigation of 'Lobbygate' was not a resounding success, due in part to its narrow terms of reference. There was no conclusive evidence that any of the ministers or their aides mentioned by the lobbyists had acted improperly. But in the highly publicised case of Jack McConnell, now First Minister, the exoneration was based on evidence which committee members considered to be limited. Coming so early in the life of the new Scottish politics, the media – which seized upon the case and gave it exhaustive attention – and the wider public came away with the distinct impression that the probity of Scottish public life was in question. The proximity of the worlds of politics and public relations and lobbying was widely judged to be at the heart of the matter – just as it had been in the repeated sleaze cases at Westminster during John Major's administrations.

The 'Lobbygate' affair led to an inquiry being set up by the then First Minister, Donald Dewar. This looked into the award of PR contracts in the public sector and it did little to counter charges of cronyism or reassure observers. Even *PRWeek* (28 January 2000), the generally tame trade journal for the UK public relations industry, hinted that a whitewash had taken place.

The Standards Committee returned to consider lobbying once again in May 2000. With 'Lobbygate' behind them, it was evident that members of the committee believed that outside interests required some regulation. The 'Lobbygate' inquiry undoubtedly shaped committee members' views as to how relations with outside interests should be handled at Holyrood. As the public storm abated, Standards Committee member Lord James Douglas-Hamilton wondered whether lobbyists as well as MSPs should have a registration scheme and code of conduct (Standards Committee 1999: col. 233). While the principle of registration received this early airing, the practicalities of who should be registered, and how, confronted the committee. It was clearly signalled that regulation would target commercial lobbyists. The committee were uncertain whether in-house lobbyists for corporations, trade associations and the voluntary sector should be included, and whether such a register would attract wider parliamentary support.

# TALKING SHOP

In May 2000, the Standards Committee agreed a phased consultation on the issue, beginning with Members' experiences of, and attitudes towards, lobbying. Forty-seven MSPs responded to a survey which revealed lobbying to be a commonplace activity at the Scottish Parliament. MSPs seemingly showed little interest in regulating the practice (Standards Committee 2000: 7). In October 2000, the Standards Committee issued a public consultation document seeking views on the organisation and experience of lobbying the Scottish Parliament in its first year. Those who responded were largely insiders to the world of Scottish public affairs and were mostly satisfied with the status quo. The Parliament was proving to be an accessible institution to the growing policy community in its orbit, and while some sought further guidance on how MSPs would prefer to be lobbied, nobody except the present authors appeared to favour registration.

At this point it seemed the prospects for registration of lobbying had receded, but this was to change as the committee opted to take oral evidence from representative bodies, including the Association of Professional Political Consultants in Scotland (APPCS), the Association for Scottish Public Affairs (ASPA), the Scottish Civic Forum, the Convention of Scottish Local Authorities (COSLA), the Scottish Council for Voluntary Organisations (SCVO) and the Scottish Trades Union Congress (STUC).

The substance of the oral evidence heard by the Standards Committee concerned the possible pros and cons of regulation. In our evidence for the Stirling Media Research Institute, we argued that a register of all lobbyists would bolster the code of conduct governing MSPs and make a telling contribution to the probity, openness and transparency of Scottish politics. In essence, we proposed that both MSPs *and* lobbyists should be regulated. The SCVO opposed regulation, repeating the conventional wisdom that this would create a barrier to participation by giving those registered an 'elite' status, though without offering any convincing evidence for this proposition. The Scottish Civic Forum also opposed regulation of voluntary sector lobbyists for the same reasons but accepted that regulation of 'lobbying for hire' was a different matter (Standards Committee 2001b: col. 769). The STUC's oral evidence expressed concern that a register of lobbyists might compromise Parliament's accessibility, although the registration of only fee-based or commercial lobbyists was deemed acceptable. The STUC wished to ensure equality of access for resource-poor groups.

The limitations of voluntary self-regulation were exposed when ASPA and the APPCS spoke on behalf of the lobbying industry in Scotland. ASPA, with members drawn mainly from consultancies, law firms, and in-house lobbyists, conceded that they represented a 'relatively small percentage' of those lobbying the Parliament (Standards Committee 2001b: col. 734). When asked 'What on earth would be the use to MSPs of a voluntary code of which many organisations are not part?' (ibid: col. 753) the APPCS were similarly unable to satisfy the concerns MSPs raised about those not subject even to voluntary sanctions.

Members of the committee were unimpressed to learn during questioning that Beattie Media, central figures in the 'Lobbygate' affair, had been members of ASPA and subject to self-regulation. When probed about their investigation and complaints procedures it became evident that ASPA had quietly swept the matter under the carpet, preferring to let the scandal die down when Beattie Media's lobbying arm was wound up during the Standards Committee's investigation. Alan Boyd, convener of ASPA at the time of 'Lobbygate', insisted that as the association had not received a complaint against Beattie Media, it did not investigate. Chairman Mike Rumbles MSP contrasted the response of his committee, which did not have a remit to investigate Beattie Media but did so speedily once evidence came into the public domain, with ASPA's failure to police its own membership.

The committee was interested to hear why ASPA had been founded. When committee member Tricia Marwick MSP suggested that ASPA was set up to 'see off any future regulation that the Scottish Parliament might introduce' (ibid: col. 743), Boyd replied that it had actually been an attempt to replicate the open, transparent and participative culture of the Parliament amongst lobbyists. This account is somewhat at odds with the minutes of an early ASPA meeting at which Boyd suggested: 'We can allow the Parliament to regulate our own affairs [or] we can get our act together and write a code which will allow us to regulate on our own' (Schlesinger et al. 2001: 212).

The mood during ASPA's evidence grew fractious when Boyd, a former president of the Law Society of Scotland, warned the committee of possible conflicts between their focus on giving private advice to clients on public policy issues by commercial lobbyists and certain rights to privacy protected by the European Convention on Human Rights (ECHR). Although at the time considered by some committee members to be a red herring, invoking the ECHR was to become a favoured refrain of those opposing registration for the duration of the consultation, and this possibility clearly shaped the registration scheme eventually favoured.

In their evidence to the committee, the APPCS quickly distanced themselves from ASPA. They stated that none of their members were affiliated to ASPA, that they did not represent legal firms with public policy arms, that they published a register of their clients and that they had acted on allegations of impropriety during the 'cash-for-access' or 'Drapergate' scandal at Westminster in 1998, immediately launching an investigation and suspending two firms from their association. The APPCS were asked to explain why they now favoured self-regulation in Scotland, as opposed to their previous support for a statutory register during the Nolan and Neill inquiries. Robbie MacDuff, secretary of the APPCS, claimed that evidence from other parliaments suggested that registration had not worked effectively. However, there is evidence that statutory registers can and do work and even the APPCS recognised that certain registers had failed due to industry non-compliance and obstruction (ibid: col. 759) – a situation that might well apply in Scotland.

During its questioning of the APPCS, it became evident that the Standards Committee was trying not to replicate the Westminster lobbying model. After taking evidence, the committee decided upon another phase of consultation, this time explicitly focused on how a registration scheme might work in practice, rather than revisiting the principles of regulation, which had by now been well rehearsed.

## LOBBYING FOR LOBBYING: ANATOMY OF A CAMPAIGN

As submissions came in during August 2001, they were accompanied by media reports, editorials and behind-the-scenes lobbying. The underlying strategy by the lobbying industry's trade associations (APPCS, ASPA and the Institute of Public Relations), who had met and coordinated their responses over the summer, was to take the spotlight off themselves, shifting it firmly onto the politicians and seeking to discredit the committee's arguments. The same objective was pursued by the bodies representing other professions engaged in lobbying (such as the Institute of Chartered Accountants of Scotland, ICAS). The APPCS and IPR at a UK level all began to take an active interest in this phase of the consultation.

The opening salvo had come on 9 May 2001, when lobbyists briefed *Business a.m.* over the perceived shortcomings of the likely Standards Committee proposals. The paper played down the importance of 'Lobbygate' as 'overblown'. Angela Casey, convener of ASPA and managing director of Countrywide Porter Novelli in Edinburgh, cast doubt on the committee's grasp of the realities and alleged that the commercial lobbyists were being used as scapegoats. The trade associations ought not to be exempted, she argued. In another broadside, Hazel Moffat of Saltire Public Affairs held that 'if there is a lack of trust, the MSPs have nobody to blame but themselves' (*Business a.m.*, 31 October 2001).

On 2 July 2001, *Holyrood* published an article by Robbie MacDuff that restated his organisation's preference for a voluntary code but also indicated its willingness to help shape a statutory registration scheme. He went on to argue (in line with the APPCS's submission to the Standards Committee) that lobbying by trade associations and companies should also come within the net. This reflected concern – which was to be reiterated – that 'in-house' lobbyists would be untouched by any likely legislation, thereby severely disadvantaging commercial lobbyists alone (MacDuff 2001: 24).

On 13 August 2001, the deputy director of the accountants' trade body, ICAS, was quoted as saying that 'The committee has gone way beyond its remit', while *Business a.m.* (13 August 2001) editorialised in ICAS's support, claiming the committee's ideas did not 'add up'. The arguments were repeated in the accountants' trade journal, *Accountancy Age*, the same week (16 August 2001). A day later, *PRWeek* (17 August 2001) reported that the Scottish Parliament might be acting illegally by attempting to regulate lobbying. It was noted that the PRCA and the APPCS had submitted evidence and that the former believed that the proposals contravened the 1998 Human Rights Act.

The view that regulation might breach the European Convention on Human Rights is questionable. Article 8 of the Convention, on privacy, is intended to protect personal privacy, not that of large corporations or other such bodies. To breach the Convention, it appears, would require a government to take actions deemed to be 'disproportionate'. A requirement by the Standards Committee to disclose lobbying tactics and spending would be intended to prevent the exercise of undue influence on Parliament. According to the Scottish Human Rights Centre, such disclosure would be 'probably the least intrusive and most effective means of achieving this end' (personal communication, August 2001).

In another refrain to be repeated, commercial lobbyists also attacked the exemption of in-house public affairs as unfair to consultancies. *PRWeek*'s editorial accused the Standards Committee of 'a knee-jerk reaction to the Beattie Media scandal' (17 August 2001). The leader went on:

> It looks bleak for PA [Public Affairs] consultants, but the constraints could be halted. The Human Rights Act, which brought the European Convention on Human Rights into UK law, comes down hard on those who limit freedom of expression or restrain trade. The Parliament could find itself up against greater barriers than even it is proposing.

On 19 August 2001, in an evident counter-strike, the *Sunday Herald* reported Mike Rumbles as saying, 'We want to take on those who practise the dark art of spin and make sure there is no threat to the reputation of the Scottish Parliament' (19 August 2001). The Standards Committee was reportedly considering 'naming and shaming' firms contravening its proposed registration scheme and barring their access to MSPs. The rather dramatic headline was to be recycled in the coming months as lobbyists sought to defend self-regulation. In the following week's letters page, Ian Coldwell, chairman of IPR (Scotland), denounced the committee's proposals as a threat to the Parliament's openness (*Sunday Herald*, 26 August 2001).

Coldwell's letter was part of an orchestrated campaign. On 20 August 2001, *Business a.m.*, *The Herald*, and *The Scotsman*, which had all been briefed on the matter, reported the views of the Scottish Council for Development and Industry (SCDI), which attacked the Standards Committee's proposals. In a covering letter, Alan Wilson, SCDI chief executive, stated boldly that the Council did 'not believe that a registration scheme for commercial lobbyists in the Scottish Parliament is necessary or workable. Nor . . . that such a process would be effective in ensuring transparency in the lobbying process. The focus should instead be on MSPs themselves.'

SCDI emphasised problems of definition and of enforcement, saying that 'it would be more realistic to scrutinise the lobbied than the many forms of lobbyist', and called for a strengthening of the code of conduct for MSPs – which had already been suggested by the Standards Committee. The idea that there should be any ethical expectations about lobbyists was rejected (Wilson 2001). *The Herald* (20 August 2001) ran an editorial supporting SCDI's argument. The leader entirely bought the Council's line, saying that it had no particular axe 'to grind because it does charge a fee for lobbying on the behalf of its wide membership' (echoing the words of that organisation's own submission). It endorsed SCDI's view that the scheme was unworkable, putting the onus on MSPs. In fact, the editorial missed the point because the committee had already decided on the principle of regulation.

Although purporting to be impartial, this attempt to sway informed opinion was actually handled by David Whitton, the one-time spin-doctor for Donald Dewar and now a PR consultant and columnist for the *Record*, who had been retained by SCDI to handle the release of its document.

Far from being a source of neutral advice, therefore, SCDI did have a partisan agenda and self-interest. Its executive board has a number of lobbying organisations on it, such as Countrywide Porter Novelli, the multinational corporation with a leading role in ASPA. The PR directors of Railtrack, Shell and EW&S Railway are members, as are a number of accountancy and law firms with lobbying interests. In its own submission, SCDI indicated its unhappiness with any principle of disclosing clients as some of its members 'prefer to remain anonymous and current Data Protection legislation would prevent publication'. SCDI's chief economist and policy manager, Ian Duff, in a letter to *The Scotsman* wrote that the Council had taken the view that regulation of lobbyists was a bad idea since June 1998 and had said so in a submission to the Consultative Steering Group; he maintained that this view was supported by a cross-section of SCDI's membership (*The Scotsman*, 1 September 2001). Yet SCDI had not submitted any evidence to the previous two consultations held by the Standards Committee.

SCDI's report and the related press coverage were picked up by the BBC's *Newsnight Scotland*. Jack Irvine, executive chairman of Media House International, was fielded to put the lobbyists' case in a live debate. Meanwhile Beattie Media were again making headlines for all the wrong reasons as press reports claimed they were implicated in a dirty tricks campaign against trade unionists seeking to represent workers at the National Semiconductor plant in Greenock (*Sunday Herald*, 12 August 2001). Moreover, questions regarding the probity of public sector PR contracts resurfaced in a report that Beattie Media had hired a former chief executive from West of Scotland Water (*The Herald*, 31

01). The appointment was seen as a crude attempt to secure PR work prior to the amalgamation of Scotland's three water authorities.

The summer season of discontent continued with a further story in the *Sunday Herald* (26 August 2001) which reported on the setting up of the Scottish Parliament Business Exchange (SPBE), backed by the Parliament's Presiding Officer, Sir David Steel, and the chief executive, Paul Grice. The central purpose of the organisation was reported as improving links between business and politicians on the lines of Westminster's Industry and Parliament Trust. The *Sunday Herald*'s headline ran: 'Want access to MSPs? The price is £6000', the figure referring to the sum committed by each of the founder members which included Pfizer, ScottishPower, Royal Bank of Scotland, BAA Scottish Airports, Deutsche Bank, Shell, BP, Conoco, British Energy, Scottish & Newcastle and Tesco. As lobbying and potential kickbacks for politicians were the post-'Lobbygate' frame, the story was structured on those lines. This theme was pursued the next day in *The Herald* (27 August 2001). Then, in a column, the paper's Scottish political editor, Murray Ritchie, asked 'When is a lobbyist not a lobbyist? Answer – when he's a member of a posh institute' (28 August 2001). Casting no aspersions, he called for complete openness in dealings between lobbyists and MSPs, a slight shift from the *Herald*'s original editorial line. The answer to Ritchie's question came from Paul Grice, chief executive of the Parliament. He argued that the business exchange was not a body for lobbyists and that it would encourage MSPs to gain experience not just in the business world but in the public sector and in NGOs. Indeed, he maintained, SPBE members would be expressly forbidden to lobby (*Sunday Herald*, 2 September 2001). Much lobbying involves the pursuit of contacts and seeking 'face time' with decision-makers. It is a trade that thrives on opportunities to network with the powerful. Therefore it will be extremely difficult to ensure that its members rigorously abide by any prohibition on lobbying.

By October 2001, the lobbyists and their business sponsors were regrouping at a seminar held by SCDI under the Chatham House rule, a convention described as 'a musty rubric which lets me tell you what was said but not by or to whom' by the *Scotsman*'s Keith Aitken, who was at the meeting. Lobbyists met the Standards Committee's chairman, Mike Rumbles, at the seminar and took the opportunity to lobby privately on behalf of lobbying. They evidently pursued a new line of argument, complaining that 'MSPs are more inclined to heed the public's perception than those of business' (*Scotland on Sunday*, 23 September 2001). Claiming that the Parliament was 'anti-business' seems to have had some effect.

# WHERE NEXT?

By the close of 2001, the Standards Committee had agreed to the principle of limited regulation. Even this required determination in the face of concerted opposition. Although it marks an important development, there are some key shortcomings in the approach taken. The proposed register will only require lobbyists to declare the names of staff involved in lobbying and the clients for whom they are acting, information already required by the APPCS's voluntary code. Failure to comply will result in 'naming and shaming' rather than fines or any other sanctions being imposed on rogue lobbyists.

By concentrating on commercial lobbyists the committee has left untouched the place of in-house public affairs activity. Were consultants to face too much scrutiny, lobbying would most likely be conducted from inside large corporations and public organisations that fall outwith the proposed rules. Trade associations and the entire voluntary sector also escape the net. There are good reasons of political expediency for this. There is a particular reluctance to deal with a voluntary sector that wraps itself in the protective flag of civic Scotland. The significance of ignoring the in-house lobbyists seems to have eluded the committee – or perhaps it simply thinks this is too big a nut to crack. The committee are keen to satisify themselves that the lobbying process is transparent for MSPs, perhaps forgetting that the wider public might appreciate a more complete account of relations between all lobbyists and decision-makers in Scotland.

The commercial lobbyists are right in one key criticism: if there is no level playing field for all significant attempts to influence public policy and mobilise resources to this end, regulation is too narrowly conceived. That is unfair and it is also short-sighted. Those left outside the rules will be able to conduct their business without the same measure of accountability as those caught within them. Our picture of the exercise of political influence in Scotland will be that much less complete. The public and Parliament will be that much less informed. Anomalies will appear and questionable cases will arise that will throw this incomplete attempt to address the issue into disrepute.

The Standards Committee, in any case, has quite a political struggle on its hands. Not only does it have to see off its critics in the lobbying industry and devise a workable scheme, it also has to convince the entire political class that its approach is right. The committee has gone through a major learning process in developing its approach. It has taken some two years of deliberation to arrive at its present destination, which in our view is a poorly conceived attempt to apply the principles of openness and transparency. The committee has been headed off at the pass by industry opposition. The wider political class in Parliament remains uneducated in the arguments and may need some persuasion to adopt the committee's line. The Scottish Executive will doubtless watch the process closely because if the Standards Committee successfully establishes a new benchmark for relations between at least some lobbyists and MSPs, eyes will turn to the Executive, and questions will be asked as to why it should conduct itself differently.

Of course, MSPs do have a fall-back position that will please the lobbyists' lobby. They can look again at their code of conduct and tighten it up even further. There is no doubt that this would be easier to police than using a registration scheme. There are 129 Members to scrutinise as against numerous daily acts of lobbying. There is no doubt, too, that MSPs as public representatives should be seen to be acting with propriety. But should the lobbyists' argument simply be accepted? That is doubtful. The Parliament was created to improve democracy in Scotland and not for the convenience of lobbyists. For politics to acquire widespread respect, those who try to influence the political process need to be rule-governed as well as those who legislate and take executive decisions. Only then is there any chance of the game being seen as reasonably clean, with some positive consequences for public confidence.

The lobbyists have repeatedly argued that some of the Standards Committee's proposals would fall foul of the Human Rights Act. Legal opinion on this is, at best, equivocal. Significantly, though, it was precisely its own toughest proposals that the Standards Committee abandoned when deciding on the kind of information to be registered. Details on the resources devoted to shaping legislation – lobbyists' fees, expenditure and their communication techniques – were rejected by the committee as they sought to balance the interests of lobbyists and their clients against the wider public interest in parliamentary transparency. The minimal form of registration proposed for Scotland may, at best, lead to a marginal increase in transparency and openness. A register stripped of meaningful information is of little use to the Scottish public. The committee has indicated that it will keep the scope of the register under review, but it will be difficult to demonstrate the benefits of registration on the basis of current proposals. It is likely that the scheme will go the way of others that have been tried in various legislatures: where a register is uninformative and therefore unused, it falls into disrepute and is eventually scrapped altogether.

Some lobbyists like to argue that the Scottish media will act as our watchdogs over both politicians and lobbyists. On this score, since 'Lobbygate' – a story actually broken by a London paper – the record has been patchy, to say the least. With the odd honourable exception – the *Sunday Herald* and the BBC's *Newsnight Scotland* – what is most striking is the ease with which Scotland's quality press has simply fallen in line with the lobbyists' lobby. The lobbyists' case has been recycled without any serious challenge or analysis. In the run-up to devolution the political press was assiduous in denouncing lobbyists and in distinguishing itself from them. That critical bite has become a compliant bark – which is another reason why some general principles are needed.

# 7

# SCOTLAND'S PUBLIC SECTOR

## Margaret Ford

The anatomy of Scotland's public sector has undergone several rounds of structural change in the last 20 years. There has also been profound cultural change, the consequences of which are only now being fully felt. This chapter charts those changes and recognises that the Scottish public sector now stands at an important crossroads: whether to continue to advocate a comprehensive model of public sector provision, delivered largely within a traditional model of publicly funded services, or to develop a more explicitly mixed economy, with increasing private and voluntary sector provision. But perhaps this dilemma is too stark. Maybe there is a tartan third way. If government wants to 'do less, better', how might that be achieved?

## HOW WE GOT HERE

Scotland's public sector has been subject to significant structural change in the last few decades. Local government has been reorganised twice: in 1975 and again in 1996. In 1975 the creation of Regional and District authorities separated strategic services from those required to be delivered locally. The professional local government organisations that emerged continued to develop for almost 25 years before political pressure led to the creation of 32 all-purpose unitary authorities. The National Health Service in Scotland has experienced more concentrated change over a shorter period of time. The introduction of general management in the mid-1980s created separately managed units within previously coherent organisations – area health boards. Shortly thereafter, the introduction of the internal market in the early 1990s fractured the coherence of the NHS in two important ways: it encouraged competition amongst neighbouring hospitals, developing duplication of resources and arguably diluting standards of clinical care; and it pitted GPs against hospitals as the former group were allowed to become fundholders, able to exercise considerable financial muscle previously unknown in the NHS.

With the election of Labour to government in 1997 a third major change occurred, as most aspects of the internal market were immediately dismantled, less than seven years after its inception. Further changes introduced at the end of 2001 will lead to the total abolition of the market structure, but may well leave behind a cultural and process legacy which will be more difficult to shift.

In the same 20-year period, Scotland has seen the creation of major quangos: the rise of the super-agency. The creation of the Scottish Development Agency (SDA) in 1975 heralded a new kind of arm's-length organisation responsible for both policy advice and service delivery. Deliberately created to have wide-ranging powers, the SDA was followed by Scottish Homes in the mid-1980s and Scottish Natural Heritage in the early 1990s, when the SDA itself transformed into Scottish Enterprise. All of these Executive NDPBs (Non-Departmental Public Bodies) wielded considerable financial and policy muscle and, at a time when the political complexion of Scotland was different at central and local level, these bodies provided for government a set of vehicles by which to deliver policies otherwise unpopular in blethering-class Scotland, such as the large scale voluntary transfer of public housing.

The overwhelming desire for devolution found expression in the referendum campaign of 1997, when the issue of the democratic deficit was finally addressed. The creation of the Parliament and Scottish Executive marked a seismic shift in the landscape in Scotland's public sector. Therefore, in 2002 a Parliament, unified health boards, unitary local authorities and some public agencies dominate the political landscape, arguably providing a coherent set of public management arrangements. The framework and opportunity for strategic management is now in place – but is the political will? With the third First Minister and administration in two years, what are the intentions of Scotland's politicians? What characterises the real nature of power in Scotland's public sector and where does that really rest? We may understand the anatomy of the new Scotland, but what about the physiology?

## UNFINISHED BUSINESS?

Scotland is a small, compact nation with lots of government. Much of the argument for a democratically elected Parliament emanated from a sense of political alienation, especially during the period 1979–97. However, much also emanated from a sense that there was an unelected state developing where people who were not directly politically accountable for their actions influenced day-to-day decisions over health, housing and the economy. And generally they had extensive resources at their disposal.

The creation of the Parliament, with its unique form of committees, coupled with a greatly expanded ministerial team based in Scotland, presents a real opportunity to radically review the role and function of arm's-length bodies such as NDPBs, executive agencies and NHS trusts and boards. The various attempts at constructing a 'bonfire of the quangos' have, by focusing on short-term political capital, entirely missed the point. Instead of concentrating on a streamlined governance system incorporating ministers, committees and appropriate delivery vehicles, the argument has narrowly focused on appointments to boards, with debate concentrating on a fixation with 'cronies' and how they were appointed.

This is a pity because the machinery has never had greater coherence. The Scottish Executive agrees its priorities in its *Partnership for Scotland* (Scottish Executive 1999a). Individual ministers identify their own programmes and targets. These are communicated to their civil servants and any arm's-length organisations responsible for delivery. Ministers are accountable for the actions of their departments and of those arm's-length bodies at their direction. Parliamentary committees hold to account those ministers and officials and scrutinise their performance and conduct.

This set of processes suggests some unfinished business: what is the appropriate role for unelected boards in the new Scotland? Arguably, if the political direction is clear and there exists the machine to deliver it, why introduce another layer of political perspective and management when local government, for example, provides an infrastructure for local delivery?

A purist would argue that there is no political or democratic justification for unelected boards in the new Scotland. Removing them might sharpen up management accountabilities, discourage unhelpful interpretation of government policy and speed up delivery. Above all, so the argument goes, it would be constitutionally appropriate. Government is, and should be, directly accountable for its actions or the actions of its agents. If there are times when expert advice is required (for example, from subject or industry specialists) then let government access it as just that: advice. The resulting governance structures might well breed a new generation of self-reliant and motivated public sector leaders, responsive to Executive direction and tightly focused on delivery.

There is plainly some merit in this line of thinking, but it also overlooks some important realities. Principally it overlooks the fact that government does not always want responsibility for every operational decision, such as closing hospitals. Some decisions, for example on aspects of economic development, are genuinely best taken locally. It also overlooks the fact that many highly talented people want to contribute to public service, but have absolutely no wish to become politicians: a fact often ignored in the media caricature of 'cronyism'. However, the new coherence offered by the constitutional and management arrangements now in place increases the pressure for a more thoughtful look at the appropriate role and responsibilities of unelected bodies in Scotland, and the role and responsibilities of people leading those bodies. And there are some outstanding individuals operating in key places right across the public sector in Scotland, part of a generation of public sector chiefs who have been brought up to appreciate that leadership, as well as management, is important in government.


## THE PLAYERS

In 2002 there are 32 unitary authorities, 15 unified health boards, 29 NHS trusts, a dozen or so special health boards, over 50 advisory and executive NDPBs and executive agencies. There are emerging a handful of real thought-leaders in this group. Muir Russell, Scottish Executive Permanent Secretary, guided the change to a devolved administration. His laconic style belies a strong strategic sense, incredibly finessed process skills and a very sure touch for what will play in Scotland. A public servant to his core, he is regarded as not only the best in Scotland, but amongst the very best in the Home Civil Service. Under his leadership the machine is changing, although not nearly fast enough for some. The Scottish Council Foundation has been especially critical of the Executive for its lack of strategic thinking and old-fashioned modes of delivery (Boyle et al. 2001). But this criticism underestimates the complexity and sheer volume of effort that has been required to translate the devolution vision into practical reality. The machine adapted to the radical change to a Scottish Parliament and has kept a steady course over three years and three different administrations. Although he might protest at the term 'leadership', it is nevertheless what Muir Russell does.

In the middle of George Street in Edinburgh, another quiet revolution has also been taking place. Audit Scotland was formed from the merger of the Accounts Commission and National Audit Office to provide a single watchdog for the activities of the Scottish Executive. Led by the forensic Robert Black, Audit Scotland is quietly and determinedly changing the nature of public sector audit. Broadening out from a pure focus on financial probity, the organisation is able to take a wide view of the Scottish scene: to conduct comparative studies within and across sectors; to challenge, probe and investigate; to focus on outputs more than inputs; and to drive up standards of performance across the piece. It represents a radical and powerful new approach to improving public sector performance. Alongside Robert Black is Caroline Gardner, Deputy Auditor General. Intelligent, focused and determined, Scotland will be lucky to hang on to her.

In the hot seat in the new unified NHS is Trevor Jones, the recently appointed and still largely anonymous NHS chief executive. Jones presides over a newly unified NHS structure with 15 unified boards. The new arrangements aim to put the internal market finally to rest. He is regarded as one of the most astute NHS managers in the UK. Arriving in Scotland in the mid-1990s, Jones just had time to understand the changing political landscape and adjust his personal style for a more open and scrutinised system.

Michael Docherty is the chief executive of South Lanarkshire Council, consistently one of the best performing councils since reorganisation. The structure of Scottish local government at first glance appears coherent. Unified authorities were intended to provide the kind of joined-up thinking, management and delivery that modern government gurus espouse. The 'unified argument' rejected the separation between strategic functions and local delivery that had been in place in 1975 and which many players in local government had admired. However, the move to unified authorities might have had more credibility had they been designed with a critical mass of population in mind. The diversity of size and geography (Clackmannanshire is 157 km$^2$ and Highlands 25,784 km$^2$) does not necessarily translate into differences in efficiencies and economies. However, strategic functions are undoubtedly more difficult to discharge without a critical mass of population or base of assets.

The low-profile Docherty leads a local authority that looks and feels strategic. Its size and central location has endowed it with quality assets in terms of its elected members and its officers. This team has quietly and determinedly developed the new organisation into an exemplary council. Docherty manages the politics and the organisation with an equally sure touch – the mark of the best local authority bosses.

At the other end of the government spectrum is the new Parliament. Paul Grice is a Whitehall civil servant who moved to Scotland in the early 1990s and started to rocket up the hierarchy in St Andrews House. A key member of the devolution team, he was regarded as a natural choice as first chief executive of the Parliament. Naturally gifted, he has a remarkably even temperament and quiet, personal influence. His role has been to create the administration that serves the Parliament on a day-to-day basis and, given that there were no rules to start with, he appears to have done a pretty good job. Inevitably, the public outcry over the spectacular overspend on the Parliament building has clouded the fledgling administration's other achievements and Grice and his political masters will find that they struggle to have these achievements recognised.

Other public sector leaders of note must include Bill Morton, the man to whom the Scottish Executive turned to sort out the Scottish Qualifications Authority (SQA). A long-time SDA/Scottish Enterprise staffer, Bill Morton's bluff exterior belies his intellectual power. One of the few public sector leaders (alongside Grice) who combine keen policy skills with genuine management expertise, he has handled the transformation of the SQA with characteristic thoroughness and modesty.

Joan Stringer is the very model of a modern Higher Education (HE) principal. Having steered Queen Margaret College to HE status, she attained the distinction in March 2002 of becoming the first female principal of a Scottish university when she was appointed to Napier. Professor Stringer is one of the few people at the top of the public sector with a professional background in public administration, her own research field. Aside from running her institution, she has contributed widely to public life, embracing such roles as Equal Opportunities Commission Scotland commissioner and she was a key member of the Consultative Steering Group.

This group, by dint of their influence, the positions they hold, or their power as role models, are among the key players in Scotland's public sector today. But there is another important aspect of life in Scotland's public sector that could contribute significantly to its effectiveness. The scale of the country means that there are well-developed networks that operate across the public and into the private and not-for-profit sectors. Government interacts closely with academia, business and voluntary organisations, with the principal players more often than not sharing the same educational or professional backgrounds. This network can at times feel parochial and self-satisfied, but at its best can make results happen incredibly quickly. The development of effective models of public sector partnership in Scotland (in economic development, urban regeneration, tourism and so on) owe as much to the personal networks of individuals as to the quality of the processes.

Seen at its best in the response to foot-and-mouth disease in Dumfries and Galloway, the effective management of the crisis arguably owed much to the already well-developed partnership arrangements between the police, local authorities and Scottish Executive. (Dumfries and Galloway is an excellent example of a strategic local authority in terms of scale and approach.) A major opportunity for Scotland's public sector lies in its scale and the potential of its networks. As we develop the next generation of leaders, more deliberate effort might be given to making these as productive as possible.

## WHO'S NEXT?

Finding the next generation of public sector stars might be difficult. In their important 1998 report *Reinventing Management*, Bolger and Pease reported a marked lack of enthusiasm amongst new graduates or undergraduates towards a life in the public sector (Bolger and Pease 1998). Far from representing a positive career choice, public service was frequently regarded as an option of last resort. Part of the rationale for creating the Scottish Leadership Foundation (a not-for-profit leadership development organisation) was to provide a profile and stimulus for enhancing the concept of public service. It aims to do this by, *inter alia*, encouraging new qualifications, private/public exchanges and high-quality development opportunities. But Scotland still has no recognised centre of excellence, no focal point where people can go to learn and prepare for a career in public service. In the Irish Republic, the highly regarded Institute of Public Administration intimately connects undergraduate and postgraduate qualification with ongoing professional development. Where is its like in Scotland? What is stopping the better universities from investing in a similar infrastructure here, as the scale and conditions are almost identical to Ireland?

The Scottish Executive genuinely seems to be making a difference where it can. It has appointed external people to its management board, seed-funded the Scottish Leadership Foundation and, alone amongst UK Civil Service departments, entirely opened up its Head of Division recruitment (a key management level) to external candidates. But there is more to be done right across the public sector, and the lack of meaningful resources for training and organisational development is particularly hampering progress in the important area of local government.

## WHAT'S NEXT?

What kind of public sector will future leaders inherit? There is a live debate about the scope and funding of public services, with a noticeable gap emerging between UK and Scottish political postures. There has been less public political appetite for private sector involvement in Scotland, with the Scottish Labour Party markedly more sceptical about its value than the party at UK level. Some imaginative options have come from the SNP in the form of their proposals for public service trusts, the key feature being that the assets of such trusts revert to the public sector at the end of the contract period.

Whatever the rhetoric, the reality is that there are all kinds of partnerships going on in Scotland. Already, many public sector processes have been subject to change. Fifteen years of compulsory competitive tendering and market-testing (in all its forms) has brought challenges and opportunities to local and central government and NHS bodies that they could not ignore. And although the so-called 'best value' regime has suffered from over-engineering and a disproportionate focus on inputs, some interesting results have emerged from it. Today's Scottish public sector has already become a mixed economy. Bowhouse Prison, Hairmyres Hospital, Edinburgh Royal Infirmary, numerous housing associations and trusts such as Weslo, Glasgow Schools Partnership, and Edinburgh Council's IT outsource are but a few examples of the partnership nature that is increasingly characterising today's public sector.

## WHAT IS THE FUTURE FOR PRIVATE INVOLVEMENT?

For all the rhetoric, it seems unlikely that the involvement of the private sector will diminish in Scotland over the next few years. There are a number of reasons for this but chief amongst them is the broad acceptance that general taxation will not provide the levels of capital needed to modernise and reinvent many services still characterised by their Victorian design and mid-twentieth-century management. There is not the political will to increase taxation, and as long as Scotland remains part of the UK, this is not likely to change substantially. There is some debate now opening up about increased taxation for NHS revenue funding, but the marginal nature of its impact and continued Treasury paranoia about hypothecation will ensure that there remains strong demand for private finance, particularly for funding capital projects.

A second reason is that even the most ardent sceptics would privately concede that there are some outstanding examples of private sector involvement, particularly in construction. Contrast the disastrous experience of the publicly funded and mismanaged Parliament building with the privately funded and managed Kilmarnock Prison, delivered to quality, on time and on budget; or the new Hairmyres Hospital, delivered well ahead of schedule and on budget. The truth of the matter is that there are some things that the private sector does much better than government. This is partly to do with expertise and core business, partly to do with incentives and partly to do with managing the balance of risk. However, government should be learning all the time to work with the private sector in the right way.

The right way need not be prescriptive. The one thing that characterises successful partnership projects in Scotland is that they are all negotiated as one-off projects. As the client, the public sector sets the specification. If that specification means that the asset reverts to public ownership (as in the case of the intelligent Glasgow School Partnership), then it can be set up that way. Equally, no one has decreed that PPP requires screwing down the employment conditions of public sector workers. And there is no requirement for this to be the case. Perhaps our paradigm needs to acknowledge that in the business of relationships with the private sector, government needs to be clearer and more confident about its own aims, and better at understanding what the private sector is best at. Building hospitals is certainly part of it. On the available evidence, cleaning hospitals plainly is not.

Government also needs to acknowledge its own shortcomings. Too often the client is not sufficiently 'intelligent' or informed to specify the right type of contract; too often the political imperatives change and too often procurement practices are more focused on satisfying short-term inputs rather than medium- or long-term outcomes.

A model for a different approach might begin with clarity about the expected nature of private sector involvement. Identifying the right roles for the private and public sectors would be a good start, with some honesty around the real expertise of each. Equipping both parties with the right skills and knowledge would assist enormously: exchanges of staff between sectors ought to be the norm, rather than the exception in a country the size of Scotland.

Government could also offer more encouragement to the private or not-for-profit sectors to come forward with new or innovative schemes. Suppliers' frustration often lies in the process of responding to half-baked invitations to tender for work or services. Government could innovate by creating a clearing house within the Scottish Executive where diligence could be carried out on innovative schemes proactively developed by external organisations. As long as the parameters were clear and intellectual property rights were safeguarded, it is likely that many organisations would come forward with ideas for improving public services. The public sector need not have a monopoly on ideas for modernising government.

Finally, it would be important to have a clear political steer about the expected treatment of public sector workers: the housing transfers pioneered by Scottish Homes in the early 1990s proved that transferring from the public sector need not be done at the expense of public sector workers' terms and conditions. Scotland's public services are in dire need of investment. Our municipal forefathers in Victorian Scotland displayed vision and drive, creating outstanding public infrastructure. It is surely time that this generation of public sector leaders rose to the same challenge: doing less but doing it better; government doing appropriate things but enabling others to do what they do best; acting as intelligent clients when appropriate but as service-deliverers when that is clearly right; restoring self-confidence and raising the management game across the public sector in Scotland to deliver the best kind of affordable public services.

We need to have more ambition and radicalism. A group of Labour MPs (Healey et al. 2001: 152–3) reviewing UK Labour's first-term record made the following points for a second-term agenda on the public sector:

● Mission, buy-in and local discretion
● Building local capacity
● The perils of centralisation
● The need to balance incentives and equity.

These points are just as relevant to Scotland. We need to develop genuinely responsive and, proactive leadership at a national and community level, acknowledge the limitations in schemes, zones, pilots, initiatives which can lead to exhaustion and raise questions about policy sustainability, and recognise deficiencies in 'evaluation culture' as a panacea for everything (Davies et al. 2000; Exworthy and Berney 2000).

Centralism can allow control and equity, but also create a lack of responsiveness, and, no matter how targeted or ring-fenced funding (see the debate on McCrone) is, anomalies and inequalities arise. Developing a change culture requires a new approach by the centre which:

● Strengthens government's central strategic capacity
● Aids the shift in the senior civil service from administration and rule

enforcing to a negotiating body
- Creates space and capacity for local innovation and autonomy
- Develops a 'fast track' across public agencies based on nurturing performance excellence, multi-agency working and getting results.

We have the best chance for a generation to achieve this. The appointment of Andy Kerr as Minister for Delivery is a step in the right direction. The structure of Scotland's government is small and manageable. We have almost 20 years' experience of working with private and other partners, and there is expertise and finance keen to work with government. With a new political generation at the helm of the Scottish Executive, there is an opportunity to get the clarity and strategic coherence that can underpin a genuine renaissance in Scotland's public sector. This will require a new vision of the public service from government, trade unions and customers to develop a modern idea of public services which creates new alliances, relationships and dialogues (Goss 2000; Quirk 1999). This will be a challenge to the institutional inertia which can be found in any agency, and which inhabits parts of the public sector, trade unions and civil service.

Is there the political will and courage? The very early days of Jack McConnell's administration appear promising: all the talk is of sharpening the focus, managing initiative overload and doing less, but better. The body language and the tone seem to hold out the prospect of a more strategic approach to government. If Scotland is to grasp the opportunities now open to it, the timing could hardly be better.

8

# SCOTLAND'S VOLUNTARY SECTOR

*Eleanor Burt and John Taylor*

## INTRODUCTION

### On the political fringes

Embedded within the nation's political economy and wider civil society, Scotland's voluntary organisations have been historically positioned to impact upon Scotland's economic performance, on the quality of life of its citizens and on the political health and direction of the nation. Three factors in particular, though, have conspired to locate Scotland's voluntary organisations on the fringes of political influence rather than its centre. First, Scotland's voluntary sector has been geographically distant from the 'seats of power' residing within Westminster, Whitehall and, more recently, Europe. Second, the 'philosophical distance' of Scotland's voluntary sector from the entrenched right-wing Conservatism that was for such a significant period the dominant force in contemporary national politics within the UK has also served to isolate the sector. Third, the scale, scope and diversity that makes Scotland's voluntary sector so vibrant and so rich an asset to the Scottish nation brings significant infrastructural challenges to a sector that speaks with a multitude of different voices. Now, at the start of the new millennium, a new political climate, together with devolution, is offering contemporary Scottish voluntary organisations significant new opportunities to contribute to the shaping of public policies and legislation – opportunities that could situate Scotland's voluntary organisations within the centre ground of government in Scotland.

### On the cusp of change?

Early indications suggest that the dialogue that is being established between the Scottish Executive, the Scottish Parliament and the Scottish voluntary sector is having positive outcomes. But are the changes we are seeing fundamental or superficial? Is the Scottish voluntary sector set to have a stronger, independent voice in the political arena? It is early days, and the basis for what follows is necessarily one of informed speculation based upon discussion with leading academics, key people within the Scottish Executive, the Scottish Parliament and the Scottish voluntary sector. As Scotland's voluntary sector sits upon the cusp of a new era in Scottish government and politics, such speculation is both vital and timely. The Scottish voluntary sector has reached a watershed. Policy decisions, regulatory initiatives and legislative developments that are made over the next few years will have implications for Scotland's voluntary sector for some considerable time to come. More fundamentally, as Scotland's voluntary sector is deeply woven into the fabric of the Scottish polity, economy and society, these same policy decisions, regulatory initiatives and legislative developments will have consequences, too, for the citizens and communities the sector seeks to represent, involve and serve.

## A MAP OF SCOTLAND'S VOLUNTARY SECTOR

### Infrastructure
Scotland's voluntary sector, as with the UK sector generally, is something of a 'loose and baggy monster' (Kendall and Knapp 1995) in its scale, scope, size and diversity. While this leads some to question whether there is legitimacy in referring to it as a sector at all, more practically it raises questions about the extensiveness of the infrastructure required to represent the estimated 44,000 organisations, more than 600,000 regular volunteers and 100,000 salaried employees that it comprises (SCVO 2001a). Various over-arching bodies in the form of intermediary organisations, forums and networks have emerged whose purpose is to represent and support in various ways both particular communities of organisation (for example, community care providers or environmental groups) or communities of interest (for example, associated with poverty and health) within the Scottish voluntary sector. While there is a range of these over-arching bodies at national, regional and local level, due to the size, shape and continually evolving nature of Scotland's voluntary sector it is improbable that there could ever be anything close to comprehensive coverage of such a sector.

### Representation
Related but more significant issues concern the extent to which over-arching bodies are able *either* to represent their diverse and complex 'communities' of organisation or 'communities' of interest, *or* to enable them to shape their own collective responses to public policy issues. These issues are exacerbated when peak bodies are separated from the voluntary organisations that they represent by one or more layers of intermediary agencies in an institutional structure ill-

suited to support the levels of interactivity, deliberation and debate that are key components of effective representation. The deep philosophical and cultural differences that exist even amongst apparently like-minded voluntary organisations add a further dimension to this already challenging issue. Organisations will perceive 'problems' differently and will seek both different 'solutions' and quite different outcomes. Many of the issues that concern Scotland's voluntary sector are cross-cutting or holistic in nature, thereby adding another complicating factor. These sorts of issues demand new forms of networked communication that the sector does not, as yet, have the technological capability to underpin (Burt 1998; Burt and Taylor 2001; Saxton and Game 2001).

Even more fundamental questions revolve around the capability of any single organisation to represent this hugely differentiated sector or to help shape its collective responses. As the peak body seeking to represent Scottish voluntary organisations, the Scottish Council for Voluntary Organisations (SCVO) is in a challenging position in this regard. However, while the willingness of the Scottish Executive and the Scottish Parliament to engage in dialogue with the SCVO is broadly welcomed, there are some within the voluntary sector who question the extent to which the SCVO is sufficiently representative of Scotland's voluntary sector in all its hues. The SCVO's ability to represent the very substantial number of small local organisations at the heart of Scotland's voluntary sector is of particular concern in some quarters, given that the proximity of local organisations to their communities makes them well placed, in principle, to represent them within the public policy process. While the Council for Voluntary Service Scotland advises the SCVO on matters of concern to these organisations, as well as representing their interests more broadly within the polity, it is an extremely small organisation sitting in the midst of a very large and geographically dispersed organisational network. Whether the newly strengthened network of local Councils for Voluntary Service will enhance the political 'voice' of Scotland's local voluntary sector is a question for the longer term.

Interestingly, the Kemp Commission (1997), in its independent review of the future of the voluntary sector in Scotland, favoured a single body to represent the sector on generic issues. Kemp recognised that issues associated with voluntarism and volunteering extend beyond the voluntary sector per se, and were the province and responsibility of a separate body, Volunteer Development Scotland (VDS). The Kemp Commission questioned both the rationale for having two separate lead bodies and its efficacy. While Kemp recognised that the SCVO and VDS have quite distinctive roles and responsibilities, the commission was concerned about the overlapping aspects of their roles and responsibilities. These, the commission argued, could distract the SCVO and VDS from their main purposes, drawing them into a situation in which they found themselves competing not only for funding and other resources but, more importantly, for influence within the public policy process. There are now indications that the issue may be revisited by the Scottish Executive in the future.

In principle, each of Scotland's voluntary organisations has direct access to the Scottish Executive and the Scottish Parliament. In reality, however, the majority – including, in particular, the small, local organisations – do not have the resources or capabilities necessary to exploit this opportunity. Those who do have regular access to the Executive tend to be the small elite of relatively 'large nationals' with incomes in excess of £1 million per annum and have the resources and capabilities to sustain necessary levels of engagement (Brown 2001). Whilst even these large organisations may lack the capabilities or capacity to sustain necessary and effective levels of participation in the public policy process in the longer term, their ability to engage directly within the political centre ground places them in an influential (and potentially powerful) position relative to the majority of Scotland's voluntary organisations.

Evidence from numerous opinion surveys over the past 30 years shows declining public confidence and trust in governments and other public sector institutions. By contrast, the voluntary sector is for the most part more trusted by the public (Kemp Commission 1997; NCVO 1998). A pre-eminent concern for Scotland's voluntary sector must be to retain and even enhance this comparatively strong reputation as it engages closely within the heartlands of Scottish politics.

Who sits on the governing boards of Scotland's voluntary organisations? Do board members have undeclared connections with other voluntary organisations, with government and other areas of the public sector, or with the private sector? Are they involved in activities that could conflict with the aims and objectives of the voluntary organisations upon whose boards they sit? The Kemp Commission called for registers of interest to be established and maintained by voluntary organisations. More recently, the Scottish Charity Law Review Commission (2001) reinforced this recommendation, calling for it to be made available within the public domain. If crucial questions concerning not only the ability but also the legitimacy of Scotland's voluntary organisations to influence the future of the nation are to be addressed, achieving such transparency and accountability is paramount.

## ACHIEVING POLITICAL VOICE

A mood of cautious optimism is permeating Scotland's voluntary sector at the present time. This reflects a view that while matters are moving broadly in the right direction, it is early days and significant challenges still lie ahead. Foremost amongst these challenges – and especially deserving of caution – are judgements about the deep culture change required to develop and sustain a climate in which voluntary organisations are able openly and constructively to challenge the policies and practices of the governmental and other public sector institutions upon whom they are dependent for at least a proportion of their funding. Second, caution must be applied because it is too early to evaluate the extent to which the voluntary sector is having real influence in shaping political thinking within either the Scottish Executive or the Scottish Parliament. Third, caution is advised because some of the most crucial issues that the Scottish voluntary sector faces can only be addressed at European and UK levels. As Scottish voluntary organisations direct their energies towards the 'government on the doorstep', they run the risk of averting their eyes from Europe and Westminster.

Four major initiatives are currently under way that signal commitment on the part of the Scottish Executive and the Scottish Parliament to strengthen the independent voice of Scotland's voluntary sector within the political centre ground of Scottish government. They do not confer influence but they do begin to establish a climate and conditions in which influence can be achieved and exerted. We turn to these now.

### New institutional arrangements within the Scottish Executive

New propinquity between government and the voluntary sector is being sought by placing clear responsibility for the voluntary sector with the Minister for Social Justice. The pre-existing Voluntary Issues Unit has been expanded and brought within the boundaries of the social justice department, where it is overseen by the recently constituted Voluntary Issues Management Board comprising senior civil servants and senior figures from Scotland's voluntary sector. Other recent key initiatives linking state and volunteer include the Voluntary Sector Forum, alternately convened by ministers and the chairperson of the SCVO; the Active Communities Forum comprising representatives from a number of core voluntary organisations; and the Millennium Volunteers Consortium likewise.

The presence of new institutional arrangements of this kind does not of itself result in an influential role for Scotland's voluntary sector in the political process. When account is taken of the substantial public monies which some of these bodies oversee, however, it would be naive not to accord some degree of influence to those organisations represented within the new institutional arrangements. To take only a few examples, the Millennium Volunteers programme received £695,000 in 2000/1; the Active Communities Initiative will receive £1.65 million in 2001/2, increased from £650,000 in 2000/1; while the newly established Black and Ethnic Minority Infrastructure in Scotland (BEMIS) received £100,000 in 2000/1.

## Culture and compact

If voluntary organisations in Scotland are to speak out confidently from positions of independence and autonomy, moves to safeguard and ensure their independence must be underpinned by a culture shift that is endorsed by, and permeates deeply, Scotland's formal political institutions. Budgetary controls, compacts, regulatory initiatives and legislation, even when acting in combination, cannot bring about such shifts. However, such initiatives can send powerful signals not only that change is required, but of the level of profundity that is accorded to such change. In a number of respects *The Scottish Compact* (Scottish Office 1998) may not have achieved as much as some hoped or anticipated. Nonetheless, its formal endorsement by both the Westminster parliament and the Scottish Executive lends weight to their acknowledgement, first, that voluntary organisations have a responsibility to speak out on behalf of the communities that they serve, and second, that they should be able to hold governmental and other public sector bodies more readily to account. Even though some civil servants and local authorities have been less quick to embrace the spirit of the compact's message and slower still to practise it, *The Scottish Compact* nonetheless sets down important markers supporting political engagement by Scotland's voluntary organisations.

## Legislative shift

Although the detail is open to precise interpretation, the spirit behind the recommendations of the recent Scottish Charity Law Review Commission (SCLRC) marks a further step forward in signalling a more liberal attitude within Scotland towards the engagement of charities in influential political activity.

Currently within Scotland, the participation of 'charities' within the polity is subject to significant legislative and regulatory restrictions that originate in English law: for example, 'charities' must not engage in 'party political' activity, they must not have 'political purposes' and any 'political' activities in which they engage must both further and be subordinate to their 'charitable' purposes (Burt 1998; Burt and Taylor 2001). As around 27,000 of Scotland's 44,000 voluntary organisations are subject to these constraints (SCVO 2001b), this represents a vastly significant restriction of 'political voice'. Nevertheless, many voluntary organisations submit more or less willingly to these constraints in order to enjoy the fiscal and other benefits that come with charitable status.

Under the proposals put forward by the SCLRC, Scottish voluntary organisations may in future seek registration under the new status of 'Scottish charity'. As fiscal eligibility is a matter that is reserved at UK level, 'Scottish charities' seeking eligibility for direct fiscal relief will remain subject to the political constraints outlined above. However, if the SCLRC proposals are accepted in their current form, it appears that 'Scottish charities' that do not apply for eligibility for fiscal benefit but which, nonetheless, now have access to other benefits that accrue to organisations accorded 'charitable status' will be subject to fewer restrictions upon 'political' engagement.

The SCLRC provides further momentum, therefore, towards the emergence of a more liberal regime within Scotland, in which the active engagement of charities within the Scottish polity is not only welcomed, but encouraged. A more radical approach, though, on the part of the SCLRC, one committed wholeheartedly to liberalisation, might have adapted the concept of 'public trust' as it exists under Scots common law as the basis for defining charitable activity. Adapting the principles underpinning the concept of public trust would have made a much wider range of voluntary organisations eligible for the status of 'Scottish charity' (Ford 2000), including, though only in theory at this stage as it has still to be directly tested under Scots law, organisations that English law excludes from charitable status because their purposes are considered to be detrimental to the 'public benefit' (for example, organisations that seek an end to vivisection) (Barker et al. 1996). Drawing upon the principles that underpin the concept of public trusts in Scotland could also have liberalised the rules regulating involvement in 'party political' activity – a concept which is open to interpretation at the best of times.

While the SCLRC proposals signal support for a more politically active voluntary sector, the extent to which liberalisation will occur in practice within Scotland will remain constrained and partial as long as Scottish charities seeking eligibility for fiscal benefits must comply with English law governing charitable activity.

### Financial dependency and Social Investment Scotland

Scottish voluntary organisations received around 35 per cent of their income from governmental and other public sector bodies in 2000/1 (SCVO 2001a). In a sector estimated to have an annual income of £1.74 billion in 2000, rising to a little over £2 billion in 2001, this is a substantial sum. Even allowing that a proportion of this income is allocated directly from UK government departments, it nonetheless suggests significant levels of dependency throughout Scotland's voluntary sector upon the Scottish Executive, the Scottish local authorities and other public sector institutions within Scotland. While the proportion of the income that particular voluntary organisations receive from these sources will vary widely, its overall effect is to induce high levels of dependency. Ultimately, the most challenging question for those who recognise the fundamental contribution that Scotland's voluntary sector has to make in the evolution of a distinctive Scottish polity is how to ensure the independent voice of Scotland's voluntary organisations in a situation in which many are not only heavily, but also crucially, dependent upon public sector funding.

Providing access to new and independent forms of funding, such as loan income of the type provided by the recently established Social Investment

Scotland, is one way out of this dilemma. However, it seems unlikely that there will be many voluntary organisations able, or even willing, to embrace loan finance as a viable alternative to other forms of income. This leaves aside the question whether it will be a sufficiently attractive option for mainstream banks and other financial institutions to allow this income stream to grow. Whatever the funding profile of Scotland's voluntary sector in the years to come, the sector will inevitably contain organisations that remain deeply dependent on public sources of income.

## ESTABLISHING THE CLIMATE FOR CHANGE

It is easy to attribute the putative and proposed changes that we have outlined here as simply the product of devolution. The judgement of those best informed is that devolution has been of some significance. It is not doubted that the new Parliament and its Executive are keen to make their mark, thus lending momentum to the encouragement and endorsement of fresh and innovative thinking of the sort reviewed here. Underpinning this keenness is the cross-party support that the voluntary sector is currently experiencing within Scotland, due perhaps to some MSPs having first-hand knowledge of the sector gained through previous involvement in a professional, managerial or volunteering capacity. At the same time, geographical proximity to devolved government means that the Scottish voluntary sector is better placed than it has ever been to develop relationships and to engage in the public policy development process in a sustained way, albeit in relation only to devolved matters.

More significant than devolution, however, may be the new political climate associated with the Labour administration at UK level, and the pivotal position of Labour within the Scottish Executive and the Scottish Parliament. Many of those with whom we have spoken perceive Labour to have a greater understanding of the voluntary sector than its Conservative predecessors, as well as a stronger commitment to it. At the same time there is a view in some quarters that Scottish voluntary organisations may share some philosophical affinity with Labour Party ideologies (Old and New) and, therefore, find it easier to establish a degree of common ground. If this is the case, it further suggests grounds for the development of collaborative relationships as opposed to those underpinned by confrontation.

The willingness of Scotland's voluntary sector to seek out and embrace the opportunities that devolution offers is also crucial and its capacity to sustain its present levels of involvement is a matter of serious concern (McTernan 2000). Supportively, however, the substantial financial investment made by the Scottish Executive to bring forward technology-related initiatives, including the development of a dedicated voluntary sector web-portal, is a purposeful step towards enhancing the sustainability of the voluntary sector's political voice. By 'wiring-up' the sector, foundations are being laid that could transform the sector's infrastructure and representational arrangements in ways increasingly attuned to the requirements of 'information age' government.

## CONCLUSIONS

We now appear to be witnessing a number of radical new developments in the history of Scotland's voluntary sector. At the heart of these there seems to be a genuine commitment on the part of the Scottish administration to engage voluntary organisations in the governance of Scotland. Moreover, this commitment is underpinned by measures intended to cultivate a more liberal attitude throughout the public sector towards the acceptance of a more politically active voluntary sector. That conditions are being established to allow at least some of Scotland's voluntary organisations to play a more influential role in the governance of Scotland is not in doubt.

Why encourage a more liberal regime, though, and why now? First, we can speculate that liberalisation is being borne of a new and shrewd understanding that the voluntary sector remains relatively highly trusted by citizens whose confidence in the formal institutions of government is declining. Second, there is anticipation within government that the voluntary sector could prove effective in resolving major social 'problems' that fall between the interstices of public and private provision. Third, and related to these first two points, there is doubtless an equally shrewd awareness that for a meaningful and effective partnership to be achieved between government and voluntary sector in Scotland voluntary organisations must be able to speak from a position of independence and confidence.

The Scottish voluntary sector has, indeed, reached a watershed. It is time for voluntary organisations to reflect carefully upon their values, and it will do no harm to revisit them in the years to come. Entry to Scotland's political heartlands is welcome and should be embraced – but at what price? Voluntary organisations will need to ensure that values do not become blurred, that relationships do not become 'comfortable', that (unconsciously and gradually) criticism does not give way to compliance. This would be damaging for the sector, as well as for Scotland.

# 9

# THE LEGAL PROFESSION

*Andrew Cubie*

It seems to be a mark of a mature democratic society that there is an abundance of respect for 'the law', but little for the legal profession. Most of us as lawyers have long accepted that, along with journalists and politicians, we do not enjoy the popularity ratings attributed to nurses, doctors and footballers! The fall from grace of almost any member of the legal profession is met with a barrage of predictable comment about avarice and opportunity; easily then applied to the profession at large. It is sad, therefore, that according to research published last year up to 40 per cent of Scots had either a negative view of their legal system or felt no pride in it (Genn and Paterson 2001). This is inconsistent with the valiant efforts of many over the centuries to sustain a distinctly different set of legal principles in Scotland. This chapter will address the following questions: has our legal system been tainted by association with lawyers rather than being tarnished itself? Has it adapted to the challenges of contemporary society, increasing interdependence and the importance of European law? And has the legal profession risen to the challenge to reflect more widely the increasingly diverse society we live in?

Scotland is largely well served by its legal profession and those who lead it today. There are, of course, faults: a tendency for many to be resistant to change; an 'old boys' network' which is the mark of most ancient professions, but now much diminished; an unrepresentativeness in relation to wider society; and structural arrangements often little understood by the wider public.

Governments need lawyers, both to draft appropriate statutes and regulations to implement policies and then, if appropriate, to enforce the resulting legislation. Vitally, other lawyers need to stand resolutely against excessive taking of power. In Scotland we have never had a shortage of individual lawyers with intelligence and integrity prepared to risk reputation, advancement or exclusion from the establishment to resist abuses of power or challenge the cosy consensus that exists in any elite.

# LEGAL NATIONALISM

Much energy and thought has been expended to sustain the law of Scotland. Our traditions and differences could have been swamped in the Westminster parliament and in the final civil appeal court of the House of Lords, had it not been for those who have argued for the law of Scotland to be appropriate to our particular social, political and economic condition. In this regard the Scottish legal profession, as such, has stood as a bulwark in our ability to be regulated differently, civilly and criminally, from England. It was not always the case: during much of the eighteenth century and the first half of the nineteenth century the House of Lords as an appeal court was dominated by Scots appeals even though there were rarely any Scots-trained judges sitting there (Paterson et al. 1999: 88). Inevitably the result was to allow English common law to intermingle with indigenous Scots law. This came about not through English pressure but by the free actions of the Scottish Bar, who understandably preferred the interests of their appellant clients to a more nebulous commitment to the purity of Scots law. Again, at the height of Empire and 'North Britain', there was pressure to bring the Scottish legal system closer to English law, headed by the Glasgow Law Amendment Society. It argued that 'there were important aspects of Scots law which were not suited to the present economic condition and this view was strongly endorsed and supported by the leaders of the city's business community . . .' (Devine 1999: 286). Even at the height of British integrationist arguments in Scottish society in the 1850s, this view did not prevail in the legal profession.

However, the majority of Scots lawyers have over centuries articulated what has been called 'legal nationalism' (Grant 1976: x). They have occupied one of the institutional pillars of Scottish identity post-1707: a key group in the 'negotiated autonomy' of the Union (Paterson 1994). James Kellas, the respected political analyst, commented: 'Law and politics have always been closely intertwined in Scotland, and after 1707 the Court of Session and the Scottish Bar took over Parliament House in Edinburgh' (Kellas 1989: 184). The Scottish Bar and judiciary have played a critical role in the governance of Scotland post-1707: before the establishment of the post of Secretary of State in 1885, the Lord Advocate administered Scottish affairs in government – reflecting the importance of the legal profession in a 'stateless nation' (Kellas 1989: 184; Paterson 1994).

Lindsay Farmer writing in *The State of Scots Law* (2001: 151) reminds us of the phrases used by Andrew Dewar Gibb in 1944 in considering legal nationalism to have four principal elements in its application to Scotland:

- A belief in the inherent strengths of Scots law
- A belief in the exceptional character of the system
- That it was a legal system ideally matched to the needs and personality

of the Scottish people

● The conviction that the system should be safeguarded against those influences (principally, but not exclusively, English) thought likely to dilute its identity.

The distinctive characteristic of the legal nationalist, he asserted, was 'that this commitment to a distinctive Scottish legal identity did not necessarily entail any support for nationalist politics' (2001: 151).

This book is about power, influence and status in contemporary Scotland. The legal profession is a powerful group in any society, and perhaps more so in a small society with the potential of 'village Scotland' (Young 2002). Individual lawyers also exercise considerable power, both as politicians and as articulate advocates of causes. That articulation remains, at least for the non-chamber component of the profession, their calling. Training in the law helped shape the abilities of the late Donald Dewar, Jim Wallace QC, David McLetchie WS and Sir David Steel: each of whom rose or has risen to the leadership of their parties. The skills of the legal profession can be a major advantage in parliamentary debates, as David McLetchie demonstrated in his harrying of Henry McLeish over the 'Officegate' allegations in November 2001. Beyond those who lead, the list of those with degrees in law and/or who have practised the law in Scotland, and who are active in politics for Scotland, whether as MSPs, MPs or MEPs is lengthy. They form a large part of Scotland's political classes beyond the well-kent faces of the late Donald Dewar and John Smith; for example, a significant number of the SNP group in the Scottish Parliament have law degrees and subsequently in most cases practised as lawyers, including Roseanna Cunningham, Nicola Sturgeon and Kenny MacAskill.

## THE INSTITUTIONS OF THE SCOTTISH LEGAL PROFESSION

The Scottish legal system has been one of the distinctive parts of civil society since 1707. The most important organisations are the Faculty of Advocates, the Law Society of Scotland, the Society of Writers to Her Majesty's Signet and the Solicitors in the Supreme Court. There are also solicitors' bodies in some of the main cities, partly to offset the influence of the Edinburgh legal profession: the Royal Faculty of Procurators in Glasgow and Society of Advocates in Aberdeen (who are nothing to do with advocates).

The Faculty of Advocates is one of the most respected and prestigious parts of the Scottish establishment, based in stunning premises by Parliament House in Edinburgh. The Faculty has a long lineage, dating back long before 1707. Its library is its most regarded asset and its collection led to the establishment of the National Library of Scotland. Its main officers are the dean, vice-dean, the treasurer, the clerk and the keeper of the library. The dean is elected after a ballot of all advocates, usually thereafter going on to become a High Court judge . The current dean, Colin Campbell QC, is responsible for just over 420 practising advocates in Scotland. Over 90 of them are Queen's Counsels (QCs), the most prestigious and well-paid members of the Faculty of Advocates, with the rest working as juniors. The path to being an advocate is a long, arduous one, with 10 to 15 years' work before 'taking the silk'. The entry system is an open and competitive one, which after a law degree usually involves two years of traineeship with a solicitor's firm, followed by a year 'devilling' for a qualified advocate (who is known as 'the devilmaster').

In recent years the Faculty has begun to modernise in an increasingly competitive legal environment, and has introduced a Faculty Directory listing the areas of expertise of individual advocates. John Sturrock QC has created an internationally regarded programme of training, induction and continuing development of advocates, and with John Campbell has encouraged alternative dispute-resolution schemes in arbitration and mediation.

Solicitors are the largest part of the Scottish legal profession: on 31 October 2001 there were 10,917 compared to 7,922 ten years previous. And while most work in Scotland, a small number can be found across the world, predominantly in the English-speaking world, in the USA, Canada, Australia and New Zealand. The 11,000 or so solicitors in Scotland work within 1,000 private practices, 600 with local councils, 565 for central government, 134 for public agencies and 316 in industry.

The Law Society of Scotland is a much more recent institution, established in 1949 to regulate the legal profession in Scotland and headed by a president, currently Martin McAllister. For example, it runs the Scottish Solicitors Guarantee Fund, which acts as a protection for the public against dishonesty and fraud by solicitors. In recent years, the Law Society has faced a number of significant challenges. One has been the pressures on civil legal aid and the issue of whether the costs of hiring a lawyer are higher than the rate of civil legal aid. These pressures and the need for cross-subsidy of legal work can restrict access to justice, one of the key pillars of any legal system, and thus have an effect on the esteem in which the law is held.

Another is the changing corporate make-up of Scotland, which is addressed elsewhere in this book. In summary, the post-war story of Scotland has been the loss of corporate headquarters through mergers and acquisitions, and this has a consequential effect on the scope and scale of Scottish coporate legal advising. One solution adopted by many Scots law firms has been to open offices in London and elsewhere.

Prior to the Law Society of Scotland, the profession contained a number of centres of power such as the Society of Writers to Her Majesty's Signet (the WS) and the Solicitors in the Supreme Court (SSC), as well as Faculties of Procurators associated with Sheriff Courts. The WS Society pre-dates the

Union, dating back to the founding of the Royal College of Justice by James VI in 1532, and has been responsible for centuries for stamping the Royal Signet on legal papers. The Signet Library was established in 1813 and is located in Parliament Square in one of the most attractive parts of central Edinburgh, while across from it sits the Solicitors in the Supreme Court library.

The highest civil court is the Court of Session, made up of an 'Inner House' of 10 and an 'Outer House' of 22. It is situated in Parliament House, Edinburgh, and the same judges also act as the High Court of Justiciary, which from time to time goes on the 'circuit' across Scotland. Scotland's top judge thus has two titles: Lord President of the Court of Session (head of the civil court) and Lord Justice General (head of the criminal court). The position is currently held by the Rt. Hon Lord Cullen.

Scotland's judges are one of the central elements of the elite which sits at the heart of the Scottish establishment and which influences and defines what happens in Scotland across a range of areas in a series of formal and informal networks. They are still almost entirely middle-class, middle-aged men, with a tradition that has historically not been hospitable to Catholics. They have also been predominantly drawn from a select band of Scotland's best private schools (Fettes, Loretto and Edinburgh Academy), although this is changing. An important networking and socialising place is still provided by the New Club, based in Princes Street, Edinburgh, to which historically most of Scotland's judges, significant landowners, bankers and businessmen have also belonged.

Since devolution judges have been appointed by the First Minister on the recommendation of the Lord Advocate. However, in future all High Court and shreival appointments will be advertised and the selection process will be undertaken by a Judicial Appointments Board consisting of five lay and five legal members who will produce recommendations for the First Minister. High Court judges are usually selected from the Faculty of Advocates. Some reformers have called for a change to a more European-based professional career structure where judges work their way up from the lower courts, but this has little support in the Faculty or the Law Society. The current system accordingly prevents some of Scotland's most bright and able minds from becoming judges.

The footsoldiers of the Scottish judiciary are the 200-plus sheriffs and part-time sheriffs who are organised via the six sheriffdoms: Glasgow and Strathkelvin; Lothian and Borders; North Strathclyde; South Strathclyde, Dumfries and Galloway; Tayside, Central and Fife; Grampian, Highlands and Islands. Each is headed by a sheriff principal who presides over sheriffs in the sheriffdom. The lowest courts are the district courts established by the District Courts Act 1975 where lay magistrates are limited to imposing fines and short jail sentences.

In certain areas of legal practice and development legal representative groups have had a strong influence. Thus on a regular basis the Scottish Executive, Legal Aid Board and the Law Society meet to discuss the current and future arrangements of the legal aid scheme. These are called 'the tripartite meetings', which are held in private without minutes being made public, a practice which perhaps does not sit easily with today's commitment to open government.

The Scottish Office's old Home Department has become the Justice Department in the Scottish Executive, with the Scottish Courts Administration becoming part of the same department as the Prison Service and Scottish Court Service. The Minister for Justice, Jim Wallace QC, shares some responsibilities with the Lord Advocate. The degree of departmental change pre- to post-devolution has been small, with the degree of continuity more marked (Parry 1999).

The Procurator Fiscal Service is based on the six sheriffdoms, each headed by a regional procurator fiscal, with fiscals, assistant fiscals and depute fiscals below them. They have nominal responsibility for investigating cases, although this is usually left to the police; the fiscals then decide whether to prosecute or not. The Fiscal Service works closely with the police service, based on six joint boards made up of councillors from different authorities (Strathclyde, Lothian, Central, Tayside, Grampian and Northern) and two others that are based on unitary councils (Fife, Dumfries and Galloway).

Key individuals do exercise influence in the shaping and development of the legal profession. The newly appointed Lord President, Douglas Cullen, is a man of enormous standing well beyond Scotland. His influence stems not only from his personal skills, but also because of the seniority of his position in legal circles in Scotland. Without his exceptional experience of public inquiries dealing with complex, highly topical and sensitive issues, the televising of the Lockerbie appeal would not have come about. His concern for the survivors and relatives of Piper Alpha was tangible amidst the rigour of his recommendations for change in offshore safety. That concern was as evident for the relatives of Pan Am Flight 103, who were eager to witness the appeal process. Without the televising of the appeal they would have been unable to follow in detail the arguments of both the Crown and defence.

## A CHANGING PROFESSION

The socio-economic characteristics of the legal profession are much commented upon, and have seen considerable change in the last two decades or more. I qualified as a solicitor in Scotland in 1969 when, for a total Scottish population which is little changed in 33 years, there were only a quarter of the number of lawyers there are in practice today in Scotland. My colleagues in the 1960s were drawn from a very narrow base of background and schooling. The division between the Scottish Bar and the Solicitors Branch was immense. The manner of doing business for colleagues who had begun their legal careers prior to World War II had changed little in the intervening years. There was still a notion that clients should be pleased that you, as a lawyer, were willing to take them on. Even business cards were not permitted until the late 1970s. This was a profession sure of itself and its place in Scottish society, but which had little understanding of the pressures building up for change.

Scotland, underneath the surface, was changing dramatically in the 1960s. The rising expectations of the public, fuelled by better living standards and education, demanded new standards of accountability and transparency across society, and the legal profession was no exception, but in Scotland it was slow to respond. In particular, the legal profession needs to reflect the make-up of the society it seeks to serve, represent and ultimately defend. Whilst the profession is now significantly more diverse in its make-up, it does not yet fully represent contemporary Scotland. Whilst the majority of students studying law at our universities are now female, the need to broaden the social background of participation remains. Within the practising profession of the 424 advocates at the Scottish Bar, 90 (or 21 per cent) are female. For those solicitors holding practicing certificates, the total number at 31 October 2001 was 8,768, of whom 3,364 (or 38 per cent) were women. The increase in female solicitors has been steady and impressive over the last ten years, having previously been 28 per cent in 1990. All of this is also reflected in the age range of the profession, with the majority of solicitors in their thirties and forties as a result of the expansion of the profession in the last 15 years; as a broad rule, the younger members are more likely to be female, the older more likely to be male.

The broadening and widening of access to university places and the funding of students in those places, which was at the heart of the work of the committee which I chaired for the Scottish Executive in 1999, had to me great relevance so far as the legal profession is concerned (*Independent Committee of Inquiry into Scottish Funding* 1999). While there are presently approximately six times the number of applicants for places on law degree courses at Scottish universities than places available, it must be to the advantage of society that a greater social and ethnic mix in legal study and practice is achieved to reflect wider society.

Whilst financial circumstances are of huge significance there is also an academic barrier to wider access to the study of law in Scotland. Admission to Law faculties is based on Higher exam results alone and the admission requirements are formidable, particularly for many students from less advantaged backgrounds. Strathclyde and Aberdeen universities, via various access programmes, have signalled a desire to tackle this, but there is a long way to go. It is possible that the new law schools will provide a route for lower-income students to enter the profession, although they may choose instead to tap into the more profitable markets of graduate entrants, part-time or post-graduate degrees.

Having obtained a degree, further study is required to obtain a Diploma in Legal Practice – less than 60 per cent of applicants receive partial or total funding – which is then followed by a traineeship, where applicants continue to exceed availability. The Professional Competence Course has now become mandatory for trainees, costing the individual or his or her employer 10 per cent of salary cost, to be rounded off with a Test of Professional Competence. The introduction of more exacting training is a welcome development, but without bursaries or other support mechanisms the law will continue to be most accessible to the middle classes.

The judiciary, at least so far as the wider community see it at work in Sheriff Courts up and down the land, is thought to be little changed in decades. In *Paths to Justice Scotland*, the public view is reported to be that the shrieval bench is male, elderly and out of touch (Genn and Paterson 2001). The parody of 'Who are the Beatles?' is much less true today, but the pressures on the judiciary to understand the nuances of an increasingly diverse and divided society are intense. There has indeed been an enormous change in the selection, induction, training and monitoring of sheriffs, although presently too little of such change is known to the general public.

It will take time for more senior positions to be occupied in better balanced gender terms, let alone socio-economic background or ethnicity. There is, however, change in the wind which has undoubtedly been stimulated by the proximity of Scottish Parliamentarians since 1999. Recent appointments to the bench of Anne Smith and of Elish Angiolini as Solicitor General are to be greatly welcomed. In particular, the appointment of a female solicitor from the Procurator Fiscal Service was a bold move, clearly made on merit and widely acclaimed by the profession as a whole. Inevitably, confronting change in the established order led some voices of noisy complaint to be heard, not least from some Advocate Deputes. The new Solicitor General was, however, entitled to relish the significant volume of letters of support and welcome received from the majority of the Faculty of Advocates and the judiciary.

The members of the Justice 1 Committee of the Scottish Parliament have currently much to do, as in June 2001 they commenced a major inquiry into the regulation of the legal profession in Scotland. The committee, which will report later in 2002, is considering the effectiveness of the current approach to and framework of regulation of the legal profession and of legal services in Scotland. It seems likely that it will recommend greater powers for the Scottish Legal Services Ombudsman.

This is one of the first significant exchanges between the profession and the Scottish Parliament. We must acknowledge that regulation and discipline regimes require to be more open, but also understand that the provision of quasi-legal services by others also needs regulation to allow for probity, confidentiality and competence which are at the heart of an independent legal profession. This is essential when the implications of the Enron debacle reach into Scotland because of the links between some of our largest law firms and the major accounting firms.

Scotland faces many choices and challenges at the start of a new century.

Post-devolution, it has to develop a body of expertise in the Parliament, legal profession and wider community about what makes good, considered and coherent laws which can aid a better governed, fairer Scotland. Within this, law-makers and the legal profession must reflect on the need to legislate for diversity in a legal and political system which has traditionally not been very sensitive to recognising minority rights of groups such as Gaelic- or Urdu-speakers (Dunbar 2001). The mark of any successful democracy is how it safeguards minority rights.

Perhaps the biggest challenge comes from Europe and the incorporation of the European Convention on Human Rights. This has already (via the Starrs *vs* Ruxton case) raised issues about temporary sheriffs' right to hear trials because the Lord Advocate takes a role in the Executive's appointment of them. Their temporary nature and reappointment each year called into question their impartiality. The Appeal Court of the High Court of Justiciary upheld the claim, leading to the suspension of temporary sheriffs, who represent 25 per cent of the shrieval bench, causing the loss of 6,000 court days (O'Neill 2000). Legislation was required to establish appointment procedures for part-time sheriffs which would not be open to ECHR challenge. A new kind of legislative and judicial system will be required by European law and ECHR, which is very different from the certainties of Westminster.

A profession can only truly call itself such if it has a robust and enforced code of discipline. As a profession we should accept, not resist, greater external scrutiny in our governance. Many understandably find the dual roles of the Law Society as regulator and representative body uncomfortable. This will be examined in the long-anticipated report of the Justice 1 Committee. However, we should note that the level of complaints in Scotland about solicitors' conduct is proportionately about one-sixth of those in England and the professional indemnity insurance record of claims is vastly better.

The review by the Justice 1 Committee will recognise in our pluralist and increasingly open society the concerns of the wider community about the need for greater accountability in regulation of the legal profession. This will not damage the legal profession if it is capable of a positive response and, indeed, may help to enhance its standing, assisting to lay the ghost of unseen influence by the profession to rest. With a single-chamber Parliament the vigilance of an engaged and respected legal profession is essential to allow for the kind of power-sharing between the new institutions of post-devolution Scotland and civic society which was envisaged. I hope that in our new Scotland the legal profession, confident in itself, but adapting to and embracing change, is able to accept greater scrutiny, create greater respect for Scots law and its lawyers, contributing to the making of a better democracy and law-making.

# 10

# WHO DECIDES ON SCOTLAND'S HEALTH?

## Chris Spry

## INTRODUCTION

Health is a major issue for Scotland. The NHS will cost £6.687 billion in 2002–3, the largest single block – almost one-third – of the Scottish Executive's expenditure. With 136,000 staff, it is by far Scotland's biggest employer. The health status of Scots is well below European averages – in many parts of Scotland staggeringly below (Mitchell and Dorling 2002; Shaw et al. 1999). The tentacles of health and healthcare reach far and wide – they are a major focus of research for Scottish universities and have complex interconnections with the worlds of social care, education, housing and community development.

### What is health?

Although the NHS has a role in diagnosing, treating and caring for people who are ill, the factors that determine health – for good or ill – lie in a profound chemistry of individual and social circumstance. Economic status, quality of housing, social relationships, genetic inheritance and each person's self-confidence about their own lives are key ingredients. So if it is health we are interested in, then power and influence over health are diffuse and hard to measure. The Scottish Council Foundation report – *The Possible Scot* – argued that health improvement required a new flexibility in health impact assessment in public policy (Stewart 1998). The Scottish Executive's approach to pursuing social justice aspires to action on the interconnectedness of the circumstances influencing people's lives and well-being.

### The NHS in Scotland (NHSiS)

If we focus on healthcare itself, what do we see? With the exception of nursing home care for the elderly, private healthcare is a negligible presence in Scotland. The NHS has a virtual monopoly of healthcare provision – state-run, funded through taxation and free at point of use (other than some people paying for prescriptions, dentistry, eye tests and spectacles). It appears a straightforward hierarchy. Led by a Minister for Health and Community Care, Malcolm Chisholm, accountable to the Scottish Parliament, the NHSiS is organised through 15 NHS boards, with 28 trusts responsible for planning and running health services.

Driving the process of policy development, resource allocation to NHS boards and performance monitoring, is the Scottish Executive Health Department (SEHD), headed by a chief executive working in concert with a Chief Medical Officer, Chief Nursing Officer and supported by a typically thorough civil service machine. Two of the three chief executives in the last decade (Geoff Scaife and present incumbent Trevor Jones) have been career NHS managers. The third, Don Cruikshank, has had extensive business experience both before and after his tenure.

Chief Medical Officers also tend not to emerge from within the civil service. The present CMO (Dr Mac Armstrong) was a west coast GP who went on to high office in the British Medical Association before becoming CMO. His predecessor (Sir David Carter) had been Professor of Surgery, first in Glasgow, then in Edinburgh, before he became CMO.

Although the relationship between the SEHD and NHS boards is usually conducted through circulars, working groups, conferencing (on policy themes), meetings and routine correspondence, it is punctuated by high-level meetings of NHS board and trust chairs and chief executives with the minister or SEHD chief executive when issues have become 'hot' or if performance is poor. Lying behind this pattern is the fact that chairs and non-executive members of the NHS boards are appointed (and can be removed) by the minister.

Chief executives are usually career NHS managers, although doctors, nurses and other NHS professionals occasionally venture into this risky role. In these days of greater openness and accountability, chief executives tend to carry the can if essential targets are not met or if something goes seriously wrong. The chief executive posts in Glasgow and Edinburgh are particularly demanding, with a significant public profile (although any chief executive is a well-known local personality). Until the 1980s the predecessors of today's chief executives enjoyed considerable security of tenure and often great longevity in their posts. This serene insulation from a demanding world is now history. Turnover is high – of the 15 health board chief executives in post in 1996, only three remained in place unchanged by late 2001. There was an influx of managers from other public and private sectors into NHS chief executive posts in the 1980s but most found their experience and skills did not translate across well into the NHS.

# WHO INFLUENCES SCOTLAND'S HEALTHCARE SYSTEM ?

Power and influence in Scotland's healthcare can be seen through a series of key relationships and tensions:

- doctors and managers
- hospital consultants and GPs
- the medical model
- the networks and influences of traditional stakeholders
- the emergence of regulators
- the consumer's relationship with healthcare
- the new democratic processes in Scotland
- the power of the 'big idea'

## Doctors and managers

Doctors have traditionally been the most powerful players in healthcare, the key shapers of their own professional practice and the service's relationship with users. However, over recent decades NHS managers have exercised growing influence through the power to control expenditure on major equipment, staff recruitment policy and allocation of key capacity, such as wards and operating theatres. They are also the local agents for implementing ministerial policy, which has become more explicitly demanding. Yet the power of managers has often been inhibited by reluctance to take on medical opinion when it opposes a manager's objectives. A chief executive who loses the confidence of clinicians is vulnerable. A vote of 'no confidence' might be enough to topple a chief executive. More often a fall occurs when a chief executive gets into general difficulty and cannot survive the crisis without doctors' support. The other more usual source of friction or mutual disengagement comes from pressure on resources.

The NHS was underfunded until Gordon Brown's first Comprehensive Spending Review and 2002 Budget (Wanless 2002). NHS managers' power resided in an extended period of economising and reining back on service improvement and expensive new technologies – negative rather than positive power, constraining rather than visionary. The better managers rise above these limitations, forging alliances with doctors in the process. Often, however, financial stringency drives wedges between doctors and managers, each failing to engage convincingly with the other – to the detriment of the ambitions of both. One consequence is that the NHS hierarchy is disconnected. Doctors conduct their practice in what they regard as inadequately resourced circumstances, whilst the management engages in intense activity over policy development, organisational restructuring, 'implementation' and reporting on 'performance'. Clinical staff, who conduct their work mostly untouched by all of this, are mainly enthusiastic about their work but disenchanted with 'the system' and frustrated at limitations in resources available to them.

## Hospital consultants and general practitioners

The medical profession is not a monolith. Some specialities are regarded as superior to others. Hospital doctors – as specialists – sometimes struggle to empathise with the skills of their generalist colleagues, the GPs; and GPs often regret the narrow view their hospital colleagues take of patients, ignoring their complex social, domestic and emotional hinterland. When complex choices between competing priorities for investing in services or uncomfortable quests for improving service efficiency or effectiveness arise, opinion among doctors can be difficult to interpret. Strong advocates of particular investment choices or resolute defenders of a threatened status quo are usually vocal. Those who disagree with them are usually more muted or subtle, especially if external populist opinion favours the vocal advocates or defenders.

## The medical model

The NHSiS functions with 'the medical model' at its heart, placing the doctor–patient relationship at the centre, with the doctor as expert and the patient as grateful recipient of the doctor's wisdom and skills. In this now rather anachronistic caricature, nurses, physiotherapists, dieticians and other healthcare professionals work in support roles – under the doctor's leadership. Encounters between patients and hospital services in particular were often episodic, making it difficult to build up long-term relationships in which the patient was seen as a social being with wider responsibilities and problems.

However, the medical model has increasingly been challenged (Benzeval et al. 1995). Service-users are better informed and more assertive. Nurses and other professionals are increasingly valued in their own right, and nurses can now legally prescribe a range of medicines on their own clinical judgement. Many individuals need both health and social care from agencies and professionals beyond the control of doctors. It is not uncommon for 'the medical model' to conflict with 'a social care model', particularly concerning the elderly, the mentally ill, children and people with disabilities. Sometimes this contributes to deficiencies in communication between different professions and agencies, undermining properly synchronised care.

The rise of consumerism, the cultivation of individual and community assertiveness as part of the Scottish Executive's philosophical commitment to social inclusion and the impact of scandals such as that surrounding children's heart surgery in Bristol, have eroded the medical model, exposed weaknesses in social care models (where provider agencies are still predominant) and are giving birth to new models. Consumerism in healthcare is still in the early stages of its upward trajectory but will become a major force in the future.

## The networks and influences of traditional stakeholders

Despite these new forces, the power and influence of traditional stakeholders remains formidable. The medical establishment has its twin pillars in the Royal Colleges and the British Medical Association (BMA). The Royal Colleges of Surgeons and Physicians in Edinburgh and the (single) Royal College of Physicians and Surgeons in Glasgow, along with the various UK Royal Colleges, faculties and associations for specialities in medicine and surgery, are responsible for the accreditation of specialists aspiring to consultant posts. The UK Royal College of General Practitioners has developed similar accreditation disciplines for GPs. Royal Colleges approve both education programmes and junior doctor posts, which provide the necessary training experience and in turn help shape clinical practice in Scotland and the UK.

A decision by a Royal College to refuse accreditation of junior doctor posts in a hospital can critically affect the clinical viability of local services. Withdrawal of recognition for training can mean no junior doctors, making it harder for consultants to cover. The hospital becomes unattractive for recruitment and retention of good quality consultants, not only because of the difficulties with cover but because training juniors adds stimulus to a consultant's own clinical practice. It is usually enough for the threat to exist to spur change to comply with College requirements. Only rarely does the sanction of withdrawal of recognition get applied. But now that the UK government, Scottish Executive and European Union (through the Working Hours Directive) have set tighter limits on doctors' hours, the stage is set for the exertion of powerful (but unpopular) change over the very configuration of Scotland's hospital services.

The BMA, the doctors' trade union, continues to be a formidable negotiator for employment conditions. Their contractual terms and conditions give protections and leeway in shaping their clinical practice that are jealously guarded. Doctors' contracts make it difficult to introduce the flexibilities and local deals commonplace in other sectors. Most GPs are independent contractors providing services to the NHS and need to protect the soundness of their business. The BMA's power in contract negotiations remains strong – although devolution in the UK is creating a new dynamic. Hitherto contracts for GPs and hospital doctors have been UK-wide, but it is doubtful whether this is still in the interests of either the Scottish Executive or Scottish doctors. Scottish GPs have fewer patients than their English counterparts and feel their remuneration (largely driven by list size) is disadvantaged. In England, negotiations on consultants' contracts take account of the significant levels of private practice in southern England – it would be strange if this factor continued indefinitely to affect the contractual position of doctors in Scotland.

Thus despite the wider social and political changes that are gradually undermining the traditional power base of doctors, the influence of the medical establishment continues to be strong. At its pinnacle are those eminent in their own clinical field who sit on the higher councils of the Colleges or the BMA, or doctors who find medical politics a satisfying way to leaven an otherwise gruelling clinical practice. However, those at the pinnacle preside over a large sub-structure of committees, and rapid communication within the profession sometimes makes it difficult for both managers and politicians to anticipate how an issue might develop.

The university medical schools in Scotland's cities exercise influence too. The power exerted by medical school academics can be significant, and the appointment of a new professor with a strong interest in a leading-edge aspect of medicine, surgery or research can bend the way the NHS locally uses its resources. Conversely a long-established academic might act as a block on development, unable to see that things have moved on since they first established their position. Sometimes a medical school can be influential over a number of clinical agendas, bending NHS priorities in the process (for example, Dundee's pioneering research and development thrust of the 1990s). Yet a medical school might also go through a less influential period vis-à-vis its local NHS partners. The key variables lie in the academic and clinical drive of the collectivity of professors, their influencing skills and cohesion, and the leadership qualities of the dean of medicine and the university principal.

This focus on the power of doctors and their often uneasy relationships with managers (and politicians) should not distract us from recognising some significant other actors in the NHS power stakes. Some have almost as venerable a history. Trade unions, for example, have experienced a decline in their influence since the 1970s. With the Thatcher government, although national pay negotiations and local industrial relations mostly continued as before, the unions were relatively sidelined. Competitive tendering was introduced for catering, cleaning, portering and laundry services but the unions' ability to resist it was limited. The flirtation with local pay determination by NHS trusts was seen as a threat by the unions. In the same period NALGO, NUPE and COHSE merged to form UNISON, the largest and most prominent union, with 150,000 members in Scotland (45,000 in the health sector). Similarly MSF merged with the AEEU to form Amicus, with 75,000 Scottish members, 8,500 of which are in the health sector. Meanwhile the Royal College of Nursing, with 33,000 members in Scotland, made some progress as what was then perceived by government and media to be a more 'acceptable' face of staff representation. It, however, joined with the BMA to argue against several of the government's management reforms. In the 1990s the espousal of the private finance initiative (PFI) by the Major and Blair governments was seen as a threat to pay, conditions and pensions for many NHS support staff. UNISON, the GMB and MSF, in particular, mounted a sustained campaign, having some success in persuading ministers to improve protections for staff. Low pay, especially for nurses, cleaners, porters, kitchen and laundry staff is also a cause célèbre for the unions but achieving enduring improvements remains elusive.

The new government in 1997 heralded a significant change in the position of trade unions in the running of the NHS. They spoke of 'partnership' in relation to how citizens, service-users, staff, various statutory services and government should work together to create new approaches. At national and local levels partnership forums were set up to give staff representatives meaningful influence. The rhetoric was that this was not 'staff consultation' given a new lease of life – but rather a bold new step to involve staff at the genesis of policy rather than at a later stage. Reality has not quite lived up to the rhetoric but trade unions are now seen as constructive players in the 'great game' of health policy-making. When the new NHS boards were set up in 2001 one seat at the boardroom table was created for an employee nominee from the local Partnership Forum.

Local authorities, of course, share responsibilities with the NHS in public health, care of the elderly, the mentally ill, children, people with disabilities and those with addictions. Joint planning mechanisms give them a major share in decision-making. Since 2001 they too have had a place among the membership of their local NHS board. This differs from the position in England where local authority influence is exercised through Local Authority Scrutiny Committees, which hold the NHS to account.

Stakeholder representation on NHS boards is today stronger. Although Greater Glasgow is larger than most boards its composition is fairly typical. Its non-executive members in early 2002 comprised a retired professor of orthopaedics, the dean of the medical school, a GP, a pro vice-chancellor (of Glasgow Caledonian University), five very senior local authority councillors, an employee nominee, a solicitor, a banker, a recruitment consultant and someone holding a senior position in the Children's Reporter Administration. At least three were also involved in health or social care charities. Alongside these were seven executive directors (the chief executive, four trust chief executives, and the directors of public health and of finance).

### The emergence of regulators

The Accounts Commission and the Health Service Commissioner (Ombudsman), although well removed from the day-to-day running of the NHS, occupy strategic vantage points in observing NHS efficiency, effectiveness and responsiveness. The Accounts Commission oversees audit arrangements for public services in Scotland and reports to the Parliament through its Audit Committee. It reviews NHS accounts and its value-for-money audits of services as diverse as ambulances, community care, day surgery and mental health make it significant in holding the NHS to account. It can force issues off the back burner, it can highlight the need to change policy or practice and it does so authoritatively, potently connected to the raw edge of parliamentary scrutiny and as a trigger of media interest. The Accounts Commission has gained this influence not just through its position in the system but through the generally high quality of its analysis and judgement.

The Ombudsman concentrates on complaints from individuals not satisfactorily resolved by the routine complaints system. Although published Ombudsman reports on complaints protect the anonymity of complainants, that protection does not apply to the NHS body involved. Adverse reports by the Ombudsman provide sharp exposure for NHS management and when something is systemically wrong the spur to action is strong.

The last decade has seen the rise of the regulator in the NHS just as much as in other areas of public services and utilities. The Clinical Standards Board for Scotland (CSBS) and its English counterpart, the Commission for Health Improvement (CHI), were created to monitor and improve clinical standards and the patient experience. They look set to be highly influential. However, they operate quite differently. The CHI exercises a wide-ranging inspectorate role looking at the clinical performance of the hospital as a whole whereas the CSBS focuses on specific sets of clinical standards for particular diseases. The CHI has also been operating longer than the CSBS and already has a reputation for being rigorous and frank; it is not yet clear what pattern CSBS reports will settle into but they are likely to highlight under-investment and weak local leadership. These new regulators, appointed by ministers but at arm's-length from them, are drawn partly from the NHS itself and partly from related disciplines in universities and professional practice, with usually a small consumer presence. Their success will depend on the selection of people to join the teams which examine local services, their training in the role and the rigour of the standards and assessment techniques they use. In the main these teams will be drawn from both healthcare professionals and managers.

The creation of a Health Technology Board for Scotland (HTBS) mirrored its English counterpart NICE – the National Institute for Clinical Excellence. Both were established to evaluate expensive (usually new) medicines or clinical technologies of uncertain efficacy or cost effectiveness. In the public mind their mission is to tackle 'postcode prescribing' (variations in the availability of treatments in different parts of the country) but in reality the challenge is more complex. Much of what is practised in healthcare is, strictly speaking, scientifically unproven. Meanwhile drug companies are subtly adept in their marketing strategies in shaping public opinion. NICE and the HTBS have not been around long enough to establish a settled pattern in their range of scrutiny, the scientific quality of their analysis or their impact on local clinical and managerial behaviours, but potentially their contribution to sifting the effective from the ineffective could be significant. Although the CSBS and HTBS started life as separate organisations, they are now combining in a single body to be known as the Quality and Standards Board for Scotland. In England the CHI and NICE remain separate but this may be reviewed.

The rise of the regulators not only reflects a trend in the service and utilities sectors generally but is also a reaction to a series of recent scandals which have dented public confidence in the NHS. The Bristol children's heart service is the most prominent but others have involved poorly supervised screening services, surgeons with poor results inadequately challenged by local clinical and managerial colleagues, and places where relationships have broken down, making the service mediocre in the process. Not only has this led to the new regulatory mechanisms – and review of the General Medical Council – it has also coincided with a growth in consumerism.

### The consumer's relationship with healthcare

Each NHS board area has a Local Health Council (LHC) with membership drawn from a wide spectrum of local community and voluntary sector interests. LHCs have a right to visit local services and to give voice to the interests of patients, carers and the public. They are consulted on significant proposals for change in local health services, and where closure or change of use is involved their support or opposition is an important consideration for the local NHS board (and the Scottish Executive, if the issue is referred nationally). LHCs have been around so long that some local community activists regard them as a part of the NHS establishment, striking a balance between being well informed, representing patient perspectives and helping the public to recognise the need for change. The Scottish Executive response is to overlay, at national level, a Scottish Health Council to provide staff support, training and advice on good practice to LHCs (whose members will still be 'appointed locally' but with involvement from the national body). There will also be a Health Service User Forum in each NHS board area. These proposals went out to consultation in the spring of 2002.

Meanwhile in England more dramatic reform of equivalent mechanisms is being advanced. They too have local Patients Forums and a national Commission for Patient and Public Involvement but at local level within the NHS itself will be a powerful Patient Advisory and Liaison Service (PALS), modelled on a highly successful pioneer service first developed in Brighton. Abolition of health councils is part of the reform.

People with a chronic illness may look to local (or national) self-help groups as better placed than LHCs to advance their opinions. Such groups often have productive relationships and influence with the clinical team providing their care. NHS staff themselves increasingly reach out to engage better with users in delivering and planning services. The very term 'patient', for so long an iconic concept, is losing its primacy. For decades the NHS asserted that 'patients' were the prime focus of its efforts but that preoccupation obscured the essentially passive nature of the role. A tide of change is running in which people are better informed, less accepting that all clinical staff are equally competent, more knowledgeable of their rights and more demanding than was the case with preceding generations. The balance of power in healthcare relationships is changing.

This tide of change is also seen in the way that local communities regard changes in the pattern, location and style of services. This arises not only over hospital changes or relocation of services but when new but 'unpopular' services are being proposed – for example services for mentally ill people or drug-users. NIMBYism and populism are in the ascendant in the current socio-political environment. But it is more than that – the NHS itself often seeks to give communities more control over their own local services as part of a process of strengthening social inclusion in Scotland. Not surprisingly, local communities often come to different conclusions about how to meet local needs, how to use resources made available by the NHS for local health projects and what attitude to take towards Scottish Executive policies. Here is a recipe for continuing controversy as local NHS boards intent on implementing the policy of the Scottish Executive, or pursuing an evidence-based approach or constrained by the opinions of local healthcare professionals, meet implacable alternative views in the community. These encounters will become an increasing feature of local civic life, particularly as Scotland already has a strong tradition in community activism.

### The new democratic processes in Scotland

The creation of the Scottish Parliament has changed the balance of power in the NHS in ways that we are only just beginning to understand. The NHSiS receives the biggest amount of expenditure. It is a service often used when people feel at their most vulnerable, is a highly complex service with plenty of scope for things to go wrong, and has become an electoral football that is firmly in the public eye. The Parliament itself has a range of devices for scrutinising the NHS and seeking to influence both its major national and local policy decisions. The Health and Community Care Committee is the most obvious but the Audit Committee has significant powers in considering audit reports and probing them in great depth. The Public Petitions Committee attracts pressure groups lobbying on specific issues. The Social Justice Committee can explore what the NHS is doing in fields such as addiction services or the promotion of better health through community development. The Parliament has stimulated a very different approach in the NHS for consulting meaningfully about ideas for service change. Citizens' juries, focus groups, public involvement in planning processes and greater openness generally are all signs of this. Individual MSPs also take great interest in local NHS matters.

And yet those simpler power plays of the past cannot be swept away. The conditions that gave rise to them still exist. The relationship between ministers and their advisers is still subject to conventions. The responsibility of managers to meet their financial duties cannot be dismissed. The need for hard choices to be made on the basis of rationality and equity cannot be abandoned merely because they are unpopular. The tension when scarce resources have to be rationed will continue for as long as scarcity remains a reality, and with that tension comes the need for managers and doctors, in particular, to balance a bewildering range of competing requirements. That these long-standing patterns from the past have been joined by a wider range of other influences and sources of power does not diminish them – it just makes the whole thing more multi-dimensional and complicated. Getting the 'right answer' on many health issues requires either extraordinary luck or an extremely rare talent for steering a sophisticated course through numerous competing demands. As the NHS becomes more genuinely responsive – as it is striving to do – so the noise of controversy will get louder, not quieter.

### The power of the 'big idea'

So is anyone 'in charge'? Clearly, at one level, the minister and those managing the NHS boards ultimately carry the can. But the NHS is one of the most complex examples of pluralism in a pluralist society. The 'great game' is carried out within a goldfish bowl of ministerial policy and targets, cash limits, local judgement and problem-solving amidst shoals of interest groups. Success is partly about meeting targets, partly about credibility, within a context of socio-economic, technological and cultural influences that usually remain largely unobserved but which exert great power. The NHS is slow to adopt new technology but the current of that technology is unstoppable. Social attitudes inexorably affect the way the NHS conducts itself. Initiatives such as general management (1980s), the NHS internal market (1990s), 'partnership' (1997 to today) do not just reflect government thinking of the time, they resonate with deeper undercurrents in contemporary society (Bruce and Forbes 2001). They bubble their way into the NHS, usually as the latest 'big idea' viewed with wary scepticism by many, but in truth they reflect something far more profound.

Scotland has seen historically higher public spending per head than England as a result of need and institutional pressure: Scotland currently spends £1,270 per head versus £1,040 in England (*Scotland on Sunday*, 21 April 2002). Gordon Brown's 2002 Budget has dramatically increased public spending on health for the next five years. Scottish health spending is currently 8 per cent of GDP, ahead of the EU average of 7.8 per cent and with £3.2 billion investment in the next five years is set to rise to 9.5 per cent. This new funding will require a shift by NHSiS managers and staff towards more proactive, responsive arrangements, but difficult choices over scarce resources will still have to be made.

The tantalising question for the future is how much divergence will be seen between the NHSiS and elsewhere in the UK. The way policy, power and influence interact in the NHS has been broadly similar throughout the UK, but this may not continue. The Scottish Parliament, the more 'communitaire' spirit of Scotland and a growing sense of national self-assertion are likely to mean that not only are different things happening in the NHSiS but that undercurrents below might become markedly different too.

# 11

# EDUCATING THE SCOTS: THE RENEWAL OF THE DEMOCRATIC INTELLECT

*Jane W. Denholm and Deirdre Macleod*

In 2002, the attainment of a 'lifelong learning society' is a commonly accepted aspiration for Scotland, and a widely used modern term for describing the concept of 'the democratic intellect' (Davie 1961). This chapter describes the main features of the school, further and higher education sectors in Scotland as they have evolved over the past decade and offers some thoughts on how the Scottish Parliament, together with the institutions themselves, might in future develop this agenda.

Education is a major public service, with expenditure in 2001–2 of £1.672 billion by central government and £2.953 billion by local government. A range of imperatives has driven change in education over the past two decades, including the perceived need for economy, efficiency and effectiveness in public services, greater accountability to stakeholders, and increasing attempts on the part of governments to inject dynamism into the system itself and individual education providers' attempts to more firmly integrate business and education, and make education a more instrumental service for its consumers. Particularly over the past decade, the topography of schools, further and higher education provision in Scotland has changed significantly.

## SCHOOLS AND THE FORSYTH SAGA

State school education in Scotland is a national system administered locally through 32 local authorities. This reverses the previous pattern of reducing education authorities which culminated in 12 regional education authorities between 1974 and 1996. Before that, the 1918 Education Act had streamlined the Victorian system of 987 local school boards into 38 education authorities.

The late 1980s and 1990s witnessed a continuation of the key Thatcher government policies to roll back the state, reducing its responsibility for many public sector functions, and to weaken the power and influence of local government. The earliest examples of this in education in Scotland were to be seen in the primary and secondary schools sectors, with the introduction of opting-out, devolved school management and school boards.

Devolved school management forced local authorities to devolve direct control of at least 83 per cent of school-level expenditure to schools while schools were also empowered to opt out of local authority control and be funded directly by the Scottish Office. The establishment of school boards, comprising consumer as well as producer interests, replaced school councils. Although an improvement on the powerless school councils, these boards had limited powers compared to corresponding school governing bodies in England. In addition, as part of the emerging new 5–14 school curriculum, national testing of Primary 4 and Primary 7 age pupils was proposed.

Each of these initiatives formed an important component in education minister Michael Forsyth's enthusiastic strategy to inject a more consumerist and individualistic ethos into the system but each initiative was substantively captured and diluted by the main teachers' trade union, the Educational Institute of Scotland (EIS). This body often harnessed the support of parents and other groups, often including disaffected local authorities, to the extent that Forsyth's 'parental genie, when unleashed . . . did not produce the results expected' (Munro 1999: 211). In practice the self-governing legislation was 'a monument to irrelevance' (Pickard 1999: 230), as only two schools opted out of local authority control, compared to several hundred in England. One of those has since opted back again: the other being St Mary's Primary in Dunblane. The powers of school boards were substantively contained; national testing met national resistance and, with the blessing of parents, finally bowed to the professional expertise of individual teachers.

The EIS, the most influential of the teaching unions, was set up in 1847 and has 53,000 members; its general secretary since 1995 has been Ronnie Smith. The Scottish Secondary Teachers' Association (SSTA) was formed in 1946, has 7,748 members plus 1,000 associates and its general secretary since 1996 has been David Eaglesham. The unparalleled success of the EIS in mobilising opinion from other groups, especially parents, ensured the watering down of education legislation and laid it open to charges of being reactive. One commentator described it as 'probably the only union in Scotland without diminished influence following the Thatcher/Major years' (Munro 2002: 213). The EIS in the 1980s and 1990s gave voice to the anger and powerlessness teachers felt at the increasing demands put upon them, combined with the devaluation of the profession by government. As a Glasgow teacher is described in the opening words of James Kelman's *A Disaffection*: 'Patrick Doyle was a teacher. Gradually he had become sickened by it' (Kelman 1989: 1).

The power of the EIS has continued post-1997. The mid-1990s were characterised by the development of the Higher Still reforms which were a response to the findings of the Howie report of 1992, that the upper secondary curriculum was not serving Scotland as well, when compared with international competitors, as had been believed (see Peat and Boyle 1999). Pleading the need for more time, the EIS successfully staved off reform twice. Such is the gestation period of schools reform that wrangling over Higher Still continues, with fundamental disagreements over assessment still going on.

## A TOPOGRAPHY OF SCHOOL EDUCATION

School education begins at age five and Scottish schools offer a comprehensive education, catering for all levels of ability until the official school-leaving age of 16 and up to age 18 for those who choose to stay on. Schools and education policy are the responsibility of the Scottish Executive Education Department.

There are nearly 3,000 publicly funded schools in Scotland. There are 2,293 primary schools, 389 secondary schools and 195 special schools. In addition, there are 162 independent schools (67 primary, 60 secondary, 35 special). State primary school pupils number 429,300, secondary 316,400 and private 30,192. The state sector employs 47,500 teachers, including 21,300 in primary schools and 22,200 in secondary schools. The Scottish Executive and local government spend £2 billion annually on primary and secondary schools.

Scotland's Catholic schools were enshrined in the 1918 Education Act, which brought them into the state system. They represent 349 primary and 59 secondary schools, mostly found in the west of Scotland. They have been shrouded in controversy and prompt accusations that they formalise sectarianism, for example as seen in the 'Rome on the Rates' allegations of the 1920s and 1930s. Supporters point to a range of findings, including research which shows that Catholic schools act as an aid to social cohesion and inclusion in Catholic communities (Paterson 2000c).

The private sector has nearly doubled in the last 20 years, from 16,000 pupils in 1980 to 30,192 in 2000. Scottish public schools are generally more day than boarding schools, but significant parts of Scotland are shaped by public schools, most obviously, Edinburgh: 24 per cent of the capital city's secondary pupils go to private schools, and they also shape certain walks of life, such as senior levels of the judiciary. The private sector has a 10.6:1 teacher-pupil ratio versus 19.1:1 in state primaries and 12.1:1 in state secondaries (Pearson 1999: 97). Not surprisingly, pupils at private schools obtain more qualifications: 70 per cent of private pupils get three or more Highers compared to 23 per cent in the state sector. However, although they are more English-orientated it is a myth that Scotland's private schools are Oxbridge-focused – over two-thirds of private pupils going to university remain in Scotland compared to 94 per cent in the state sector (Pearson 1999: 99).

This is a time of great change in Scotland's schools. Glasgow City Council is undertaking a comprehensive infrastructure modernisation of every one of its 29 secondary schools via use of the public-private partnership, levering in millions of pounds over the next 25 years. A very different example can be provided by Perth and Kinross Council's plan to work closely with the nine private schools in the area, recognising the services, jobs and money they bring to the area. Such a scheme would be unthinkable in Labour central Scotland, even in Edinburgh, but a decade ago Glasgow working in such an ambitious way with the private sector would also have been unthinkable.

The Scottish school examinations system is overseen by a single agency, the Scottish Qualifications Authority, formed by an amalgamation of the former Scottish Examinations Board and the Scottish Vocational Education Council in 1987. There are two major qualifications: the Standard Grade in a range of academic subjects is taken at the end of fourth year when learners are aged around 16; in addition, upper secondary school examinations were reviewed in the early 1990s, with the Higher Still reforms introduced in the late 1990s coming fully on stream in 2000/1. The reforms retain elements of the traditional Higher which have been restructured and augmented into a framework of five levels ranging across Access, Intermediate 1, Intermediate 2, Higher and Advanced Higher.

Influential institutions include the General Teaching Council (GTC) set up in 1966 as a result of a committee of enquiry chaired by Lord Wheatley into concerns over 'uncertificated teachers' which recommended the registration of state teachers. It is one of those quintessentially inclusive Scottish bodies, with 49 members on its council drawn from the teachers' side, local authorities and government. HM Inspectors of Schools in Scotland comprising 87 HMIs and five chief inspectors, inspect schools and publish reports. Whereas in England, Chris Woodhead, the previous head, impatiently pushed for change and challenged teachers' unions, in Scotland HMI are known for their understated reports and for not being parent-friendly. The Scottish Consultative Council on the Curriculum was established in 1965 as the main advisory body to Scottish ministers on primary and secondary curricula and is now a part of Learning and Teaching Scotland. As an independent, external body with a tripartite membership, it was the one of the driving forces behind Higher Still.

COSLA's Education Committee is the main negotiating forum bringing together local authorities and teachers. One of the most important posts is that of COSLA education convener, and in the past it has been held by such figures as Ian Davidson, now MP for Glasgow Govan. The convener also sits as the chair of the management side of the Scottish Joint Negotiating Committee which determines the terms and conditions of teachers' pay. Finally, parents are represented in the Scottish Parent Teacher Association, a body whose influence confirms that parent power is rarely expressed in the producer-dominated, institutionally heavy world of Scottish education.

## FURTHER EDUCATION

The main activity delivered by Scotland's further education colleges is vocational education and training. Colleges provide a wide range of provision, including access courses which can lead to higher education, adult basic literacy and numeracy and other adult and community learning programmes. Colleges also provide programmes of general education for all ages, but mainly for younger age groups. They also have a statutory responsibility under the Further and Higher Education (Scotland) Act to make provision for learners with special educational needs.

A particular feature of provision in Scottish further education colleges is the delivery of a significant volume of higher education-level provision. In 1999/2000, just under 17 per cent of enrolments in colleges were for higher education programmes. Around 30 per cent of higher education students are studying in further education colleges. Over 97 per cent of these learners are undertaking one- and two-year National Certificates and Diplomas and more than half of those studying higher education courses in further education colleges go on to continue study in higher education institutions. In six colleges, higher education enrolments constitute over one-quarter of total enrolments.

Over the past ten years, several important changes in governance and administration have affected the further education sector. On 1 April 1993, further education colleges became independent, incorporated bodies responsible for their own management and governance and directly accountable to central government, through the Scottish Office. Policy statements from the Scottish Office setting out broad guidance to the new sector emphasised the importance of improving further education in Scotland, creating a better trained and qualified workforce, raising the educational attainment of 16–18-year-olds, improving the quality of provision overall, contributing towards the expansion of the higher education sector and improving efficiency and value for money.

These concerns have remained broadly stable over the course of the period since incorporation. However, there have been a number of changes of emphasis, mainly since 1997 and the advent of the UK Labour administration with an even more vigorous emphasis on access and participation, social exclusion, quality improvement, governance and management. Very few of the policies developed and implemented in the Scottish further education sector could have been said to have been particularly Scottish, in terms of either influence or design. They were pursued with equal vigour in England. One key difference, however, related to funding policy and the way in which it was used to contribute to expansion and efficiency. In England, massive growth was fuelled by the demand-led element of the funding formula and franchising from 1994 to 1995, whilst Scotland strove to achieve efficiency and value for money in other ways.

Apart from the above intense activity in the early 1990s, the government left the further education sector very much to its own devices, particularly so when compared in relative terms to the attention received by the schools sector over the same period. This fitted with the laissez-faire, market-orientated economic and social policies of the government more generally. Colleges were expected to find ways of becoming closer to their market, to become more entrepreneurial in diversifying their sources of income and some have argued that '. . . colleges' behaviour has been characterised by competition, expansion, cost-reduction and vigorous marketing, whilst on the other hand, incorporation has had a liberating effect on colleges as they have strengthened their identity and esteem and have developed income streams from beyond the public purse' (Leech 1999: 304).

There are 46 further education colleges in Scotland – 42 of these became incorporated bodies on 1 April 1993 under the provisions of the Further and Higher Education (Scotland) Act 1992. They are funded by central government via the Scottish Further Education Funding Council; Bell College in Hamilton joined on 1 April 2002. A major development has been the UHI Millennium Institute, a formal collaboration of the higher educational provision of 14 further education colleges spread across the Highlands and Islands, with aspirations to achieve the status of a new University of the Highlands and Islands.

## HIGHER EDUCATION

The 1990s also witnessed important structural changes in the higher education sector. At the same time as it bestowed university titles upon four new universities (Abertay followed in 1994), the FHE Scotland Act 1992 brought the Scottish universities and the other higher education institutions together as a single sector for funding purposes for the first time. New funding councils for higher education were created for all three UK home countries, with the Scottish Higher Education Funding Council as the buffer body between government and the sector in Scotland. While the new universities welcomed these changes, the extent of paranoia and anxiety on the part of the eight older established Scottish universities cannot be underestimated. The vagaries of the former funding body for UK universities, the University Grants Committee, were many, but there were real fears of parochialism, detachment from southern-based research funding streams and that the new funding body by its nature and history might be both more interventionist and closer to the former central institutions.

In the event, SHEFC has proven to be an unexpected success. Distinguishing itself in the eyes of the sector, it 'successfully tackled a number of crucial and sensitive policy issues', and formulated 'a funding framework which was credible and robust' (Universities Scotland 2001: para. 2). This modus operandi – to consult the sector by written means and through extensive use of advisory groups and committees drawn from sector experts – convinced the sector early on that it needed to have a forum for collectively considering issues and making representations. Thus, as could hardly be envisaged from a distinctly polarised binary sector in 1990, the Committee of Scottish Higher Education Principals (now known as Universities Scotland) – a representative body for all higher education institutions in Scotland – was created.

Not long after the establishment of SHEFC, growing pressure on public expenditure led to the official abandonment of government policy to expand places available in higher education. The huge expansion of higher education student numbers, delivered by both further education colleges and higher education institutions from the 1980s through to the early 1990s (when numbers almost doubled), was replaced by a policy of 'consolidation' of student numbers imposed on higher education institutions from 1993/4 and 1994/5 for further education.

The National Committee of Inquiry into Higher Education was established in the spring of 1996, under the chairmanship of Sir Ron Dearing, to consider and report on the size, shape, purpose and funding of higher education. Unlike its closest predecessor, the Robbins Committee, it immediately created a Scottish Committee under the chairmanship of Sir Ron Garrick, chief executive of the Weir Group and a highly respected figure amongst industrialists and the educational world. The Garrick Committee ensured that the UK national committee was accurately informed of Scottish practice, as well as generating its own thinking and adapting national committee decisions for a Scottish context. Very importantly, it also largely successfully protected the Scottish system from the more hawkish elements of the national committee. The position and financing of the Scottish four-year honours degree was a cause of much debate and the resulting fudge which led the Scottish Office to guarantee to pay the tuition fees of Scottish students for the 'extra' year of study, so equalising the costs of a degree across the UK, led in turn to further anomalies which arguably kept the general issue of tuition fees alive and on the agenda until it became the first political football of the new Scottish Parliament.

In 2000/1 there were approximately 190,000 learners in higher education institutions enrolled on courses leading to qualifications or credit. There are also around 100,000 continuing education places largely comprising non-certificated classes for adults in a wide range of subject areas. The shape and size of the Scottish higher education sector has changed significantly over the past decade. This has largely been driven by a combination of a change in government policy, recognising the educational benefits of incorporating teacher education within a wider university environment, and the general effects of a universal funding formula for teaching and learning applied by SHEFC. Thus the five independent monotechnic teacher education colleges, and two smaller colleges, merged with larger multi-faculty universities. In addition, two new higher education institutions have been designated.

There are currently 20 higher education institutions in Scotland. Fourteen of these are universities, including the five former polytechnic central institutions which were designated as such by the Further and Higher Education (Scotland) Act 1992 and the Open University, which retains its links to the UK Open University in Milton Keynes but which, from 2001/2 has been funded as part of the Scottish higher education sector. At the same time, public financing of the UHI Millennium Institute was also brought into the funding ambit of SHEFC. The Scottish Agricultural College is the only higher education institution which continues to be funded directly by the Scottish Executive via its agriculture department. The sector also comprises a university college, two art colleges and a conservatoire.

The total annual turnover of the Scottish higher education sector is over £1.4 billion of which, in 2002/3, £703 million is attracted through direct grant from the Scottish Higher Education Funding Council. The rest is competitively earned from public and private sources. The sector employs over 36,000 people.

## THE SCOTTISH PARLIAMENT AND EDUCATION

Growing recognition on the part of all advanced capitalist countries of the importance of education and training in underpinning the economic prosperity of the nation has led to a re-examination of the nature of their education systems, with consequent structural readjustments. As outlined earlier, the UK and Scottish education systems have been no exception, instituting major structural changes throughout the past 20 years. In addition, over the past decade there has been a growing consciousness of the need to ensure that all people have the opportunity to reach their full potential by gaining the skills that they need for employment and for updating existing skills.

The establishment of the Scottish Parliament in 1999 represents a real opportunity to identify the important issues and deliver a lifelong learning society. First the Executive, and then the Parliament, split portfolio responsibilities for schools education from post-compulsory education. In a popular move with universities and colleges, the Executive created a ministry for Enterprise and Lifelong Learning which acknowledged the key and increasing role of further and higher education institutions in equipping the workforce with skills and generally powering the so-called knowledge economy.

In its first term the Parliament has endorsed the recommendations of the McCrone report, which represents a huge national commitment to school education, although unresolved issues about resource implications and responsibilities have led some to speculate that it may begin to unravel in practice. Teachers won a 21.5 per cent pay rise over three years and a 35-hour week in return for more flexible working; critics, including Gavin McCrone, have argued that teachers have not kept their side of this bargain. In another development, Jack McConnell, in his short period as Education Minister, acted swiftly in the face of the much publicised failure of the Scottish examinations system and the Scottish Qualifications Authority to deliver accurate results to candidates on time, stemming a major crisis of confidence in the system as a whole (Paterson 2000b).

Education has long been considered to occupy a special place in the hearts of Scots and this belief is underpinned by a self-sustaining tradition of there being a 'democratic intellect' (Davie 1961). This has been found in the 'lad o' pairts' (with no consequent 'lass o' pairts'), 'the Kirriemuir career' and respect and authority for 'the dominie' (the school teacher as leader in the community) (McCrone 1992; Howson 1993). All of these myths have emphasised the opportunity in education regardless of background, and reinforced the belief that Scotland was an egalitarian society.

From the revelations of the Howie report in 1992 that over half of all fifth-year pupils left school with none or only one Higher (Scottish Office Education and Industry Department 1992) to OECD reports which showed Scotland far down the international league table of attainment in maths and science and the fact that one in five adults in Scotland has poor basic levels of literacy and numeracy, it is now clear that relatively high participation rates in higher education compared to the rest of the UK have masked huge areas of non-participation and excluded groups. In 2001, only 31 per cent of all Scotland's S6 pupils left with three Highers or more, ranging from a high of 52 per cent in East Renfrewshire to 19 per cent in Glasgow. In the words of Jack McConnell, Scotland has to 'close the gap', but we also need to ask whether anyone needs another 'great education debate' to do it. Scotland has had to reconsider the basis for some of its taken-for-granted myths – that the system is better providing more people with higher and better quality qualifications than those in the rest of the UK. In 2002, too many Scots still regard learning as 'not for them' and have no intention of returning to any sort of learning.

On top of these substantive qualitative issues, the failure of process manifested by the malfunction of the Scottish school examination system in 2000 attracted wide media coverage and severely dented Scotland's educational image, externally engendering a palpable amount of *schadenfreude* on the part of other UK commentators and internally shaking the faith of ordinary Scots in the system.

Yet, despite these confidence-sapping events and revelations, education remains a service high in the public consciousness. In 1999 student hardship, as encapsulated by the issue of tuition fees, became the coalition deal-breaker in the newly established Scottish Parliament, arising from a popular widespread sense of social justice and concern for the education system. Amid the confusion, misunderstanding, political opportunism and downright hypocrisy that surrounded this debate, there was a real issue which clearly captured the zeitgeist of Scottish opinion and resulted in a renegotiation of tuition fees and, more substantively, a reintroduction of grants for students from the poorest backgrounds.

In 2002, there is a healthy acceptance that Scotland can and should do better and a widely drawn consensus – subscribed to by all political parties – that the way to achieve improvement is through the creation of a lifelong learning society in Scotland. The past decade has been characterised by educational soul-searching in the form of numerous reviews of different parts and features of the education system, the most recent of which is the Scottish Executive's National Debate on Education – a major review of the future of school education. Incredibly, in the past year there have been no fewer than five separate reviews of aspects of the post-school education and training sectors: the Scottish Higher Education Funding Council's own reviews of its teaching and research-funding methodologies; the Enterprise and Lifelong Learning Committee's inquiry into those reviews; SHEFC's strategic review of higher education; the Scottish Executive's quinquennial review of SHEFC, including a general review of the role of Scottish higher education; and the Enterprise and Lifelong Learning Committee's ongoing Inquiry into Lifelong Learning.

Lindsay Paterson, assessing the impact of the Scottish Parliament on education, observed: 'Devolution has allowed us not to do what David Blunkett and Estelle Morris have done down south. There will be no specialist schools, probably no private money in school management, and there will be a much less aggressive regime towards teachers, and of testing and target-setting. Pre-devolution, these ideas would have spilled across the border, but not now' (*The Scotsman*, 22 April 2002). Whether this is a good or a bad thing, breaking with consensus or reinforcing myths, at least now Scots are deciding priorities for themselves.

The renewal of the democratic intellect – the nearest Scotland has to 'the American dream' (McCrone 1992: 92) – is central to the remaking of Scottish education. A useful contribution has been made by the Scottish Parliament Enterprise and Lifelong Learning Committee's vision that lifelong learning can 'create a culture where everyone has the desire and the opportunity to continuously develop their knowledge and skills, thus enhancing their quality of life and the well-being of society' (Enterprise and Lifelong Learning Committee 2002: para. 29). Any revised version has to acknowledge the ambiguity of the democratic intellect historically and how it has sat side by side with conservative inertia, inequalities and privilege. There is scope for a new agenda across Scotland, as Keir Bloomer has noted, when he asks how we can maintain 'a broader view in a climate where education is increasingly seen in utilitarian terms, with the priority being to raise levels of academic achievements' and emphasise as well 'the social, economic and physical development of young people?' (Bloomer 1999: 167). Two years later, Bloomer sees signs of optimism in the adoption of a more self-critical approach: 'the "wha's like us" attitude is dead. Scottish education has stopped congratulating itself and started thinking' (Bloomer 2001b).

# 12

# NETWORK SCOTLAND: THE POWER OF THE QUANGO STATE

## George Rosie

There is a conundrum at the centre of public life in Britain. It concerns those bodies we all know as 'quangos' (quasi-autonomous national government organisations) but which Her Majesty's ministers insist on calling NDPBs (non-departmental public bodies). On the one hand, quangos are thoroughly disapproved of by all and sundry. The Right is inclined to see them as the tentacles of central government which strangle initiative and enterprise. The Left sees the quangocracy as an unelected abomination stuffed with the cronies and placemen of whatever party happens to be in power. Both Left and Right denounce quangos as an unnecessary expense, things that should be got rid of as soon as possible.

On the other hand, almost everyone with an idea of how Britain and/or Scotland should be run seems to want to become one of the quangofolk. Whenever an agency needs bodies there is never any shortage of applicants. And it is certainly not the money that attracts them. In February 2002, for instance, the Scottish Environmental Protection Agency (SEPA) had vacancies on its regional boards. Applications were invited from anyone with a bit of experience of the wider world who could spare a day per month. For this SEPA were offering an annual wage of £1,569 'plus your expenses'. The big-spending Scottish Higher Education Funding Council (SHEFC) was only slightly less thrifty. It was offering board members £210 a day.

Not, you would be right to conclude, the kind of money calculated to bring the firebrands and heavy hitters of Scottish life leaping out of the heather to batter down the doors of SEPA and the SHEFC. Nevertheless, the quangos have no problem of stocking up with new board members. Cachet counts. It may not be everything, but it is certainly something. There seems to be a distinct attraction in joining the ranks of the great and good even if it is only as a part-time board member of the Scottish Advisory

Committee on Underwater Hearing Aids for West Shetland Salmon-Sexers.

There is no such body, of course. But cheap quango jokes are easy to make. That is part of their allure. And probably one of the reasons that so many solemn and sensible folk on all shades of the political spectrum are keen to see quango numbers cut to 'manageable' proportions. On the face of it, they have a case. According to the Cabinet Office, at the last count (in March 2001) there were 1,035 NDPBs in the UK, which were run by around 30,000 quangofolk who dispensed more than £24 billion of our money, which is more than the Ministry of Defence spends on keeping the alien hordes at bay.

But sometimes it is hard to see why so many get quite so hot under the collar about the quangocracy. One of the charges invariably levelled is cronyism. But is there anything intrinsically wrong with men and women who are sympathetic to the aims of an elected government trying to ensure these aims are carried through by serving on a quango? As for political preference, what government in its right mind is going to appoint its known political enemies to positions of power and influence where they can use that power and influence to thwart government policy?

## A SHORT HISTORY OF THE QUANGO

Weir and Beetham offer the following definition of quangos:

> . . . quangos allow central government fairly easily to set up mechanisms outside existing structures . . . They are in this sense the flexible friends of central government. The creation of new hierarchies of control in school and further education shows how quickly this political scaffolding can be rigged up. (Weir and Beetham 1998: 203–4)

Worrying about central government is a venerable tradition. It is one of the plangent themes of the Enlightenment which can still be heard, particularly in the United States. Adam Smith – who was an ardent admirer of the fledgling USA – takes it up in *The Wealth of Nations*. He wrote: 'Great nations are never impoverished by private, though they sometimes are by public prodigality and misconduct. The whole, or almost the whole public revenue, is in most countries employed in maintaining unproductive hands' (Smith 1813: 143).

To the sage of Kirkcaldy, government officials were just such 'unproductive hands'. Unless their numbers were curbed, Smith warned, '. . . all the frugality and good conduct of individuals may not be able to compensate the waste and degradation of produce occasioned by the violent and forced encroachment' (ibid: 152). Which is a bit rich coming from a man with a government sinecure in the Customs Department.

But Smith seemed to have been writing in vain. Within 50 years of his death in 1790, quango-like bodies were sprouting all over Britain. By 1832 the British government had in place the National Debt Commission, the Board of Customs and Excise, the Board of Taxes and Queen Anne's Bounty Board. In Scotland, up popped the Board of Manufacturers, the British Herring Fishery Board, the Board of Supervision and the Lunacy Commission. As Britain grew in size and complexity, through the nineteenth century and into the twentieth, so did government in all its ramifications.

The statist enthusiasms of the Attlee, Wilson and Callaghan governments added to the total, of course. Although the Tories are sniffish about the value of quangos, when they were in power in the early 1970s and 1980s they never hesitated to conjure them up when it suited their ends. Just how many quangos we ended up with has always been a moot point. But one survey by the free-marketeers of the Adam Smith Institute in 1979 counted more than 3,000 quangos employing more than 46,000 people (mostly unpaid) and costing the taxpayer £7.28 billion a year.

Since then the numbers have been reduced, as successive governments have tried to slash and burn the bureaucratic undergrowth. But there are still enough quangos and quangocrats around to induce apoplexy on the political right and much head scratching in the ranks of New Labour. The most recent Cabinet Office blurb on the subject of 'public bodies' declares that the government is '. . . committed to keeping the number of public bodies to an absolute minimum and to ensuring that those which remain are open, accountable and effective'.

It is interesting that the regime of Margaret Thatcher made little impact on quangoland. In fact, the Thatcher government created quite a few of its own, notably the 14 development corporations that were set up around England to try to inject some life into flagging local economies. Their record was patchy, to say the least, and most were quietly wound up before the Tories were thrown out in 1997. A few were touched with scandal that is still being investigated.

But the one Thatcherite quango that has to be judged a success is the London Docklands Development Corporation (LDDC). By dint of an extraordinarily generous bundle of enterprise zones, tax-breaks, rates-breaks and massive public spending on roads, railway and underground, the unelected Thatcherites of the LDDC were able to transform a huge slice of rundown docks on the Isle of Dogs into one of Europe's glittering financial centres (to the fury of the City of London).

## THE SCOTTISH STATE

Scotland, of course, has its very own quangocracy. North of that meandering line between Tweed and Solway the Scottish Executive presides over a total of 36 'executive' and 53 'advisory' quangos plus a clutch of nationalised industries and public corporations, an assortment of tribunals and a whole raft of National Health Service boards and trusts. The Executive says that the quangos under its wing spend something like £6.5 billion a year (some observers say it is closer to

£9 billion) and are run by 3,500 appointees. This figure includes the 2,000 or so men and women appointed to the Children's Panels.

No Whitehall ministry presides over the range of quangos that falls to the Scottish Executive. The executive variety range from big-spending giants such as Scottish Enterprise and the Scottish Higher Education Funding Council to minnows such as Scottish Screen and the Deer Commission for Scotland. Similarly, the advisory category stretches from familiar outfits such as the Scottish Law Commission and the Historic Buildings Council to obscure boards such as the Fisheries (Electricity) Advisory Committee (now doomed) and the Scottish Advisory Committee on Distinction Awards.

On top of which are the troika of publicly-owned corporations – that is, the East of Scotland Water Authority, the North of Scotland Water Authority and the West of Scotland Water Authority – which are soon to be rolled into one all-Scotland water authority. Not forgetting what is left of Scotland's nationalised industries – Caledonian MacBrayne Ltd, Highlands and Islands Airports Ltd, and the Scottish Transport Group (whose sole function is to wind up the pension schemes of the ten bus companies that were privatised in the early 1990s).

Most of our cash (around £6.7 billion of it) is swallowed up by the quangos which have grown up around the National Health Service. The 15 NHS boards and 28 NHS trusts are well-enough known, along with organisations such as the Scottish Ambulance Service, the Mental Welfare Commission and the Health Education Board Scotland. But there is also the Common Services Agency, the Clinical Standards Board, the Scottish Hospital Trust, the Scottish Council for Postgraduate Medical and Dental Education and the State Hospitals Board (which supervises the running of the State Hospital at Carstairs in Lanarkshire).

However, the NDPBs (the civil service hates the word quango) run by the Scottish Executive are only part of the story. Many others impact on Scotland but fall under the remit of various Whitehall departments. Take, for example, the BBC, which belongs to the stable run by the Department for Culture, Media and Sport (DCMS). The BBC has a presence in Scotland, of course, but all the money and all the big decisions are handed down from London. BBC Scotland has no power to make strategy, as the row over the 'Scottish Six' proved.

The BBC is not the only DCMS quango that makes itself felt in Scotland. So too do the Independent Television Commission, the Broadcasting Standards Commission, the Radio Authority, Channel Four, the Great Britain Sports Council, the National Lotteries Charities Board, National Lotteries Commission and the British Tourist Authority (the body usually blamed for the dismal state of Scotland's tourist industry). Almost all of the new Food Standard Agency's executive and advisory NDPBs operate UK-wide.

# DEMOCRATISING THE NETWORK STATE

The quango state will be with us for a long time to come (Parry 1999). Alex Neil, the MSP for Central Scotland, one of the SNP's leading lights and one of quangoland's more passionate critics, has harsh words for the country he loves. 'Scotland is a crony state,' he says. 'It's an incestuous little country. There's a kind of 'Ah ken his faither' mentality that is deeply rooted, particularly in the culture of the Scottish Labour Party.' In Neil's opinion, this political culture is one of the reasons that Scotland is finding it so hard to root out quangos. 'Labour can see nothing wrong with it,' he insists. 'It's the way they have always worked. They just do not see it as corrupt or corrosive or wrong.'

The other common charge – following the Adam Smith line – is that these organisations cost money. But for the most part their boards are manned by part-timers who are paid a pittance plus expenses. The top lawyers who sit on the Scottish Criminal Cases Review Commission are paid £217 a year for their pains, except for their chair Professor Sheila McLean, who collects £372. Would the quangos be any cheaper if they were staffed entirely by well-paid, fully pensioned senior civil servants? It seems unlikely. More importantly, would those civil servants have anything like the expertise and knowledge of the big bad world that the quangurus bring to the table? That seems even more unlikely.

Scottish Enterprise, for example, includes some heavy hitters among its board members. The chairman is Sir Ian Robertson, previously the chief executive of Scottish Power. The deputy chairman is the highly regarded economist Professor Neil Hood. Also on the board are Brian Souter, boss of the hyper-aggressive Stagecoach Holdings, Christine May, leader of the Fife Council, top accountant Eric Hagman, Campbell Christie, one-time general secretary of the STUC, and Jim Sillars, ex-politician and now flying high among the world's chambers of commerce. Together they represent an accumulation of skill, experience and contacts that no coven of civil servants could muster.

Again, Alex Neil is not impressed. He takes the view that the unelected state has to be brought under control. 'We've got to get to grips with these bodies,' he says. 'They are an extension of executive government. And as such they are very important. They decide priorities. They set agendas. And, among them, they spend almost £9 billion of taxpayers' money. That's almost half the total Scottish budget. Distributed by people who are not only unelected but are virtually unsupervised. That's a situation that has got to be changed.'

Neil is a passionate believer that the polity of Scotland would be much improved if quangoland was subjected to supervision by the elected members of Holyrood. Which is why he cooked up his Public Appointments (Parliamentary Approval) (Scotland) Bill which had the support of the SNP, the Tories and some of the Lib Dems. At the core of Neil's bill was the plan to set up a cross-party 'Public Appointments Committee' (PAC), under a non-executive convener, which would scrutinise candidates for Scotland's quangos. Neil is too much of a practical politician to argue that the board of every little quango in the land should be approved by the PAC. But he does argue that the conveners of the big spending bodies should be assessed and approved by Holyrood.

'I'm talking here about organisations like the water companies, the health boards, the education funding councils, the big development agencies. Scottish Enterprise, for example, dispenses a budget of around £500 million. Highland Enterprise does £70 million. The Scottish Environment Protection Agency – SEPA – spends another £20 million. It all adds up to a great deal of money, public money. The Parliament should have a say in who runs them.'

One of the arguments against Neil's bill was that his appointments committee would clog up the system and cause parliamentary log jams. 'That was rubbish,' Neil says. 'We did the sums. Most of the appointments to these bodies are for three to five years. We worked out that we would need three or four confirmation hearings a year, probably for no more than 40 minutes or maybe an hour each. It's done in the States. It's done in Ontario. It's very successful in the European Parliament. And it does not clog up the system.'

He is even more scornful about the argument that the system he wants to see in place would 'politicise' the process by which men and women are appointed to Scotland's quangos. 'When they were in power the Tories stuffed these organisations with Tory supporters,' he says. 'Now Labour are stuffing them with Labour supporters. That's the way politics works. If that's not a politicised system I don't know what is.'

Neil's bill prompted a response from Dame Rennie Fritchie, the newly appointed Commissioner for Public Appointments to the British government. She told the Holyrood committee looking into it, that the kind of confirmatory hearings proposed by Neil 'may have the effect of discouraging many people from a diverse background from applying for public appointments'.

This, Alex Neil announced to the Scottish press, was absolute rubbish. 'The thing that will act as a deterrent,' he declared, 'is if people think it's not worthwhile applying because if you're not part of the old boys' network or a member of the Labour Party, you don't stand a chance of getting a job.'

Interestingly (and perhaps worryingly), Neil suggests that his bill met with the quiet but deadly hostility of Scotland's top civil servants. 'The civil service hated the idea,' he says. 'It strips them of their influence. They worked on ministers endlessly to stop it happening. And these ministers failed to control their civil servants.' Neil is of the opinion that it is 'high time' that someone had a good hard look at the way the civil service operates in Scotland.

If what he says is true, the mandarins of St Andrews House did a pretty effective job. When Neil's bill was put to the vote on 7 February 2002, it fell by 13 votes. Neil is sanguine about (or at least resigned to) the hostility of Labour MSPs but quite upset about the Lib-Dem members who voted against, despite pious words about quango reform in their election manifesto. 'I'm told that the non-MSPs on the Lib-Dem executive are furious,' Neil says. 'They wanted the bill. They'd promised reform in their election literature. But when push came to shove, Jim Wallace sold the pass to keep in with Labour. He did his duty by the coalition. Now we are more or less back where we started.'

Not quite. It seems that Neil did not labour entirely in vain. There is a widely held (if rarely voiced) view that it was Neil's bill that nudged the Scottish Executive into sharpening up its own reforms with a plan to install a full-time Commissioner for Public Appointments who will screen candidates for quangos with the help of 25 'assessors'. In the middle of February 2002 it looked as if Elizabeth Filkin, the one-time Westminster watchdog who was ousted by the hostility of Westminster MPs, would be interested in becoming Scotland's first Commissioner for Public Appointments.

On the face of it, a non-partisan commissioner and a team of assessors seemed like a workable solution. But as soon as the names of the 15 new assessors were announced, it was discovered that 12 of them were Labour Party supporters. Naturally, the SNP and the Tories began to kick up a fuss, only to be assured by Peter Peacock, the Deputy Minister for Finance and Public Services, that the new assessors 'were appointed strictly on merit after a rigorous and open process'.

## CULLING THE QUANGOS

Interestingly, no one involved in the quango debate on either side of the border seems to have dug out a document entitled *The Hunting of the Quango* which was published in 1995 by the Adam Smith Institute. The author was Sir Philip Holland, one-time Tory MP and junior minister, and a man who seems to have spent most of his retiral stalking through the thickets of quangoland. His publications include *The Quango Explosion* (1978), *Quango, Quango, Quango* (1979), *Costing the Quango* (1979), *The Quango Death List* (1980), *The Governance of Quangos* (1981), *Quelling the Quango* (1982), and *The Hunting of the Quango* (1995).

Holland comes at the subject from the right field, of course, but he is always worth reading. He makes a number of interesting points and one of them is that 'Opposition politicians waste their ammunition or they concentrate their fire on political affiliation . . . instead of drawing attention to all those non-departmental bodies that serve little or no useful purpose' (Holland 1995: 23). In other words, the real problem with quangos is not their inevitable political bias but the proliferation of the useless and the next-to-useless.

Holland came up with a few corkers in his research. One of them was the Advisory Panel on the Importation of Sexually Explicit Films for Health Purposes which, it seems, set up a squad of nine top medical professionals to decide which foreign blue movies might be useful for psychotherapists and psychiatrists in the 'treatment of psycho-sexual conditions'. A deal had to be hammered out with Her Majesty's Customs and Excise over whose job it was to prevent lewd material coming into the country and 'corrupting the morals of the lieges' (as Scots legalese used to have it).

But when Holland investigated this intriguing little panel of experts he found that they were unpaid, that they had never met and that they had never produced an annual report because nobody had ever asked them to watch a single blue movie. Not even for medicinal purposes. But, as a body the Advisory Panel had existed from 1986 until 1994, when the Department of Health finally pulled the plug.

In Holland's view it is this kind of bureaucratic lunacy that is the real curse of quangoland. He also makes the point that getting rid of many quangos is much easier said than done. Quangos born of primary legislation require more primary legislation to kill them off, which, of course, takes up valuable parliamentary time. This is the problem now facing the Scottish Executive in its attempts to dump its redundant quangos.

In June 2001 the Scottish Executive produced a document entitled 'Public Bodies: Proposals For Change' which, among other things, lists those quangos earmarked for the chop. But many of these doomed bodies require legislation by the Scottish Parliament before they can be buried. This does not only apply to the well-known quangos. They do not come much more obscure than the Fisheries (Electricity) Committee but the Executive's report points out that 'Since this Committee is appointed by statute, in accordance with "The Electricity Act 1989", abolition would require legislation' which would happen 'When the legislative timetable allows' (Scottish Executive, 2001c).

Among the quangos standing on the tumbrils waiting for Holyrood's guillotine to fall are: the Scottish Medical Practices Committee; the Scottish Hospital Trust; the Building Standards Advisory Committee; the Independent Schools Tribunal; the Ancient Monuments Board for Scotland; the Historic Buildings Council for Scotland; the Scottish Conveyancing and Executry Services Board; and the three water authorities which are to be rolled up into one. Just how much time each of these abolitions will consume no one seems sure. But there is enough business there to keep our MSPs voting for a while.

Sir Philip Holland found a neat way around this time-consuming problem – 'sunset legislation'. This is a legislative species which is common enough in many states of the USA where quangos have a built-in lifespan. If, at the end of that time, they are found to be redundant, they quietly pass into history without fuss or bother. If, however, a state administration wants to keep them, it has to get the legislature to agree. Holland even drafted a measure he called the Public Bodies (Termination) Bill, which put a three-year life span on new quangos and a four-year span on existing ones.

To date, Philip Holland's ingenious ideas have not been taken up by New Labour. Instead, the government – both north and south of the border – has preferred to immerse itself in the long and complex process of investigating each and every quango to decide whether it is worth funding. And, if not, then trying to find the parliamentary time at Westminster and Holyrood to dump it. Which means, of course, that the quangos and the quangocrats will be with us for a long time to come.

# 13

# FRONTLINE SCOTLAND

## Trevor Royle

During the Cold War, Scotland was like a huge, permanently anchored aircraft carrier, its land mass bristling with weaponry, high-tech electronics and, of course, the big bad wolf of the nuclear bomb. From east to west – from Edzell by the Braes of Angus or Mormond Hill in Strathdon to the nuclear submarine bases at Holy Loch and Faslane, from the Royal Air Force radar station at Saxa Vord in Shetland to the Royal Aircraft Establishment at West Freugh near Stranraer – Scotland was infested with the technology of war. Add on the Royal Air Force stations at Kinloss and Lossiemouth in Moray, the fighter interceptors at Leuchars in Fife, the naval base at Rosyth just down the coast in the Forth estuary and Scotland was a veritable Cold War warrior – and, no doubt, a prime target for the planners in the Kremlin.

That was certainly how British and NATO commanders saw the country (Spaven 1983). The 19 million acres of the Scottish land mass would have been the first obstacle any advancing Soviet naval fleet would have faced in a break out through the Iceland–Greenland gap to the North Atlantic. It would have been over the northern seas and in Scottish skies that the air battles would have been fought and it was from the US and British bases on the Clyde that the nuclear submarines would have launched the response by way of Polaris missiles, each one of them capable of destroying Hiroshima several times over. If Scotland had not existed, NATO would have been hard pressed to invent it.

## SCOTLAND AFTER THE THAW

Come the fall of the Berlin Wall and the collapse of Communism, as free-market economies swept inexorably through eastern Europe, Scotland was supposed to stand down too (Royle 1992). And, in a sense, it did. The sinister matt-black hulls of the US nuclear submarine fleet slipped out of the Holy

Loch, presumably never to return; the secret US listening post at Edzell shut up shop, as did the Royal Navy's base at Rosyth, and the army lost two Highland regiments to amalgamation. The biggest change was that the senior Scottish naval and air force commanders lost their NATO role and the joint maritime headquarters at Pitreavie Castle in Fife was closed down, put on sale and its Cold War command bunker sealed. Even low-flying decreased – from 11,608 hours in 1995 to 7,866 in 2001. This was the peace dividend and, although many regretted the loss of famous regimental names and the spending power that evaporated with the closure of bases, the country had at least become a little safer. Except, of course, it has done no such thing.

Take a spin along the switchback road from Helensburgh to Arrochar and the naval presence of the Clyde Submarine Base at Faslane and the Armaments Depot at Coulport do not just announce themselves, they stand there and demand to be noticed. The high walls, barbed wire and chainlink fencing keep the curious at bay, and the bland institutional buildings are suitably anonymous, but the naval presence is not so amorphous that it does not excite emotions. For some, pride in naval power might be one, but for most people the overwhelming feeling is probably a high-octane cocktail of suspicion, fear and dislike. Small wonder that the area is a magnet for protests, some of them violent: the Cold War might be history but the base on the shores of Loch Long still keeps Scotland on the front line.

At 2001 and 2002 demonstrations, church leaders united with trade unionists and politicians to demand the closure of the base and the scrapping of the Trident weapons system, which is three times more powerful than its predecessor, Polaris, and a darned sight more expensive to operate. According to the latest Ministry of Defence figures, the missiles and their warheads cost the taxpayer £277 million a year. But, according to the Scottish CND, the figure is closer to £1 billion. For that, argue those for whom Trident is anathema, the government could put at least £1,000 a year into every classroom for the next quarter of a century.

The mass protests attracted high-profile publicity, as did the earlier trial in 2000 of two female saboteurs who escaped sentence because the sheriff-substitute deemed nuclear weapons to be illegal under international law. Although the decision was not upheld and although the demonstration was momentary, the unease conjured up by the Clyde Submarine Base refuses to go away. When it was developed during the Cold War, the US-built Trident was regarded as a weapon of deterrence. It provided the threat of overwhelming retaliation or, as General Thomas Power, commander of the US Strategic Air Command, put it in the 1960s: 'The whole idea is to kill the bastards. At the end of the war, if there are two Americans and one Russian left alive, we win.'

Fortunately, those days and philosophy have long gone but that does not leave Trident irrelevant. Far from it. The missile system and its submarines are still integral to Britain's defence policy and in a number of scenarios could be fired in anger. At the top end of the tariff, it could be used independently or as part of NATO's policy of 'last resort', when a submarine could fire off its complement of 16 missiles, each armed with multiple warheads, to wreak overwhelming destruction on a nuclear aggressor.

Closer to the bottom end, and in a scenario which is more likely, it could be deployed 'sub-strategically' with as little as one warhead per missile. These circumstances might include attacking a country found to be developing weapons of mass destruction (chemical, biological or nuclear), for which there is no comparable retaliation; warning a country which is committing acts of aggression; or punishing a country for refusing to stop reckless criminal behaviour. Recent confrontations with Iraq, Yugoslavia and President George W. Bush's war against terrorism all fall variously into these categories and, if the crises had spun out of control, British defence policy would have allowed the use of Trident missiles.

Having spent huge amounts of money on its development – some £12 billion – British defence experts are unwilling to see Trident scrapped or put on the table in arms limitation or reduction talks (Hennessy 2002: Ch. 2). They argue that it offers good value for money; that it is a tried and tested system which is more accurate and more powerful than anything used before, and that membership of the nuclear club is a prerequisite for keeping the country's seat as one of the five permanent members of the UN Security Council. All this is true but, of course, it comes at a price, namely that these weapons are not just symbolic: one day they might be used in anger. Just ask any crew member of the old Polaris boats which operated out of the Clyde throughout the Cold War. Whenever they went out on patrol they were on a war footing for the duration of the trip; they knew that they might have to press the button to release their missiles against computer-generated targets, and the same holds true for the crews of the four Clyde-based Trident boats – *Vanguard*, *Victorious*, *Vigilance* and *Vengeance* – one of which is on patrol at sea at any given time.

The presence of the Trident submarine squadron at Faslane is the most potent symbol of the defence establishment in Scotland but it is not the only one. Although there were cutbacks in the 1990s, the services' presence is still obvious and it carries with it significant spending power: in 2001 the Ministry of Defence estimated that its expenditure in Scotland amounted to £600 million. Over 20,000 defence-related jobs are based in Scotland, 12,000 service personnel and 8,000 civil servants (Law 1995). The Faslane and Coulport naval bases are the biggest single employers in the west of Scotland, although this might cease to be the case if proposed job cuts are pushed through in 2002 following privatisation of dockyard facilities. Aid to the community is also offered and all three armed services are tasked to help the emergency services, local authorities and government departments in time of crisis. In 2001 the army provided personnel and an operational structure to deal with the culling of farm animals during the foot-and-mouth outbreak. The army's bomb disposal unit in Edinburgh regularly helps police with suspicious objects and unexploded ordnance, and the Royal Navy and RAF are both involved in search and rescue operations. In 2001 the RAF Mountain Rescue team at Leuchars, Royal Navy Sea King helicopters from Prestwick and RAF Sea Kings from Lossiemouth were called out over 600 times and saved some 400 people in distress. The Aeronautical Rescue Co-ordination Centre based at Kinloss is the only one of its kind in the UK.

Defence manufacturing is also a factor. Scotland accounts for 8 per cent of the UK's jobs, the largest single employer being BAE's shipyards at Scotstoun and Govan, while Thales Optronics in Glasgow is the biggest supplier of electro-optical systems and equipment, including periscopes, airborne and armoured-vehicle surveillance systems and thermal imaging cameras. Rosyth became a political football in the 1990s as it vied with Devonport to win the contract to service the Royal Navy's nuclear submarines and, although the site eventually lost out, it remained as a dockyard under the management of Babcock Engineering Services Ltd and secured contracts to service Royal Navy warships, including the carriers HMS *Invincible* and HMS *Illustrious*. Despite consistent rumours of cutbacks or closure, it remains a major employer in Fife, with a workforce of 2,000.

## THE ROYAL NAVY

Throughout the Cold War the Flag Officer Scotland was also responsible for Northern Ireland and operated under the acronym FOSNI. In the reorganisation of the 1990s the remit was extended to include northern England as far as the Dee–Humber line and in Scotland itself the navy shrank. In 1996 it pulled out of Rosyth, a naval base since the First World War, and its resident warships – the self-styled 'Scottish Navy' – were deployed elsewhere. The four Type 42 destroyers went south to Portsmouth, while most of the Minor War Vessels – minehunters, minesweepers and patrol ships of the Fisheries Protection Squadron – were moved to HM Naval Base Clyde at Faslane to join the resident Swiftsure squadron of hunter-killer submarines – soon to be replaced by Astute Class boats equipped with Tomahawk cruise missiles – and the four Trident boats. The base is also home to the NATO tri-service Joint Maritime Course three times a year, for which it provides berthing and command-and-control facilities.

The Flag Officer Scotland, Northern England and Northern Ireland (FOSNNI) was reduced in rank from vice-admiral to rear-admiral and he now has his headquarters at Faslane. FOSNNI is responsible for the following installations and facilities: HM Naval Base Faslane, including the Royal Naval Armament Depot at Coulport; Superintendent Ships at Rosyth; NATO Fuel Depots at Campbeltown, Loch Striven and Loch Awe; the Oil Fuel Depot

Garelochhead; HMS *Caledonia* at Rosyth (responsible for support of naval personnel); and the Navy Buildings at Greenock. Although the Royal Navy does not have the same emotional or territorial links with Scotland as those enjoyed by the army's infantry regiments, four of its warships are connected to the towns and cities after which they have been named: the Type 42 destroyers HMS *Glasgow* and HMS *Edinburgh*, the Type 23 frigate HMS *Montrose* and the minehunter HMS *Inverness*. The Swiftsure class fleet submarine HMS *Spartan* is affiliated to Rothesay and the Trident submarine HMS *Vanguard* to Islay and Jura. Many of the Minor War Vessels, especially the Island Class ships of the Fisheries Protection Squadron, operate in Scottish coastal waters and their crews enjoy a close rapport with the fishing community.

## ROYAL MARINES

HMS *Condor* at Arbroath in Angus is home to 45 Commando Royal Marines and forms part of 3 Commando Brigade, Royal Marines, which is the Royal Navy's amphibious infantry on permanent readiness to deploy across the globe, a core component of Britain's Joint Rapid Reaction Force. Condor is also home to the Fleet Royal Marines Protection Group (formerly Commachio Company), which was formed in 1980 to provide specialist security forces for the protection of the navy's strategic nuclear weapons. In March 2002, 45 Commando was deployed in Afghanistan in support of US forces to track down Taliban and al-Qaeda terrorists as part of Operation Enduring Freedom.

## THE ARMY

Scotland's military presence is integrated into the UK land command structure with its headquarters at Wilton near Salisbury. With the reduction in army numbers which resulted from successive cutbacks in defence spending by the Conservative government in the 1990s, Scotland lost its separate command and with it the post of GOC Scotland. In 2000, under the terms of Labour's Strategic Defence Review, all military units in Scotland came under 2nd Division, commanded by a major-general who looks after Scotland and Northern England, as far south as the Humber. (He also retains the historic title of Governor of Edinburgh Castle.) As a sop to Scottish sensibilities, the headquarters were based not in York but at Craigiehall, outside Edinburgh.

The 2nd Division comprises four brigades, two in England (15 North East Brigade and 42 North West Brigade), two in Scotland (51 Highland Brigade and 52 Lowland Brigade) and a garrison at Catterick in Yorkshire. Other army establishments in 2nd Division's area of responsibility include the Army Personnel Centre in Glasgow (responsible for managing the careers and postings of all army personnel), the Army Foundation College at Harrogate and the Infantry Training Centre at Catterick (which conducts phase two training for all infantry soldiers). The 2nd Division also has responsibility for reserve and cadet forces. In Scotland there are 60 reserve force units, with 4,600 personnel and 230 cadet detachments involving 9,500 members, the majority aged between 12 and 22.

Of the two Scotland-based brigades, 51 Highland has under its command a regular infantry battalion based at Fort George near Inverness, one Territorial Army infantry battalion with its headquarters in Perth and in its area there is a Yeomanry Squadron based at Cupar, a Royal Engineer Squadron based at RAF Leuchars and a Field Ambulance based in Dundee. In 2001, there were claims that the brigade would be axed but these were denied by the Ministry of Defence. The other formation, 52 Lowland Brigade, has its headquarters in Edinburgh Castle and has two regular infantry battalions under its command, both based at Dreghorn and Redford barracks in Edinburgh. The Territorial Army elements include an infantry battalion, a Royal Artillery air defence regiment, a Royal Signals regiments and a Field Hospital.

Despite cutbacks and a reduction in personnel which has seen the army's strength drop from 147,000 in 1991 to a projected figure of 108,500 in 2005, Scotland still provides 13 per cent of the British Army. There are still six line infantry regiments – the Royal Scots, King's Own Scottish Borderers, Royal Scots Fusiliers, the Black Watch, the Highlanders and the Argyll & Sutherland Highlanders – plus a foot guards battalion, the Scots Guards, and an armoured regiment, the Royal Scots Dragoon Guards. However, recruiting has become a problem and, with numbers falling, some regiments, notably the Royal Scots and the Highlanders, have been reinforced with Gurkha and Fijian riflemen.

## THE ROYAL AIR FORCE

Since the very beginning of flight, Scotland has been involved in military aviation. The first air base was constructed at Montrose in 1913 and that same year saw the foundation of a naval sea-plane base at Cromarty. Today the Royal Air Force presence in Scotland remains strong and has not produced any significant post-Cold War casualties – all three bases remain operational. RAF Leuchars still houses two squadrons of F-3 Tornado interceptor aircraft (43 and 111 Squadrons) and, following the closure of Pitreavie, is the headquarters of the Air Officer Scotland. The base also houses the RAF Mountain Rescue Unit and the Air Transportable Surgical Unit, and is home to the Aberdeen, Dundee and St Andrews University Air Squadron. Since the al-Qaeda terrorist attack on the US, two Quick Reaction Alert armed fighters are held at readiness at Leuchars to police the UK Air Defence Region as part of the UK's contribution to NATO.

RAF Lossiemouth houses three squadrons of GR1/4 Tornado strike aircraft

(12, 14 and 617 Squadrons) and one operational conversion unit – XV (Reserve) Squadron. A helicopter rescue unit, D Flight, 202 Squadron, is also based there, and two ground defence units – 51 and 2622 (Highland) Squadrons, RAF Regiment. Kinloss houses the entire fleet of Nimrod MR2 maritime patrol aircraft (120, 201 and 206 Squadrons) and an Operational Conversion Unit – 42 (Reserve) Squadron. Gliding is also catered for through 663 Volunteer Gliding School.

Originally opened in 1952 as an Air Defence Radar Unit, RAF Buchan in Aberdeenshire is home to a Control and Reporting Centre (CRC) which co-ordinates all aspects of air defence for the Northern UK Air Defence Region, working closely with similar units in Scandinavia. CRC Buchan is frequently involved in multi-national training exercises involving the Royal Navy and other NATO navies. The radar station at Saxa Vord in Shetland also comes under the jurisdiction of the Air Officer Scotland, since 1994 in the rank of air-commodore.

Although service personnel no longer wear uniforms in public, other than when they are on duty, the presence of the three services is central to Scottish life and the country's landscape. In addition to the bases and facilities already listed, other parts of the nation's life and landscape are also touched by the defence establishment. The army has training facilities at Garelochhead in Argyll, Barry Buddon in Angus, Cultybraggan in Perthshire and Castlelaw in Midlothian. The RAF and other NATO air forces use bombing ranges at Tain and Cape Wrath and the Royal Aircraft Establishment operates a weapons development facility from West Freugh. Each August the army in Scotland lends assistance to the Edinburgh Military Tattoo and through 52 Lowland Brigade provides troops for ceremonial duties such as the opening of the Scottish Parliament or visits by the Royal Family to Holyroodhouse and Balmoral.

However, a conundrum lies at the heart of the relationship between Scotland and the defence establishment. The MoD makes much of the fact that 'Scotland makes a huge and very important contribution to UK defence', but the fact remains that the Scottish Parliament has no responsibility for defence matters and there is no separate Scottish defence organisation as such. The formulation and execution of defence policy is the responsibility of the MoD in London and the three services in Scotland are under the operational command of headquarters in England: the Royal Navy at Fleet Headquarters at Northwood near London, the army at Wilton and the RAF at Strike Command headquarters at High Wycombe in Buckinghamshire. This arrangement prevents the Scottish Parliament from taking executive action, and it might even stifle debate, but it will not stop MSPs and their constituents from thinking about the subject and its relevance to their country.

This is not just idle speculation: defence and foreign policies have a relevance to any debate about Scotland's future. Recent polls suggest that some 60 per cent of the population want no truck with Trident, and the SNP is committed to sending the weapons bag-and-baggage out of Scotland and withdrawing from NATO if they ever come to power in an independent Scotland. Many in the

Scottish Labour Party are equally uneasy; scratch the surface of party unity and there are few Labour takers for Trident.

But what would happen if there were a crisis involving Scottish-based Trident boats? It need not be a direct confrontation with another nuclear power; it might just be another of those near-wars which plague our times and which require the short sharp shock of airstrikes. Only this time the government deploys a Trident boat, its D-5 missiles armed with low-yield tactical nuclear warheads which can do the job just as easily, and perhaps even more cheaply, than fixed-wing aircraft. In March 2002, Prime Minister Tony Blair gave notice that Britain might use its nuclear weapons in operations against rogue states such as Iraq. If that happened, given the opposition to nuclear weapons, the Parliament might be hard-pushed not to debate the issue. For sure, the orders would have come from London but the locus would still be Scotland and in no small measure Scots would be involved in the process. The missiles might fall on targets far away, but the submarine would still have to find its way back to Scotland and an uncertain reception.

It is not just the Trident submarines which give pause for thought. Scotland's regiments are British military assets yet they are still recognisably Scottish and invariably they attract public interest when they are deployed on operational duties. Whatever their nationality, their soldiers are still liable to be killed in action. Could the Parliament remain silent if, say, the Royal Scots or the Black Watch lost heavy casualties on peacekeeping or anti-terrorist operations? When the Arbroath-based 45 Royal Marines Commando was deployed to Afghanistan in spring 2002 commanders warned that there would be casualties (happily there were none). Likewise, could a Scottish Parliament have ignored the fact that, in the face of widespread protest, Scottish-based warplanes were used in punitive airstrikes of the kind undertaken by the Lossiemouth-based 12 Squadron which attacked Iraqi targets during Operation Desert Fox in December 1998?

Even if scenes such as those were never to be played out, the presence of the Clyde base is such an affront to so many people that it remains central to any Scottish debate about defence. There have been consistent calls for the base to be closed down and reopened somewhere else, England for preference, but such a scenario is unlikely. Not only would Westminster turn down the idea as intolerably expensive – the base on the Clyde cost £1.9 billion and it would take at least three times that amount to reconstruct it elsewhere – but it is also unworkable, as neither Plymouth nor Portsmouth has the room or the infrastructure to support such a move. The Americans were more sensible. When they set up house in the Holy Loch they brought most of their own facilities with them in the shape of a moored tender, a decision which had more to do with common sense than any cent-pinching in Washington. At the time of the deployment in the 1960s, the Americans were far from certain that their British hosts would always be onside, a sensible precaution since it seemed to them that an incoming Labour government would adopt a policy of unilateral nuclear disarmament.

Then, as now, the presence of the nuclear submarines is a key to the predicament facing Scotland if it ever became independent. If its government was committed to expelling Trident – likely, if controlled by the SNP – the new administration would find itself in direct conflict with Westminster. The consequences would be dire. Such is the complexity of naval operations that an expulsion order could hardly be acted on immediately. At least one boat would be at sea, the base contains sophisticated electronics and then there is the whole irreducible issue of the nuclear warheads and the boats' power plants. Removal would take years and, as it would cost some £4 billion for England to create another base, it is not difficult to imagine the resentment the decision would cause south of the border.

The aggravation could be eased by a leasing arrangement which would allow the Royal Navy to retain the base as a diminishing investment but it would leave long-lasting scars. After 300 years of union there would still be a special relationship and England would remain Scotland's main trading partner. All this could be put in jeopardy. In the spring of 1999, Dr Malcolm Chalmers, a leading analyst at Bradford University, pointed out to a Scottish defence seminar that any decision to close Faslane would 'force crippling costs on England, creating resentment and souring relations between states whose peoples have close personal and cultural ties'.

The decision might not appeal either to the people of Argyll and Dumbarton. Many might object to the submarines squatting on their shoreline but the men and women who run and service the boats bring much-needed spending power into the area. Back in the 1980s, the commander of the submarine base silenced doubting trade union leaders by providing evidence of his squadron's spending power. It was in the region of £100 million a year. Did they really want to forfeit that in exchange for their unilateralist opposition? The answer was, apparently, no.

That is the main problem facing the defence debate in Scotland. From a moral perspective, there is much opposition to the presence of weapons of mass destruction and to the country's role in Britain's strategic obligations. On the other hand, it cannot be denied that the creation of ploughshares will never be achieved without financial penalties affecting many hundreds of working people.

At present, all of the serious talking has taken place at Westminster and, under the terms of the Scotland Act, that is how things will proceed. This is both the reality and a challenge: defence cannot be compartmentalised; it intrudes into too many aspects of political life. The Finance Committee might wish to question the impact on Scotland of Westminster-ordained defence cuts, and the Transport and Environment committee could have things to say on low-flying and the effect on health of so much nuclear hardware. Like the four black-hulled boats on the west coast, defence is an issue which is on our doorstep; and like them, too, it is unlikely to go away without the devil of a debate.

# 14

# WHAT INFLUENCES SCOTTISH BUSINESS?

*Christopher Hope*

You might have thought that the Scottish business sector was in good health at the start of the third millennium. After all, why should it not be? The nation attracts more than its fair share of state funding for health and education through the complicated Barnett formula. It has its own legal and education systems, and a new Parliament, with a number of underemployed MSPs to understand business's needs. But the reality is a bit different. Scotland has a depressingly low business start-up rate and a declining number of publicly listed companies which is numerically outgunned by other UK regions (Peat and Boyle 1999; Rice and Johnstone 2000). Add to that a declining population and a sluggish GDP – it only grew by 0.3 per cent in the 12 months to the end of June 2001 – and it is no wonder that one London-based economist described Scotland as a 'third world' economy in mid-2001 (*The Herald*, 28 August 2001).

## FORMAL INFLUENCES

The influences which account for Scottish business's underperformance are, in my view, threefold: formal, informal and historical. Perhaps the most influential formal influence is a state-funded agency called Scottish Enterprise, which tries to stimulate the economy in central and southern Scotland. (The northern parts are looked after by a different body, Highlands and Islands Enterprise.) Formerly known as the Scottish Development Agency, Scottish Enterprise can plough £390 million every year into the economy to create new jobs, a figure which is the envy of other English enterprise agencies such as Yorkshire First just south of the border. The agency says it turns £1 of public funding into as much as £2 through a network of local enterprise bodies in its business creation activities, but the ratio is less generous in other areas. It also has a number of enterprise bodies which are designed to attract overseas companies to Scotland, as well as helping Scottish businesses to start exporting.

However, Scottish Enterprise has historically been criticised for being over-bureaucratic and hindering more than it helps. The agency has also been condemned for ordering review after review after review. So it was no surprise that a radical overhaul was ordered within the first year of the new Parliament. To its credit, the remedial work seems to show some sign of working. New chief executive Robert Crawford – the highest paid public official in the entire United Kingdom – has presided over a period of far-reaching change and transformation. Scottish Enterprise has undergone a root and branch reform, with the network taking greater control of its regional offices. Discredited initiatives have been scrapped and the focus is now on attracting companies which can bring in quality jobs.

The Scottish Executive (Scottish Enterprise's paymaster) is another formal influence on Scottish business, as is the UK government, and in particular the Chancellor of the Exchequer and Treasury, who set the overall economic framework for the UK, determining income tax, national insurance, VAT, corporation tax and broad public expenditure priorities (including the Scottish Block Grant) (Danson and Gilmore 2000). In the first years of devolution, with Gordon Brown, a Scottish MP, at the Treasury and a Labour–Lib Dem administration at Holyrood, the two governments and parliaments have broadly followed the same agenda in relation to business and the economy, but this will not always be the case.

Most of this impetus for change has been channelled through the dynamic force of Wendy Alexander, the Enterprise minister from November 2000 until May 2002. Alexander has been a rare thing among ministers, in that she actually had some experience of the area she governed. This daughter of a Church of Scotland clergyman is also a former management consultant who came into politics to work closely with her friend, the late First Minister Donald Dewar, to draft the legislation which gave Scotland its Parliament.

Alexander at full throttle was a formidable sight, rattling out policy at a terrific speed while hurriedly leafing through her briefing papers. But her problem was that she was an outsider, unschooled in the world of local Scottish politics from where most of the ministers in the devolved administration have sprung. This could leave her open to being spun against by jealous colleagues, and on the outside looking in. A bit like business's relationship with the Executive, in fact, which still regards the new government with suspicion. In February 2002, for example, the new owner of Edinburgh broker Torrie and Co. accused the Executive of not being 'business friendly', adding: 'There is a worry that you could see fund management business drifting away [as a result]' (*Business a.m.*, 27 February 2002).

His main fear was – erroneously – that the Executive might start to impose anti-business taxes when it has no real power over taxation. Devolution might

Buisness suspicions of
Executive - not doing enough

have improved transparency and access to officials to find out why decisions are taken, but it takes a little longer to build trust. In April 2001, for example, Motorola, the mobile phone giant, confirmed that it was closing its assembly operation at Bathgate, West Lothian, with the loss of 3,100 jobs. This sparked a frantic round of negotiations as Alexander shuttled back and forth between Edinburgh and Motorola's HQ in Chicago to try to persuade Motorola to change its plans. Yet while Alexander was engaged in fruitless talks with the directors at Motorola, 3i's Scottish arm was separately offering Motorola an eleventh-hour rescue bid (*Business a.m.*, 1 November 2001). The venture capital firm was considering buying the plant, bringing in new management and setting up a contract manufacturing plant for mobile phone handsets. Some of the jobs would have been saved.

But Motorola turned down the plan and the plant was closed. This begged a question: why did 3i not tell the Executive about its plans? If nothing else, it would have given Alexander something to work with when negotiating with Motorola's top executives. The answer was depressingly simple – because ministers would not have understood what 3i was trying to do, according to one industry source.

Another formal – but far less effective – influence on business comes from the 129 elected members of the Scottish Parliament. Before MSPs were elected in May 1999, there were high hopes. Business people lined up to tell them how the budding relationship might work. But it was never consummated. Business did its best, though. The Scottish branch of the Confederation of British Industry organised a series of seminars to bring MSPs up to scratch on business issues when they were first elected. But the relationship soon soured after the CBI published a document calling for the Parliament to be more 'unashamedly pro-business'. One MSP retorted: 'CBI Scotland will make no friends by being critical' (*The Scotsman*, 16 May 2000).

Business did not give up on the relationship. In November 2001, CBI Scotland organised a programme for MSPs to work in business on an exchange programme. Some of Scotland's highest profile companies such as the Royal Bank of Scotland and British Energy took part. But three months later, only 14 out of the 129 MSPs had volunteered. John Slater, policy manager at Edinburgh Chamber of Commerce, spoke for many when he said: 'It is disappointing that MSPs have not taken up this opportunity. Can they suitably represent those businesses if they do not understand the issues?' (*Business a.m.*, 22 February 2002).

## INFORMAL INFLUENCES

The second influences are a loose collection of informal pressures, known by some as the 'Scotia Nostra'. It is characterised by Scottish companies stuffing their boards with fellow Scots and only using other Scottish firms for advice. This is, perhaps, understandable – it is good for the Scottish economy to use other Scottish firms. But it is also dangerous – these Scottish firms are not gaining the insight which might come from using people from outside the country. Worse, it suggests there is a barrier to companies which want to expand into Scotland – and, if nothing else, business hates barriers.

Never is the feeling of a large club more apparent than at one of the many business dinners and awards nights that takes place in Scotland every year. Last year there was an average of one major business dinner every eight weeks, many doling out awards to fellow Scottish companies. How about the Deloitte and Touche Fast 50 awards, the Scottish Council for Development and Industry Gala Dinner, the Scottish plc awards, the Entrepreneurial Exchange dinner, the Insider corporate elite dinner or the London Stock Exchange Scottish dinner, to name a few? Scotland has one of the most over-rewarded business communities in the UK. No doubt the firms deserve their awards – yet all the while Scotland's macro-economic performance is in the doldrums.

Mixing with rivals and business advisers can help to boost sales. But at what point does a networking dinner become little more than an exclusive club into which newcomers are not welcome? And this exclusiveness can damage Scottish business. It is not hard to see why Scottish business feels set apart from the rest of the UK. Scotland is a small country, with only one land border and its own banknotes, as well as its distinct legal and educational systems. This fosters a cosiness which is far from healthy. Many lawyers, accountants, venture capitalists, corporate financiers and bankers were at school and/or university with their clients. No doubt their help is required to guide Scotland's new companies, but over-reliance on a small pool of advisers can be the enemy of growth for firms.

This is not to suggest that there is anything underhand in their dealings. Merely that in a small pond it is hard to grow into big fish. Tough advice is harder to dole out to people you might know from your school days (or, more likely, from the golf club bar). The close links between advisers and businesses reach an apogee in the business dealings of Sir Angus Grossart. Sir Angus is a very successful businessman, who runs a small and highly influential merchant bank in Edinburgh called Noble Grossart, which makes investments and advises companies on strategy. But Sir Angus was also depicted in *Business a.m.* as a large pink octopus with his tentacles spreading across the page. It was not hard to see why. Sir Angus's presence is felt across the top Scottish companies. He holds down board positions with Scotland's biggest bank, the Royal Bank of Scotland; with Scotland's biggest brewer, Scottish & Newcastle; and with Scotland's biggest newspaper, Trinity Mirror, owner of the *Daily Record* and *Sunday Mail*. He is also linked to arguably Scotland's biggest football club – Rangers – by a seat on the board of Murray International, the firm owned by Rangers boss David Murray. He is on the board of Edinburgh Fund Managers, one of Scotland's biggest financial institutions.

145

Not only that but Noble Grossart – 80 per cent controlled by Grossart – hands out corporate advice to a host of other big Scottish companies such as the Macfarlane Group, Burn Stewart, A.G. Barr, Miller Group and Stagecoach. There is nothing wrong with this – Sir Angus should be roundly applauded for being a flexible executive – but for one man to have so much influence across Scottish business is seen by some as unhealthy. The suggestion, however erroneous, that Scottish business operates via its very own code and rules damages its image outside the country.

Take one example. In late 1998, Geoff Ball, the chairman of a small Edinburgh-based house builder called Cala, was getting very depressed by the low price of his company's shares. So he decided to take matters into his own hands and make the company private by buying back its shares from the stock market, at a premium. He made an offer to shareholders of 165p per share, well above the existing share price. But Miller Group, a local rival construction company, had different ideas and tabled a 175p counter-offer to buy the company. The stakes were raised and Cala came back with 190p. Finally, Miller tabled a final offer of 200p in cash – more than twice the original valuation of the company before bidding commenced – valuing the company at £98.6 million. Cala looked dead in the water – until one of its legal advisers realised that if it also offered 200p, Miller would be unable to counter with an offer because its earlier 200p bid had been stated as 'final'. The two companies were at an impasse. And in June 1999 they both went to the market. Ball's team won the day, as fund managers sold their shares to him ostensibly as a reward for making the deal happen.

Everyone should have been happy – the management had won their company back and shareholders had doubled their money. Except it was a tainted triumph, with London fund managers grumbling that it looked like a 'classic Scottish stitch-up'. It was not – but that did not matter. As far as some fund managers were concerned, all of the advisers, solicitors and banks were from Scotland. And that meant that it was a bunch of Scots helping out another bunch of Scots. They had a point – one fund manager from Edinburgh admitted: 'It's the usual "mugged in the New Club" scenario' (*The Scotsman*, 24 April 1999).

## A THIRD INFLUENCE

So far I have detailed two sets of influences – formal and informal – which, in my view, serve to constrict business growth in Scotland. There is also a third influence, which stretches back more than 300 years. It was recently raised by the prominent new economy businessman Ian Ritchie in a thoughtful speech to an annual dinner for Scotland's financial community in October 2001. Scottish business was too conservative, he said, and has been for three centuries. In the late seventeenth century, Scotland was an independent, vibrant country, with a reputation for taking risks. So, a group of Scottish financiers came up with an idea: to build a waterway in the Gulf of Darien across Central America to provide a new and fast trade route for ships plying between the Atlantic and Pacific Oceans.

Sadly, the project rapidly came unstuck after pressure from the East India Company, the then market-leader, resulted in support being withdrawn at the last moment by the Dutch and the English governments. Scotland carried on alone. But it was a disaster. The Scottish financiers lost all of their money, 2,000 Scots lost their lives trying to build the canal and only one out of the sixteen ships which had left Scotland to build the canal returned home. By the time this happened, most of Scotland's capital had been invested in this ill-fated adventure, leaving the country virtually bankrupt. So this proud nation was forced to seek a merger with its larger rival – England – in the Treaty of Union in 1707. When an emasculated Scotland joined the Union, she had a fifth of the UK's population and only one-fortieth of her wealth.

One hundred years later, of course, the Americans built the Panama Canal, pretty much to the plans drawn up by the Scots, and it turned out to be a huge commercial success. But the failure of the Darien project has cast a long shadow across Scottish business, Ritchie argued. True, the nation has since won back its reputation for being prudent with money: Scotland has £350 billion worth of funds under management – the seventh-largest concentration in the world – which grew by 10 per cent in the year to June 2001. No mean feat for a country smaller than Finland. But at what cost? Ritchie argued that, perhaps with notable exceptions such as the Royal Bank of Scotland's successful £20 billion bid for NatWest bank in February 2000, risk-taking is frowned upon. 'We have brains, energy and money and despite all that we have one of the most sluggish economies in the Western world. What is wrong with us? The main thing is a collective lack of confidence in our own abilities,' Ritchie said. 'Scotland's financial community was not investing in its own back yard,' he added, citing the example of PPL Therapeutics, the firm behind the cloning of Dolly the sheep, which was seeking new funding not from Scottish financiers but from foreign investors (Ritchie 2001).

Therefore, there are three broad sets of influences which impact on Scottish business. Formal ones, such as Scottish Enterprise, the Parliament, the Executive and UK government; informal ones, such as the damagingly close links between advisers and businesses; and historical ones, such as the loss of confidence illustrated by the Darien mentality. These influences have not, in my view, had a beneficial effect on Scottish business. Witness, for example, Scotland's very low business birth rate compared to other regions in the UK. Scottish Enterprise ploughed £140 million of public money into a strategy for improving the rate between 1993 and 1999, but with little effect: only 2,124 new start-ups were created out of a target of 25,000.

Witness, too, the continuing instances of Scotland's growing businesses

147

selling out to rivals rather than taking the more risky ways forward, such as floating on the stock market. No wonder, then, that Scotland has a very low number of listed companies – only 65 – compared to other areas of the UK. And they are not doing well. Research by *Business a.m.* claimed that more than half of Scotland's quoted companies – 34 out of 65 – were reporting falling profits or rising losses (*Business a.m.*, 19 March 2002).

Of course, some of this underperformance can be pinned on difficult economic conditions, but that perennial lack of confidence cannot help – and it was starkly illustrated by a debate held by 3i at its Glasgow offices in late 1999. The venture capitalists invited Scottish companies in which it held investments to discuss the best exit for its funds: float or trade sale. The debate was robust, with speakers from either side of the argument. But at the end almost all of the businesses voted for a trade sale. One of the lone voters who voted for a float later blamed the result on the 'jam today' approach of Scottish businesses. Why risk even more and build a global business, when you can still settle for a few million and a life on the world's best golf courses? It must be tempting but, long-term, the effects are damaging: lack of indigenous business growth, and only a handful of global companies headquartered in Scotland, creating an over-reliance on overseas businesses coming in to Scotland. And these companies can wipe out entire local economies when a downturn comes, with the squiggle of an accountant's pen. It is not all gloom, though. In the past couple of years, Scotland has started to address some of these failings. The Scottish Executive and Scottish Enterprise seem more business-savvy and responsive to business's needs.

Business too is changing. Some of Scotland's companies have now become truly global players, such as ScottishPower and the Royal Bank of Scotland. It is interesting to note that if the Royal Bank's shares increase by a few pounds to £24, then the company will be worth more than Scotland's GDP. The company is already worth more than all of Scotland's plc base put together. On a more ad hoc basis, Scotland's growing technology base is allowing rich entrepreneurs such as Brian Souter, Tom Hunter and John Boyle to bring on a new generation of hungry business people such as Kevin Dorren, Chris Gorman and Brendan Hyland. Hunter, who made £290 million when he sold his Sports Division chain of sports shops, has even put his money where his mouth is by ploughing £5 million into a Centre for Entrepreneurship at Strathclyde University.

Scotland is slowly changing in ways unforeseen even a decade ago, but not quickly enough for the challenges it faces. The fixation with traditional manufacturing has lessened, but not disappeared. The roll call of Singer at Clydebank, British Aluminium at Invergordon, British Leyland at Bathgate, Scott-Lithgow in Greenock, Ravenscraig and Kvaerner in Govan, where announcement of closure was followed by campaigns, government intervention and the flourishing of subsidies, has diminished. There has also been a significant shift away from what was once a near-complete obsession with comparing the Scottish unemployment rate in relation to the rest of the UK, which lasted for a large part of the 1960s and 1970s (Young 1999: 77–8).

However, we need to beware contemporary orthodoxies and conformity as well as the conservative mindset of Scottish business and policy-makers. Scottish Enterprise's 'smart, successful Scotland' (Scottish Enterprise 2001) has, as well as opportunities, limitations in its vision of the Scottish economy. The debate on Scotland's future prospects has to get beyond the generalisation of a high-skill, high-wage, knowledge economy to reflect the diverse realities of the Scottish economy: the growth of the public and service sectors, and of predominantly female, part-time and often low-paid work (Warhurst and Thompson 1999; Keep 2000).

Much more far-reaching change is needed if Scotland is to compete in the world market. Scotland's attitudes to entrepreneurship have hardly shifted in the last 20 years. A mere 2.4 per cent in a 1999 MORI poll said they are committed to starting their own business, while a further 8 per cent are already in business and 18 per cent are enthusiastic about starting a business. That leaves seven in ten Scots who have no interest in starting a business: 38 per cent who could, but do not want to, and 32 per cent who do not want to (Mackay et al. 2001). This entrepreneurial deficit is particularly acute in urban Scotland and, in particular, in the central belt. The stock of firms per 10,000 people is highest in parts of rural Scotland (Highlands, Borders and Dumfries and Galloway) and lowest in urban central belt Scotland (Glasgow, Dundee, Lanarkshire, Dunbartonshire, Renfrewshire, Falkirk and Fife) (Peat and Boyle 1999: 76).

The reasons for this are not simple and not solely due to the predominance of traditional industries earlier in the twentieth century, nor the historic low levels of home-ownership in Scotland until recently; with the latter, Scotland has seen a huge shift towards owner-occupation in the last 20 years without any shift towards a more business-friendly culture. One significant factor has been the strength of a public sector employee culture which has been particularly strong in the central belt. This has paradoxically grown stronger in the last 20 years as the economy and home ownership in Scotland have transformed; this is in part a product of the Thatcher years, where the Scots middle-class professional interest groups, predominantly in the public sector, positioned themselves as the principled defenders of Scotland's national interest.

Scotland's experience of migration does not aid the process of change. London and the south-east have been aided by the experience of immigration by highly skilled, educated and motivated workers who have transformed the economy and culture of London. Scotland, with the exception of some areas of Glasgow, has not had this process, and with Scotland's population predicted to decline from 5.1 million to 4.6 million by 2040 as the UK population increases, Scottish public agencies will have to start thinking about repositioning Scotland as an attractive place to come to work and live in.

It is within the above context that the resignation of the Enterprise Minister

Wendy Alexander in May 2002 has to be put. Alexander, as has been previously discussed, was seen as a bright, driven, dynamic minister. Ian Ritchie, commenting on the overload of Alexander's portfolio of enterprise and lifelong learning with transport, said it was 'completely and utterly barmy. Clearly, in retrospect, it was designed to overload her and switch her off because McConnell wanted to keep her in place' (*Scotland on Sunday*, 5 May 2002). Alf Young commented on her undoubted drive: 'Talking to Ms Alexander about her political mission was sometimes akin to being swept along by a focusing, provocative torrent of ideas, connections and vulnerabilities, all laced with bubbling laughter and indiscreet asides' (*The Herald*, 4 May 2002). However, we need to divorce the style from the substance, and ask in Wendy Alexander's own words whether her setting of the strategic priorities for Scottish Enterprise, universities, further education, careers and transport amount to 'a national consensus that a faster growing Scotland is the key to delivering a fairer Scotland' (*Business a.m.*, 1 May 2002). This was the central difference between Alexander and McConnell, and it is far too early to tell if all Alexander's endeavours these last few years will amount to anything but good intentions and impressive plans.

If nothing else, devolution has forced Scotland to start to address its long-term problems – both formal and informal – which have held back Scottish business from delivering on its potential. But whether it will be a catalyst to help the nation's business community bury its historical ghosts is still too early to tell.

# 15

# SCOTTISH BANKING, FINANCE AND INSURANCE

## *Andrew Collier and Gerry Hassan*

Scotland – a small country – has a disproportionate amount of profile in banking and consumer and corporate financial services across the globe. There are a number of reasons for this, some purely historical and others resulting from a determined and growing desire to develop a presence in markets at home and abroad.

## A SHORT HISTORY OF SCOTTISH BANKING

Scottish banking pre-dates the Treaty of Union, with the Bank of Scotland being established in Edinburgh by an Act of the Scottish Parliament in 1695 (interestingly, it was a Scotsman, William Paterson, who founded the Bank of England the preceding year). Richard Saville's monumental history of the Bank (Saville 1996: 251) describes this period thus:

> The system established by the Bank of Scotland Act of 1695 provided mechanisms for building a substantial basis of credit on a relatively small capital by the issue of paper money. This advance was buttressed by the institutions of society, politics and the legal system and, although it encountered many difficulties, was able to develop into one of the most important parts of the credit available to agriculture, industry and commerce.

The Royal Bank of Scotland was founded by Royal Charter on 31 May 1727 and opened for business in Ship Close, Edinburgh, in December 1727 with deposits of just over £111,000. Among its innovations, the Royal claims at various times in its history to have invented the overdraft, to have been the first clearing bank to have introduced a house purchase loan scheme for customers and to have pioneered automated banking machines.

The two Edinburgh banks concentrated most of their business and credit in the city, creating problems for business in the rest of the country, and in 1746 the British Linen Company was formed to offer banking services to this sector, pioneering the idea of branch banking. The growth of industry and commerce in the early nineteenth century saw a growth in banking, with the establishment of the Union Bank of Scotland in 1830 and the Clydesdale Bank in Glasgow on 7 May 1838. The Clydesdale became over time Scotland's third major bank and the first bank to introduce adding machines in 1899, mobile branches in 1948, and to advertise on television in 1958; it also became the first with personal loans (1958), cheque guarantee cards (1966) and security cameras (1971).

The first savings bank was founded in Ruthwell in Dumfriesshire in 1810 by the Rev. Henry Newman, leading to the establishment of the penny savings banks. The savings bank movement slowly evolved, with the savings bank of Glasgow the largest in the UK, but others quite small, and by the 1960s there were concerns about the profitability of some accounts. This led to the 1973 Page report which recommended reorganisation under a holding company with a wider range of services, which led to the Trustee Savings Bank in 1975.

By the turn of the twentieth century banking had contributed to making Scotland one of the most successful economies in the world: overseas investments stood at £300 million in 1900 and £500 million in 1914. Scots money found its way across the globe: to America, Canada, Australia and New Zealand, rebuilding Chicago and buying American land and property. Dundee's jute barons invented the investment fund as a mechanism for directing profits into overseas investments (Walker 1979). Lenman says of this golden age of Scots capitalism: 'It was commonplace of late Victorian comment that Scotland invested abroad on a scale per head with no parallel among the other nations of the United Kingdom' (Lenman 1977: 192).

Scotland at this point was shaped by regional clusters of capital which emphasised the distinctiveness of Scots business and banking; of the Dundee jute barons of Cox, Baxter and Fleming, the Edinburgh banks and the Glasgow network of the Tennant's companies, the Caledonian railway and Clydesdale Bank. Post-1945, the influence of the old dynastic Scots families had begun to weaken, but up until the 1970s Scots business interests were held together by an alliance of the big three banks: Bank of Scotland, Royal Bank and Clydesdale. The banks played a major part in the reproduction of a Scottish business elite which did not need to 'network', where all the key players, the civil service and politicians, knew each other intimately, and which sustained the 'negotiated order' of Scottish society (Moore and Booth 1989).

# A BANKING REVOLUTION?

Since the 1970s, the world of Scottish banking and finance has been totally transformed from a very cosy, comfy world into one of the most competitive and successful sectors of the Scottish economy. In 1986, the TSB, despite opposition from a wide spectrum of Scottish opinion, was privatised, leading to the formation of TSB Bank Scotland plc. Assurances were given about its Scots distinctiveness and staff levels, but these were not kept and job losses and restructuring downgraded its Scottish operations. In 1995, the TSB Group merged with Lloyds Bank leading to the creation of Lloyds TSB Scotland. Susan Rice, chief executive, was previously managing director of the Bank of Scotland personal banking division. She was born and grew up in Rhode Island, New York, as far away from Edinburgh clubland as possible, and was recently voted the most powerful woman in Scotland by the *Sunday Herald* Business section (*Sunday Herald*, 31 March 2002).

The Royal Bank of Scotland's £21 billion takeover of NatWest in 2000 was a seminal moment for Scottish banking, taking the firm to a size which dwarfs every other Scottish company, let alone those in the financial sector. The Royal Bank is now the fifth biggest and the third most profitable bank in the world after the awesome-sized Citibank and the Hong Kong and Shanghai Banking Corporation. It has been aided by the leadership of former Scottish Development Agency chief executive Sir George Mathewson and ex-Clydesdale Bank chief executive Fred Goodwin. Goodwin, who was rated the third most influential person in Scotland in a recent poll and is a product of Paisley Grammar School and Glasgow University, was nicknamed 'Fred the Shred' after he made savings of £653 million in the first year of merger (*Scotland on Sunday*, 14 April 2002).

The NatWest takeover was hugely important to the Royal Bank, elevating it instantly from a medium-sized and relatively provincial European player into something else. It is now a major global player with a powerful international focus. Its size means that it is able to leverage much bigger deals than would otherwise have been the case. We can now expect the Royal's involvement in international banking transactions – perhaps in partnership with other global players – to be much more profound, especially in the US, where it has a growing presence in sectors such as oil and gas.

In an industry where global consolidation is everything, the Royal's strengthened market position should ensure it continues to grow and be a major player both within the UK and Europe. Nevertheless, the Royal is not making a one-eyed dash for global business. It continues to place great importance on its home market, particularly in the business sector. Much of the specialist corporate work has to be done through Edinburgh or London, but it does maintain a team of relationship banking managers which allows it to service the corporate market, from the smallest local business customers through to the giant multinationals.

The merger between the Bank of Scotland and the Halifax to create HBOS has caused anxieties. Its name may be unwieldy, but there is an undoubted logic to the merger. The Bank of Scotland has its real strength in corporate, structured and institutional banking, with its retail branch network largely confined to Scotland. The Halifax, on the other hand, is extremely strong in mass-market retail banking, though it, too, has a corporate presence, including a strong PFI/PPP team which has now been brought under the Bank of Scotland umbrella. For instance, the Halifax's innovative funding of the public-private partnership deal to fund the redevelopment of 29 Glasgow schools – the largest project of its kind in the UK – has now passed seamlessly to a new team at Bank of Scotland Structured Finance.

The synergies between the two are undeniable, and the marriage looks to be a promising one, combining the strengths of both operations. HBOS has taken over the Bank of Scotland's traditionally strong business lending book, which is now worth nearly £35 billion. However, while its head office functions have been reserved in Edinburgh, the balance of power has shifted to Yorkshire. Peter Burt, executive deputy chairman of HBOS, ranked sixth in the most powerful list, was educated at Merchiston Castle School, Edinburgh, St Andrews University and the University of Pennsylvania, joined the bank in 1975 and rose through its ranks. He will face a difficult period, taking the firm through new challenges emanating from merger and attempting to find a new corporate HBOS identity.

The Clydesdale Bank was owned by the Midland Bank from 1950 and for years suffered from underinvestment and a lack of managerial vision. In 1987, Midland sold the Clydesdale to the National Australia Bank (NAB) for £360 million, and a significant period of growth and investment followed in which the Clydesdale was able to make higher profits than its two bigger rivals, the Bank and Royal Bank. The Clydesdale has not, however, seen its structures revolutionised in the past couple of years. Under NAB, Clydesdale's development has been unspectacular but solid. It has worked hard to build up its corporate presence, although its range of available solutions is narrowed by the fact that it has historically preferred to provide debt finance rather than equity. It now majors strongly on tailored business solutions, some of which are refreshingly innovative, and its branch-based retail network remains strong.

One criticism which has been made of the Clydesdale is that since the NAB takeover, there has been too much of an Australian influence at top levels; the recent appointment of the unmistakably British Grahame Savage as chief executive may help to change that perception. The Clydesdale's reputation in the Scottish marketplace was not helped, however, by remarks from its former head and now NAB chief, the Australian Frank Cicutto, that Scotland had been in recession for 200 years. Cicutto's intervention was unfortunate because, in reality, NAB does have a significant investment in Scotland. Its European headquarters are in Glasgow, and it employs several hundred people in the west of Scotland who undertake administration, shared services and call-centre functions.

Scottish merchant banking's most famous name is Sir Angus Grossart, who set up Noble Grossart in 1969 with Sir Iain Noble, and which grew in the 1970s with investment from Sir Hugh Fraser and North Sea oil. In the 1980s it financed Eddie Shah's newspapers and David Puttnam's films, as well as advising on some of the decade's biggest flotations, such as TSB and ScottishPower. Grossart was educated at Glasgow Academy, Glasgow University and trained as an advocate, practising at the Scottish Bar between 1963 and 1969. He has succeeded by keeping his core business small, and was recently voted the most influential man in Scotland by *Scotland on Sunday*. Whether or not this is true, he unquestionably has a wide reach into different parts of Scottish life: he is on the boards of the Royal Bank, Scottish & Newcastle, Murray International, Edinburgh Fund Managers, Trinity Mirror, Hewden Stuart and the Scottish Investment Trust, as well as having been a member of the boards of Scottish Opera and the Edinburgh Film Festival.

Although the numbers employed in Scottish banking have fallen in recent years from 42,000 in 1990 to 37,000 today, and the wider world of financial and insurance services employed 255,000 people (including banking) in 1997 versus 288,000 in 1995, the industry has massively expanded over the last few decades. This is reflected by the fact that in 1971 financial services represented 3.1 per cent of Scottish GDP (compared to 30.3 per cent for manufacturing), but in 1998 took 19.1 per cent (versus 21.5 per cent manufacturing). Financial and business services now cover a range of activities, with only one third of jobs in banking and insurance and the rest accounted for by legal and computer services, accounting, property services and industrial cleaning. The most rapidly expanding sector has been computer-related services, which grew by 78 per cent between 1991 and 1996 (Peat and Boyle 1999: 128).

The macro-economic statistics tell the same positive story. In the period 1995–2002, total output from the Scottish economy has risen by something less than 12 per cent (the comparable figure for the UK is 19 per cent). The service sector has risen by a greater figure, 18 per cent, while the growth in business services and in finance has been no less than 30 per cent.

## AN INTERNATIONAL MARKETPLACE

Scotland's role as a major financial centre means that the industry now has a truly international feel. Interlopers such as State Street Bank, First Direct and J.P. Morgan now employ significant numbers, although many of these business are seeking not to directly and deliberately attack the indigenous Scottish banking base as much as to use Scotland as a base to leverage new UK and European business.

These institutions are not under any illusions that they can take on the Royal Bank or HBOS. They do not see it as their function to take on the incumbents in an already well-developed marketplace where there are large barriers to entry. Instead, they see Scotland as a prime spot on which to muster their forces in order to fight on a much bigger battlefield. The reasons for their location here are relatively mundane, although sound enough in business terms: office space remains relatively cheap in many parts of Scotland compared to the centre of London and – an important factor in operations such as call centres and back-office processing – good staff are still easy to find. Employee loyalty also tends to be higher north of the border than in the south-east of England, where levels of 'churn' – leaving one company to join another – can be extremely high. These factors, combined with the Scottish reputation for quality banking and for product innovation, have helped to explain the presence of a large number of the new operations which have been established recently.

A Royal Bank offshoot, Direct Line, was one of the first companies in the UK to realise the potential of dealing with customers directly via the telephone. Standard Life Bank and Scottish Widows Bank, both offshoots of highly regarded Edinburgh life institutions, were pioneers in offering basic, no-frills telephone accounts with highly competitive rates of interest. This concept has been further developed by a new Edinburgh-based operation, which has refined the concept of direct consumer banking in what it claims is a revolutionary way. Jim Spowart, the managing director of Standard Life Bank and a man regarded as one of the most innovative bankers of his generation, was poached by the Halifax to launch its new Internet and phone bank, Intelligent Finance.

Under Spowart's supervision, Intelligent Finance has grown into one of the most successful banking operations the UK has ever seen. Adopting a simple but novel (at the time) policy of allowing customers to offset their credit balances in one account with their debit balances in another, so reducing interest payments, caught the imagination of the public in a huge way. In its first full year of business, the operation captured no less than 9.2 per cent of the entire UK mortgage market, achieving £9.5 billion worth of new business and attracting more than 70,000 current accounts.

Spowart, who has always worked within the Scottish banking sector and was determined to locate his new operation north of the border, has created more than 1,400 jobs in Edinburgh and Livingston. He has put pressure on the Edinburgh labour market and helped to create a shortage of suitably qualified people in the city (so pushing wage rates up); but in Livingston, 15 miles away, it has been a different story, with Intelligent Finance moving in quickly to take redundant workers from the Motorola mobile phone plant and retrain them as call-centre operatives.

Intelligent Finance was a huge gamble for the Halifax, as it is possible that the operation may simply have shifted customers from one part of its group to another, incurring huge costs without adding any value. In the event, this does not seem to have happened. Most of the new bank's customers have been attracted from outside Halifax/HBOS.

The start-up costs for Intelligent Finance run into hundreds of millions, but banking is a long game and the losses to date are in the business plan. It is scheduled to break even within the next two years, after which it will start making considerable profits for HBOS. Significantly, IF has not been affected by restructurings within the group as a result of the Halifax/BoS merger: it has been allowed to retain its operational independence, which shows the confidence group chief executive James Crosby and his colleagues have in Spowart's style of management.

## BEYOND CHARLOTTE SQUARE

Edinburgh has historically been seen as the home of Scotland's financial services sector, and it still has the greatest visible presence. It retains the lion's share of the companies and supporting professions, many of them located in the industry's traditional home in Charlotte Square and the surrounding terraces of the New Town. Further measure of the city's success in capturing financial services business can be seen in the rapid development and success of the Exchange financial district off Lothian Road.

However, the industry now spreads well beyond the capital. Glasgow also has a strong history of delivering financial services, though this has tended to be eclipsed in recent years by Edinburgh's remarkable success. Nevertheless, it has attracted big-name players such as Abbey National, and financial services remain a key and growing part of the city's economic mix. The city also has plans for its own financial district at the Broomielaw on the Clyde waterfront.

Aberdeen, too, has a vibrant financial services sector, albeit much smaller than the ones which have developed in Glasgow and Edinburgh. Aberdeen Asset Managers remains one of the country's most important, successful and focused fund management houses, and there is also a considerable amount of corporate financing activity taking place. This is particularly true at present, where the local economy is highly buoyant due to the stable oil price, with opportunities open to independent niche-market players and the desire of some early entrants into the offshore industry to now exit their companies and hand the reins over to a new generation.

One of the biggest areas of activity in the Scottish financial sector is fund management. At the time of writing, some £326 billion in funds is managed in Scotland. Most, though not all, of this money is managed from Edinburgh, the historic capital not just of the country but of the fund management sector. That figure represents a slight drop on the £350 billion or so reported the previous year, but most of that decline is down to worldwide factors such as the lacklustre state of world stock markets rather than for any specifically Scottish reason.

157

Despite the blip caused by world markets, growth of funds under management over two years has been 16 per cent, and over a decade it has been 100 per cent.

This is a remarkable performance, and we have to ask how Scotland has achieved it. History and tradition are clearly important – the notion of Scots prudence with other people's money – but giving someone your cash to invest involves a trust which goes beyond the record of history. There is, rather, a recognition that we have an instinctive understanding of investment opportunities, combined with an inherent ability to react well to unpredictable events. Scots investment fund managers may not have a worldwide reputation for taking any screaming, high-octane gambles, but they do not have a reputation for disaster either.

The two largest players in life insurance and pensions are Scottish Widows and Standard Life. Scottish Widows has now merged with Lloyds TSB to create the second biggest life and pensions business in the UK. Under the stewardship of the canny and highly respected Mike Ross, it has retained its autonomy within the group and remains free to make its own decisions. Scottish Widows provides an excellent example of how a company can be controlled from outside Scotland but still have an effective position within it (in fact, one of the reasons for the huge growth in funds under management north of the border was that Scottish Widows Investment Partners received a hefty £50 billion from Lloyds TSB's own asset management business, Hill Samuel Asset Management, as part of the takeover deal).

Standard Life also continues to flourish with an impressive track record and a reputation for quiet but continued and stable success. It also prizes its status as a mutual, owned not by shareholders but by its members. Attempts by the veteran carpetbagger Fred Woollard to break his way into the company's sanctuary by forcing an end to its mutuality were resoundingly defeated by the membership, but the company did not escape without damage to its reputation. Standard Life realises it has to learn lessons from the episode and that someone could mount another attempt to force demutualisation. The issue is resolved for the moment and, under its avuncular new chief executive Iain Lumsden, the organisation aims to double in size in the next five to ten years.

## THE FUTURE

The Scottish banking sector has long been one of the most important pillars of the Scottish establishment. There has been a distinctiveness about the Scottish financial system (Callaghan 1997); it has a very different ethos 'fed by the social and cultural cohesion within the sector' whereby Scottish banks appear 'more responsible, knowledgeable and sympathetic towards their small firm customers than English banks' (Clay and Cowling 1996: 73). However, while this is true to a degree, it is also part of the elaborate set of myths that make up Scotland

158

and a very different story can be told in which banks and financial institutions are part of the problem of facilitating a more entrepreneurial culture in Scotland.

A 1992 Scottish Enterprise report on Scotland's poor economic record identified that some of the responsibility lay with the banks. They had established such an 'utter dominance' of Scotland as to be regarded as 'near-monopolists' who acted with 'extreme caution in seeking high levels of owners' capital and security and low levels of risk'. Venture capitalists were criticised for 'their reluctance to fund start-ups' and the contribution of 'business angels' has been limited by a lack of accurate information and worthwhile prospects: 'networking is often ineffective in Scotland, which can make it difficult both for angels trying to find investment opportunities and for entrepreneurs seeking angels' (*Scottish Business Insider*, November 1992: 6–8).

There are particular problems between banks and the financing of small and medium-sized firms, with the banks' attitude described by one analysis as 'sterile, uncommunicative and unimaginative' (Cowling et al. 1991: 18), while a Federation of Small Businesses survey found that 20 per cent of small to medium firms felt that banks had a 'low or very low' understanding of their needs. However, this is a two-way problem in which the banks' conservatism is matched by unwillingness on the part of some firms to secure external funding. The banks' attitude is part of a wider defensive financial behaviour (Boyle et al. 1989) which characterises large acres of Scottish public life and the economy – risk aversion, short-termism and asymmetric information – and which acts as an inhibitor on raising the business start-up rate and encouraging entrepreneurship.

The financial sector will face numerous challenges over the next decade or so. One is the changing framework of regulation with the Financial Services Authority (FSA) and the Cruickshank report commissioned by Gordon Brown which reported in March 2000. Cruickshank confirmed that UK banks operated as a cartel and called for an independent regulator to ensure that consumer interests were protected, but his report has been quietly dropped by Brown. Even so, the degree of regulation is too much for many in the financial world (Perman 2001). Another is the advent of the euro and European Monetary Union, which, if the UK joined, would mean shifting from a common currency of 60 million to one of 13 nationalities and 350 million people. The banking and financial communities are divided on this issue, but Scotland trades more with the EU than does the rest of the UK: 73 per cent of Scottish exports go to the EU, compared to 58 per cent of UK exports (Jones 2001).

The Scottish banking and financial sector has undergone far-reaching changes in the last few years, perhaps more so than any other sector of Scottish life. It has gone from being an environment that operated as a relatively distinct Scots 'closed shop' to one that operates and succeeds on the international stage. In this transformation, some of the old-fashioned, quaint and romantic Scottish features and traditions – seen in such customs as the Royal Bank of Scotland's

Ladies Branch in Princes Street, Edinburgh – have been lost; these have become international and transnational companies with a sense of Scottishness only in their history. The Royal Bank's takeover of NatWest and the Bank of Scotland merger with the Halifax were the final chapter in an era of Scottish banking that was drawing to a close. It was an era marked by caution and successful stewardship of financial institutions: of grandee figures such as Viscount Younger and Sir Jack Shaw, who sustained their banks as major benefactors of Scottish life and culture, and the arts in particular, and the movers and shakers such as Sir Angus Grossart and Iain Robertson, who have in effect been replaced by the faceless figures of the Edinburgh-based financial houses. The old institutions were successes on a number of criteria, but they inhabited a Scotland that lost its pro-business climate and became characterised by an anti-entrepreneurial culture. It remains to be seen whether a new generation of bankers and financiers leading internationally owned and operated companies can more aid the cultural shift in Scotland that is needed to survive and prosper in the global age.

# 16

# A NEW ENTREPRENEURIAL CLASS?

*Eleanor Shaw and Jonathan Levie*

## INTRODUCTION

The importance of entrepreneurship in today's developed economies cannot be overstated. It encourages innovation and creativity and uses scarce resources to exploit unmet market demands. In a changing technological, political and organisational environment, entrepreneurship is recognised as vital to the economic wealth and health of Scotland's economy. Unfortunately, recent research suggests that, relative to its economic counterparts, Scotland demonstrates low entrepreneurial activity (Galloway and Levie 2002). The most recent Global Entrepreneurship Monitor (GEM) analysis of 'total entrepreneurial activity' ranks Scotland in the lowest of three country groupings (see Table 1 below).

**Table 1: National Total Entrepreneurial Activity (TEA) Scores**

| TEA BAND | NATION |
| --- | --- |
| High (15–20) | Australia, Brazil, Korea, Mexico, New Zealand |
| Medium (10–14) | Argentina, Canada, Finland, Hungary, India, Ireland, Italy, Poland, South Africa, United States |
| Low (5–9) | Belgium, Denmark, England, France, Germany, Israel, Japan, Netherlands, Norway, Portugal, Russia, Scotland, Singapore, Spain, Sweden, Wales |

*Source: Galloway and Levie (2002)*

Scotland's perceived entrepreneurial poverty is not a phenomenon of the twenty-first century. Over the past half-century a number of driving forces have created a 'dependency' culture within Scotland that has contributed to Scotland's poor entrepreneurial activity. Reliance on jobs created by large organisations, together with the fear of business failure and the insecurity caused by the likely loss of benefits when moving from unemployment to self-employment, are among the drivers which have created a 'dependency' rather than an 'entrepreneurial' culture within Scotland (Wylie 1999).

This situation has not always existed. Business history identifies Scotland as home of the television, breeding ground of penicillin and inventor of steam engine technology. Many of the recently published 'post-devolution, arrival of the millennium' histories of Scotland describe a nation of successful industrialists, radical political thinkers and a hotbed of enterprise and innovation (Devine 1999; Lynch 2001). In tracing the economic and social history of Scotland, it seems that a once enterprising economy boasting a wealth of natural resources, an array of entrepreneurial talent and the capacity to exploit its island position has become dependent on employment provided by large firms and the interventions of a, at times, paternalistic government.

This chapter provides a map of entrepreneurship in Scotland and explores the changing role and importance of entrepreneurship. It opens by positioning current discussion and debate about Scotland's entrepreneurial potential within the historical context of Scotland's entrepreneurial past and considers the evolution and impact of successive economic development interventions. This discussion argues that current debate will benefit from recognition of the diverse nature of entrepreneurship and adoption of wider conceptualisations of entrepreneurship that acknowledge the many contexts within which it can be found. Drawing upon recent research, including the findings of the most recent Scottish GEM study, the chapter moves to identify and describe Scotland's 'new' entrepreneurs. These findings suggest that, within Scotland, entrepreneurship is without a 'class' structure: it is a process and behaviour that cuts across gender, industry, size, type, age and location of organisation. Importantly, these findings reveal that, within Scotland, entrepreneurship is found within a diverse range of contexts. Finally, it considers who influences entrepreneurship in Scotland.

## HISTORICAL CONTEXT

A review of the economic and social history literature reveals that Scotland has a strong entrepreneurial heritage that permeated most industries and professions. In engineering, James Watt is credited with inventing the technology necessary for the steam engine and Neilson revolutionised iron manufacturing with his 'hot blast' system. In shipbuilding, Scotland's rate of innovation was high for most of the 1800s and the Clyde achieved a worldwide reputation for improvements made to modes of propulsion and pioneering new materials for construction (Devine 1999). Scotland's current position as a leading centre for financial services was assured with innovations of the eighteenth century such as the Royal Bank of Scotland's introduction in 1728 of the first 'cash accompt' or overdraft, as it is known today. In philosophy, history, law and economics too Scotland gained an international reputation throughout the eighteenth century for contributions made to a diverse range of intellectual fields of inquiry that William Robert Scott in 1900 termed the 'Scottish Enlightenment'. Scots who made world-class contributions to the eighteenth-century European Enlightenment include David Hume and Francis Hutcheson (philosophers); Adam Smith (economic theorist); Adam Ferguson and William Robertson (historians) and James Hutton (geologist) (Herman 2002).

Economic history provides much evidence to suggest that, historically, Scotland has benefited from a diverse range of entrepreneurial behaviours and witnessed entrepreneurship in a variety of contexts. Considered alongside current disappointing indicators of Scotland's entrepreneurial activity, it can be argued that as Scotland has developed it has lost some of its entrepreneurial capital. Certainly, throughout the UK, from the days of the Industrial Revolution figures for self-employment declined until the 1980s when the number of people establishing their own firms increased by around 60 per cent to 13 per cent of the UK workforce (Brooksbank 2002). One factor contributing to the demise of Scotland's entrepreneurial capacity was the significant number of jobs provided by larger-sized employers. This became strikingly apparent during the recession of the 1980s that also witnessed concerted efforts on the part of government and economic development agencies, including the Scottish Development Agency (SDA), to promote business ownership as a route out of unemployment.

Within Scotland, interventions to support economic development were introduced before this time. The Scottish Development Council was established in May 1931 with the remit to 'examine and endeavour to solve the industrial, commercial and economic problems' that the country then faced (Lynch 2001: 574). In 1946, the Scottish Council (Development and Industry) was established with a remit to create jobs and promote economic diversification. The Scottish Development Agency (SDA) was created in 1975 and charged with the responsibility of generating investment in industry, providing publicly owned factories and environmental recovery. In 1977, the attraction of foreign investment was also added to this remit. The SDA's Small Business Division was a relative backwater, known to insiders as 'sleepy hollow', and entrepreneurship generally had a relatively low profile in Scotland. Focus tended to be on supporting the unemployed in creating jobs for themselves. In November 1987, the SDA's new chief executive announced that much of the SDA would be regionalised 'as part of a reorganisation to make the agency more responsive to local demand' and to counter a popular view that the SDA was biased towards the Strathclyde region and Glasgow (*Financial Times*, 28 November 1987).

In 1988 Margaret Thatcher was lobbied by Bill Hughes, a Scottish businessman, leading member of the Scottish Tory Party and chairman of the

CBI in Scotland. To reform regional development agencies in Scotland, the SDA was replaced by Scottish Enterprise (SE) in 1991. One of the pressures for this institutional change was a feeling amongst many business people that the SDA was a large public organisation with a huge property portfolio and an agenda which business could not control. A perhaps ironic consequence of the change from SDA to SE was that, through its network of local enterprise companies (LECs), Scottish Enterprise secured greater control over and indeed superseded many local enterprise trusts and local initiatives by formalising their funding under the Scottish Enterprise umbrella. Local business people did, however, become involved and formed a majority on the boards of LECs.

The new chief executive of Scottish Enterprise, Crawford Beveridge, a former senior executive with Sun Microsystems in California, was struck by the low rate of new business creation in Scotland, and started a debate on Scotland's business birth rate. Following wide consultation, a Business Birth Rate Strategy was developed and launched in 1993. Though no additional money was allocated to new business creation support, with only about 4 per cent of Scottish Enterprise's budget being spent in this area, there were some shifts in funding. In particular, new efforts to affect culture change were instituted, and public attitudes to entrepreneurship were monitored. An initiative established with public sector support in 1995 (the 'Year of the Entrepreneur' in Scotland) and which quickly became self-supporting was the Entrepreneurial Exchange – a networking organisation 'by entrepreneurs, for entrepreneurs'. This network provided a forum for entrepreneurs to meet and discuss issues in common. By 2001, it had over 400 members and 40 events per year and, while not a lobbying organisation, was increasingly making representations to the Scottish Executive on matters of interest to its members.

In the early 1990s, entrepreneurs in Scotland were and felt unloved and undervalued. However, as the Business Birth Rate Strategy unfolded, media attitudes and interest shifted and became much more positive. But attitudes among the general population seemed to change much more slowly and new business creation rates, having risen up to 1997, started to decline in line with the rest of the United Kingdom as rates of GDP slowed. By early 2001, the new Scottish Executive was beginning to exert its powers in setting local economic development policy, while at the same time there was increasing discontent within the business community with the effectiveness of the Scottish Enterprise network, particularly in the area of support for entrepreneurship.

In June 2001, the Fraser of Allander Institute at the University of Strathclyde produced its report into the effect of the Scottish Business Birth Rate Strategy (BBRS). The report concluded that original targets had been over-optimistic, that relatively little new money had been spent on the BBRS, and that the strategy had had a positive but very small effect on actual business starts (less than 10 per cent of the original target of 25,000 extra new starts). It suggested a modest shift in resourcing from promoting business starts in general towards concentrating on new businesses with growth potential; sought greater recognition for the role the private sector could play; and urged a continued emphasis on enterprise education and improving delivery of information and advisory services. The report stimulated top-level debate among leaders of the entrepreneurial community on the role of entrepreneurship in the economy, and on how government and Scottish economic development agencies should promote entrepreneurship. Ian Ritchie, serial entrepreneur, prominent business angel and a director of Scottish Enterprise, set out his view in July 2001:

> Scotland has a relatively small corporate sector, and although we have some genuine world-class players such as the Royal Bank and ScottishPower, it is vital that we also have new blood coming through . . . Over the next few years, we can expect electronics manufacturing jobs to migrate to lower-cost economies such as in Eastern Europe. Without the dynamic of new high-growth, home-grown businesses, Scotland is doomed to remain a branch factory economy, and our jobs and our futures will remain at the mercy of corporate headquarter decisions in Tokyo or Chicago. So it is vital that new growth businesses are created and thrive here in Scotland. (*Business a.m.*, 5 July 2001)

Ritchie hinted that future entrepreneurship-support programmes would be aimed at high-growth, graduate-led start-ups, that enterprise education would be a particular target, and that the private sector would play a more prominent role in delivery. After the publication of the Fraser of Allander report, Scottish Enterprise consulted widely with prominent members of the 'entrepreneurial community', such as key influencers in entrepreneurship education, the media and entrepreneurial business, including new technology business entrepreneurs. The new Scottish Enterprise strategy for entrepreneurship, *Generating Entrepreneurial Dynamism*, was launched in January 2002 with three priorities: encouraging innovative high-growth new starts; encouraging more people to start businesses; and increasing the contribution of education to the development of entrepreneurship. A feature of the new strategy was the involvement of experienced entrepreneurs as 'buddies' to new entrepreneurs. It appeared that the private sector would be involved more than ever before in the delivery of public sector support to new venture creation and growth (Scottish Executive 2002).

Since the 1980s economic policy has moved from the encouragement of new firm formation mainly as a route out of unemployment towards increasing interest in improving the cultural environment for entrepreneurship, to a current sharper focus on the skills and know-how needed to successfully grow young ventures. The next development may be the recognition that entrepreneurship is wider than the process of new firm formation and growth.

## RE-DEFINING ENTREPRENEURSHIP

We have argued above that there is much historical evidence of Scotland's diverse entrepreneurial heritage and experience. However, Scottish society is still ambivalent about the value of entrepreneurship in the narrow sense of creating and growing businesses for perceived personal gain. Consequently, benefits may lie in rethinking definitions and conceptualisations about 'entrepreneurship'. The creation and growth of a new business, with associated personal financial wealth creation, is not the only expression of entrepreneurship. Entrepreneurship can take place in many contexts and be instigated by a diverse range of individuals and groups. For example, recent research has found that many of the individuals and groups establishing initiatives to address unmet social needs can be described as 'social entrepreneurs' (Shaw et al. 2002). This research suggests that entrepreneurial capabilities, such as 'vision', 'creativity', 'opportunism' and the ability to marshal resources to exploit unmet needs are not restricted to individuals seeking to establish and grow a business for personal gain. In an environment where traditional providers of public services have been criticised as bureaucratic and resistant to change (Mulgan and Landry 1995) and the Welfare State overstretched and hampered by resources restrictions (Leadbeater 1997), innovative approaches used to address social problems are just one example of the variety of contexts within which entrepreneurial behaviour and capacity can be found. Within Scotland, examples of social entrepreneurship – individuals and groups involved in entrepreneurial activity for social rather than financial gain – can be found in the work of *The Big Issue in Scotland*, Clydeline Recruitment and Maggie's Centre. Each of these organisations was established and developed by individuals motivated by the opportunity of adopting an innovative approach and creative use of resources and contacts to satisfy needs which had fallen outside of, or been let down by, the mainstay of economic and community development.

## SCOTLAND'S 'NEW' ENTREPRENEURS

While the headlines of the GEM Scottish report suggest that relative to many other economies, Scotland demonstrates less entrepreneurial activity, other findings presented within the report demonstrate that within Scotland, entrepreneurship can be found across a range of industries and is undertaken by a diverse range of people. Table 2, based on a sample of 2,000 Scots and 2,000 alumni of the University of Strathclyde, shows that the distribution of new businesses by industry sector in Scotland mirrors the international average, except in the retail and hospitality sectors, where it is lower. Table 2 also shows that university alumni are more likely to establish organisations in business services, often as advisers or consultants.

Table 2: Distribution of new businesses (under three years old) by industry sector in Scotland, among alumni of the University of Strathclyde, and among the average of 23 other nations.

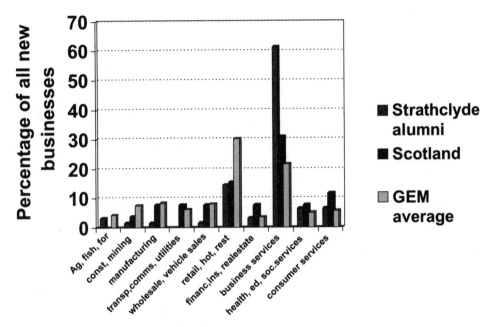

Source: Levie, Brown and Steele (2001)

The number of network organisations established over the past decade to facilitate exchange and the sharing of resources between entrepreneurs also reflects the variety and vibrancy of Scotland's new and emerging entrepreneurs. For example, the distribution of membership of the 400-strong Entrepreneurial Exchange, composed of company founders, is diverse with members coming from all industry sectors. Other networks are more local or sector-specific. The Creative Entrepreneurs Club, run from the Lighthouse in Glasgow, holds regular meetings in Scotland's major cities, attracting 50 to 100 members per event. First Tuesday Scotland claims more than 4,000 active 'new economy' members, with over 80 events per year. Connect Scotland, a network dedicated to nurturing the creation, development and growth of technology enterprise throughout Scotland, provides over 30 events for aspiring technology entrepreneurs to meet representatives of major corporates, leading academics and experienced business service providers. Established by Scottish Enterprise and Wellpark Enterprise Centre, scottishbusinesswomen.com provides an online business community for enterprising Scottish women. This electronic network supports women interested in establishing their own businesses; brokers relationships between existing businesswomen, training providers and professional advisers; and seeks to provide women in Scotland with the opportunity to network with like-minded people both in Scotland and internationally. Complementing this online network, Women into the Network offers women interested in and already running their own businesses a programme of monthly meetings and the opportunity to meet and exchange ideas with other female entrepreneurs.

Every year, *Scottish Business Insider* magazine, a prominent Scottish business monthly, publishes its 'corporate elite'. Although intended to be no more than a 'representative cross-section of those very talented people who help make Scotland plc what it is today' (*Scottish Business Insider*, November 2001), it is one measure of the social impact which entrepreneurs have on business in Scotland. In 2001, a quarter of the 200 individuals profiled had founded their own business. Table 3 shows the distribution of the founder-entrepreneur 'elite' compared with 'new' entrepreneurs (from Table 2) by industry sector.

**Table 3: Distribution of 'corporate elite' founder-entrepreneurs and new entrepreneurs by industry sector**

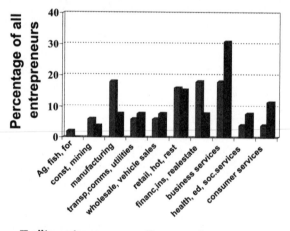

■ **elite entrepreneurs** ■ **new entrepreneurs**

*Source: Levie, Brown and Steele (2001)*

This table shows that, relative to 'new' entrepreneurs, 'elite' entrepreneurs have a greater presence in the manufacturing, finance and real estate sectors and a lower presence in business services. This may reflect the recent decline of manufacturing and rise of business services generally in Scotland, and the presence among the 'elite' of several high-profile venture capitalists who were entrepreneurs. It is notable that only 10 per cent of the 'corporate elite' founder-entrepreneurs are women, when 16 per cent of the membership of the Entrepreneurial Exchange and 30 per cent of 'new' entrepreneurs are women.

Interestingly, this latter figure is the same as the average for all 31 nations sampled in the 2001 GEM study.

A number of others in the 'corporate elite' have bought into and completely reinvigorated old firms (for example, Jim McColl of Clyde Blowers). Other corporate entrepreneurs either create new organisations within existing firms or take established firms into new and different areas, including Jim Spowart who founded Direct Line, Audrey Baxter of Baxter Foods, Maggie Morrison of Cisco, and Mary Campbell, director of British Linen Advisers Ltd. This suggests that a substantial minority, perhaps 30 per cent, of Scotland's 'corporate elite' could be described as entrepreneurs.

In the area of social entrepreneurship, Steve Ebbit, chief executive of the Glasgow Simon Community, and Mel Young, co-founder of *The Big Issue in Scotland*, provide examples entrepreneurship within a context traditionally regarded as outside the mainstream of economic activities but increasingly recognised as critical to the provision of important social services. A qualified social worker, Steve began his career as a volunteer with the Simon Community in London in 1979. Since then he has worked with a variety of projects and organisations, mainly dealing with issues affecting homelessness. Steve was named Social Entrepreneur of the Year by Glasgow Chamber of Commerce in 2000. Also working to alleviate homelessness and combat poverty, Mel Young was the only nominee from Western Europe to be nominated for a Schwab Foundation award. This award was created to honour individuals the Foundation describes as 'outstanding entrepreneurs from around the globe'. In the recent BT Vision 100 index of visionary UK firms, six Scottish firms were listed: Elemental Films, Maggie's Centre, Matthew Algie, MGM International, the Adventure Centre and the Wise Group (*The Guardian*, 18 March 2002). Of these firms, four were established only in the past seven years.

As the figures and examples presented in this section reveal, within Scotland, entrepreneurship is diverse and entrepreneurs, especially those who have emerged in the last decade, are to be found in a range of sectors and contexts. Simply put, within a modern Scotland, entrepreneurship is an activity which can cut across class, industry and location.

## THE SCOTTISH POWERBASE

Who are the most powerful entrepreneurs in Scotland? First, let us distinguish the formal and informal power structures. Formal power structures are relatively easy to identify. If we consider the membership of boards of organisations which serve entrepreneurs or decide or effect policy affecting entrepreneurship in Scotland, a few individuals can be seen to be at the heart of the power base of the Scottish entrepreneurship renaissance. These are people who are gradually taking over from an older generation of entrepreneurs, such as Ian Wood, Bill

Hughes, Tom Farmer and Angus Grossart. At the time of writing, the individual with most relevant board representation was Tom Hunter, chairman of the Entrepreneurial Exchange. Hunter had a particular passion for recreating an entrepreneurial culture in Scotland, and saw education as key to this. He was the lead funder of Schools Enterprise Scotland (which is funding at least two enterprise education experiences for every primary school child in Scotland) and board member of Young Enterprise Scotland (aimed at secondary school pupils). In 2000, Hunter also endowed £5 million to the University of Strathclyde for entrepreneurship education. The Hunter Centre for Entrepreneurship, which produces the annual GEM Scotland report, rapidly became the largest entrepreneurship centre of any university in Scotland. Hunter is also a board member of the Prince's Scottish Youth Business Trust, which provides advice and acts as lender of last resort to young entrepreneurs.

   Other individuals with at least two board memberships of relevant national organisations include: Ian Ritchie (board member of Scottish Enterprise and Scottish Institute for Enterprise); Martin Ritchie (chairman of Connect Scotland and board member, Scottish Institute for Enterprise); John Anderson (chief executive of Entrepreneurial Exchange and board member, Scottish Institute for Enterprise); and Gio Benedetti and Gordon Beattie (both on the board of the Entrepreneurial Exchange and PSYBT). Other influential entrepreneurs included Jim McColl (vice-chairman, Entrepreneurial Exchange and board member, Scottish Higher Education Funding Council) and Chris Van Der Kuyl (chairman of Young Enterprise Scotland). In addition, many other entrepreneurs serve on national and local entrepreneurship-related organisations in 2002. Examples include: Ann Rushforth (board member, Entrepreneurial Exchange and Scottish Enterprise Dunbartonshire); Chris Gorman (board member, Entrepreneurial Exchange and Chairman, Hillington Innovation Centre); Marilyn Orcharton (entrepreneur, Chair of Women into Business and past President of Glasgow Chamber of Commerce); and Elizabeth McAreavey (board member, Entrepreneurial Exchange and Executive Committee member of SCDI). Other entrepreneurs are active in advising or lobbying politicians in specific policy areas, for example David Sibbald in telecommunications, Professor Sir David Lane in science, John McGlynn in planning and Bill Fleming on bankruptcy law.


## CONCLUSIONS: ENCOURAGING ENTREPRENEURSHIP IN SCOTLAND

Scotland's entrepreneurial potential is brighter than recent figures for new business creation might suggest. Thanks to the efforts of far-sighted individuals, from both the public sector and private sector, Scotland is now seen as a world leader in entrepreneurship education. This is playing a major part in helping

Scottish society undergo this culture change from dependency to creativity.

This is not to suggest, however, that intervention to support and encourage entrepreneurship is not required. For example, in addition to entrepreneurship education, many interventions have recently been developed to support the establishment of new firms and encourage firms to grow at a fast and a high rate. These are laudable, but we can go further. The next stage could be to broaden our definition of entrepreneurship to include social, corporate and public sector aspects, and devise and implement ways of encouraging entrepreneurship irrespective of the organisational setting.

# 17

# CREATIVE SCOTLAND

*Stuart MacDonald*

## INTRODUCTION

Creative industries ought to be a hotter topic than it is. Why this should be much more than a specialised argument centred on the imprecision of the definition, the flakiness that surrounds the notion of creativity or puzzlement about the Blairite fascination for the world of the arts, generally, should be a matter for wider discussion. That it is hardly discussed outside a limited circle is due to its relegation to the margins of the arts press or occasional presence in the business pages. It ought to be a matter of national concern. At its core is a debate about the future of Scotland's most talented individuals and companies, the creativity of the Scottish nation and the ways in which technology is breaking down barriers – between commerce and culture, art and science, consumption and production – with implications for all our economic, social, educational and cultural futures.

## CREATIVE EXPECTATIONS

When, in March 2000, several hundred assorted designers, games developers, film-makers, architects, music and media consultants gathered at the new Dundee Contemporary Arts to discuss Scottish Enterprise's forthcoming Creative Industries strategy, there was an expectation that something which had been perceived as a Cinderella was at last being treated seriously. Launched six months later by former enterprise minister Henry McLeish, the vaunted strategy (ten pages in all) invoked something less than enthusiasm, despite there apparently being £25 million on offer to develop the sector in Scotland. Now that time has moved on, cynicism has supplanted that early optimism. The general mood is that the creative industries, despite being valued as worth as much as £5 billion to the Scottish economy and providing 100,000 jobs, have been and remain poorly served.

Why should this be so? And what are the creative industries exactly? Are they really important to Scotland, culturally and economically? Who are the key players? And are there peculiarly Scottish dimensions to this debate?

## WHAT ARE THE CREATIVE INDUSTRIES?

According to who you are, the creative industries can mean many things. Pragmatically, business strategist John Hawkins (2001) believes that the copyright, patent, trademark and design industries constitute the creative industries and the creative economy. New economy commentator Charles Leadbeater (1999) has termed this the 'thin air' business, whilst cultural consultants such as Comedia's Charles Landry (2000) locate the debate more widely, believing creativity to be a generic capacity central to the development of our cities. For others, such as DEMOS director Tom Bentley, the new economy, in which knowledge is the primary source of economic value, demands that creativity become a core competence requiring a radical transformation of the education system. For all of this 'third way' talk, there is an equal amount of cynicism. The Edinburgh-based Policy Institute has depicted the creative industries as a door that opens to special pleading for any industry on the basis of higher national interest (Baird 2001).

Discontinuities abound and definition appears both elusive and contentious. This is not helped by the fact that when the Department of Culture, Media and Sport (DCMS) mapped out the sector in 1997 and 2001 and 'clustered' a range of activities into the creative industries, the film industry was lumped along with antiques and games, software with architecture, music with design. Also included were the arts and cultural industries which, with their legacy of public subsidy, operate to quite different financial and business models.

## THE ARTS ARE NO HELP

In this context international comparisons are helpful only in that most countries would agree that creativity and its industries embrace the creative imagination in all its forms, but in the UK science and the patent industries are excluded. The exception to this is the government-established National Endowment for Science, Technology and the Arts (NESTA), which takes a wider view, assuming creativity is present in all new and innovative products and services. However, generally in the UK – and in 2000 Scottish Enterprise adopted the DCMS definition without demur – the word 'creative' is still used to mean something 'artistic' and 'cultural'. In Scotland, with its tiny and close-knit art world and lacking a coherent cultural strategy, the potential for confusion is never far away. Certainly, that is the quite understandable misconstruction placed on the creative industries by the Policy Institute in their otherwise excellent publication on arts funding in Scotland. However, to confuse the arts, including Scottish Opera with its presupposition of long-term (government) revenue funding via the Scottish Arts Council, with creative enterprises such as design, advertising and the commercial music business, is specious.

For example, in Scotland, for some practitioners, any problems that come with the looseness of the definition are more than outweighed by the utility of having a transferable concept 'creativity'. For designer Janice Kirkpartick (2001), this has allowed her to move beyond the UK obsession with culture and art. For her, the latter has become so specialised that it is in danger of relegating itself to the level of entertainment. Not withstanding the relevance of contemporary art, Kirkpatrick and Bentley (2001) see the need for a major overhaul in education to prioritise creativity in all subjects. Anyway, it is debatable whether looking to the arts will help. Conflating the arts with the creative industries is not useful and begs the question as to how the contemporary performing and visual arts, philosophically and theoretically stricken as they are, and which are almost totally taken up with differentiating between what is and what is not art, can add anything to creative business.

Nonetheless, taking on a wider debate which links the demand for a definition of the creative industries which focuses on creative business – and at one level this might obviate the arts – with the need to examine the role of creativity at all levels of education and, indeed, to develop a much more refined interface between education and the creative industries might be the Scottish contribution. These, however, are not the only bones of contention.

## FROM JUTE AND JOURNALISM TO JOYSTICKS AND JAM

One of the principal criticisms of Scottish Enterprise's Creative Industries strategy has been an almost exclusive focus on the development of the computer games industry in Scotland. Admittedly, Scotland has benefited from support in this area – the UK is the third-biggest market in the world after the US and Japan. What has evolved from a 'geeky' activity in teenagers' back bedrooms is now a significant industry. The University of Abertay even runs a master's course in computer games technology – the world's first – in order to feed more creative talent into the industry. Indeed, Dundee, once associated with jute, jam and journalism, is now the centre of a thriving games industry with companies such as DMA, whose *Grand Theft Auto 3* was ranked seventh in the world top-sellers. The city is also host to other big names in the business such as Viz and Denki, whose prize-winning designs more than manage to compete in the worldwide market. Elsewhere, the world's leading designers of avatars, Digital

Animation Group (DAG), based in the Lighthouse, Scotland's national architecture and design centre, have broken new ground, producing Ananova, the world's first digital newsreader, sold on to Orange. DAG is now developing a range of new avatars, including a virtual receptionist and a virtual 'signing' interpreter, thus making Scotland a potential centre of excellence for virtual human beings. DAG's avatar work is done in parallel with animation for films and e-business. And with the average weekly household spending on leisure-related activities amounting to £62.50 – according to government figures for 2001 – the demand for digital games and play is unlikely to diminish.

The success of Scotland's games industry is not in dispute but what is seen as contentious is a preoccupation with this sector over digital developments generally. Also, in a sector worth £5 billion the Scottish games industry's turnover of £100 million has to be seen in perspective. For example, because of computing technology, architecture – with approximately the same revenue value as the Scottish games sector – now operates in a global market. The digital revolution has vastly accelerated architecture's reaction speeds, which were traditionally very slow. Complex forms are suddenly economic. At one extreme Frank Gehry can produce Guggenheim clones anywhere in the world and at the other, nearer home, Scottish architects could, if innovative clients required, come up with imaginative ideas in a way that would have dazzled Mackintosh or Thomson. Digital technology also allows architects to export designs to new markets but, unlike their counterparts in the Netherlands or Denmark – countries of a similar size to Scotland but with a much more sophisticated architectural culture – Scottish architects, especially young, small practices, lack the support to compete effectively with their global rivals.

Product and fashion design are other areas which are neglected in Scotland despite the wealth of homegrown talent and its exodus annually to London, Paris and Milan. Even with the marketing platform of Glasgow UK City of Architecture and Design in 1999 the business death rate in product design, especially, should be a matter of national shame when set against the range and number of product design courses in our colleges and universities. Equally, despite the numbers of students studying textiles and fashion-related courses, Scotland has produced only one significant international fashion designer, Dundee's Kenneth Mackenzie. Suffice to say, his label 6876 is based in Paris. There are also success stories, however. Many Scottish advertising companies have successfully broken into the London-dominated market, opening up offices in the capital. These companies offer models of effectiveness, entrepreneurship, creativity and management to the more vulnerable and immature parts of the sector. They are not necessarily at the forefront of the digital revolution but their expertise – to say nothing of their fee income – is considerable.

## DISSOLVING BOUNDARIES

The prioritisation of one area of the creative industries over another is an issue but the bigger picture is that the boundaries of what constitutes a discipline are changing. Architecture or design or art are in transformation. Architecture, which is not regarded as a new media, is nonetheless dissolving into graphics, sculpture, fashion and performance because of technology. People are also consuming contemporary culture (and this has huge implications for the creative industries) in very different ways. Mackintosh is worn as jewellery or used as mouse-mat, coffee is drunk from a Colourist mug, Raeburn can be appreciated as fridge magnet or headscarf. More and more people are attending cultural events – the success of Tate Modern is but one famous example – but increasingly, and at the same time, people are consuming culture vicariously through the Web and other media. More importantly, the widespread availability of digital cameras and enabling software will allow people to become producers themselves, whether creating their own movies, music, websites, interior designs or indulging in digital play. These new consumers will require more and more creativity which, as a generic, problem-solving competency, will continue to increase in demand, far outstripping supply.

The borders between culture and commerce, production and consumption, are so permeable that the whole status of the arts – certainly the arts as defined and differentiated in SAC grant applications – is called into question. If, as economist and former SAC chair Alan Peacock believes, the government have just invented the creative industries in order to redefine the arts as part of a dumbing down process to justify spending and hike participation rates, then it looks like the middle-class cognoscenti who dominate the arts scene simply do not get it (Peacock et al. 2001). Unfortunately, the same people inhabit other quangos in other walks of Scottish life, to the detriment of the creative industries.

## EDUCATION: GAME ON?

Because of the exponential growth in technology, in particular computer games, more and more people will become involved in online learning and electronic communication than ever was the case with conventional media or traditional curricula. Rapid technological change coupled with increased demand for knowledge is creating a dramatic transformation which far outstrips the ability of all levels of the education system to keep up. Indeed, two separate think tank reports on respective sides of the border, by Keir Bloomer (2001a) and Tom Bentley (2001), have highlighted the national inertia in developing links between education and industry. Both underline 'modernisation' in education as deeply conservative, reflecting a model inherited from the industrial age.

According to these two think tank reports, reforms in education have done anything but develop the curriculum revolution the country needs, creating instead more physical infrastructure and clunky systems.

In Scotland, the problems are exacerbated by the pull of London haemorrhaging talent from our universities and colleges; a lack of inter-disciplinary courses or training synergising creative, technical and managerial skills; a pernicious, historical exclusion by the education system of creative/artistic matters; and a failure to connect science and art. There is also a complete absence of research either to aid the creative industries or to spin out new businesses and knowledge, raising the question as to whether the higher education sector, given the slowness of its reaction times, has the ability to undertake research in this area or whether the lead should be taken by the industries themselves. Crucially, there is the lack of a focus for training and skills development as well as research – a centre that might act for the diverse needs of the creative industries – which would be resistant to the vagaries of political fashion or the shifting priorities of enterprise agencies. Not least there is the social exclusion which stunts so much of Scotland's nascent talent. At root is a misunderstanding of what it means to commercialise talent, to industrialise creativity. This means engaging all sectors of the education system, from primary to higher education, in redefining creativity. It also means deconstructing it and moving it out of its artistic ghetto to embrace imagination, risk-taking, entrepreneurship and problem-solving in a range of subjects and curriculum contexts. Most important, it means learning to apply knowledge to new situations.

## INDUSTRIALISING CREATIVITY

It is in that sense that the lack of an operable definition for the creative industries betrays a deep-seated lack of understanding about 'industrial creativity'. That word shift is more than semantic. Charles Rennie Mackintosh, despite his creative genius, failed to make any impact on the design of Scottish products apart from being the unwitting legatee of a range of post-Modern tat. The fault for this lies with the high-mindedness of the British educational elite, who, in their reverence for 'fine art', relegated industrial design to the lowly category of 'commercial art'. According to historian Correlli Barnett (2001), here was a new twist to the old story of the divide between the cultural values of the common room and boardroom. This explains why there is no equivalent in Scotland of Finland's University of Industrial Design in Helsinki (UIAH), which annually develops more patents than all of the universities and businesses in Scotland put together.

## THE POLICY DEFICIT

What is required is a better understanding of what industrial creativity means. Also needed is the clear separation of the world of the arts, with its self-referencing introspection, from creative business. The august *Financial Times*, whose Tuesday Creative Business supplement focuses on media, design and communications, seems to have no problem in doing this. Once that distinction is made, talking about creativity in terms of the weightless economy becomes easier. What is apparent is that there is something missing in public policy. Policy-makers, both governmental and otherwise, know little of industrial creativity. That is because no one has studied the new generation of entrepreneurs – how they work, where they come from, what their particular needs are – nor how to engage with them. This void in policy has to be filled with more radical and innovative approaches to education and training as well as management and business support, including advice on finance and intellectual property – investment, not subsidy.

There are also crucial and immediate concerns, such as the situation south of the border where DCMS, not the DTI, has responsibility for the creative industries. The recently established Higher Education/Creative Industries Forum, set up to address shortfalls in provision, is also organised under the auspices of DCMS. Within the Scottish Executive there is a similar, perceived discontinuity. Mike Watson, the Minister for Tourism, Culture and Sport, appointed in the re-shuffle after the demise of Henry McLeish, took the remit for the creative industries from Wendy Alexander's industry portfolio. Unannounced, this took Scottish Enterprise by surprise. Officials were perplexed as to how the creative industries would sit with the rest of the new minister's brief. Either this is an example of obfuscation, lending support to Peacock and the Policy Institute's thesis that the creative industries are the arts lumped under another guise, or there really is a recognition that culture and commerce have come together and that joined-up government is actually happening. However, given the fact that the economic agency charged with developing the creative industries – Scottish Enterprise – was amongst the last to know about the ministerial switch-over, the reality is probably much more prosaic. What is more likely, now that the boundary lines are so blurred, is that no one knows how to manage the relationship between culture, creativity and the economy.

## CONCLUSION: HYBRIDS, GAP SITES AND BROKERAGE

Because creative industries – as opposed to the fine arts or cultural industries – are distinctive in that they create new value, coupled with the fact their management is tricky, grey areas and gaps abound. Added to this is the realisation that a 'cluster' is not a discrete group – they permeate, they overlap, they inter-connect, they recruit from the same pool of creative talent and such people move from one sector and from one technology to another. It is not just technological platforms that are converging, traditional skill areas and disciplines are doing the same. The big question is: how do we fill the gaps between the old institutional arrangements? Hybrid meeting places will be needed to allow people entry to the creative industries. This is not simply an issue of counter-posing creative industries to cultural consumption. It is in the cross-over between these two spheres that innovative models have to be developed – and fast.

For example, a new institution such as the Lighthouse, Scotland's Centre for Architecture, Design and the City, has come into its own in this respect. It is in many ways a different model. First, it is private and only partially reliant upon public subsidy, with over 80 per cent of its income coming from commercial activity. This is the reverse of Scotland's visual or performing arts venues. Second, it has placed itself on the proactive side of the culture–economy equation, encouraging both creative consumption and production. Third, it acts as a hub for creative industries practitioners – showcasing their work, organising network contacts, holding seminars and generally offering a significant resource. Finally, and most importantly, it is innovating creative education, with a Scotland-wide programme bringing designers into schools and creating new electronic learning resources and materials with cutting-edge digital delivery. Designers and creative professionals from all the industries are intertwined with this process. They and the Lighthouse's products and services are networked internationally. The Lighthouse is thus performing a much-needed brokerage function, acting in the middle ground between local and national policy and government, between creatives and clients, between different sectors of education.

Mongrels can act in this way – they have no pedigree to worry about, especially in the spurious debate about high or low culture. What matters is getting creative professionals to interact in a way that results in new ideas and products. It means maximising the contact between those whose energy and ideas produce things people want and the people who consume them. It means, for example, encouraging creative professionals and young people to learn from and with each other. It means nurturing the talent of the next generation to fuel what will be a never-ending demand for content and ideas for the next generation of creative industries, whatever they might be. It will mean more and more people creating their own culture.

In Scotland, what the creative industries need – a sector that is composed largely of micro-businesses, depends on freelancers (mostly from London) and which is hugely undercapitalised – is not subsidy but investment, a policy framework for their support and development which at least recognises who is working in creative business, what their unique problems are and what their unique contribution could be. They are the entrepreneurs whose talent will create the innovative products and services the country's economy needs to compete in the global age.

# 18

## SCOTTISH MUTUALS: TRADE UNIONS AND THE BUSINESS LOBBIES

### Keith Aitken

## INTRODUCTION

Whatever the prospects of the Scottish economy, it rests upon a very elaborate institutional topography (Peat and Boyle 1999). This chapter attempts to draw distinctions among the numerous agencies, institutes, and lobbying groups that comprise the Scottish economic community; to describe how they relate to each other and to the broader Scottish body politic; and to assess their effectiveness in influencing a key area of public policy within Scotland's new, devolved politics.

## THE TOWER OF BABEL

The Small Business Consultative Group for Scotland (SBCG) is neither a glamorous nor a famous body, but it is an interesting one. Its purpose is to guide public policy in relation to the support, development and regulation of Scotland's small businesses, in which mission it is broadly the Scottish equivalent of the Department of Trade and Industry's Small Business Council.

What makes the SBCG interesting is its composition. It is chaired by the Minister for Enterprise, Lifelong Learning and Transport and its independent advice is ensured by a spread of member organisations: the Federation of Small Businesses (FSB), the Forum of Private Business (FPB), the Institute of Directors (IoD), the Confederation of British Industry (CBI Scotland), the Scottish Chambers of Commerce (SCC) and the Scottish Trades Union Congress (STUC). Looking at this list, outside observers might remark that this tripartite mix is distinctly reminiscent of what in the 1970s was called the corporate state, a jabberwock assumed slain by Margaret Thatcher. They might think that, as a small and not particularly diverse economy, Scotland seems to squeeze an awful lot of representative bodies around its policy table; and that, given a new politics supposed to embody innovative forms of consultation, the SBCG sounds and looks terribly like the usual suspects.

Our observers would be right, though in each case there is more to say. Scotland did retain more than is commonly supposed of the old consensual structures through the Thatcher years, even though it spent much of that time protesting noisily about how they were being destroyed in an affront to Scottish collectivist tradition. For example, the Scottish Economic Council, which advised Secretaries of State right through the Thatcher and Major eras, was really the last shard of the Department of Economic Affairs, Harold Wilson's quixotic attempt to shut the Treasury out of economic planning.

Certainly, when real power needed exercising in Scotland prior to 1997 a ruling party perpetually short of elected friends tended to pack quangos with compliant boardroom trusties, and to marginalise or exclude dissident voices. The boards of the enterprise networks – elaborately got up in commercial trappings – were required by statutory prescription to draw two-thirds of their membership from private sector panjandrums. Across the course of the 1980s, the STUC's representation on Scotland's health boards fell from 36 seats to none (Aitken 1992). Yet civic coalition, ostentatiously symbolic of representative authority, formed around both topical issues – such as industrial closures – and longer-term objectives, as witness the Standing Commission on the Scottish Economy and the Scottish Constitutional Convention (STUC 1989; Boyle et al. 1989). Politically, these civic militias were defined chiefly by their antagonism to the Conservatives; not surprisingly business kept its distance, assertive, though privately unsure of its influence in the corridors of power.

Scotland's population of business bodies remains formidably dense. Those jostling for elbow space at the SBCG are barely the half of it. There is, for example, the oldest, broadest-based and least reticent of all, the Scottish Council for Development and Industry, headed since 1996 by Alan Wilson, who has risen through the ranks after joining it in 1980. It affects to speak on behalf of the whole economic polity. There is also Scottish Financial Enterprise, elegant tribune of the money-changing classes led since 1999 by Ray Perman, previously a financial journalist. And there are more professional and trade associations than you could shake a stick at. Some play significant parts in economic debate: Scottish Engineering conducts an often newsworthy quarterly survey of manufacturing mood. Others are immensely grand. The West of Scotland Branch of the Institution of Civil Engineers may not be on every lip, but it attracts more than 850 dinner jackets to what is resonantly billed as the biggest annual dinner of the oldest professional institute in the world. Yet there is dissonance rather than harmony in numbers. Though the main business lobbies meet each other periodically in pursuit of common purpose, there is as much mutual suspicion as empathy. Many of the groups, and many more of their corporate members, regard one another as competitors rather than comrades in adversity. An extreme example is the loathing that seethes between food producers and food retailers. The priorities of small and big businesses, likewise, rarely coincide. Many groups also have overlapping memberships and compete for subscriptions. All are modest in terms of membership and have been affected by the post-war loss of corporate headquarters in Scotland (Scott and Hughes 1980).

To a disturbing degree, the influence of a Scottish business lobby often seems to be determined by the gravitas of the individual at its helm. Little was heard for years from the Scottish Chambers of Commerce until they appointed the voluble Lex Gold as chief executive in 1995. Gold, a three-shift quote-maker of many causes, came from the equivalent post at CBI Scotland. Scant mutual affection is evident with his successor there, Iain Macmillan. Similarly, the diminutive Bill Anderson parted company with FSB only to resurface at its sworn rival, the FPB. To ask either of those organisations why small businesses need two representative bodies is to hear at length the shortcomings of the other.

## MAMMON ON THE MOUND

Plurality of hymn-sheets is one reason why the business lobbies have made what is widely seen as a disappointing early impact on the counsels of devolved Scotland. This disappointment is felt across the political spectrum and by many elders of the business tribe itself. Policy inputs by business lobbies, though plentiful, are perceived to have been ineffectual, inconsistent, reactive, predictable and sometimes less than astute. Nationalist MSPs attribute this to a lack of internal policy devolution within the business lobbies and this is certainly true of some. The frequency with which the CBI's pugnacious director-general, Digby Jones, flies north to rebuke Scotland for economic underperformance does Macmillan's clout on the Mound few favours. Some organisations are also severely hidebound by a need to avoid offending anyone within a diverse membership, and policy consequently suffers from the blandness of the lowest common denominator.

There is a view – to which some MSPs subscribe – that the poor quality of business inputs should be blamed in part on the Parliament and its committees, because they have been insufficiently challenging to low-grade submissions. Prior to devolution, Scottish public debate was conducted in informal, knockabout terms through the media. Exposure depended on topicality and tartness rather than on scholarship, and newsdesks lacked the time and inclination to question the provenance of pithy copy. This created among business (and other) lobbies both an opportunity to make a big noise with small resources, and a temptation to present a few thoughts assembled over lunch as the calibrated wisdom of the sector. A parliament with an inquisitorial and proactive committee culture should expect better. If access is for all, opinion must be weighed on quality, not rank or privilege. Yet, the business lobbies continue to be heard, and expect to be heard, as of right. The committees are thus accused by some of being excessively tolerant of licensed mediocrity. It is also clear that the Executive finds the old institutional landscape a still convenient route map when consultation is required, or if a sudden taskforce needs whistled into being.

There are problems with this criticism, though. It is not the job of the Parliament to school those who would influence it. The main business-related committee, Enterprise and Lifelong Learning (or ELL), is actually one of the more self-willed and energetic. It scored a major coup in forcing a wide-ranging review of the enterprise networks in 2000, long before ministers had intended anything of the sort. The review, one might add, was provoked in part at least by pressure from certain business lobbies, notably FSB, which harbours a seasoned (and not disinterested) belief that the networks devote too much money to large and foreign-owned companies. Finally, it is open to question whether, as currently resourced, the business lobbies would be able to raise their game very readily even if the Parliament required it of them.

Yet even if devolution has not greatly enhanced the quality of economic debate, it has unquestionably changed the style and grammar. The biggest change is access. The STUC attended more than twice the number of ministerial meetings – around 50 – in the first year of the Parliament than in the whole 18 years of Thatcher and Major. The SCDI was likewise heard to boast, at its 2001 AGM, that policy submissions were running at almost one a week. These interactions take preparation, however commonplace they become. Facts need to be assembled, strategies formulated, papers drafted, journalists briefed. The pressure on enthusiastic but scant human resources is intense.

Access alone is not influence. It is no longer an end in itself. Those now in command of these organisations grew up in an age when the primary objective of agitation was to catch the attention of London, and simply being noticed was a triumph. Adjusting to changed circumstance is hard, and the business lobbies suffer a further handicap. Business was persuaded, and persuaded itself, to acquiesce with a Scottish Parliament on the basis that devolution did not really matter. It therefore saw no pressing need to adapt its structures, methods or policy in readiness for a new Scottish politics. The electorate's expectations were likewise depressed. Critics who fret at the lack of public fervour for Scotland's new institutions forget the long years voters spent being told by home rule parties that a devolved Parliament would not be capable of doing anything remotely alarming. Devolution was sold by its advocates (and deplored by the SNP) on the basis of what it could not, rather than could, do.

As it became increasingly obvious that Labour would win the 1997 election, and would deliver on its promise to devolve, Scottish business (having mostly opposed home rule) began to reassure itself, with the happy connivance of pro-devolution politicians, that the Parliament would be unable to do it any great harm. The question of whether the Parliament could improve the commercial environment scarcely arose. Assurances were sought, and given, that the key economic powers – fiscal policy, monetary policy, regulation – would remain reserved to Westminster. The business-related remits to be devolved were the same ones the Scottish Office had run for decades. Therefore, business saw little need to review or revise its relations with the machinery of Scottish government.

What it failed to take into account was that many policy areas of high business importance – education and training, transport and infrastructure, local taxation and planning, agriculture and fisheries, tourism and economic development – would now be determined by new legislative processes, new and ambitious politicians, and new forms of consultation. It was not just a question of opportunity missed. Some interest groups, such as the environmental and voluntary sectors, recognised quickly the potential for influence – perhaps because the previous regime had ignored them even more than it had the business lobbies. They upgraded their policy and communication processes and learned to build supple alliances behind targeted objectives. Not all these civic organisations have agendas entirely compatible with the keenest priorities of Scottish business. To take just one example among dozens, the green agenda of restricting access for motor cars to city centres swiftly gained a momentum that the various Chambers of Commerce viewed with dismay. Business lobbies have yet to develop an effective response to these civic strategies.

Formal routes to influence, for sure, are not the whole story. The Scottish business community has an enthusiasm for informal 'networking' that borders on the mystical. Scarcely an evening passes in Glasgow or Edinburgh's big hotels without a gathering of the community's finest, often to present one another with awards. Were competitiveness measured in dinner-jacket hours or engraved glass, Scotland would be a tiger economy. Politicians too do a good deal of their business by informal networking. What is little evident is that these respective networks yet intersect nearly as readily as one would expect in a small, homogenous and substantially self-governing nation. Business dinners are something of a closed circuit. Though politicians are often invited along as speakers or as trophy guests, there is little sign that they feel much need to fraternise more systematically. The grandest networking event in the Scottish economic calendar has traditionally been SCDI's Annual Forum, yet it attracts only a handful of MSPs. The frequency with which the same few boardroom grandees crop up on quangos, working groups and consultative boards also tends to suggest that political acquaintance has not penetrated terribly deep through the cigar smoke and Macallan fumes of business networking.

# THE EMPIRE STRIKES BACK?

Many of the key devolved economic functions are delivered at one remove, through executive agencies. By far the most significant agencies are Scottish Enterprise and Highlands and Islands Enterprise, successors to the warmly recalled Scottish Development Agency and Highlands and Islands Development Board. Their role is multi-faceted. As creators (within given political parameters) of development policy, they are objects for critical assessment and challenge. As evangelists for new ideas and strategies, they also both shape and participate in debate. In recent years, for example, they have beguiled the nation with such novelties as clusters, competitive place and e-commerce. Finally, because they are required to operate in ostentatious partnership with the private sector, they have been important conduits for business input to policy. This importance may now be diminishing.

Their self-designation as networks reflects an aspiration to be the practical forum wherein all economic wisdom comes together selflessly to forge strategies that advance the common weal. It is not an aspiration universally accepted at face value, particularly by those (from the SCDI to the local authorities) who have lost powers and prestige to the enterprise bodies and who sometimes find their virtuous advances hard to stomach. Co-existence is not helped moreover by the networks' tireless capacity for structural and ideological upheaval. They labour in perpetual transition, buffeted both by frequent political review and by their own restless urge to adapt, and be seen to adapt, to changing business dynamics (fashion would be another word).

The biggest change came in 1991, with the transformation of the SDA and HIDB into SE and HIE. Under the Conservatives, the old agencies had been driven far from their interventionist, remedial origins in Harold Wilson's administration. They had been directed to target opportunity rather than need, to restrict interventions to the catalytic minimum, to gainsay the market only on its proven failure, and to make a commercial return on activities. None of this placated business critics, some of whom persisted in damning them as relics of the state's socialist delusion that it knew more than business about business. But the agencies remained useful to ministers, both as purveyors of optimistic inward investment press conferences and as an arm's-length recourse for showing due concern when industrial calamities occurred.

Accordingly, the reforms sought to retain the usefulness, while giving business critics a sense of ownership. First, they married economic development to responsibility for training, an act of administrative devolution that no one in Scotland was going to oppose (though policy control initially remained with Whitehall). Second, they revamped the agencies' district offices into local enterprise companies (LECs), a nationwide web of employer-dominated commercial analogues charged with formulating insightful local strategies and thereby allocating funds for all but the biggest national projects. The LECs in turn reported to central boards composed to the same private sector-led formula.

Crawford Beveridge, the Edinburgh expatriate lured from serious earning in Silicon Valley to be the first Scottish Enterprise chief executive, used to insist dutifully that he ran a commonwealth, not an empire. It was not always a comradely commonwealth. The business titans recruited to grace the LEC boards chafed to find that Treasury money could not be treated quite as dashingly as corporate petty cash, and that substantive projects required central authorisation. The core administrations in Glasgow and Inverness, conversely, watched in powerless dismay as the anticipated creative inter-LEC competitiveness descended into silly rivalries. LECs demanded ever-greater autonomy, even when a shared resource was the sensible way to spend taxpayers' money. Many considerable players – local authorities, the voluntary sector, the professions – felt increasingly alienated from Scotland's economic development apparatus. There were nagging concerns about the proper insulation of directors' commercial interests, not least among business people whose rivals served on the self-perpetuating LEC boards. Such issues reached a head when HIE's admired chief executive, Iain Robertson, accepted a senior post in the building company of the outgoing HIE chairman, Sir Fraser Morrison, one of several such lucrative career moves for senior enterprise personnel. An ever-widening range of critics also felt that the networks were becoming so obsessed with reconciling the contortions of their structures that they had lost the ability to forge effective national strategies.

Since 1997, and particularly since the appointment of Robert Crawford as Beveridge's successor, the commonwealth has regained some of the dynamics of empire. There is a new emphasis on national strategies, albeit drawn up after painstaking consultation, and new obligations upon LECs to channel local endeavour into delivering these strategies. The networks' current ministerial mission is the alliterative grail of *Smart, Successful Scotland* (Scottish Enterprise 2001). The LECs have been required to standardise their branding, their procedures of governance and, through initiatives like the Business Gateway, their core programmes of business support. Increasingly, their role is to provide the personnel for 'virtual' teams, which ensure consistent application of national strategic priorities. Crawford's new senior management structures have created unambiguously linear decision-making flows. All the overseas-related operations – inward investment, trade promotion, Brussels representation, globalisation and the little-loved Scotland the Brand – now function within a single directorate, Scottish Development International, under the command of former Locate in Scotland director Martin Togneri. Ostensibly such change is about synergies, but it also concentrates and centralises strategic power. Late in 2001, Crawford unexpectedly announced that three LEC chief executives were to be raised above their peers with a coordinating remit, as yet imprecisely defined, in respect of LEC activities. If the other LEC chief executives were thrilled by this development, they concealed it well.

There is a clear perception within the business community that the pendulum of influence over the enterprise networks has swung away from them and back towards the politicians and development professionals. Business disquiet has grown more voluble, though scarcely more coherent. It ranges from the FSB's standing complaint about the resources spent on big inward investors, to a no more compelling, though equally familiar, suggestion from merchant banker Sir Angus Grossart that the networks would do better to invest in successful established companies rather than frittering the cash on fledgling businesses of doubtful prospect.

Ministers have responded to these conflicting criticisms in a number of ways. In 2001 they announced the creation of a network of local economic forums (LEFs), partly to restore ownership feelings towards economic development among public and third sector bodies. The nominal purpose of the LEFs was to eradicate wasteful duplication and competition, and to provide the sort of local market insight that was once the nominal purpose of the LECs. Two ministerial LEF taskforces, covering the HIE and SE areas respectively, assumed a prefectorial oversight. It is too early to reach a judgement on the worth of this initiative, the impact of which has thus far been patchy. In June 2001, the FSB was threatening to boycott several LEFs before they had even met, because of a perception that vested interests were being placed ahead of meaningful reform. The Executive's declared vision of forum members 'honestly and critically assessing who does what best . . . genuine give and take . . . working together more effectively' does not want for ambition.

Early in 2002, First Minister Jack McConnell also gave a nod towards the perennial business demands for more of the Enterprise budget to come the way of indigenous firms. He announced that a smaller proportion of Regional Selective Assistance, the principal development incentive provided by the state, would in future be spent on inward investment. There was an air of opportunism, and of imprecision, about this announcement. A combination of cyclical and structural change in the global economy had ensured that there was less internationally mobile investment around anyway, and less chance of Scotland landing it. Therefore, inward investors were already making much reduced demands on the RSA pot. Nevertheless, the announcement went down well with Scottish business.

The relationship between Scottish Enterprise and the business lobbies is a perpetually uneasy one on both sides. For some of the business organisations, the taint of state ownership makes the Enterprise networks inescapably suspect as interventionist. Despite new procedures for taking their counsel, the business lobbies in turn are privately seen by some in SE as wearisomely conservative. What is certainly true is that SE has a budget (approaching £400 million) and an array of executive powers that the business lobbies can only view with envy. This imbalance seems destined forever to hamper efforts to build a greater *esprit de corps* across the Scottish economic community.

# FOR FEAR OF SOMETHING WORSE

The way in which Scottish business has adapted to the new politics has rarely been the stuff of wonder. There is recognition that the change is irreversible, and acceptance that business's traditional political ally, the Conservative Party, is unlikely to hold much sway in the near future over the public policy agenda in London or Edinburgh. In autumn 2001, reports surfaced that some figures were toying with the idea of a Scottish Business Party, although the idea was not received with any very evident excitement in corporate cricles, or anywhere else.

As the Parliament approaches the 2003 election, the prevailing business attitude is to acknowledge that things might have been worse, and to maintain vigilance to ensure that they do not become so. If that adds up to acquiescence rather than enthusiasm, then it is only fair to recall how recently there was outright hostility. On the other hand, it remains some way short of wholehearted commitment.

At the time of writing, even that mood has been unsettled by the resignation of Wendy Alexander. One of McConnell's reforms on becoming First Minister was to lump Transport in with Enterprise and Lifelong Learning. Given the campaign by the tourism industry for a dedicated minister, one might have expected business dismay at the downgrading of a portfolio that is important to them. Instead, they enthusiastically welcomed its transfer to the department and the minister – Gordon Brown's protégée Alexander – that they most trusted. It is not clear that this view drew upon a measured analysis of wise governance. Alexander's fluency in the aspirational management-bubble of the Enterprise networks, and her genuine appetite for ideas, seemed to betoken a receptiveness to business concerns. Her successor, Iain Gray, is seen (justly or not) to be rather more steeped in Labour's traditional associations with the public and voluntary sectors. He may find it hard to rebuild business confidence.

The business community's response to the challenge of the new Scottish politics has yet to impress. The harsh judgement would be that business has failed to apply the lesson it has so often commended to the public – namely, that the mature way to deal with any threat is to view it instead as an opportunity.

# 19

# THE SCOTTISH MEDIA

## *Juliette Garside*

Attempting to pin down exactly what makes a member of the media pack influential can seem as hopeless as trying to beat the Queen of Hearts at croquet: there are few rules, and those there are tend to change according to who is playing. The task is daunting also because of the complex network of rivalries that have helped to shape the industry over the years.

I have tried to write this chapter from a neutral standpoint, but before I do I should declare my interests: my employer is the *Sunday Herald*, which is owned by SMG. SMG also owns Scottish Television and Grampian Television and, of course, the *Sunday Herald*'s daily sister paper, *The Herald*. SMG's television stations are naturally rivals of the BBC's in Scotland, and the group's newspapers compete most directly with *The Scotsman* and *Scotland on Sunday*.

As the above suggests, in order to determine influence in print or broadcast media, it is always essential to find out who the media owners are. Of course, owners do not always try to exert their influence on editorial content. The Northcliffe group tends to take a hands-off approach to its local papers, such as the Aberdeen *Press and Journal*. The reclusive Barclay brothers, who bought *The Scotsman* in 1995, have always pursued an anti-euro agenda. But, having found a champion for their cause in publisher Andrew Neil, they prefer to leave the other policy decisions to him and remain out of the fray on their island hideaway in the Channel.

Scotland has long been blessed with a powerful and lively newspaper publishing industry. Over the decades the *Sunday Post*, helped by Oor Wullie and other much loved cartoon strips, and the *Daily Record*, with its moral conservatism and socialist sympathies, have had an enormous impact on national tastes and opinions (Hutchison 1978). Both papers have carried their influence well beyond Hadrian's Wall, spreading into the north of England and, with the Scottish diaspora, as far afield as Canada and Australia.

And yet today, the majority of Scotland's national and regional newspapers are owned by foreign companies. The editors and managers of Scottish papers owned by English companies, such as the *Press and Journal*, or of English papers with tartanised editions such as the *Scottish Sun*, argue that they are given the freedom to decide editorial policy without interference from London.

The BBC, in particular, suffers from the fickleness of the factors which determine influence. Figures do not make comparisons easy, but the amount of regional television the corporation produces for Scotland is roughly equal to the number of hours produced by Scottish Television. Auntie invests a growing chunk of money in programmes made for and by Scots, and yet has found it difficult to convince her northernmost audience that she is not simply the cultural arm of the English colonial machine.

In the Scottish media, as elsewhere, traditional hierarchies do not always apply. Owners may have a say over editorial policy, but prominent journalists and commentators are usually better known to the public and therefore can exert considerable influence. The *Daily Record*'s ubiquitous sports pundit James Traynor, and *The Herald*'s business commentator, Alf Young, arguably have more sway with football club chairmen and Edinburgh bankers than the owners of their papers do. Scottish journalists and presenters enjoy a huge prominence within the London-based media today, with Kirsty Wark presenting *Newsnight*, Kirsty Young glamming up *Channel 5 News*, and James Naughtie now the *Today* programme's leading light. Not to mention Sheena Macdonald, Nicky Campbell, Lorraine Kelly, Carol Smillie and Gail Porter.

Scots émigrés are also increasingly successful as English media company-owners and directors. Granada Media is run by two Scots, Charles Allen and Steve Morrison, the latter of whom cut his teeth at STV. Former *Daily Record* and *Sunday Mail* managing editor Murdoch MacLennan left to head Associated Newspapers in 1994. Alex Graham is managing director of one of the top-flight production companies, Wall to Wall Television. In film, Douglas Rae has produced the Billy Connolly and Judi Dench hit *Mrs Brown* and *Charlotte Gray*, FilmFour's most expensive venture to date, through his London-based company Ecosse Films.

But influence in London does not automatically translate into influence at home. Of all the above, only Kirsty Wark and Douglas Rae regularly return to Scotland to work or create jobs for others. Wark has put her weight behind a Glasgow-based television production company which she set up with her husband, Alan Clements. Rae, by bringing his ideas and productions to Scotland (he has developed a successful relationship with BBC Scotland, producing its long-running series *Monarch of the Glen*), has helped inject cash into local communities.

Of course, influence can also be unseen. Within a country the size of Scotland, public life can turn into a minefield of conflicts of interest. As the film industry is still fairly small, it follows that many of those involved in making films are also members of the film quango Scottish Screen. Perhaps unavoidably, grants will occasionally go to projects in which Scottish Screen council or committee members, or their friends, have an interest, and accusations of cronyism invariably follow; a situation which caused the previous chief executive, John Archer, to resign.

Personal and professional lives have also been known overlap in the worlds of politics and media (Schlesinger et al. 2001). In a country of some five million people, it is almost a fact of life that senior journalists and MSPs will meet and occasionally form relationships. When SNP leader John Swinney and BBC political correspondent Elizabeth Quigley announced that they were stepping out, she simultaneously requested a transfer to general reporting duties so that nobody could accuse her of conflicts of interest.

## THE BROADCAST INDUSTRY

The regulation of broadcasting, unlike the more important areas of health, policing and education, has not been devolved to Holyrood. When Westminster was debating which powers the Scottish Parliament should have, private and publicly-owned broadcasters successfully argued that they now have to compete on an international stage, fighting to sell their channels and programmes abroad while foreign broadcasters enter the UK via cable and satellite. Having to respond to more localised regulation would hamper business, both the BBC and SMG claimed.

It would also have been awkward for both organisations in other ways. The worst-case scenario for the BBC would have been a Nationalist-dominated Parliament calling for the break-up of the organisation and the formation of a Scottish Broadcasting Corporation. For SMG shareholders, life could have been made more complicated had Holyrood politicians wanted to break up its dominance of the media in Scotland by forcing it to split into smaller pieces, or indeed by MSPs preventing the sale of its television business, should it come to that, to an English or foreign broadcaster.

Nonetheless, the general movement of power to Edinburgh and the creation of the Parliament are already changing the face of broadcasting in Scotland. Under pressure from politicians and independent producers based outside the south-east of England, Channel 4 increased its quotas for regional production in 1997, and set itself the target of producing 30 per cent of its programmes outside London by the end of 2002. The BBC, meanwhile, introduced voluntary quotas for production outside London, and makes greater use of independent production companies, which potentially means more work for Scottish production houses.

Making TV shows outside of London is, of course, cheaper but Wark Clements co-founder Alan Clements, who has benefited from the quota system, believes none of this would have happened without devolution: 'If there hadn't been pressure for political change, do you think that Channel 4 would have a 30 per cent quota for outside London?'

Talk of quotas sounds abstract and bureaucratic, but the effect has been a gradual migration of talent and jobs out of the south-east. Previously those wanting to get ahead in television had to move to London. Today, the quotas have made businesses based in centres such as Cardiff, Liverpool, Birmingham, Manchester and Glasgow viable. More and more London-based Scots are returning to their homeland, many of them to Glasgow, the biggest centre of TV production in Scotland. They are finding work with local companies such as Ideal World and Wark Clements, which have grown exponentially over the last five years. London-based production houses such as Heart Ryan and Mentorn Barraclough Carey have also opened offices in Glasgow to take advantage of the quotas. Not everyone north of the border thinks this is fair, but these outsiders bring experience, create jobs and tend to employ Scottish talent.

Clements believes part of the battle for Scottish programme-makers is lack of cultural confidence, even post-devolution. He says there is a feeling, both in the local media and amongst commissioners in London, that Scottish producers should only make programmes about Scotland. 'There is still a cultural cringe, there is still a sense of self-loathing about the Scots, and I think a lot of it is to do with the media. Parochial is a word we reserve only for ourselves. And yet my impression of the English is that they are much less interested in the world around them than the Scots.'

Stuart Cosgrove, who, when he is not presenting BBC Radio Scotland's *Off the Ball*, runs Channel 4's nations and regions office from Glasgow, complains that he has a hard time convincing the Scottish press that Glasgow or Aberdeen production companies can and should make films about events outside of their homeland, as London outfits do. In 2001, Wark Clements made a documentary about a murder committed by Italian fans of the US rock star Marilyn Manson. Cosgrove says: 'It was made in Italy, about an American satanic rock star, by a Scottish company. It becomes very difficult to convince the media in Scotland that that has significance for the development of the Scottish media industry. They are trapped into an opt-out culture, whereas Channel 4 is an opt-in channel, and I find that immensely frustrating. There is a civil war between the various branches of the media in Scotland.' His ambition is to continue to grow the independent production sector in Scotland, which at the moment lags some way behind English regional powerhouses such as Leeds and Manchester: 'I want to have Scotland recognised as a place where business can be done within our industry. Scotland has 10 per cent of the population of the UK but it doesn't have nearly 10 per cent of the production companies.'

Things have changed since Cosgrove left the independent sector for a job at Channel 4. Eight years ago, his own company, Big Star, had a turnover of £1.1 million. It was the largest independent in Scotland at the time. These days the biggest Scottish indies, Wark Clements and Ideal World, have turnovers of between £7 and £10 million. Cosgrove can take some credit for the growth of the independent sector in Scotland. His influence is dependent more on sheer force of personality than on heading up a significant workforce here. He does not directly commission programmes or personally set the quotas. But he created the role of head of nations and regions, set up the office in Scotland, galvanised producers and helped persuade Channel 4 to take Britain's northernmost production companies seriously. Scotland's share of the Channel 4 production budget has gone from £5.5 million four years ago to £10.5 million today.

While Clements and Cosgrove believe 'cultural cringe' is holding Scotland back, John McCormick, BBC controller since 1992, is convinced that political devolution was only made possible by a surge in cultural confidence. 'The Parliament is part of a wider process which is about the self-confidence of Scotland,' says McCormick. 'The Parliament is the most important station on that journey about Scotland in the twenty-first century, but devolution of power has to be preceded by cultural confidence.'

The BBC, though, does indeed have a new-found confidence. McCormick has been able to argue for more money for Scotland, on top of the regional quotas. There has been an extra £10 million for news, and £14 million a year is on its way for entertainment shows, one of which will be a new Scottish soap. Unlike *High Road* over on Scottish Television, the BBC's soap will be set in the urban central belt. Thanks to BSE, foot-and-mouth and the organic movement, rural life is arguably more dramatic and gritty than urban living these days. But the cultural cringe mentioned by Clements is usually sparked by representations of Scots as a couthy, crofting, tartan-wearing people. With this in mind, the BBC's urban soap may find favour with Scots viewers.

To help understand the wider perspective, we need to emphasise how things have changed in recent memory and in the longer term. BBC Scotland has always had a curious status in the Corporation:

> The BBC Regions were too large to represent communities with a common sense of social and cultural identity. Scotland was a nation of regions and so could not easily be treated as a social region as the BBC sought to do. In Scotland, the BBC was given the status of 'National Region'. It was regarded as a Region because Scotland represented only one part of the unitary BBC covering the whole of the United Kingdom; it was regarded as a National Region because it served a nation, thus distinguishing it from one of the BBC's English Regions. (McDowell 1992: 32)

Radio Scotland was only established in 1978, but now it would be impossible for chattering-class Scotland to do without it, while BBC Scotland began 'a Scottish news service for viewers in Scotland' in August 1957, one day before STV came on air (MacInnes 1993: 90).

McCormick has argued for extra funds on the basis that BBC1, the flagship channel, has generally not performed as well in Scotland as it has in the rest of the UK. The most recent figures show that while in the UK as a whole BBC1 overtook ITV last year for the first time, in Scotland the channel still lags behind STV and Grampian. McCormick says the BBC is something of a public knocking-horse in Scotland, suggesting it is still sometimes perceived as an arm of the English colonial machine. This presents him with a problem post-devolution, because the approval of Holyrood politicians is important.

> The Scottish Parliament is allowed to debate any subject it wants. It is an expression of the voice of the people of Scotland, even on reserved matters. Let's say there was an emerging view in the Scottish Parliament about a broadcasting issue. I think it would be listened to by Westminster. When the BBC charter comes up for renewal in 2006, the Parliament may want to have a say on what basis it should be renewed.

The control of broadcasting from Westminster does throw up the occasional absurdity. As with the much debated issue of whether BBC Scotland should have its own six o'clock news show, the Liberal Democrats, the Scottish National Party, the Tories and the BBC's governing council in Scotland campaigned for a 'Scottish Six' pre-devolution, with no success. Now the issue is being debated again, but in Westminster, where the television sets do not broadcast BBC Scotland. The issue could be debated at Holyrood, but while Labour politicians in Edinburgh are prepared to divert from the Downing Street line on matters like free personal care for the elderly, they have so far avoided direct confrontation on this particular issue.

The extent to which devolution has affected SMG, Scotland's largest media company, is debatable. SMG owns the Scottish and Grampian television stations, *The Herald*, and *Sunday Herald* newspapers, and Pearl & Dean cinema advertising. In 2000, it bought Virgin Radio and Ginger Television from Chris Evans, and a stake of just under 30 per cent in Scottish Radio Holdings (SRH), Scotland's largest commercial radio group. If media-ownership laws are relaxed, SMG has made no secret of the fact that it is hoping to buy the rest of SRH, further extending its influence within Scotland and the radio sector.

The focus at SMG since the current chief executive, Andrew Flanagan, took over in 1997 has been on expanding the company through acquisition. Within that period SMG has grown significantly and changed its name twice, from Scottish Television to Scottish Media Group (to emphasise its expansion into newspapers and the north-east, with the acquisition of Grampian Television) and then to SMG (to underline the fact that it owned businesses not just in Scotland but across the UK). The expansion has been about self-preservation as much as shareholder value. With the gradual consolidation of ITV into two main companies, Granada and Carlton, many city analysts believe it is only a matter of time before SMG is swallowed by one or other of the big fish. Granada already holds a 17 per cent share in the company.

The bigger SMG is, the harder it will be to take over. If the company is forced to sell its television assets to avoid an aggressive suitor, then it will still be able to continue trading as a publisher, radio broadcaster and outdoor media-owner. Recently, however, there has been a renewed emphasis on programme-making. It is important politically for the company to be seen to be creating jobs in Scotland. Making programmes here is one of the best ways of doing that. So the drama department has been moved from London to Glasgow, and the factual and children's departments are also based there now. The entertainment division is still run from London, but money is being invested across all departments in developing new ideas and winning commissions. These changes may well help to placate Holyrood critics, but they also have a commercial logic. With advertising revenues in freefall across the media, owning a television broadcasting licence is not enough to make money. Income must be supplemented by selling programmes. At the moment, *Taggart*, *Wheel of Fortune* and *High Road*, thanks to foreign sales, are the television division's only significant revenue-generators putting forward a 'marketable image' of Scotland (Caughie 1982: 114).

Commercial radio in Scotland has always been dominated by one group, Scottish Radio Holdings. As well as owning Radios Clyde and Forth, it controls NorthSound around Aberdeen, Radio Tay in Dundee, stations in Ayr, the Borders, England and Northern Ireland, and local papers in Scotland and Ireland. But changes are afoot. The Guardian Media Group last year acquired Scot FM, which broadcasts right across SRH's central belt heartland. Under its energetic chief executive John Myers, GMG's Real Radio station in Wales has already overtaken BBC Radio Wales' audience. Myers has just overseen the re-launch of Scot FM as Real Radio in Scotland, and he is hoping for a repeat performance, threatening to 'rip the liver' out of BBC Radio Scotland. It is more BBC Radio 2's listeners, however, that Myers is really targeting. If he is successful, he will draw advertising away from SRH.

Launched in 1973 with the Radio Clyde franchise, SRH grew up alongside SMG in relatively peaceful co-existence. Media-ownership rules which prevent ITV broadcasters from owning radio stations in their area discouraged either company from making a move on the other. But, in December 2000, anticipating a relaxation of the rules in the forthcoming Communications Bill, SMG began buying up SRH shares. Now, thanks to the recession in the media sector, the future looks uncertain for both companies, and a little bleak for those who believe in a plurality of media-ownership. For SNP media spokesman Mike Russell, the choice is stark: 'The companies shall either succumb to a Sassenach invasion, or merge into one dominant Scottish player.' A look across to Edinburgh and its banking sector suggests an alternative model. The Royal Bank of Scotland took on the City of London Goliaths to win the bidding war for NatWest two years ago, while Bank of Scotland's merger with Halifax has created an uneasy balance: Halifax executives were put in charge of the new company, HBOS, and the headquarters were moved to Edinburgh. Scotland's broadcast media, unlike most of its newspapers, need not end up in foreign ownership.

## THE NEWSPAPER INDUSTRY

Aside from the flurry of recruitment and reshuffling that preceded the opening of the Scottish Parliament, the biggest changes in the recent history of Caledonian newspaper publishing took place a decade ago, long before devolution. In the late 1980s and early 1990s, News International, the *Daily Express* and the *Daily Mail* began tartanising their Scottish editions, investing in teams of Glasgow-based journalists, price-cutting campaigns and marketing north of the border (MacInnes 1992; Smith 1994). Until then, the English paper which had made the most significant investment in Scotland was Lord Beaverbrook's *Daily Express*, with its art deco headquarters in Glasgow's Albion Street. But the *Express*'s most northerly operation was closed in 1974 and did not reopen until 1992. Last year, the Glasgow office suffered cuts again, on the orders of the paper's new proprietor, Richard Desmond.

According to the most recent representative circulation figures, the 20 London-based daily and Sunday papers have a combined circulation of 1.5 million in Scotland. The tartanised products are still outsold by the genuine articles, with the ten regional and national Scottish-based papers having a total circulation of just over 2 million.

But dissect the figures another way and a very different picture of who controls the Scottish press emerges. Of the Scottish-based papers, *Business a.m.* is owned by the Swedish Bonnier family, *The Scotsman* and *Scotland on Sunday* belong to the Channel Islands-based Barclay Brothers, the *Daily Record* and *Sunday Mail* are owned by Trinity Mirror, an English company, and likewise the *Press and Journal*, which belongs to Northcliffe Newspapers. Northcliffe is part of Viscount Rothermere's *Daily Mail* and General Trust, which, of course owns, the *Daily Mail*.

All of which means that the only Scottish newspaper publishers with a significant toehold in their own market are the Dundee group D.C. Thomson, publisher of *The Courier* and the *Sunday Post*, and the *Herald*'s parent company, SMG, in Glasgow. Their papers have a combined circulation of 640,000 in Scotland. In other words, only 18 per cent of papers sold in Scotland are owned in Scotland. Nationalists would argue that this is not in the interests of the Scottish people. Outside owners, they claim, will occasionally champion their own interests rather than those of their readership. One oft-cited example is the *Scottish Sun*'s decision to switch its support away from the SNP in 1997. On 23 January 1992 the *Scottish Sun* had diverged from its London edition, to support the

Scottish National Party, a move it announced under the headline 'Rise now and be a nation again'. The switch boosted its popularity in Scotland. But, for the 1997 general election, after a struggle which went to the very top of News International, a three-line whip was imposed by Rupert Murdoch and the *Scottish Sun* came out in favour of Blair, 24 hours after the London edition had. The paper did campaign for a 'yes, yes' vote in the referendum on devolution, despite London's scepticism, but the *Scottish Sun* wore the red rose in its buttonhole again when it came to the 2001 general election. It made for an awkward editorial in the Scottish edition, where editor Bruce Waddell had to tack a few pro-Nationalist sentiments onto London's ringing endorsement of Labour. The first part of the editorial told readers that Labour should make the most of its political capital and call the election as early as possible, while the second part added for the benefit of Scottish readers that: 'the election is a whole different ball game in Scotland . . . the SNP can still have much to offer . . . their say could shape our future almost as much as Scottish Labour' (*Scottish Sun*, 15 May 2001).

Things are a little different at the *Press and Journal*. The paper, under its editor of ten years Derek Tucker, has never endorsed a political party at election time, unlike the group's flagship title, the *Daily Mail*. 'The *Press and Journal* has always been non-aligned,' says Tucker. 'I personally don't believe it is my role to tell people who to vote for. We feel it is a decision for each individual. We "hate" all politicians equally.' If a Northcliffe editor did suddenly decide to come out in support of Labour or the SNP, it is not unreasonable to assume there might be a little resistance at headquarters. Even the *Evening Standard*, with its majority of Labour-voting readers, only grudgingly came out in favour of Tony Blair at the last general election. Tucker says that he would never make a decision to back a political party without consulting the Northcliffe executives. 'I do take the view that the political orientation of a paper is a proprietorial matter, not an editorial one.'

Andrew Jaspan, editor of the *Sunday Herald*, says the company's owners take a hands-off approach to editorial policy. He maintains that he and Mark Douglas-Home, editor of *The Herald*, are left to make their own decisions. 'One of the reasons I thought the *Sunday Herald* might work was that if we could demonstrate to readers that we were open-minded, people might actually find that quite appealing,' says Jaspan. Of course, SMG journalists have to tread carefully when reporting developments within their own company. Anything printed in *The Herald* or *Sunday Herald* will be assumed by the City to have to approval of their owners, and could therefore affect the share price.

Diktats about which political party to support at election time do not mean that owners have more influence than editors. Particularly if a paper snipes at the party it is meant to be supporting throughout the rest of the year, as the *Daily Record* arguably did under its former editor, Martin Clarke. But, as Jaspan points out: 'Even if the editors have day-to-day control, it's the big policy decisions that set the mood music of a publication.'

Mark Hollinshead, managing director of Trinity Mirror in Scotland, says the effect of devolution on newspaper sales has been negligible: 'It was over-hyped in terms of the structural impact. What's been interesting is the venom with which the tabloid press have started to look at politicians.' Hollinshead's comment is a reference to the media frenzy which surrounded the resignation of First Minister Henry McLeish last year, following revelations about his office expenses, and his successor Jack McConnell's decision to come clean about an extra-marital affair.

The *Daily Record*, one of Hollinshead's charges, proved itself capable of plenty of venom when editor Peter Cox lost out to *The Sun* on the McConnell scoop. Cox was locked in conference with McConnell for a few hours the day before he went public about his extra-marital affair, but it was *The Sun* that got advance warning and broke the news. The *Daily Record* editor retaliated by running stories and commentary attacking McConnell. He printed the results of a poll which suggested 86 per cent of readers were against him becoming First Minister. Relations between the two have since thawed, however, with the *Daily Record* resuming its traditional pro-Labour stance.

The Scottish Parliament's impotence when it comes to selling more papers has not deterred the *Daily Record* from devoting plenty of space to politics in its pages. For Hollinshead, this makes strategic sense. 'We know certain stories will not sell choirs and choirs of newspapers but there is a responsibility for the paper to report the facts and reflect the views of the nation. It's about positioning for the hearts and minds of the readership rather than the treadmill of tomorrow's sale. Devolution has made us more acutely aware of that responsibility.'

Politics is unlikely to sell more tabloids, but it has not sold more broadsheets either. Investment in staff, new Saturday sections and promotion has helped *The Herald* hold firm against the general downward drift in newspaper circulation figures, while the *Sunday Herald* is but three years old and still finding its circulation climbing northwards as it consolidates its readership. Meanwhile at the *Scotsman*'s headquarters in Edinburgh, investment estimated at £5 million and a policy of positioning the paper as a UK national initially paid off when the circulation briefly reached 100,000 in early 2001. But by December 2001 circulation was back down to 77,000. Rivals argue that publisher Andrew Neil's grudgingly pro-devolution, anti-public sector stance alienated a section of the paper's core readership. A quick succession of editors (there have been five in as many years) alienated the staff, too, with many jumping ship to join *Business a.m.*, the new Edinburgh-based paper. The ship has been steadier at sister title *Scotland on Sunday*, but the paper is having to fight hard to hold its own against the well-resourced tartan edition of *The Sunday Times* on the one hand, and the relatively new *Sunday Herald* on the other.

One might think that with a single political body to unify the country, Scotland could also have at least one truly national paper. But Scottish reading habits remain regionally divided, with the *Press and Journal* holding sway in the north-east, the D.C. Thompson-owned *Courier* still hugely influential in Dundee, and *The Herald* and *The Scotsman* consigned to their Glasgow and Edinburgh citadels. The *Daily Record* is probably the closest thing to a truly national organ, but its heart remains with its headquarters, in the west. *Business a.m.* launched in 2000 as a daily national business paper. Although based in Edinburgh and drawing a large section of its readership from the city's financial services industry, it has no particular geographical affiliations. As such, it is a genuinely national paper, but its circulation of around 12,000 means that its influence is restricted to a small niche of readers.

Occasionally, speculative business plans have been drawn up proposing to merge *The Scotsman* with *The Herald*, most recently by former *Scotsman* editor Tim Luckhurst, but devolution has not really added impetus to this possibility. Most publishing executives are of the view that merging the papers would simply alienate their respective east- and west-coast readerships, perhaps driving even more readers towards the English broadsheets or mid-market tabloids.

Devolution may not have altered the balance of ownership of the Scottish press, but it has almost certainly increased the influence of individual journalists, in both broadcast and print media. On matters of health, housing, education and the police, political achievements and failures are far easier to monitor because the decisions are now taken in Edinburgh rather than Westminster. The influence of newspapers does have its limits, however. During the debate over Section 28 (or Clause 2A, as it was known in Scotland), the *Daily Record* threw is considerable weight behind Brian Souter's campaign to prevent the discussion of homosexuality in classrooms. The furore that ensued took up more column inches than any other legislative debate has in three years of home rule, but the liberalisers ultimately won the day.

The surest indicator of influence in the unpredictable wonderland of the media is ownership. Devolution may have increased the profile and influence of journalists based in Scotland, but it has not changed the fact that the majority of the media remains in the hands of owners based outside of the country, and whose broader interests may not be those of the Scottish people.

# 20

## WORD POWER: THE IMPORTANCE OF ARTS AND LITERATURE

*Angus Calder*

This chapter concentrates on the Cinderella of arts funding – the Scottish word, as printed or as staged by actors; and the predicament of wordsmiths – writers. 'Cinderella', of course, is both skivvie and princess. Say to a new acquaintance at a party that one is a 'writer' and one's interlocutor usually assumes that one is a novelist hoping to meet Prince Charming – a big public and then big contracts, such as have given Iain Banks, Irvine Welsh, Ian Rankin and J.K. Rowling the freedom to flaunt celebrity lifestyles, if they wished.

Sensibly, these people do not. Charles Dickens, writing superstar of his day, famously feared failure. This was not just paranoia. Walter Scott had failed like a great elm crashing. In the 1960s, I interviewed J.B. Priestley. He was then past his sell-by date as a best-selling novelist, and also out of fashion in the West End as a playwright, but could still command large sums as journalist and broadcaster. Anyway, well-heeled, he had wisely invested not in a country house but in a 'cottage' – so-called, though commodious – in Stratford upon Avon. Puffing a large pipe, he asked, rhetorically, 'This man, Orwell, why do they make such a fuss about *him* these days? *I* said the same things as 'e did . . .' This, as it happened, was largely true. But a major component of Orwell's posthumous cult status was a perceived equation between his integrity and his struggles to make a living before – too late – he published two fables which brought him world fame.

When I think 'writer' it brings to mind not just Ian Rankin, still modestly housed in Edinburgh, but a splendid dramatist fuming to me about the disgusting rates which his kind get for new plays from theatres subsidised by the Scottish Arts Council. I think of Alasdair Gray, in a pub in the Byres Road on the day we first met some 20 years ago. His *Lanark* had just been published and one star reviewer, Anthony Burgess no less, had acclaimed it as the best Scottish novel since Scott, but Alasdair was lamenting the incapacity of his brave

Scottish publisher to give him enough money to live on. I mentioned my own publisher in London, Liz Calder (no relation). That worked. Yet for all his fame and prizes since, Alasdair has never been seriously affluent. I think of a doughty magazine editor fuming with rage over an Arts Council grant too small to support a necessary assistant at minimum-wage rate. And I also think that as a freelance writer myself, I am – like any actor, however starry – in an archetypal buyer's market. If I fall ill, or my work seems not quite the thing, there are five, ten, fifty people out there, each competent to fill any slot I leave vacant.

## MARKET FORCES AND POWER

During a large public lamentation over the sad fate of the Scottish wordsmith not so long ago, Allan Massie said that people should stop whingeing and give the public what they want, serve the market. But I think Allan would concede that one of the characteristics of the best writing is that sooner or later it creates a new market, beyond bland tosh saleable just now. Words are at their most powerful at the moment when they are not what people expected, or even find acceptable.

Which brings us to a major subject in this volume: power. The arts are always involved with power. This is obvious in the case of major conductors – Furtwaengler and Karajan – who played for the Nazis, or great poets and composers who died or somehow survived in Stalin's Soviet Union. It flavours the cases of other great conductors permitted by their bourgeois sponsors to torture fine musicians in rehearsal, and of glowing American abstract expressionists and feisty jazzmen drawn willy-nilly into the Cold War.

We have in Scotland less unattractive examples of political power wielded through art. One is the long-term impact of MacDiarmid's lyrics and rantings in 'Lallans' Scots since he published them in the 1920s. The impact of the folk song revival spearheaded by Hamish Henderson in the 1950s, that of John McGrath's play *The Cheviot, the Stag and the Black, Black Oil* in the '70s, and that of Gray's *Lanark* and *1982 Janine* in the '80s likewise appear to all profound commentators to mark indispensable stages towards the emphatic results of the election and referendum in 1997.

Shelley was not daft when he remarked that poets are the unacknowledged legislators of the world. It is because writers' words – printed, staged, or sung – are so powerful in focusing and creating consciousness that legislators praise them as essential to Scotland's vitality (and the land's appeal to so-called 'tourists'). The opening of the new Scottish Parliament in 1999 was adorned not only by Sheena Wellington's rendering of Burns' great anthem, 'A Man's A Man for A' That', but with a poem by the just-dead, much-loved Iain Crichton Smith, and another by a schoolgirl from Thurso, such a cracker that I might have reflected, 'Oh damn – here's another one coming up to flood the buyer's market for words . . .'

Where are brave new words taking us now, with that devolved parliament won? The impact of Irvine Welsh in the early 1990s followed those of Tom Leonard and James Kelman in the '80s: the real and often foul language of actual Scottish poor people was presented in what could be called 'works of art'. In case anyone is disposed to deny that Welsh is an 'artist', I would point out that no publisher motivated solely by commercial considerations would have touched *Trainspotting* in 1993, when it appeared with the distinguished London imprint of Secker and Warburg. Its subject matter and language were way out. Like Kelman, but in a less stylised, more directly mimetic way, Welsh overran fiction with the actual talk of the schemes and the pubs. The book's vast popularity meant that readers in other countries confronted the desperate real lives of Scotland's disposed-of people.

Meanwhile, gender has come to the fore in Scottish fiction in a new and positive way. The long-term effects of the women's movement have found powerful expression here. It is not just that some of our female writers have attracted great critical acclaim – Janice Galloway, A.L. Kennedy, Dilys Rose, Jackie Kay and many more. Male novelists have foregrounded female characters, too. This had occurred, momentously, in the 1930s when Lewis Grassic Gibbon, in his great *A Scots Quair*, made 'Chris Caledonia' his moving emblem of a vanishing peasant culture. But 'condition of Scotland' fiction lapsed thereafter. Splendid as were Elspeth Davie, Alexander Trocchi, George Friel and the amazing Muriel Spark, their fiction steered away from massive statements about this country. Robin Jenkins, who was not averse to them, found publishers, let alone readers, hard to acquire. There was a breakthrough in the 1970s, though, with William McIlvanney's massive *Docherty* and its definite popularity.

Gray and Kelman weighed in during the 1980s with their new editions of Scottish human nature. But none quite reflected changes of vision wrought by Germaine Greer and the feminist movement. I may as well testify here that I myself, born in 1942, had my pro-feminist viewpoint formed before *The Female Eunuch* was published, and got British women's poetry of the twentieth century badly wrong when I was anthologising it, twice, for different purposes, around 1980.

Roots in a Scottish working class where patriarchy and matriarchy had separate spheres determine McIlvanney's outlook. Gray's highly individual sensibility projects women as subjects of wariness, as well as of admiration. Kelman acknowledges gender issues fully, but in fiction typically centred on damaged and victimised males. Even when Irvine Welsh tried to play a pro-feminist hand, disastrously in *Marabou Stork Nightmares*, impressively in that very powerful book *Filth*, distance between men and women was what came over.

It is noteworthy that in a lengthy recent newspaper interview with Welsh's cult successor, Alan Warner, an intelligent journalist did not even bother to raise what even ten years ago might have seemed the obvious questions – why are the man's first three novels all written from within the points-of-view of female protagonists, and what made him think he could get away with it? *Morvern Callar* (movie now coming to good cinemas your way, after a prize at Cannes) is exceeded in chutzpah by the magnificent *The Sopranos*, given to us as from a team of audacious schoolgirls in a school choir from Oban headed for Edinburgh. Other males have recently sailed over the gender high-jump with ease. Andrew Greig, in his startling *When They Lay Bare* develops a female protagonist as enigmatically powerful in her way as Warner's Morvern. James Robertson empathises brilliantly with Major Weir's tragic, incestuous sister in his Covenanting novel, *The Fanatic*. Now Peter Burnett has come out in *The Machine Doctor* with an eponymous heroine who is intellectually brilliant, crazily imaginative, and sumo-strong on attitude.

Burnett's book is a satire on Aberdeen civic politics and the new information era together. It takes on New Labour and Internet-mania while providing an indelibly vivid view of life on an exceptionally nasty housing scheme. Set in a future where Aberdeen Council, in thrall to a local version of Bill Gates, seeks to give everyone in the city a computer to establish 'connectivity' and promote supermarket shopping, it is obviously a book which could not have been published before the twenty-first century. Burnett mimics brilliantly the newspeak of business and bureaucracy, devises other parodic idiolects, renders the dialect of schemes as vividly as Welsh, and displays an astonishing combination of bizarre imagination with sturdily humane values.

Is anti-Blairism likely to be the characteristic subtext of Scottish fiction in the 2000s as anti-Thatcherism was in the 1980s? I hope so. Meanwhile, Burnett's easy relationship with science and technology was prophesied by MacDiarmid and realised by Edwin Morgan, whose poem 'The Computer's First Christmas Card' dates back to the mid-1960s. Morgan now has a clear, though not plagiaristic, heir in Ian McDonough, whose *The Clan McHine* (published in 2002) startreks with grace between Brora and the Big Bang, meeting all manner of quarks and quirks on the way.

## A SCOTTISH PUBLISHING INDUSTRY?

Peter Burnett is published by Thirsty Books, a small imprint based in Argyll. But notoriously, all other novelists mentioned above, even if they started with Scottish 'houses' (or cottages, rather), have gravitated ineluctably to publication in London. Quite simply, just two Scottish publishers, Mainstream and Canongate – leaving aside the strange, special case of Edinburgh University Press and its literary imprint, Polygon – compare in size and ambition to medium-sized London houses. Neither is famous for forking out to writers the kind of advances which a north-eastern Scot, Robin Robertson, working for Cape, has had to find for A.L. Kennedy, let alone Welsh. Alasdair Gray was so deeply grateful to Canongate for conspiring with him in the production of his beautifully designed blockbuster *Lanark* that he still returns to them between excursions to London. But Scotland has cause to be grateful to Cape and Bloomsbury for further superbly produced books crafted by him under the aegis of Liz Calder.

Liz Calder once helped me also to produce a lavishly illustrated doorstopper while she was at Cape. I do not think it a betrayal to go to London to find publishers to pay me advances large enough to keep me in power cards. We live in a country with about a tenth of the reading public found in England, and with a correspondingly impoverished publishing industry. London publishers have the market power to attract reviews and distribute books efficiently. Yet Canada, with a similar problem vis-à-vis the USA, has sorted out more of a national publishing industry than we have. I think we could build up our valiant medium-sized and small firms, if we set our minds to the task.

However, it is worth remembering that the sudden arrival of African writers on the UK and world stages from the late 1950s owed almost everything to Heinemann, through its specialist African Writers Series and its subsidiaries in Kenya and Nigeria. The commercial basis was a developing 'textbook' market, as schools expanded in post-independence Africa, and sometimes Heinemann's decisions might appear, though they were not, cynical. But I do not think that world bestsellers such as Chinua Achebe and Ngugi wa Thiong'o were, or are, ashamed to have first appeared under the imprint of a firm from the former colonial power. It might be no bad thing for Scottish writing if more English firms had subsidiary offices or imprints in Scotland, with prompt cheque books, offering decent advances.

Such firms might even risk publishing poetry, where the position is grievous. Michael Schmidt of Carcanet, who has published Edwin Morgan and Iain Crichton Smith and presides over the final stages of Alan Riach's great MacDiarmid 2000 project, says that Scottish bookshops seem uninterested in books from him by rising but not celebrated authors. Polygon have published quite a lot of poetry, but do not market it. Canongate have produced a little. Otherwise, we are left with small imprints for whom distribution is a major difficulty. Of course, the best-known younger Scottish poets, published in London, win lots of prizes. This obscures the plight of those not favoured by Faber, Chatto or Cape. About half a dozen people in England sort out which Scottish poets shall have high profiles.


# DEMOCRATISING ARTS AND LITERATURE FUNDING

One problem is that literature gets a small share of Scottish Arts Council funding. The SAC has done a lot of good, but short commons (for theatre, a writer's art, as well as for fiction and poetry) have produced some much-derided decisions, handed down by committees of unelected and unaccountable persons whose proceedings are private. I go along with the suggestion that funding of opera, ballet, big orchestras and the new national theatre organisation, should be directly in the hands of the Scottish Parliament. After a committee or committees of MSPs had deliberated, with expert advice, Parliament could vote adequate funding for three years ahead. It is hideous to think of a nation of Scotland's character, home of the largest arts festival in the world, without the resources to stage world-class opera, as the Scottish Opera *Ring* will be if it is completed in the same magnificent style as the two instalments which we have seen. But Wagner is inherently expensive, and he should not be competing for funds from the same kitty as the next great short-story writer from Motherwell.

Should Parliament also take charge of literature? Perhaps not, though it is our country's most distinctive and enduring glory, and indeed defines what Scotland is at any given moment. Either by direct Holyrood debate or via the mechanism of the SAC or some other quango yet to be devised, a seven-figure grant for literature – in the broadest sense of the word – should be made annually. This would transform the position of worthy Scottish publishers tempted, but not able, to publish brilliant 'uncommercial' titles, and could give quite a number of authors a living to compare to those of bank trainees, though hardly to those of arts administrators. Is it impudent of me to suggest that while matching the RSNO grant from the SAC of £2.6 million might seem appropriate, to round up to £5 million might make a more significant and lasting contribution?

Consider what happens just now. A couple of new publishing ventures received Lottery money. Neil Wilson, publishers, received £80,000 to publish new Scottish fiction under the 11:9 imprint (invoking Scottish referendum day not al-Qaeda's terrorist activities). Alex Finlay got similar support for Pocket Books, to make beautifully crafted little volumes in the spirit of international avant-gardism. As I write, both ventures are defunct parrots. Finlay, I gather, has done as much as he wants with his conception, and is turning elsewhere. 11:9 has brought out lots of new fiction, but has not hit the jackpot commercially – nor, sadder still, amongst reviewers.

Meanwhile, without Lottery funding, good-standard literary magazines plug away. Scotland has more of these, proportionate to population, than England. This has a history. Walter Cairns, a wonderful SAC Literature Director back in the 1980s, pursued a diametrically opposite policy to that of the Arts Council in Cardiff. In Wales, two or three magazines have had lavish grants. In Scotland, the short commons available were split so that any new magazine which could start itself up in promising fashion would get useful SAC support.

This once-admirable policy is now ensnared in the new era of marketspeak. Accountants bewitch arts administrators into asking not, 'How good is it?' but 'How many does it sell?' Modestly funded magazines may publish the heirs and heiresses of MacDiarmid and MacCaig and Spark, but they cannot afford the apparatus of advertising and administration required to build imposing circulations. (In Scotland, the ceiling seems to be around 15,000 for the likes of *Scottish Field*, maybe 2,000 for a 'little magazine'. Multiply by ten to get the English equivalents.) Nor can Scottish magazines pay established freelance authors ready and even eager to contribute to them more than a token pittance, if anything at all.

It is not, and never has been, the primary function of literary magazines to sell large numbers of copies. T.S. Eliot's *Criterion*, edited by the most prestigious literary figure in Britain, who happened, furthermore, to head a successful publishing firm, never sold more than a few hundred copies – but it did take note of, and publish, the piss-poor Scottish writer who called himself 'MacDiarmid'. The value of the work done by *Chapman* and *Cencrastus* in the 1980s is measured not by circulation at the time, but by the splendid new writers they helped to get started, and by frequent references nowadays in scholarly articles which are about such writers, or which explore the impact of word power and fresh political and cultural thinking on Scotland after the 1979 referendum.

It would be an excellent thing if good magazines such as *North Words*, published in Easter Ross, and *Markings* from Kirkcudbright, were seen in more bookshops and acquired more subscribers, so long as the expense and tedium of handling distribution did not drive them out of business.

Paying authors matters. I once received from a Scottish magazine a cheque for £2 in respect of five poems which it had published. I should have framed it, but was so broke at the time that I banked it. Why did the magazine bother? Well, it had to, you see – the SAC had made its grant conditional on payment to authors.

Gerry Cambridge, editor of *Dark Horse*, recently wrote an editorial comparable in its way to Dr Johnson's celebrated patron-spurning 'Letter to a Noble Lord'. The SAC had given his magazine more than he had asked for. Why? So that he could pay authors. He sent the extra money back. His points were: (a) that, split between all his contributors, payments would be insultingly small (contributors include some heavyweight US writers); (b) he himself would have to administer these payments on top of all his hefty work producing the magazine. The SAC itself employs people to administrate. If they want writers to be paid, why cannot they see to this themselves?

We live, you will observe, in the land of Lilliput. A Scottish publisher is really excited. 'Great news today . . .' 'What's that?' asks his interested interlocutor. 'We're getting our titles displayed on the Stornoway ferry . . .' In Gulliver-land, London, publishers get excited over sales of American rights, film rights. In Brobdignag, New York, I guess it is the scale of the sale which sometimes calls for early Martinis.

What can be done? I am not suggesting that a few million bucks, about as much as a mediocre footballer for Rangers or Celtic gets in wages in one year, should be voted to go direct to such unpredictable creatures as actual writers. Whereas money given in advance to support performances by theatres and orchestras will almost certainly produce those performances (though it cannot guarantee bums on seats or high quality), the state could hand out a few thousand pounds to the fine novelist who would promptly suffer from prolonged writer's block. Unless Holyrood wishes to imitate the ways of football clubs who fork out huge sums for players who crock themselves in training and barely appear on the field of contest at all, I would suggest the following procedures.

In relation to magazines, they should be asked to bid for funds to enable them to 'market' themselves as much, or as little, as they may wish to do. Payment of authors – irrespective of circulation – could be at going rates applicable right across the board: £x per line of verse, £y per 100 words of prose. This would make it worthwhile for leading writers to contribute (and meet deadlines!) and this in turn would surely serve to heighten profile and increase circulation.

With regard to books – and here I include not only fiction and poetry but also serious works of history, biography, art history, philosophy and so on – the SAC already gives modest sums to publishers, in advance, for books accepted or commissioned. With serious money available, publishers could be invited to apply, on a realistically costed basis, for funding in three stages. (1) To give the author an advance to support her or him during composition or assembly of the book. (2) On delivery, when the publisher gives the author another payment and receives also money to cover costs in editing and producing the book. (3) On publication, when the author gets another dash and the publisher needs cash for publicity and distribution. This does not rule out waste, but limits possible loss, as when an author cannot deliver, or falls out with the publisher – things which every major house has to take for granted. Finally, theatres could apply for funds to remunerate authors of commissioned plays on a similar tripartite basis – commission, delivery, production – but in this case, all monies go to the author.

This process would not guarantee the sales of large numbers of any given titles, or full houses at any theatre. But it would enable Scottish publishers to match the more moderate advances paid by London counterparts, and to rest easy that an excellent manuscript, well edited and printed, is not going to head them towards bankruptcy when sales, irrespective of quality, are disappointing. (There are many stories of very important books which fail to take off commercially in the first instance.) It would also mean that London publishers were competing against levels of payment arranged in Scotland, rather than vice versa, and it should encourage some of them to set up Scottish subsidiaries, as I suggested above might well be desirable.

Much rhapsodising by distinguished suits has gone on about the wonders performed by Scottish writers in the last three or four decades, in bringing prestige to our wee land and expressing or reconstructing our national consciousness. If suits put money where mouths have been, your prize-winning Scottish author might even be able to afford a restaurant meal in Iceland, where they know how to reward creative people.

# 21

# THE SCOTTISH PERFORMING ARTS

*Joyce Macmillan*

In one sense, the main features of Scotland's performing arts landscape are obvious to any casual observer of the nation's political scene. In the front rank of fame and notoriety stand the two national performing companies, Scottish Opera and Scottish Ballet, the subjects of what seems like an unending series of rows over their funding, purpose and policy. Just behind them ranks the Royal Scottish National Orchestra, less prominent in public debate largely because its presence as part of the national life is more widely accepted, and less rudely challenged. In the world of theatre, most regular readers of Scotland's broadsheet press would probably note the presence of the Citizens' Theatre in Glasgow, the Royal Lyceum in Edinburgh, perhaps Dundee Rep – home since 1999 to Scotland's only permanent ensemble of actors – and the nation's leading theatre for new work, the Traverse. Many would touch, with a vague sense of nostalgia, on the tradition of small-scale touring theatre in Scotland and the legacy of the late, great John McGrath's 7:84 company, with its mission to bring radical left-wing theatre to community centres and village halls across the country. Some would also refer to the continuing debate on whether Scotland should have a national theatre. Most would mention the Edinburgh Festival and Fringe, the Western world's greatest festival of the performing arts, a huge and influential feature of the Scottish cultural landscape for the last 55 years.

Beyond this front rank of organisations and events, the average well-informed citizen would probably perceive a hazy hinterland of smaller dance and theatre companies, orchestras, ensembles, choirs, festivals; as well as a range of impressive arts venues, from the Glasgow Royal Concert Hall to His Majesty's Theatre in Aberdeen or the Edinburgh Festival Theatre, not linked with any performing company. Behind all this activity, he or she would be aware of the presence of the Scottish Arts Council, the most prominent national source of public subsidy for the arts, with a budget (in 2002/3) of £36 million in Scottish Executive grant-in-aid, and around £20 million from the National

Lottery. Many people would also be aware of the growing importance, particularly for the most prestigious arts events, of sponsorship from businesses and trusts. And some would recognise the huge, if less obvious, arts funding contribution of Scottish local authorities, which are estimated to spend between two and four times as much again as the Scottish Arts Council on everything from direct grants to professional performing companies, through a huge range of educational and community activities, to the maintenance and renovation of many important arts buildings.

To sketch this kind of outline of the Scottish arts landscape, though, is only to provoke a fresh round of argument about the assumptions on which the mapping is based. In every healthy culture, the twin questions of what constitutes art, and which kinds of cultural activity should receive public subsidy, are endlessly contested; and nowhere more so than in Scotland, where the conventional definitions of 'high art' can be seen not only as old-fashioned and socially exclusive, but also as externally imposed, and insensitive to the specific needs, traditions, forms and dynamics of Scottish culture. There are many Scots, of course, who would contest the idea that the 'high arts' agenda has been externally imposed at all; Scottish Opera, for example, was founded by Alexander Gibson in 1962 out of a deep amateur–professional tradition of orchestral playing and choral singing in Glasgow. But the debate continues as to whether the standard international repertoire in these areas represents a useful and vital form of cosmopolitan culture in which Scotland must play a part, or a decaying and socially exclusive old-world phenomenon fatally detached from the energy of contemporary popular culture, in Scotland as elsewhere.

## SUPPORTING ARTS

The story of official arts funding in Scotland over the past decade has therefore revolved around a series of efforts, in an age of broadly static resources, to shift the balance of support to reflect these changing definitions and priorities; and around the substantial frustration of these efforts by the huge structural inertias built into the system. Essentially, everyone wants to free up money to reflect new times and priorities; but no one seriously wants any of the major arts companies to go bust. The result is that the Scottish Arts Council's three largest clients – Scottish Opera, Scottish Ballet and the RSNO – absorbed 40.6 per cent of the SAC's total grants budget in 1982, and still absorb 39 per cent of it today. With hindsight, it is possible to argue that the one funding bonanza the arts did experience during the 1990s, the National Lottery Arts Fund which came on stream in 1995, could have been used to achieve a massive shift in emphasis in arts funding, including much more radical forms of cooperation with the commercial cultural industries. But in its early years, the Lottery was widely perceived as an unreliable source of revenue which should not form the basis for long-term funding policies; and even today, the money tends to be used either for one-off building projects, or to support special cross-cutting initiatives such as the annual Creative Scotland Awards.

The Scottish Executive's *National Cultural Strategy*, published in 2000 (Scottish Executive 2000a), also pays lavish lip service to the new agenda in the performing arts, and the Executive has signalled some willingness to make limited extra funds available for new initiatives, notably increased support for traditional arts and the gradual development of a national theatre project. But the jury is still out on whether the Scottish Executive will follow many other European regional governments in making increased and enthusiastic support for the cultural life of the country, along revised twenty-first-century lines, one of the strong signature policies of devolved government; and at the time of writing, in the spring of 2002, the signals from Culture Minister Mike Watson and his team seem more tentative than exuberant.

So where does this broad pattern of funding and support leave the major players on the performing arts scene? To begin with the area traditionally least affected by government policy, it has to be said that, despite many strong statements of intent from both the Executive and the SAC, the world of live rock and pop – by far the most important form of live cultural experience for most young Scots, and the one which probably has most influence on their negative or positive perception of Scotland as a living force in contemporary culture – remains overwhelmingly dominated by Scotland's two major commercial rock promoters, DF (Dance Factory) of Glasgow and Regular Music of Edinburgh. Regular Music has an annual turnover around the £5–6 million mark, and attracts around 400,000 paying customers a year; DF, which runs the annual T in the Park summer festival as well as most of Glasgow's major rock and pop concerts, is about twice the size, with an annual turnover of around £12 million. Both organisations are seen as doing their best, within commercial constraints, to promote Scottish-based bands and interesting international work alongside the normal run of money-spinning pop events.

There is concern, though, particularly in Edinburgh, about the shortage of small-scale venues in which new young bands and artists can perform without major financial cost. Several significant Edinburgh venues have fallen or are about to fall victim to the city's commercial and residential development boom, which is placing an ever-stronger squeeze on the kind of informal city centre spaces where performance can flourish. The collapse late in 2001 of the small-scale Glasgow promoter 13th Note – which operated two small venues in Glasgow specialising in Scottish independent music – is also an ominous sign of the difficulty of sustaining smaller rock venues against strongly marketed large-scale competition.

Some hope that SAC's latest announcement, in March 2002, of its intention to strengthen its support for 'previously underfunded areas of music such as traditional music, jazz, rock and contemporary classical music' may lead to some funding for small-scale independent rock venues, which are widely seen as the key to development and creativity in this field. So far, however, most SAC and local authority activity in this area has been confined to the provision of facilities, instruments and tuition for young musicians; there is no rock equivalent of Scotland's Assembly Direct jazz organisation, funded by the SAC to the tune of £140,000 a year to promote live jazz performance around the country. And if more money for rock and pop music does come on stream, the challenge will be to find ways of giving strategic support to those areas of the commercial scene most likely to encourage local talent, without seeming to take over or institutionalise 'worthy' strands of rock activity in ways that can only diminish their appeal to young audiences.

The Scottish traditional music scene, on the other hand, is beginning to emerge as one of the major success stories of the last decade. There's no doubt that forces outside Scotland – notably the huge 'Celtic tiger' boom in Ireland's economic and cultural life, amplified through North American culture and echoing around the globe – has helped energise the Scottish traditional arts scene in unprecedented ways, linking it to a global network of interest in Celtic culture, and 'world music' generally, which barely existed a generation ago. But Scottish artists and arts entrepreneurs have been quick to seize the moment; and from the grassroots level of the burgeoning Feis movement – developing small local festivals of traditional music and arts across the Highlands and Islands and elsewhere – to the hugely successful Celtic Connections Festival now held every January in Glasgow, they have been key players in the development of a completely new approach to traditional cultures, an approach which is deeply connected to the past but focused on the future, willing to experiment with an amazing range of musical styles and cross-overs, closely associated with the use of new technology in the production, distribution, marketing and discussion of music, and inspired by international connections which range round Europe's Atlantic arc from Galicia to Shetland, and also reach eastward into the Nordic countries, and westward to the Americas.

In only eight years, with minimal amounts of public subsidy, Celtic Connections has grown into a booming three-week festival which attracts audiences and media attention worldwide, and which sold more than 80,000 tickets in 2002; an economic survey conducted in 2001 estimated that it brought an additional £3 million into the economy of the city of Glasgow, at a time of year which has traditionally been the graveyard of the Scottish tourist industry. And while it would be wrong to overstate the role of public funding in supporting the traditional music boom, there is no doubt that the gradual improvement in SAC funding over the decade, the growing enthusiasm for traditional arts among local authorities – many of which have now appointed traditional-arts officers – and the Scottish Executive's provision of an additional £1.5 million of funding for traditional arts over three years from 2001, are helping to strengthen the career infrastructure for traditional artists, and to create a critical mass of full-time creative workers in this area.

# THE SCOTTISH ARTS ESTABLISHMENT?

In terms of the politics of the performing arts in Scotland, there is no doubt that it is the relationship between the Scottish Executive, the Scottish Arts Council and the major subsidised producing organisations that continues to dominate the debate, particularly in the fields of opera and ballet, where purely commercial performance barely exists, and where the Scottish scene is dominated by a single national company.

Scottish Opera remains the subsidy queen of the Scottish arts scene, effectively the only professional opera company in the country and funded by the SAC to the tune of £7.5 million pounds in 2002/3, out of a total company turnover of around £11 million. This sum represents more than every other classical music organisation in the country put together, and something between £90 and £100 of subsidy for every single seat sold by the company during the year (Peacock et al. 2001). Scottish Opera essentially strong-armed its way to this level of subsidy, in the period 1998–2001, by running up a substantial financial deficit while producing work of unchallengeable international quality; this at a time when, after painstaking negotiation, Scottish Opera and Scottish Ballet were about to merge into a single management under the same chief executive. The Scottish Executive and SAC were left with no option but to let the new joint company go bankrupt or bail it out; and in November 1999 the then Minister for Education, Culture and Sport, Sam Galbraith, famously came up with the money in the shape of a £2-million rescue package.

Today, Scottish Opera remains an artistically respected but financially cash-strapped operation, still underfunded by international operatic standards, yet often resented on the Scottish cultural scene for its perceived failure – despite the activities of its small-scale touring company Opera-Go-Round, and its substantial education programme – to deliver a high rate of return to all the people of Scotland. It remains, together with the RSNO, Scotland's flagship 'high arts' company, attracting almost £1 million of commercial sponsorship annually, featuring regularly in the Edinburgh International Festival, attracting fervent support from sections of the Scottish establishment, and staging around six major operas a year, including new work by Scottish-based composers such as James MacMillan and Sally Beamish; and so far, no Scottish administration has dared to let it go to the wall.

Scottish Ballet, by contrast, is in a less happy position. Radically underfunded throughout its 33-year history by comparison with Scottish Opera, the ballet attracted a Scottish Arts Council grant of £2.8 million in 2002/3, out of a total company budget of less than £5 million. For the last decade, the ballet has struggled to maintain an international standard of work in classical dance; and in 2000/1, the Scottish Ballet Board developed a plan to abandon the attempt to run a full classical ballet company in Scotland, and instead to take advantage of the growing Scottish audience for contemporary dance by taking the company in that direction. This decision has been the subject of bitter dispute, but on balance, it now looks as though the decision to transform Scottish Ballet into a contemporary dance troupe will go ahead from 2003/4.

The situation is complicated, however, by the fact that Scottish Ballet is not Scotland's only professional dance company. The existence of a thriving Scottish contemporary dance scene – including a cluster of medium- and smaller-scale dance companies led by Janet Smith's increasingly impressive Scottish Dance Theatre of Dundee, and with a fresh focus in the beautiful new Dancebase building in Edinburgh's Grassmarket – intensifies the debate as to whether Scotland needs a Scottish Ballet transformed into a national contemporary dance company; and the dazzling programme of international contemporary dance now available at the Edinburgh Festival Theatre – perhaps the finest state-of-the-art dance stage in the UK – has set a standard which Scottish Ballet may find it difficult to match.

And the world of orchestral music in Scotland is facing similar problems, although there can be little long-term doubt that the two major players – the Royal Scottish National Orchestra, with annual SAC subsidy of £2.6 million on annual turnover of around £5 million, and the Scottish Chamber Orchestra, with SAC support of £1.44 million on a total budget just under £3.5 million – will survive. Like many British orchestras, though, both organisations are struggling both with a musicians' salary bill which has risen faster than the available funding throughout the last decade, and with major issues of marketing and audience-building for all but their most popular programmes; nor is Scotland's other leading orchestra, the independently-funded BBC Scottish Symphony Orchestra, immune to these problems, although it seems secure for the time being.

## FESTIVALS, THEATRES AND THE ARTS COUNCIL

Festivals, by contrast, have been the great success story of Scotland's subsidised performing arts scene in the last decade, flourishing in communities across Scotland, from the famous St Magnus event in Orkney to the Highlands and Northlands Festivals, the Perth Festival, the Dumfries and Galloway Festival and many others. The only significant casualty of the decade was Glasgow's Mayfest, once the UK's second-biggest arts festival, wound up in the mid-1990s after a serious loss of direction and impetus – and finally of commitment on the part of Glasgow City Council – following the massive effort of Glasgow's year as European City of Culture in 1990.

The flagship, on the other hand, is the mighty Edinburgh International Festival, which, with its Fringe, now sells around 1.3 million tickets in Edinburgh in August for a dazzling range of performances encompassing the official and fringe festivals, as well as major film, jazz, folk and media events. The official festival, under the direction of Brian McMaster, has become something of a model twenty-first-century 'high' arts event, innovative, creative and intelligent, with ticket prices for world-class music, theatre and dance kept low by international standards, and a £7.4 million budget perfectly balanced between box-office income, commercial sponsorship, and public subsidy both from the SAC (£890,000 in 2002/3) and Edinburgh City Council (around £1.4 million).

As for the Edinburgh Fringe, this is the astonishing phenomenon that turns Edinburgh's August festival into the single biggest arts event in the world; an open-entry, come-if-you-can festival which sold almost 900,000 tickets over four weeks in 2001, and crams itself into every available performance and street space in the city. After 15 years of breakneck expansion in the 1980s and early 1990s, the Fringe now seems to have stabilised in size around the 600-company mark (or just over 20,000 performances of some 2,000 shows), perhaps because of the growing pressure on Edinburgh city space. But the Fringe remains one of the most remarkable cultural phenomena on earth, bewildering and magnificent in its scale and variety; and a half-century of exposure to this tremendous, unsought gift of an arts event has helped to internationalise the Scottish cultural scene in ways that could never have been predicted when the Edinburgh Festival was launched in 1947, with a mission to promote peace among the war-weary nations of Europe.

Of all the performing arts, though, the one that most powerfully reflects and encompasses all the tensions described above is theatre. Defined from the outset as one of the 'high arts' subsidised by the Arts Council, theatre in Scotland has nevertheless always retained powerful links with popular and grass-roots culture across the country, and has emerged in the last half-century as a major creative interface between the classical performance tradition in Britain and Europe, and the stuff of everyday life in Scotland. Unlike classical music and dance, theatre in Scotland retains a strong commercial dimension, ranging in scale from tiny comedy clubs, through the annual pantomime season, to the year-round programme of major West End and Broadway musicals at the 3,000-seat Playhouse in Edinburgh, now run by Clear Channel Entertainment as one of the most successful commercial stages in Britain. Beyond that, Scotland has a thriving tradition of amateur and community drama, represented both by the independent Scottish Community Drama Association (assisted by the Scottish Arts Council to the tune of £50,000 in 2002/3) and by local authority-supported community and youth projects throughout the country.

Even within the professional subsidised sector, theatre in Scotland is the only 'high art' traditionally produced in many centres across Scotland, and in theatres which are often as strongly supported by their local authorities as by the arts council (Cameron 1993). In 2002/3, the Scottish Arts Council funded eleven building-based producing companies – three in Glasgow, three in Edinburgh, three in Tayside, and one each in St Andrews and Mull – as well as eight major national touring groups, including 7:84, Suspect Culture, TAG Theatre and Theatre Babel. It also supports a score of other small-scale theatre companies through project funding, co-funds a programme of large-scale touring theatre (mostly from London) at receiving theatres such as the King's in Edinburgh, His Majesty's in Aberdeen and the Eden Court in Inverness, and supports mixed arts programmes, which include theatre, at venues such as the Tramway in Glasgow, the Lemon Tree in Aberdeen and Cumbernauld Theatre. The total SAC drama budget for 2002/3 – excluding support for arts centres with mixed programmes – was £7,444,926, including over £1 million of extra annual funding for theatre recently announced by the Scottish Executive to strengthen the Scottish theatre infrastructure in the run-up to the national theatre project. It is worth noting that this total enhanced sum, supporting a huge range of organisations from Caithness to the Borders, was still less than the SAC's single annual grant to Scottish Opera; and that the largest single grants made to theatre companies, to the Citizens' in Glasgow (£829,000), the Royal Lyceum in Edinburgh (£754,000), Dundee Rep (£626,000) and the Traverse in Edinburgh (£573,000) were all well under the £1 million mark.

This richly pluralistic pattern of production has been the defining feature of Scottish theatre life since the 1970s, the source of its great creative strength and its relative political weakness. Over the last generation, Scotland's producing theatre companies have done a mighty job of transforming the Scottish stage repertoire – through both new plays and classic adaptations – and generating new forms of Scottish voice in public performance, yet for most Scots without a prima facie interest in theatre, this huge achievement, and its tremendous ripple effect through the worlds of film and television, has gone largely unseen. When Scottish Opera or Scottish Ballet seems threatened with collapse, everyone who cares about Scotland's national life and status is aware of the debate. But no Scottish theatre company has that power to command national and media attention and, as a result, the whole work of Scottish theatre has traditionally gone undervalued and underfunded.

The new plan for a Scottish national theatre – first devised by the Federation of Scottish Theatres in 2000, and now moving cautiously towards implementation in 2003/4 – is therefore an attempt to give a national platform to the best achievements of the Scottish theatre community without draining resources from this diverse creative production base across the country. The aim is to set up a national theatre which is neither a building nor a company, but a commissioning body along the lines of the Edinburgh International Festival, with a pot of money which it will use to commission an annual programme of Scottish national theatre shows from existing Scottish theatre companies, and to tour them around Scotland and internationally. This is an experimental model for a national theatre, and one that has attracted a great deal of interest from other smaller countries – Norway, Sweden, Ireland – which have had problems with the centralised structures of their own national theatres; whether it can be made to work remains an open question.

Which brings us, finally, to the Scottish Arts Council itself, and the question of its continuing role in the Scottish Arts. It was only eight years ago, in 1994, that the then Secretary of State for Scotland, Ian Lang, agreed to the ending of the SAC's old status as a sub-section of the Arts Council of Great Britain, funded through Whitehall; and to the transfer of responsibility for Scottish arts funding to the Scottish Office. Throughout this period, there have been suggestions – particularly from the Nationalist camp – that the SAC ought to be wound up, as an organisation born of a bygone age of British cultural patronage, and subsumed into a modern Scottish 'Ministry of Culture' on the French model. Others have argued that responsibility for the large national companies, at least, ought to be transferred to the Scottish Executive, which already has a direct funding relationship with the National Galleries and Museums. To add to the confusion, the SAC itself – despite surviving far better than its English counterpart through the 1990s – has not been immune to the plague of managerialist jargon, overpriced consultancy and compulsive restructuring that has spread through many British public bodies during the last 15 years, and it has frequently been accused of subjecting its clients to chronic bureaucratic overload.

On balance, however, it seems likely that the Arts Council will survive in something like its present form. In the end, some degree of arm's-length funding, however modified by increasing interest from the new devolved government, is probably better for the arts than political decision-making at government level; and the new Scottish political establishment is not so popular with the public, or with artists, that a campaign for the abolition of the SAC is likely to make much headway at the moment.

And that – with a brief nod to the huge infrastructural importance of Scotland's great training conservatoire at the Royal Scottish Academy of Music and Drama in Glasgow, and to the growing prestige of the Theatre School at Queen Margaret University College in Edinburgh – is a rough anatomy of the performing arts scene in Scotland today. To say that it is in transition is an understatement; the performing arts is a volatile, dynamic world at the best of times, richly dependent on the inspirational work of gifted individuals who can sometimes change the landscape single-handed, and sensitive to every minor shift in the political, cultural and economic climate. But in a nation where, for so many centuries, the whole idea of public performance outside the pulpit was regarded as questionable, the modern performing arts in Scotland have, at their best, a tremendous freedom and radicalism about them, a thrilling post-modern sense of deep local roots combined with rich and flourishing international links that has a great deal to offer not only to the people of Scotland, but to the world. The political task, as ever, is to find the structures – of funding and of institutions – that will support Scotland's artists in that work, and allow them to soar.

# 22

## BUILDING A NATION?: THE STATE OF ARCHITECTURE AND PLANNING

*Neil Baxter*

With regard to Scotland's architecture, responses to the question 'Where to now?' are remarkably inconsistent. One unconsciously comical rejoinder, 'It's all up in the air', though piquant, is a fair summation of the state of play in a nation which has celebrated its refound self-determination by commissioning an extraordinarily self-indulgent new Parliament building.

The procurement process for our new symbol of nationhood may well, in time to come, be considered an exemplar of how not to do it (Black 2001). The financial qualifications required in the design competition excluded many of Scotland's best architects – simultaneously both offensive and an implicit denial of native creativity (entrants were required to have experience of £50 million-plus projects). The selection process, at best questionable, has been condemned by many as a 'carve-up'. The site for this totemic structure – 'our own Sydney Opera House' – is 'down in a dunny', lacking visibility (a usual prerequisite for a major totemic structure). Most notoriously of all, and most frequently criticised by press, public and opposition politicians, the budget is now over six times the original cost estimate and rising.

## A DESIGN FOR LIFE: DEVOLUTION AND ALL THAT

The process of creating the Parliament building does not bode well, and yet much has been made of the Scottish Executive's endeavour to create a legislative framework for architecture. Scotland is unique in this endeavour, but despite its innovation (or perhaps because of it), *A Policy on Architecture for Scotland*, published in October 2001, has been criticised by many as replete with generalisations and platitudes (Scottish Executive 2001d).

Sebastian Tombs, secretary and treasurer of the Royal Incorporation of

Architects in Scotland, is more optimistic, seeing the paper as beneficial, if only in placing design quality firmly on the agenda. In support of this contention, he quotes the stated intent of the document to pursue the undoubtedly positive objectives and aspirations of the framework document published in 1999 (Scottish Executive 1999b). Two years later the policy document states that: 'Design is an integral part of the process of building and should not be marginalised or considered an option' (Scottish Executive 2001d). Tombs also cites the objectives of the urban design policy statement, *Designing Places*, published in November 2001, which reiterates the aspirations of the architecture framework document (Scottish Executive 2001e). These documents, according to Tombs, reinforce the Scottish Executive's desire to pursue the highest quality in our built environment. Quite how this will be achieved is, sadly, largely left to conjecture.

The pursuit of the high aspirations of these well-meaning but woolly policy documents is within the remit of Dr Elaine Murray MSP. Dr Murray is the fourth minister with responsibility for architecture since the advent of the Scottish Parliament. As Deputy Minister for Tourism, Culture and Sport, she is, according to Tombs, an unknown quantity. With a PhD in Physical Chemistry, she seems unlikely to bring significant direct experience of working within the construction industry. However, Tombs is hopeful that she will hold the architectural brief for long enough to gain a knowledge of the complexities of the process, an understanding of its key drivers and motivations and, most important, an awareness of the long-term benefits of improving our built infrastructure.

There is no doubt that Dr Murray arrives at a time of great flux. The Scottish Enterprise Network is engaged in a process of repositioning, influenced first by the vision of its chief executive, Robert Crawford, of a Scottish nation which will lead Europe in electronic commerce. The previous Enterprise Minister, Wendy Alexander, who jocularly described herself as 'Minister for Everything', saw the importance of combining Crawford's vision with consolidating Scotland's infrastructure and environment to provide a sustainable and attractive physical setting to encourage new businesses to establish themselves and existing organisations to grow.

Elsewhere, Scottish Homes, itself the product of the early 1990s amalgamation of the Housing Corporation and the Scottish Special Housing Association, is evolving under its new banner, Communities Scotland, and the leadership of Bob Millar (a former chief executive of the major private sector developer, the Miller Group). This new organisation is not yet sufficiently well established to have defined its role.

Another major change is the advent of the Glasgow Housing Association and the permanent removal of Glasgow City Council's 80,000 homes from council ownership and responsibility. This move, the most significant shift in housing ownership in Scotland's largest city for a century, will affect all aspects of Glasgow's housing provision for decades to come. An inevitable concomitant of the stock transfer will be fundamental change in the role and funding of the city's 80 housing associations. Glasgow stands at a crucial juncture, where it can address the dreadful condition of much of its council stock, pioneer new models of involving people and draw a line under a century of municipal paternalism which has ended ignominiously. The scale of Glasgow's problems cannot be minimalised, but at least the city is now looking to the future and to new ways of working.

It would be truly tragic if this process were to thwart the best that might be achieved by the community-based housing association movement in the future. In 2001, the singular distinction of the Royal Institute of British Architect's award recognising the Client of the Year went to the director of one of Glasgow's housing associations. The achievement is all the greater when it is considered that this particular prize is open to any client for any building in the UK, from a small private dwelling right up to projects of the scale of the many white elephants created to mark the advent of a new millennium.

For Glasgow, indeed for Scotland, the award of the Client of the Year to Rob Joiner should be considered not merely an achievement worthy of note but an opportunity. As director of Reidvale Housing Association and Molendinar Park Housing Association, Joiner has worked for the last decade to achieve affordable housing of quality and distinction in Glasgow's East End. In the process, the architects who have worked with him, and their buildings, have received continuous plaudits and awards. Until last year, Joiner was also chairman of the Glasgow Building Preservation Trust, responsible for the saving and restoration of a significant number of Glasgow's most important historical buildings, most notably the mid-eighteenth-century St Andrew's in the Square, now a highly successful focus for Scottish music and culture and one of a number of catalysts in the extraordinary transformation of the area east of the city's historic Saltmarket, long considered an unsaveable slum.

Rob Joiner would undoubtedly be embarrassed by all this dwelling on his achievement. However, what is truly worthy of note is the fact that, despite all the plaudits, Joiner remains that most Scottish phenomenon, a prophet unheeded in his own land. His expertise in social policy, urban regeneration and particularly in the complexities of procuring buildings which function well, look good and which cumulatively contribute to a greatly improved urban environment are well worthy of UK recognition. Yet he has not been sought out to serve as an adviser to national government, to the Scottish Executive or even, closer to home, to Glasgow City Council.

In fact, one of Rob Joiner's major preoccupations at present is what he sees as a potentially disastrous planning position on the part of Glasgow's city fathers. Currently the massive tract of land east of the High Street and south of Duke Street at the eastern edge of the city centre is scheduled for light industrial use. As Joiner and a number of others have pointed out, this historic planning position fails to recognise significant economic and social shifts in recent years. There is currently huge demand for affordable housing in the city centre, creating a real opportunity for community development to bring new vigour and prosperity to this long-blighted area. Joiner argues that, rather than condemning this hugely important site – *the* last major undeveloped tract of central Glasgow – to a restricted, business-orientated future, a much wiser course would be to create a mixed-use development combining housing with light industrial pavilions, perhaps with some retail, leisure and conceivably a primary school to serve the new community which would be formed there.

Thus, the historically blighted Dennistoun area of the city would be reconnected to the city centre by development of an appropriate scale and quality to provide a safe and accessible new urban village. As Joiner points out, from the city centre, it is currently possible to walk five miles to the west on safe, lighted streets but only a few hundred yards to the east – a condition inimical to the urban character of Glasgow, but which would prevail if the site were redeveloped only for business use.

In the Scottish scene, which lacks the influential (if sometimes misguided) advocacy of the self-appointed regulator of design quality, Prince Charles, or the government appointee Richard Rogers, analysis must focus upon not those who are actually influencing the future of our buildings and cities at the political level, but who should be. In 1994, Rob Joiner and Fraser Stewart, director of the New Gorbals Housing Association, were hailed as innovators in housing whose example was central to Glasgow's argument for being awarded the accolade, City of Architecture and Design 1999. Yet, depressingly, eight years on from that successful bid Joiner observes that it is still the case that among Scotland's housing associations there are only a handful whose work is celebrated for the quality of its design, its innovation, or the permanent improvement it has achieved in the urban landscape.

In Edinburgh, the situation is similarly one where individual housing association developments of distinction are sufficiently few and far between to be regularly cited as exemplars, while observers simultaneously lament that their example is not being followed elsewhere. Thus, Canmore Housing Association's car-free development continues to be mentioned whenever the subject of innovation is raised but there is a tacit acknowledgement that the priority in social housing continues to be the political numbers game. As ever, there seems very little concern over architectural quality and an overriding preoccupation with the number of units which can be provided in areas of deprivation and housing need.

Lamentably, the majority of housing associations continue to focus their endeavours on the aspiration of our urban poor for a house with 'a front and back door', rather than attempting to shift the focus and introduce their constituency to the notion that flat-dwelling is a potentially desirable condition. What is created as a result are miniature versions of suburbia on brownfield sites, inappropriate in character for city dwelling and of insufficient density to sustain shops. These homes are being built for people who are, in many cases, too poor to afford the other fundamental prerequisite of suburbia – a car. It could be argued, therefore, that political pressure for the short-term fix continues on the inexorable course which it has pursued since World War II, developing without sufficient consideration for the long-term cost or social benefits, and generating sump communities which will, in time, be the slums of the future.

## PUBLIC SECTOR REFORM

If the situation in housing seems bleak, David Stark, a director of Keppie Design, one of Glasgow's longest-established architectural practices, is hopeful that significant changes in the procurement of health, education and other public buildings will bring real benefits. He argues that the advent of what were historically known as private finance initiatives (PFI), but which have recently acquired the more, politically acceptable, moniker public-private partnerships (PPP), provides real hope for the major buildings required for our educational and physical well-being – namely, schools and hospitals.

Stark emphasises that what is now sought in these acronymic endeavours is real value for money (VFM). This, he argues, is quite different from the historic tendency to adopt the cheapest solution, which was often a legislative necessity when the cost of all major public projects were met from the public purse. Stark argues for the efficacy of private procurement on the basis that traditional methods of tendering have, in recent years, resulted in innumerable instances of contractors providing extremely tight costings in the first instance in order to win the job but thereafter charging 'through the nose' for all variations which are inevitably required in the creation of large and complex buildings.

Often these scenarios have resulted in lengthy and costly litigation, a situation beneficial to neither client nor contractor and which creates a culture of suspicion and distrust. These situations are ultimately detrimental to society. In support of this argument, Stark cites the tendency of architects quoting fee costs at around 40 per cent of the fee scales recommended by the Royal Institute of British Architects. Such levels are, he argues, unsustainable and inevitably result in low-quality service and poor-quality buildings. His own belief is that, with good housekeeping, a fee level of around 80 per cent of recommended scales is viable.

The history which precedes our increasing reliance on PFI or PPP procurement is one of underinvestment in the decades from the 1960s, which ultimately led to a review of public projects by Margaret Thatcher's government. The political analysis at that time was that the required level of capital investment was simply not possible from the public purse and that other mechanisms should be sought. Thus, a new model evolved which is, according to Stark, presently being reviewed by many other nations as exemplifying good practice.

In support of his argument, Stark comments on the new Edinburgh Royal Infirmary, built (by PFI) to a higher build-quality and in a considerably tighter timescale than could ever have been achieved through traditional procurement.

He emphasises, however, that key prerequisites of such a process are the political and economic stability which allow the private sector to invest with confidence. Stark also emphasises that long-term performance is enhanced in a process which requires the contractor to fund the development and maintain it over the first 30 years of its life. During this period, the public purse repays the capital cost but also pays an agreed rate for maintenance and elements of staffing, which continue to be the contractor's responsibility. Thus, in the Edinburgh Royal Infirmary all non-clinical posts are contained within the PFI mechanism.

While PFI schemes may well give their developers an incentive to create sustainable, durable structures which function efficiently, evidence in support of their success on the design front is perhaps rather thinner. The Edinburgh Royal Infirmary incorporates, for example, a six-metre wide underground 'tugway' and additional lifts which improve internal communications, save money and enhance efficiency. The hospital procurement also incorporated an agreed allowance for art. However, the emphasis was arguably less on achieving something of real architectural distinction than on creating a building whose negative impact on the landscape was mitigated as far as possible and which addressed a complex functional brief.

David Stark reluctantly admits that many early PFI projects are unremarkable in design terms and advocates the need for design champions and design-quality indicators. This view is endorsed by Sebastian Tombs and his predecessor, Charles McKean, who have, over the last two decades, worked with the RIAS's members to preserve the autonomy of the Incorporation in the provision of governance and professional support for Scotland's architects. The Incorporation has also striven to raise awareness of the role of architects with both politicians and in society generally.

## SCOTLAND AFTER MODERNISM

In spite of this positive endeavour, Sebastian Tombs shares some of Rob Joiner's pessimism about the direction of architecture and our cities. While the advent of a new Scotland would seem to be a major opportunity for community regeneration, Tombs emphasises that the political pressure at present seems to be towards creating 'better quality ghettos'. He urges that a more holistic approach is adopted and that Scotland should endeavour to define a new architectural direction through observing the best examples of architecture achieved in the last 20 years both at home and abroad. The need for education, he urges, has never been greater. While there are always glimmers of hope, for example a recent visit by key Aberdeen councillors to see the best new housing in Glasgow, what is required are changes at policy level.

Tombs does not fully share David Stark's belief in the PFI mechanism, which he feels leads to very cautious buildings and a tendency on the part of commissioning authorities, whether they be health boards, local councils or government agencies, to abrogate responsibility. Once again, he emphasises that the 'education, education, education' mantra of Tony Blair's first election victory is the key towards achieving a successful and sustainable architectural future for Scotland.

Acknowledging the need for architectural champions, Tombs cites Rob Joiner's expertise as both urbanist and client of great skill. He also mentions his predecessor Charles McKean's continuing preoccupation with setting the contemporary striving towards excellence within its proper historic context.

Among contemporary patrons, Tombs mentions both Ian Wall, the irascible chief executive of EDI, Edinburgh City Council's highly successful development arm, and Andy Doolan, whose Point Hotel has become a model for subsequent contemporary 'Art House' developments in the capital. He also gives an honourable mention to Peter Wilson, whose proselytising endeavours through journalism, commentary, exhibitions and architecture-focused events has often created conflict with Tombs' own organisation but whose overall achievement has been to direct attention to the pursuit of excellence in architecture.

All the foregoing has been preoccupied with procurement for (if not necessarily by) the public sector – the most crucial endeavour towards the future of our cities. Private sector work, whether by developers or corporations, is similarly subject to the post-millennium identity crisis, bereft of consistency and all too often playing down to a fairly low common denominator. Too much developer housing continues to be of the 'little boxes on the hillside' variety, despite the odd, inspired, home for the future. There are glimmers of hope in recent university work, and some large corporate buildings seem to recognise the simple fact that good design is good for business, but Scotland still has to look to its past for architectural glory.

Architecture in Scotland is at a crossroads in the nation's history, as Glendinning et al. observe: 'Unlike the 1930s and 1950s, the Modernist faith in materialistic Progress, and in state-directed discipline, was no longer available as a simple answer.' The loss of these old certainties has been seen in a 'revived concern for the "national"' and 'a diverse, outward-looking future, rather than guarding a threatened "essence" of the past' (Glendinning et al. 1996: 501).

Throughout the eighteenth century and much of the nineteenth, Scotland was rightly recognised internationally as a focus of architectural excellence. The work of the Adam brothers was arguably the most significant redefining of classicism since Palladio. Our Victorian antecedents achieved many monuments of world significance and indeed Mackintosh continues to inspire new generations of young architects. Ten years ago, McKean wrote that Scotland was 'a country suffering from an advanced case of amnesia' (ibid. 517), but since then the willingness to acknowledge and draw from a wider heritage – British, European and international – has grown. Lamenting the loss of any architectural ascendancy in the past as some golden age would be folly, when there is so much change and optimism, but there is a consensus that Scotland could, and should, do better.

# 23

# THE PEOPLE'S GAME?:
# THE STATE OF SCOTTISH FOOTBALL

*Jonathan Northcroft*

## 'SCIENTIFIC SOCCER': THE SCOTTISH WAY

The first football international was a draw, but Scotland were the victors. They could not put a goal past their opponents, England, but they scored in terms of influence. Played at the West of Scotland Cricket Ground, Partick, in 1872, the game was pivotal in the way football developed into its modern form and it was the Scottish team – all 11 of them amateurs from Glasgow's Queen's Park club – who were responsible. Their use of an organised playing formation, of tactics, and of the revolutionary concept of passing the ball to one another, profoundly impressed the English, who were still playing in a more rudimentary style, closer to rugby, based on physical contact and individual dribbling. Clubs in England began importing huge numbers of players from across the border to help in teaching these ideas. By the turn of the century, when English coaches began to spread football throughout continental Europe and South America, it was the Scottish 'scientific' form of the game that they were preaching.

Fast-forward 13 decades. Where Scottish names once dominated the team-sheets of England's top outfits (Liverpool once fielded a side completely composed of Scots), there are now as many Danes and Swedes in the employ of the English Premiership's best clubs. Nor can Scotland supply enough quality footballers to keep its own leading sides viable – Rangers and Celtic started the new millennium by fielding, for the first time in their histories, teams which did not include a single Scot. The picture is the same in dug-out, dressing-room and boardroom. The Scottish Premier League's star player since 1997 has been Henrik Larsson, born of a Swedish mother and a father from the Cape Verde Islands. The top managers have been Martin O'Neill, a Northern Irishman, and Dick Advocaat, who is Dutch. The controller of the country's most successful club, Celtic, is Ireland's Dermot Desmond, who bought his shareholding from Fergus McCann, a Canadian golf entrepreneur.

Even the Scottish national team is no longer tartan territory. In February 2002, the Scottish Football Association appointed the first-ever foreign coach of the Scotland national team – the German, Berti Vogts – and because of the lack of native talent, since the mid-1990s, Scotland have been fielding English-born players, who qualify through tenuous ancestral links. When Surrey-born defender Matt Elliott joined up with his first international squad in Glasgow, it was only the second time he had ever visited Scotland. A nadir was reached when enquiries were made to see if Rangers' Lorenzo Amoruso could wear the Scottish jersey. They proved fruitless when it was revealed Amoruso had already represented Italy at competitive level, though at least his hometown had a reasonably Scottish-sounding name – Bari.

## SCOTTISH FOOTBALL: THE LAST TRADITIONAL INDUSTRY?

Scots have often prided themselves on their internationalism, on their history of looking outward to, and engaging with, Europe and the world beyond, compared to what they see as the ostrich-like tendencies of the English. But the overwhelming influence of foreigners upon Scotland's national sport has come about by necessity rather than choice. There cannot be a country in the world that has less control over how football is played and governed within its own borders, but for whom the game occupies such a central position in its cultural life. The evidence is cumulative and unmistakable. Scottish football is sick, kept alive by means of a drip-feed of coaching, playing and administrative talent from abroad.

Football is heading the way of steel or coal or shipbuilding – industries through which Scotland once led the world, but whose products the country must now import from elsewhere. Hampden Park's recently opened national football museum is in danger of becoming a mausoleum. In it, you can view an exhibit celebrating that very first football international in 1872, but when football's top 32 countries gathered in Japan and Korea in summer 2002 for the World Cup, Scotland were not among them. In the Hampden museum you can learn about the 1937 Scottish Cup final between Celtic and Aberdeen, when 146,433 spectators packed the stadium to produce the world's biggest ever crowd for a club match. Yet since Hampden reopened after refurbishment in 1999, less than half of the games it has hosted have seen full houses, despite a reduction in capacity to only 52,000.

'New' Hampden (like New Labour, a blander version of the old) symbolises Scottish football's decline and folly. Remodelling the stadium was first proposed in the early 1970s, yet there was a 30-year gap between conception and completion. Then, incredibly, laymen – the directors of the still amateur club

Queen's Park, and the pen-pushers of the SFA – were allowed to guide the project. Like Edwardian stadium-builders, they lavished money on the frontage and fittings, but paid little attention to the fundamentals, like car-parking and the sight-lines for ordinary spectators. You might not be able to see much from your narrow, plastic seat after paying £30 to watch Scotland as a punter, but at least if you decide to complain to the SFA afterwards you can go up to their offices in a smart lift.

Wales's magnificent Millennium Stadium puts Scotland to shame. Among New Hampden's many calamities has been the discovery that it is built on polluted soil (after rain during one game, players reported the mud smelt like excrement) and the heavy debts the building project accrued, which took millions of pounds of taxpayers' money to remedy, and which continue to cripple the finances of the SFA. Yet New Hampden is supposed to be the centrepiece of Scotland's bid to host the European Championships in 2008. If ever a process demonstrated Scotland's confused relationship with its national sport, it has been the saga of Euro 2008. The man who conceived it, SFA Chief Executive David Taylor, is a former member of the Tartan Army, yet he has promoted the idea in low-key, almost apologetic fashion, because of uncertainty as to the support it will get from the common fan. One First Minister, Henry McLeish, seized on the project with unbridled enthusiasm. Another, his successor Jack McConnell, could not have treated a petition to make 'Land of Hope and Glory' the Scottish anthem with less enthusiasm. Meanwhile, nobody really knows what the public think – least of all the public themselves. Opinion polls have shown a certain support for the bid, but it is hardly the talk of the streets and the pubs.

A truly self-confident nation, even a small one, would have no qualms about staging what would be a global event. Holland and Belgium successfully hosted Euro 2000, and Denmark the 1992 tournament. Taylor and McLeish were initially adamant that Scotland would go it alone, yet already the SFA have back-pedalled and have approached Ireland to stage a joint bid. Attempts to raise the £30 million necessary to build a new stadium in Aberdeen, crucial to the project, are in trouble. Done well, staging Euro 2008 could revitalise Scottish football from top to bottom – just as Euro '96 produced an explosion of interest in the game in England, from kids in the park to multi-national investors in the City of London. Done badly, a failed bid could knock national self-confidence for years.

Irrespective of the bid's success, it will prove positive if it gets Scots to re-examine the future of their national game. Back to New Hampden: is it only the Scots who could lavish vast resources upon a new stadium yet spend next to nothing on developing footballers fit to play there? This is a little bit like a Millennium Dome complex: spending millions of pounds of scarce public money and attracting corporate sponsors, while all around the basics are not invested in. Neither Italy, Germany, Spain, Holland, nor any of the

THE PEOPLE'S GAME?: THE STATE OF SCOTTISH FOOTBALL

Scandinavian countries have purpose-built national football stadiums. They prefer to direct resources into coaching schemes to improve their young footballers; while France built their national stadium on the outskirts of Paris only after a decade spent pumping money into the coaching infrastructure that enabled them to become World and European champions. Thanks to Hampden's reconstruction, Glasgow is now the only city in the world with three football stadiums that seat more than 50,000 spectators, yet Scots are provided with so few facilities for the training of players that not a single full-sized indoor pitch exists. Canada (that football colossus) is into double figures. And, of course, we only have three stadiums of such size because the teams that occupy two of the grounds, Celtic and Rangers, refuse to play Cup finals or allow national matches to be played permanently at each other's grounds. This means that in a shrinking city of 600,000 inhabitants there are enough football seats for one-in-four of the population at the same time.

All front, no substance; nice plaid, nothing under the kilt – the SFA's hubris over Hampden is merely symptomatic of the way Scottish football misdirects its energies. Some English clubs have owned purpose-built training grounds for more than 40 years, but not until 2001 did the first Scottish outfit, Rangers, open their own complex. Celtic, the Scottish champions, still train their players on a patch of public ground in a rundown area of Glasgow's East End. Henrik Larsson might find better facilities back in Cape Verde.

Scotland's smaller clubs have been equally remiss, spending what meagre income they have on transfers and stadia rather than training and development. The decline of native standards can be seen in the fact that Celtic won the European Cup in 1967 with a team comprised solely of Scots, yet just 35 years later Scotland are ranked outside the world's top 50 nations by FIFA, the game's governing body. Slovakia and Trinidad and Tobago are rated higher. Yet football continues to exert an almost unnatural hold on the nation. Per head of population, only Albanians attend football matches in greater number than the Scots, putting truth in the old Tory insult that some Scots want to aspire to be nothing more than a 'Caledonian Albania'.

## THE SCOTTISH NATIONAL TEAM

> Graeme Souness: It's a minority. It's a shame you just can't pick those out.
> Jimmy Hill: I always felt that about the England–Scotland game. Because you, er, Scots are always welcome in England, a lot of you live here, you know, and have done, and there's a great affection for the Scots and what a lovely weekend that match could be if they came down in peace when they did come. I think Londoners would give them a warm welcome and, as you say, share a glass of wine or a bottle of beer or something and make it a lovely sporting occasion.

(BBC1 discussion after the Heysel Disaster, 29 May 1985, quoted in
Moorhouse 1989: 207-8)

The Scottish national team has been the central and defining aspect of the game
in Scotland for decades. It has been associated with feelings about the state of
Scotland, national self-confidence and, crucially, relations with the English.
Given this, we need to ask the question: when is the quality of Scotland's
football going to match the quantity of those who watch it? We should,
realistically, not expect answers from the national team for several years. When
Vogts took over from the canny but cautious Craig Brown, he made revolution
his mantra and packed his squad with a collection of rookies and teenagers in a
bid to start building tomorrow's Scotland team today. Vogts, to affirm his
passion for his adopted country, told the Scottish press at his first meeting with
them to 'call me Berti McVogts', but his first game brought to mind another
'Mac', Ally McLeod. McLeod, before leaving for Argentina, was asked what he
planned to do after the 1978 World Cup. He replied 'Retain it', but was to
watch Scotland exit the tournament in the first round after being humiliated by
Peru and Iran. McVogts' debut international against France was similar – fanfare
pre-match, 4–0 down by half-time. Such a result seemed to tax the patience of
even the Tartan Army, who in recent years have carved a niche and positive
identity out of revelling in the role of hopeless, romantic losers. Maybe that is
some kind of progress after all.

Vogts, at least, is thinking along the right lines. There is such a lack of
strength in depth among Scotland's senior players, his only chance is to try and
improve our younger ones. In today's multi-million-pound football business,
power has shifted from national teams to clubs, from the World Cup to the
UEFA Champions League. Vogts, in his first game against France, faced a tussle
with Rangers manager Alex McLeish over the injured Barry Ferguson, who was
fit enough to play for club but not for country, according to his boss. Vogts,
unlike the careful Craig Brown, tried to win this battle but lost, such is the
financial power and pull of the club.

What is the importance of the Scottish national team post-devolution? For
several decades, a large part of (generally) male Scotland saw the national team
as the only visible international profile for our country and statement that we
were not English. It provided a rare forum for Scots to exercise all kinds of
complicated emotional, historical and political feelings from pride in themselves
to resentment at the more successful English. This began to change during the
period when Scotland qualified for five successive World Cups from 1974 to
1990 (never actually getting past the first round and winning only a cumulative
total of four matches, but that is not the point). At the same time, in the 1980s
and 1990s an emerging political consensus formed in support of a Scottish
Parliament, thus having an impact on Scottish identity. The Tartan Army began
to portray itself as international ambassadors, a transformation from the image

of 1970s' Scots fans as drunk and violent, and looking forward to the symbolic Wembley trip every two years (Moorhouse 1989). Now the Scots win awards for good behaviour, although there is a lingering suspicion that much of this is a reaction to the hooliganism of English fans in the 1980s. There is also much celebration still of a ritual supposedly anti-Englishness (as in 'We hate Jimmy Hill'). Post-Thatcher, post-devolution, in a football world shaped by big business and clubs, it is perhaps inevitable that the national team will be of less importance and, given their exploits and talents, this could be no bad thing.


## THE OLD FIRM IN THE MILLENNIUM

In Glasgow half the fans hate you and the other half think they own you.
(Tommy Burns, quoted in MacDonald 1994: 46)

Radical change as a means to break a cycle of failure is the policy being pursued by Scotland's leading clubs. Rangers and Celtic can draw huge attendances at Scottish home games and have significant wider communities at home and abroad (Bennie 1995 (on Celtic); Walker 1990 (on Rangers)). However, faced with mounting debts and dwindling levels of competition in the domestic game, they are both seeking to leave the Scottish Premier League and compete on a weekly basis against clubs either in England or Europe while still playing their home matches in Glasgow. Rangers chairman David Murray and his Celtic counterpart Brian Quinn both say that the question is no longer whether the Old Firm should leave Scottish football, but when.

So far, their escape plans have proved futile. The possible new competitions explored by Rangers and Celtic have turned out to be footballing Darien Schemes. First there was the 'Atlantic League', a proposed competition involving clubs from Holland, Portugal, Scandinavia, Belgium and Scotland. Next came the Euro League, a scaled-down version involving just Holland, Scotland, Portugal and Belgium. Then there was the Phoenix League, a plan to join together clubs from England's lower leagues. It proved to be one Phoenix which failed to rise from the flames.

Despite these setbacks, however, the Old Firm remain convinced their destiny lies outside Scotland. There are economic imperatives behind their thinking. The Souness revolution at Rangers, followed by McCann at Celtic, has widened the gap between the Old Firm and the rest to an unbridgeable chasm as the two try to compete in Europe (Murray 1998). Despite Scotland's mania for football, there is only so much revenue that can be generated from an audience of five million people. Television, football's chief source of income, pays Scottish clubs £10 million per season to show their league games – in England, the broadcasters shell out around 50 times that sum. The Old Firm chairmen highlight the fact that low-ranking English clubs like Leicester and

Bolton earn several times the amount Rangers and Celtic do from television. Yet at the same time the Old Firm have to compete not just with these clubs, but also with the likes of Manchester United and Bayern Munich in terms of player wages and transfer fees. Celtic, despite three share issues and greater on-field success than they have enjoyed for three decades, are currently over £20 million in debt. Rangers owe even more – in excess of £60 million. The demise of Scottish Premier TV – an attempt by the Premier League clubs to launch their own TV channel after Sky refused to bid again for the rights – brought about by Celtic and Rangers jointly vetoing the package showed the common interest they had versus the rest. The action of the ten remaining clubs in announcing their intention to resign from the SPL in two years' time showed the problems and inequalities in the Scottish game, but did not offer a way forward.

## THE OLD FIRM AND THE REST OF SCOTTISH FOOTBALL: 'THE PROVINCIALS'

> It's dangerous to draw a line and say everybody below it is out of the Scottish League. In 1959 Dundee United were second bottom of the Second Division. Some people might have said then that they should go, that Dundee can't support two clubs, etc, etc. I think you've always got to allow for clubs 'recovering' themselves.
> (Bob Crampsey, quoted in MacDonald 1994: 163)

The Old Firm's real aim is to join the English Premiership, the most heavily marketed and most widely watched competition in the world, and they argue this would allow them to become football superpowers carrying a torch for Scotland beyond its borders, in the way Barcelona represent the cause of the Catalans while playing in Spain's Primera Liga. Their argument is complicated somewhat by the fact both of the Old Firm are also seen as embodying non-Scottish constituencies – Rangers the Ulster Protestants, Celtic the Irish Catholic diaspora (Bradley 1995). But there is no doubt that with average match-day attendances which, when added together, exceed those of Scotland's other 40 league clubs combined, the Old Firm represent a majority of fans who watch club football in Scotland. David Taylor, SFA chief executive, is only admitting what many know when he acknowledges the unsustainable nature of four leagues in a population of five million, asking 'What do 29 spectators at a lower division match tell about us?' (*The Scotsman*, 30 March 2002). The state of Scottish football has never looked more perilous. John Boyle put Motherwell up for sale after investing £11 million, while in May 2002, 35 years to the week Third Lanark went out of business, Airdrie, after two and half years in administration, finally went out of existence. Two months later Clydebank followed – to be replaced by a reconstituted Airdrie club, playing under the name of 'Airdrie United'.

Rangers and Celtic have tried to leave Scottish football before, of course, but there are reasons for believing they now have a better chance of making their escape than at any time in their history. Unlike the previous occasions when they have explored playing in the English league, some English clubs have actually warmed to the idea. After a decade of unprecedented growth in terms of media and sponsorship revenue, the English Premiership has run into the problem of how to keep the expansion going, and several chairmen believe the novelty of having Rangers and Celtic in their midst would be the answer. Peter Kenyon, the Manchester United chief executive, has said, 'I'd sooner play Celtic than Southampton. People don't like change but change is sometimes necessary.'

Furthermore, for the first time there seems to be a will within Scotland as a whole for Rangers and Celtic to leave. In October 2001, a survey found that 74 per cent of Old Firm supporters and 68 per cent of fans from other Scottish clubs believed it would be better for the Glasgow giants to quit the Scottish game (*The Sunday Times*, 7 October 2001). That belief does not seem misplaced, given the way football's rapid revenue growth over the last decade has exaggerated the advantages bigger clubs have over smaller ones and all but killed competition in the domestic game. As recently as the mid-1980s, teams like Aberdeen and Dundee United were able to beat the Old Firm to Scottish Cups and championships on a regular basis and others, like Hearts, gave them stiff competition. Now Scotland's entire domestic season is reduced to whoever comes out best in that year's Old Firm derbies. The last time what is quaintly and patronisingly called a 'provincial' team won a cup was when Hearts beat Rangers in the Scottish Cup final of 1998. The last time someone outside the duopoly won the national league was Aberdeen in 1985. The 17 years since have been the longest period of Old Firm dominance since the inception of the Scottish League in 1890–91. Even Mike Watson, Sports Minister and a passionate and thoughtful Dundee United fan (author of two books on the subject), admits, 'I cannot envisage any other club other than Rangers or Celtic winning the SPL title in my lifetime' (*Scotland on Sunday*, 24 February 2002).

So remote is the chance of beating Rangers or Celtic in even a one-off game that the visit of either of the Old Firm, once guaranteed to produce a full house, now rarely makes for a sell-out at any of the SPL's other ten clubs. Though Rangers and Celtic are the main draw for television companies and sponsorship, the amount Scottish clubs earn from these sources is not so great that it would be calamitous if the Old Firm leave. Indeed, it could be argued that the SPL without the Old Firm would be so much more competitive and attractive to viewers and backers that commercial losses would be limited. Those who want Rangers and Celtic to stay argue that without them the SPL would become no more important than the Danish, Swedish or Norwegian leagues – low-revenue competitions which even incorporate a degree of semi-professionalism. But given those very leagues have a much better record of nurturing young football talent than the SPL, would that really be so bad?

Ebbe Skovdahl, manager of Aberdeen, Scotland's biggest club outside the Old Firm, believes Rangers and Celtic should go. Skovdahl managed Brondby in Denmark at a time when the club, and his country, were able to produce players good enough to become European champions, despite the financial limitations of their league. For him the attraction of an Old Firm-less SPL is strong – imagine a league where Hearts and Hibs, Dundee United, Dundee and Aberdeen, Livingston and Kilmarnock, Dunfermline and perhaps even a Highland club like Inverness could compete on more or less equal terms for the championship. According to Skovdahl:

> In the long term it [Rangers and Celtic leaving] could be one of the best things to happen. It would be far better for some of the young Scottish players and though it would emotionally upset some of our fans at first they would get over it. It's not for me as a foreigner to say whether the Old Firm should leave Scotland, but if they do they should be aware a lot of people are sure the league they leave behind would get stronger and stronger. (*The Sunday Times*, 14 October 2001)

Getting Scotland's other clubs to approve of their exit, once seen as the biggest impediment to such a move, might be the smallest hurdle the Old Firm face. But there remain huge political obstacles abroad. For the Old Firm to be allowed to play in the English Premiership they require the backing in a vote of 14 of the 20 chairmen who govern the league and, despite Manchester United's backing, they need to persuade smaller clubs such as Blackburn and Bolton to support them. That will not be easy, given that Rangers and Celtic's presence would mean two fewer places available in the Premiership to smaller English clubs. The even greater problem is securing approval from FIFA and UEFA, the international bodies who rule the game. FIFA, particularly, has voiced strong opposition to such a move. They fear that if Rangers and Celtic can leave Scotland, it would open the way for a chaotic rash of applications from big clubs in other small countries to enter more lucrative neighbouring leagues – Porto, Benfica and Sporting Lisbon fleeing Portugal to play in Spain, for example, or even Grasshoppers Zurich moving to Germany and its Bundesliga.

Rangers and Celtic hope to use the examples of clubs who already play in other countries' leagues in their favour: Cardiff City, Swansea and Wrexham play in England; two Liechtenstein teams play in the Swiss domestic football league; and the Auckland-based New Zealand Kingz compete in the Australian League. They need good politicians to state their case, but have so far been unable to secure the support of Scotland's most powerful administrator, David Will, who is one of FIFA's vice-presidents.

The rise of Will, a Brechin lawyer who still works out of offices in the town, demonstrates how Scotland has prospered best in recent years in those areas that do not involve actually kicking a ball. The chief referee of FIFA is George

Cumming, a Scot, while UEFA's head of coaching is Andy Roxburgh, the former Scotland manager. In England, the chief executive of the Football Association is Adam Crozier, a young former advertising executive from Glasgow. Though Scotland cannot find a Scot to coach their national team, the English cannot find a non-Scot to successfully manage their clubs. Only three times in the last 15 years has the Premiership been won by a team not managed by a son of Glasgow – when Arsene Wenger took Arsenal to the title in 1998 and 2002, and Howard Wilkinson won the same honour with Leeds in 1992.

But Scotland, the country whose Victorians refined the rough new game of football, whose people were the first to take football to their very hearts, deserves more than just good managers, administrators and officials. As the nation sits wedged between Peru and Angola in the world rankings, watching more football than anyone except Albanians but playing it less successfully than almost anyone except the Albanians, its national game is in need of a sea change. There are two crucial requirements. First, football thinking must become long- and not short-term, so that Scotland can start developing its own players and providing facilities – and, who knows, maybe even an international football tournament – for its populace. Second, it should be hoped Rangers and Celtic can effect their radical move, their reverse devolution, and form a new act of union with England and its top clubs, so the rest of Scotland can get on with supporting a proper domestic league again.

This might not be what genteel amateurs from the Queen's Park club had in mind when 11 of them donned Scotland's colours in that first international at the West of Scotland Cricket Ground. But it is that or having future generations traipse down to the museum in empty New Hampden to discover days when football united and delighted their country.

# 24

# THE SCOTTISH ARISTOCRACY

*Roddy Martine*

## THE CRITIQUE OF THE ARISTOCRATIC SOCIETY

In 1909, a radical young Scots journalist of the name of Thomas Johnston published an exposé of the aristocracy entitled *Our Scots Noble Families* (Johnston 1909). It proved a controversial bestseller, Johnston's view being that the Scottish aristocracy had only reached its present state of power and privilege by exploitation, theft and robbery on the grandest scale. In his later life, as the Rt. Hon. Tom Johnston, Privy Councillor, Companion of Honour, former Secretary of State for Scotland, chairman of the Scottish Forestry Commission and North of Scotland Hydro-Electric Board, he visited second-hand bookshops around Scotland and systematically bought up copies of his book. When asked by a member of his staff why he did this, he replied, 'Times have changed' (Galbraith 1995).

For Tom Johnston, the grocer's son from Kirkintilloch, times had certainly changed. Although he stopped short of accepting a peerage for himself, he was instrumental in launching the Scottish Ancestry Research Society and by the time of his death had become not only a member but a pillar of the establishment he had for so long despised. Whether or not it suits a particular political viewpoint to accept this, that is the way of the world.

Ramsay MacDonald, another dangerous young radical of the early socialist movement, attacked the myth and majesty of the landowning classes in an introduction to the 1913 edition of *Our Scots Noble Families*:

> Show the people that Our Old Nobility is not noble, that its lands are stolen lands – stolen whether by force or fraud: show people that the title deeds are rapine, murder, massacre, cheating or Court Harlotry: dissolve the halo of divinity that surrounds the hereditary title: let the people clearly understand that our present House of Lords is composed largely

of descendants of successful pirates and rogues: do these things and you shatter the Romance that keeps the nation numb and spellbound while privilege picks its pockets. (Quoted in Sillars 1975: 256)

MacDonald, even more than Johnston, ended up part of the establishment, but *Our Scots Noble Families* does provide food for thought. It is interesting to note that, through filial loyalty, Johnston ignored the powerful Border clan of Johnston and the families of the earls of Annandale and Hartfell, but most of the other great historic names are there – the Bruces, Stewarts, Campbells, Dalrymples, Douglases, Drummonds, Dundases, Kennedys, Murrays, Hamiltons and Frasers. All of them shared two driving ambitions: the acquisition of political influence and the procurement of land, the one leading to the other and vice versa.

For the greater part of the past millennium, these twin obsessions formed the bedrock and raison d'être of the aristocracy. The problems started when some among them became convinced that primogeniture alone gave entitlement to such spoils. It is simply not enough to quantify your existence on the basis that your family has occupied the same territory for generations. Arrogance and family conceit get nobody anywhere.

A thousand years ago, the population of Scotland could approximately be estimated at around 100,000. Social structure was built up on territorial families and, north of the Highland line, the clans. By the time of the Treaty of Union with England in 1707, it was calculated that, in a total Scottish population of 1,250,000, there were 154 peers (England, with five times the population, made do with 164) and more than 10,000 titled Scottish families (encompassing territorial and baronial designations). One in every 45 Scots belonged directly to the Scottish nobility.

Such a proportion of hierarchic individuals is unknown in any other nation. That is why if you ask anyone over 30 with a recognisably old Scots name – Abernethy, Broun, Buchanan, Macdonald, Macleod – anywhere in the world, from any walk of life, where they come from, the chances are you will be subjected to a text on their genealogy, suitably embellished to connect them with some ancient noble blood lines.

## THE ARISTOCRACY AND GENTRY IN A DEMOCRATIC AGE

In a twenty-first-century democracy, the concept of a non-elected corrective legislature is virtually impossible to justify. All the same, nobody should make the mistake of believing that the removal of hereditary and even life peers from the UK's upper house of representatives will dramatically alter the way in which we are governed. Nor will it significantly reduce the social influence of the aristocracy, particularly among the chattering classes. As other European countries have discovered, the abolition of titles merely creates a more rarefied breed.

At Westminster, post-House of Lords partial-reform, 19 Scottish hereditary peers remain *in situ* in a total of 90 UK hereditaries, and there is already a legitimately elected Scottish peer, Viscount Thurso (owner of 36,800 acres in Caithness), in the House of Commons for the Liberal Democrats (Cahill 2001: 277). For the Tories, in the House of Commons, there is the Marquess of Lothian's heir, Michael Ancram, and for Labour, father of the house Tam Dalyell of the Binns. In the Scottish Parliament, the Scottish Conservatives have the Duke of Hamilton's brother, Lord James Douglas-Hamilton, and Labour has Berwickshire landowner John Home-Robertson, whose ancestral stately home Paxton House, now an outreach gallery for the National Galleries of Scotland, is a statement on wealth and patronage if ever there was one.

On other levels, born aristocrats have moved with the times. The Duke of Hamilton is a qualified engineer, test pilot and designer of off-road vehicles; the Marquis of Queensberry is a former professor of ceramics at the Royal College of Art and heads up a design group; the Marquess of Bute is the racing driver Johnny Dumfries; the Earl of Erroll runs a computer programming consultancy; the Duke of Argyll and Lord Sempill are executives in the Scotch whisky industry; the Earl of Glasgow is a producer/director in television; the Earl of Lindsay is a landscape architect; Earl Haig is an accomplished painter and an associate of the Royal Scottish Academy; and the Earl of Rosslyn is a policeman. Others have successful careers as farmers, public relations consultants, businessmen and hoteliers. Far from being the idle rich layabouts of popular perception, scions of the old aristocracy have been obliged to flex their muscles in the modern world largely without the back-up of class and privilege so many of their predecessors enjoyed.

So exactly who are they, this Scottish elite? If they are genuinely such an anachronism, why do they attract such obsequious obeisance from certain quarters while inspiring such bitter resentment in others? At the apex of Scotland's aristocracy are the dukes. There are ten Scottish and UK Scottish dukedoms other than those held by members of the Royal Family: Argyll, Atholl, Buccleuch and Queensberry, Fife, Hamilton and Brandon, Montrose, Roxburghe and Sutherland. There are 11 marquesses in Scotland: Aberdeen and Temair, Ailsa, Bute, Huntly, Lansdowne, Linlithgow, Lothian, Queensberry, Tweeddale, Zetland. There are 58 earldoms, 27 of them dating back to before the Union of 1707: Airlie, Annandale and Hartfell, Balfour, Breadalbane and Holland, Buchan, Caithness, Cawdor, Crawford and Balcarres, Cromartie, Dalhousie, Dundee, Dundonald, Dunmore, Eglinton and Winton, Elgin and Kincardine, Erroll, Galloway, Glasgow, Haddington, Haig, Home, Inchcape, Kinnoull, Kintore, Lauderdale, Leven and Melville, Lindsay, Loudon, Lovelace, Mansfield and Mansfield, Mar, Mar and Kellie, Moray, Minto, Morton,

Northesk, Orkney, Perth, Rosebery, Rosslyn, Rothes, Seafield, Selkirk, Southesk, Stair, Strathmore and Kinghorne, Sutherland, Wemyss and March held by Scots, ignoring the courtesy titles used by heirs to dukedoms and marquesses. Finally, there are only seven viscounts: Arbuthnott, Falkland, Melville, Oxfuird, Thurso, Weir, Younger. Lower down the pecking order there are barons and literally hundreds of life peers, baronets and knights.

Such influence as these patrician figures realistically possess remains simply on two counts. First, a significant number, by no means all, still own the acres of land upon which their ancestors have lived for generations. It is a fact that 20 or so of them currently control more than a tenth of Scotland's land, but there are others who own nothing more than a terraced villa in Leith. Taxation and the collapse of Lloyds during the twentieth century achieved far more for the socialist dream of destroying the old order than any revolutionary uprising could ever have done. Second, and more intangibly, their names resonate with the turbulent passage of Scotland's history, some significantly more than others. This invests them with a certain romantic status, but equally becomes a terrible burden for those unable to live up to expectations.

The titles they carry are the rewards of ancestral achievements or, in the case of more recent peerages and knighthoods, their own. But ennoblement comes at a price. There are responsibilities associated with bearing both ancient and modern titles, and they have nothing to do with personal privilege. If being a lord or lady does create a certain cachet in the eyes of others, then that is as it should be. But to earn that respect, the lord and lady must be seen to contribute to the society in which they live. If not, then the entire honours system has to be overhauled, and the sooner the better.

And possibly this, coupled with the uncertainties of primogeniture, is the reason why some of them have been unable to stay the course. The dukedom of Atholl, for example, has passed to a retired mining engineer in the Traansvaal and the family seat, Blair Castle, one of Scotland's top visitor attractions, has been placed in trust for the nation; likewise, the 11th Earl of Dunmore, whose ancestors held lands in Stirlingshire and on Harris, lives in Tasmania. A significant number no longer own any land or property in Scotland and choose to live predominantly in England.

## THE CLANS

The clans are part of the 'myth' of the open, harmonious nature of Scottish society. As late as the 1960s the Countess of Erroll could pronounce:

> In too many countries the great historic families are separated from the
> mass of the people, but in Scotland we have been fortunate in that pride
> of name has never depended on wealth and rank, and in that the clan

tradition has always prevented class barriers from arising to divide our proud nation . . . We are all one family of Scots, the branches of that family being the clans and Names, and the Chief of Chiefs our Queen. (Bain 1968: 7)

The Scottish Clan Chiefs, a strange and esoteric body of men and women, are a prime example of how hereditary influence can survive when genuine authority and power is removed. At the last count, there were 124 members of the Standing Council of Scottish Chiefs, although, in theory, such hierarchical figureheads, and the clans they led, ceased to exist in the aftermath of Culloden. But it is not that easy to obliterate the loyalties of blood lines, especially in the Scottish Highlands. The further removed from it we are in this troubled world, the greater becomes the significance of kith and kin. Hence, whenever an expatriate bonds with a bottle of Scotch, Brigadoon rises. The Scottish Executive, intent on courting the so-called Scottish diaspora, must be mildly dismayed to discover that our overseas cousins are far more interested in Mac Cailein Mor than the First Minister.

Throughout civilisation, nations and epochs evolve their own hierarchies and allocate their own rewards. On and off between the fourteenth and seventeenth centuries, the Three (sometimes four) Estates – clergy, nobility and burgesses – ruled Scotland through parliament, general council and convention under the monarch until, in 1603, a Scottish king inherited the English throne and took off to Westminster as fast as his cortège could carry him. 'This I may say of Scotland, and may truly vaunt it,' he wrote from London. 'Here I sit and govern it with my pen. I write and it is done, and by a Clerk of the Council I govern Scotland now, which others could not do by the sword.' James VI had by then already survived 37 years in the snake-pit of Scottish politics. From the example of his mother, Mary, Queen of Scots, he had learned at an early age what could happen when the nobility turned hostile. He also recognised how easy it was to balance the one off against the other when he himself was out of reach, thus paving the way for the 1707 Act of Union and dissolution of the Scottish parliament. Thereafter, the United Kingdom that emerged was equally status-conscious, but there was nothing unusual about this. Every other country in Europe, and indeed Scandinavia, Asia and tribal Africa, had an aristocracy. It was the revolutions and wars of the eighteenth and nineteenth centuries which began the process that swept them away, but not entirely. To be a Graf or Freiher in Germany today, a Duc or Comte in France, a Marques in Spain, a Maharajah in India, a Sultan in Malaysia, or better still any of these in America, still means the best table in a restaurant, something that otherwise only money can buy.

In the United Kingdom, the passage of social change has been more measured, less volatile but equally brutal. At the same time, the old British aristocracy, both north and south of the border, replenished their fast diminishing wealth through marriage with the emergent dynasties of the

Industrial Revolution. Thus, a large proportion of Scotland's gentry today have coal, biscuits, beer, shipbuilding, jute and whisky to thank for their modest prosperity. And land, of course.

Land is the only thing that is permanent, and that is why there is so much resentment about so few people legally owning it, especially when there are those who believe that nobody should own it at all. That is another debate (Wightman 1999, and in this book), but it has to be said that to a very large extent it is the ownership of land, particularly in Scotland, that fuels much of the antipathy felt towards the aristocracy, on the assumption that they have a monopoly on it. But this is very unfair towards many of the surviving landowning gentry, since, in many cases, they have done a remarkably good job at land-husbandry. That is why they are still there when others are not. The problems only really began to emerge when land was sold off to incomers and financial consortia with little or no interest in the welfare of tenants. It is this situation, coupled with the exploitation of 'Minutes of Waiver' and 'Rights of Pre-emption', rarely enforced by traditional landlords, which led to the recent abolition of the feudal tenure entitling holders of a feudal superiority to acquire or exercise influence over land they did not own.

There is another aspect to this discussion that should also not be overlooked. North of the Highland line, and particularly in the north-west and Hebrides, where much of the resentment towards landowners originated, the land is poor yet has been crofted for generations. The scenery may be pretty to look at and jolly to walk over, but it yields little and the climate can be vicious for months on end. Hence, English plutocrats such as Lord Stafford, who became 1st Duke of Sutherland on his marriage to the heiress to the Sutherland estates, and even late-eighteenth-century tourists such as Dr Samuel Johnson and his sidekick James Boswell, were appalled at the primitive conditions endured by the northern crofting communities. Smallholding has little to offer beyond subsistence. Crofting has never been a viable way of life unless you hold down a second job or somebody, a rich man whose money originates elsewhere, and nowadays the taxpayer, subsidises you.

Much political sensitivity and grievance continues to exist due to the evictions inflicted upon crofters during the Highland Clearances of the nineteenth century, but it would be wrong to tar all of the Highland aristocracy with the same brush. It should also be remembered that there were a large number of landowners who refused to clear and who suffered financial ruin as a consequence. Thus, while Britain's empire was in the ascendant, it was not only the disenfranchised smallholders who were obliged to go abroad to earn a living, or travel south to seek advancement. Then, as now, Scots at Westminster made a pretty good showing, with the likes of Lord Aberdeen, William Ewart Gladstone, Lord Rosebery and Lord Balfour moving to the top and becoming Prime Minister. Others prospered in the new territories of Canada, Australia, New Zealand and Hong Kong, with, for example, the Jardine and the Matheson families returning to invest vast fortunes in their homeland.

A wealthy marriage was another option. In 1878, the fortunes of the Rosebery family were significantly enhanced through marriage into the great Rothschild dynasty. The American wife of the 8th Duke of Roxburghe brought significant landholdings in Manhattan into the family portfolio. In the last generation, the Countesses of Minto and Haddington were both heiresses to the Canadian Cooks Tour fortune.

## ENTERPRISING SCOTS, EMPIRE, ARMY AND CHURCH

The turn of the twentieth century saw self-made Scots tycoons, 'mighty magnates' such as Sir Thomas Lipton (tea), Lord Glentanar (cotton), Lord Inchcape (shipping) and Sir Charles Tennant MP (bleach) buy Scottish estates having made fortunes on the Clyde, in Aberdeen, or in Scotland's central belt (Checkland 1984). Having done so, it was invariably to London, the centre of government, that they were drawn, the latter fathering a veritable dynasty of politicians (1st Baron Glenconner and Baroness Elliot of Harwood) and aesthetes (Stephen Tennant, who although not unwell, spent most of the latter part of his life in bed, and the 3rd Baron Glenconner, who developed the Caribbean island of Mustique), including a prime minister's wife, the redoubtable Margot, Countess of Oxford and Asquith.

To add to this drain of talent, it was to English public schools that they turned for their children's education – Eton, Harrow, Rugby and Stowe. The ones who stayed behind were sent to Trinity College, Glenalmond; Loretto; Fettes, Rannoch and, more recently, Gordonstoun, but it is the perceived Anglicisation of Scottish schools that seems to arouse the most virulent response, while higher education at Oxford and Cambridge merely acerbated the situation.

The British Army too played its role in this social disenfranchisement by recruiting school-leavers for officer training at Sandhurst and Eaton Hall, near Chester, leading to short service or career commissions. At one stage there were ten Scottish regiments, largely relying on the territorial recruitment of both officers and men. For example, the Argyll and Sutherland Highlanders enlisted its conscripts in Argyllshire and Stirlingshire; the King's Own Scottish Borderers in the Scottish Borders; the Royal Scots in the Lothians, and the Black Watch in Perthshire. In addition, there was the Royal Scots Greys, Scotland's only cavalry regiment, which in 1978 amalgamated with the 3rd Carabiniers to form the Royal Scots Dragoon Guards.

The Army is by its nature hierarchical. That is how it works, and in two world wars the reputation of the Scottish Division was equal to none. Consider, for instance, the imagery of the 15th Lord Lovat leading his Lovat Scouts during the Normandy landings. Alas, for a generation whose distant memory is the Falklands War such heroism means very little. With government defence cuts and a general indifference towards military service, only six Scottish regiments remain. For the sons of regimental families there are not very many places left to go.

Finally, there is the church. Following the Reformation, many old families remained Catholic, but kept their heads down to avoid losing them. Those who did not fall in line with the Presbyterian faith embraced the Scots Episcopalian church or remained agnostic. Sons of the manse, in particular, have over the generations entered politics and been ennobled for their services. In the present generation, for example, Sir David Steel (Lord Steel of Aikwood) is the son of a former Moderator of the General Assembly, while Gordon Brown, and his acolytes Douglas and Wendy Alexander, grew up as sons and daughter of the manse.

In generations past the local laird's patronage, in tandem with the church congregation, was considered de rigueur in the appointment of a pastor, but the across-the-board nature of orthodoxy within the Scottish aristocracy speaks for itself. In the last century, the Haldanes of Gleneagles produced a Bishop of Argyll and the Isles. That towering Presbyterian, the late Lord Macleod of Fuinary, founder of the Iona Community, was a baronet in his own right; the Marquess of Ailsa's daughter is married to the Rev. Norman Drummond, minister of Kilmuir and Stencholl on Skye, and a chaplain to the Queen; the Earl of Mar's son Michael Erskine is also a Church of Scotland minister; and the baronet Sir Hew Hamilton-Dalrymple's son John has entered the priesthood in Fife.

The Church of Scotland recognises no superior, only God, and therefore the monarch, who is Head of the Church of England, either attends its annual General Assembly in person or appoints a Lord High Commissioner as her personal representative. This is an entirely ceremonial position allocated by her to a member of the Royal Family such as the Prince of Wales or the Princess Royal, or to a significant figure in Scottish life who adheres to the Protestant faith. As with Parliament, the monarchy knows it must remain detached. The lessons were learnt long ago when both Charles I and II failed to impose their views on the Kirk.

The establishment of the Scottish Parliament in 1999 offers new opportunities and challenges and brings us back to how our country is governed in future, and the role of the aristocracy, if it has one, in our public life. Perhaps the days of chivalry and lords and ladies are indeed long gone, but while we still have a monarchy, a Prime Minister and a First Minister, patronage remains.

The presence of a politically unaligned and financially incorruptible head of state protects us from the wilder excesses of party politics. However, the cronies who currently occupy the chairs of quangos and public offices are merely the twenty-first-century equivalents of the upstart barons who did so three centuries ago, only now to make themselves more plausible they have been obliged to respond to advertisements and fill in application forms. The most tangible difference is that, with more money to spend, everything becomes even more bureaucratic and more political, to the extent of having committees scrutinising the work of other committees. Whereas in the past only those with independent means could afford to take time off from their main occupations to front up an arts council, an enterprise board, or tourism initiative, some now draw sizeable salaries for doing so.

In theory, this is supposed to quash any conflict of interest, but instead has introduced a new breed of career opportunist. Gone are the days of the harmless old buffer being invited onto the board of Historic Scotland, Highlands and Islands Enterprise or Visit Scotland simply because his or her ancient title implied all those old-fashioned virtues: integrity, originality of mind, and respectability. For years, the landed gentry dominated rural councils, and not only because they had a vested interest in local affairs. They genuinely understood them. When independent voices ceased to be valued in politics, large numbers of them disappeared. Therefore, nobody can blame the present ranks of the Scottish aristocracy for no longer wanting to become involved.

One of the silliest comments made by Tory spokesman Dr Liam Fox MP prior to the last election was that the main problem with the Scottish Conservative Party lay in its being run by out-of-touch Scottish aristocrats. Equally it could be argued that the problem with the Scottish Conservative Party is that it is no longer run by Scottish aristocrats who showed greater care and sensitivities to Scots concerns than a generation of self-made men who presided over a golden era of Scottish Toryism in the 1940s and 1950s (Mitchell 1990).

Unfortunately, it is when certain of their number are at their most visible and inoffensive that they appear to incense some people the most, such as at an installation of a Knight of the Thistle at the High Kirk of St Giles in Edinburgh, or at ceremonial events at Holyrood Palace, when the dignitaries of the Royal Household are on parade. Accompanied by the Lord Lyon King of Arms, who presides over heraldic law and is appointed by the government, with his heralds and pursuivants in their gold tabards, such parades provide an opportunity to pay homage to great moments of the past. Inevitably, there are those who view such solemnity from a very different perspective.

It is the 'hereditary' bit that jars with modern public opinion. Why should these so-called establishment families be given the opportunity to show off in public? What right has any unelected person to fill a public role on the basis of heredity, even when the position carries with it little more than the obligation to dress up in a silly uniform? Such detractors would rewrite the past, if they only could. They certainly have no desire to celebrate it. They are, in fact, afraid of it, and it was just this type of neurotic paranoia that led to the official opening of the Scottish Parliament being such a disappointingly low-key affair, with only the Queen and the Hollywood actor Sir Sean Connery adding colour, style and occasion.

# THE QUEEN'S HOUSEHOLD

The centre point of the Scottish aristocracy remains, in these non-deferential times, the monarchy itself, symbolised in Scotland by Her Majesty's Household in Scotland, which each summer serves and looks after the Queen when she resides in Scotland. It is the last remnant of the old Scottish royal court, which disappeared with the Union of the Crowns of 1603. This is headed by the Lord High Constable, the Earl of Errol, the Hereditary Master of the Household, the Duke of Argyll, the Hereditary Bearer of the Royal Banner of Scotland (Lion Rampant), the Earl of Dundee and the Hereditary Bearer of the Scottish National Flag (Saltire), the Earl of Lauderdale. The Hereditary Carver, Sir Ralph Anstruther, recently died and no heir or successor so far has been appointed.

Special mention should also go to the Royal Company of Archers, who are in all but name the Queen's bodyguard in Scotland and one of the most prestigious and exclusive psuedo-military forces in the country. Their history is a rich and varied one, but they only gained the royal bodyguard responsibilities at the time of the infamous 'King's Jaunt' of George IV to Edinburgh in resplendent tartan in 1822. The night before the official opening of the Forth Road Bridge in 1967, I remember going to South Queensferry with a school friend to marvel at this wonder of engineering and stumbling upon the Royal Company of Archers rehearsing for the next day's ceremonial. 'Are those regular soldiers?' my friend asked a policeman. 'No, son, just rich gits,' he replied.

The parade was certainly colourful, with their green uniforms and feathered bonnets, but we could not help wondering what use their bows and arrows would have been under attack. This, we were told, was not what it was all about. All of them had previously served with Scottish regiments, or their fathers had, and it was a kind of old boys' club to provide the monarch with a ceremonial bodyguard on special occasions and, yes, to indulge in archery, which they practise regularly on Edinburgh's Meadows and have been doing so since 1707. Harmless enough – and seeing them lined up at a royal garden party, it is hard to imagine them as an elite taskforce whose sole purpose is to keep the working classes suitably downtrodden.

The Order of the Thistle, the personal gift of the Queen, is Scotland's greatest honour, the equivalent of England's Order of the Garter. Revived on and off over the centuries, it is restricted in number to 16 at any given time, and bestowed only upon Scots deemed to have given outstanding service to their nation. Accusations of upper-class cronyism are inevitable, of course, especially with the majority of the present complement drawn from Scotland's great titled families. Regardless, it is hard to belittle the years of selfless public service rendered by these individuals, even if they have just been dutifully following in their ancestor's footsteps. Remember, though, that this is not some meaningless trophy. It is an award for a lifetime of unselfish achievement, and extended to those who are in the autumn of their years. Thus, you have the Duke of

Buccleuch, Chancellor of the Order, who, with his 270,000 acres, is the largest individual landowner in the UK (apart from the Queen); his land comprises 167,200 acres in Dumfriesshire, 49,200 in Roxburghshire, 37,500 in Selkirk and 17,000 in England (Cahill 2001: 282). Before inheriting the dukedom he had a distinguished political career as a Tory MP from 1960 to 1973 and, following a serious accident, has worked with disabled people. The others are the Earl of Elgin, former president of the Boys Brigade and one of the most charismatic unofficial ambassadors Scotland has ever known; the Earl of Wemyss, president emeritus of the National Trust for Scotland, Lord Clerk Register of Scotland and Keeper of the Signet; the Earl of Airlie, who is the Queen's Lord Chamberlain; Sir Donald Cameron of Locheil, a former president of the Royal Highland and Agricultural Society of Scotland; Lord Macfarlane of Bearsden, honorary life president of United Distillers, who has earned his spurs through work with the fine arts and countless charitable causes; Lady Marion Fraser, former chair of the board of Christian Aid; Viscount Younger of Leckie, a former Secretary of State for Scotland and chairman of the Royal Bank of Scotland; Lord Thomson of Monifieth, former chairman of the Independent Broadcasting Authority and in a previous life, a Labour MP and European Commissioner; Sir Iain Tennant, former chairman of Seagram Distillers, Scotland; the Earl of Crawford, a former minister of state for Foreign and Commonwealth Affairs; Viscount Arbuthnott, former chairman of the Federation of Agricultural Co-operatives and of the Advisory Committee for Scotland of the Nature Conservancy Council; and Lord Mackay of Clashfern, who was Lord High Chancellor of Great Britain from 1987 until 1997.

So how can such a roll of honour fit into the picture of a modern Scotland struggling to assert itself as a dynamic, progressive nation, first within Europe, and second, within a world community? Through choice or otherwise, today's nobility may well find itself sidelined, but not altogether – and others will rise to take their place. Whatever happens in the future, especially in the wider European context, the old aristocracy of Scotland is unlikely to disappear so long as there is a misty-eyed romantic who knows enough about our history to shed tears over Flodden.

In the meantime, what the people of Scotland need to decide is how they should reward their modern men and women of achievement in the century ahead. Has anybody noticed the number of self-important individuals who nowadays use initials after their names and insist upon being called 'Doctor' or 'Professor' when their medical and academic credentials are, not to put too fine a point upon it, highly debatable? Titles and designations, whatever they may be, still count for something, especially when they are your own.

A distinguished Scot, politically influential industrialist, chairman of public corporations, self-made millionaire, charity benefactor and friend of politicians across the political spectrum recently confessed to me that his remaining ambition was not to sit in the Scottish Parliament, but to become a member of the Scottish House of Lairds. There was a twinkle in his eye, but it was obvious that he was being semi-serious. Despite his wealth and success, he still felt he deserved a public accolade for his lifetime's achievement. Perhaps times have not changed so very much after all.

# 25

# THE LANDED GENTRY

## Andy Wightman

Landed power has been central to state power since the birth of the Scottish nation. Feudalism – a system of political governance based on territorial control – was introduced by early Scottish monarchs as a means of cementing their authority. Over the centuries that followed, this system evolved into a system of land tenure which conferred inordinate power on the landed classes. In 1814, Sir John Sinclair, author of the *First Statistical Account of Scotland*, claimed that 'In no country in Europe are the rights of proprietors so well defined and so carefully protected' (Callander 1986: 5).

Landed hegemony would thus appear to be central to any analysis of power relations in Scotland. In the year 2002, however, perhaps for the first time, such a certainty can no longer be automatically assumed. David Cannadine, in *The Decline and Fall of the British Aristocracy*, argues that: 'The traditional landed class has ceased to exist as the unchallenged and supreme elite in which wealth, status, and power are highly correlated, and are underpinned by territorial pre-eminence.' He continues: 'The place that the remaining patricians occupy in the Britain of the 1990s is overwhelmingly less important than that of their forebears a century ago. Economically speaking they no longer own the majority of the land, they do not themselves constitute the wealthy elite and even the very richest of them are a minority amongst the contemporary super-rich' (Cannadine 1990: 692).

## NEW AND OLD ELITES

Whilst there has been an undeniable trend of decline in the role of the traditional landowning class, the institution of landownership and the power and influence it confers have survived remarkably intact. New money and new networks of power and influence have taken over where the older order has decayed. Collectively, the 30 richest Scottish landowners domiciled in the UK are worth £17.5 billion. Among this number features only two members of the Scottish aristocracy – the Marquis of Bute and the Earl of Wemyss. The Whitbreads, Bulmers, Vesteys and Flemings, together with the Al Fayeds, Schwarzenbachs, van Vlissingens and Schroders, represent the new Scottish landed class.

Despite changes in the personalities, Scottish landowners remain a wealthy and influential elite. The central reason for this is that, despite the steady attrition of landed power, the transformation has been a largely peaceful one in which the landed classes have been able to adapt and survive the hostile forces which from time to time, have blown their way. Such has been their success, that what characterises Scottish landownership at the dawn of the twenty-first century remains a system of land law and division of land that has been consigned to the museums of rural life in the rest of Western Europe.

Thus, whilst the aristocracy as the traditional focus of landed power may have waned, the institution of landed power has endured, a fact best illustrated perhaps by some simple statistics.

**Table 1: Percentage of privately owned rural land owned by number of owners**

| Per cent | 1872 | 2001 |
|---|---|---|
| 10 of the privately owned rural land is owned by | 3 | 14 |
| 20 | 21 | 43 |
| 30 | 34 | 95 |
| 40 | 63 | 183 |
| 50 | 118 | 343 |
| 60 | 196 | 691 |

*Source: Wightman 1996; 2002*

What is significant about these figures is not that the distribution of land has expanded in the past 130 years but that it has changed so little. In comparison with the rest of Europe where the transformation has been by orders of magnitude, the pattern of landownership in Scotland has barely changed. Whilst a few territorial grandees have lost most of their land, the houses of Buccleuch, Argyll, Seafield, Cowdray, Roxburghe, Cawdor, Lothian, Dalhousie and Stair still control about 13 per cent of Scotland. For all that landed power has lost much of what it once took for granted, Scotland's territory is still owned by a tiny fraction of the population and the impact that such a concentrated pattern of power can have at a local and regional level remains significant.

This significance is amplified by the close inter-personal relationships that persist among the landed classes, including the Queen herself. For example, the Queen is related to the Earl of Airlie through his brother, Sir Angus Ogilvy, who is married to Princess Alexandra of Kent. The Countess of Airlie is also a Lady to the Bedchamber of the Queen. The Earl of Airlie was chairman of Schroders, the merchant bank, from 1977 to 1984, whilst Bruno Schroder himself owns Dunlossit Estate on Islay next door to Lord Margadale. Another relative of the Queen, James Hamilton, the 5th Duke of Abercorn, is married to Alexandra Anastasia, whose niece is married to the Duke of Westminster. The Duke's sister, Lady Jane Grosvenor, was the first wife of the Duke of Roxburghe (her marriage to Roxburghe made her the daughter of a duke, the sister of a duke, the wife of a duke and finally the mother of a future duke!). Meanwhile, the Queen's aunt, the Duchess of Gloucester, is the third daughter of the 7th Duke of Buccleuch, whose widow is the daughter of the 13th Earl of Home. The current Duke of Buccleuch's sister is the Duchess of Northumberland, whose daughter was the first wife of the Duke of Sutherland. The Duke of Buccleuch's son and heir is Richard Walter John Montague Douglas Scott, the Earl of Dalkeith. Richard is married to Lady Elizabeth Kerr, the youngest daughter of the 12th Marquess of Lothian. Lady Elizabeth's sister, Lady Cecil Kerr, is married to Donald Cameron of Locheil (younger). The hereditary master of the Queen's household in Scotland is Ian Campbell, the 12th Duke of Argyll, who is married to the daughter of Sir Ivar Colquhoun of Luss, whose nephew is Sir Michael Wigan. Sir Ivar's sister is the widow of the 8th Earl of Arran. The great-grandson of the 4th Earl of Arran's brother married the daughter of the 4th Earl of Cawdor – which brings us back to the Duke of Roxburghe, who is one of the trustees of the Earl Cawdor's estate (Wightman 1999: 31). None of this was lost on MSPs when, in a parliamentary debate in March 2002, George Lyon MSP claimed that:

> The Land Reform (Scotland) Bill is the first step in shifting the balance of power from the rich and powerful absentee landlords to the ordinary people of rural Scotland. We should not be in any doubt that that is the nub of the debate. Will members support the ordinary people of Scotland or the absentee landlords?

Alasdair Morrison MSP did not spare the rhetoric either:

> For far too long, community confidence and development have stagnated because a few privileged landowners have so decreed. No longer can they look to the House of Lords to take care of their interests and strangle any legislative process or effort that could threaten their position. (Scottish Parliament 2002a)

Whilst the measures being debated were not particularly radical, the language deployed conformed to the traditional stereotypes that one might expect from parties across the political spectrum. Only this time it was for real. Under debate was a bill that begins to significantly alter the balance of power over land. This could never have happened at Westminster where a lack of parliamentary time and a traditionally hostile House of Lords has frustrated any attempts to reform landownership.

As a result, land has never been truly democratised and the discourse on land has been dominated by landowners, their agents, lawyers and accountants, and members of the House of Lords. The institution of landownership, as has been argued, has provided an extraordinary bastion of power and privilege which has deterred any serious attempt at dismantling. The landed interest might appear to be modest in number but it remains formidable in its influence. As the late Margaret MacPherson observed, 'it would be as easy to pare the claws of a tiger running loose in the jungle as control the laird with his factor, accountants, lawyers, friends in the Scottish Landowners' Federation and the House of Lords' (MacPherson 1985).

## LANDOWNERS WITH A CAPITAL 'L' AND A SMALL 'L'

In understanding the politics of landownership in Scotland it is important to distinguish between landowners with a small 'l' and Landowners with a capital 'L'. There are hundreds of thousands of landowners in Scotland, namely the vast majority of the middle classes. Over 63 per cent of houses in Scotland are owner-occupied and so anyone who owns land in Scotland, whether it be a house, flat, smallholding or mansion of vast estate, is a landowner (small 'l').

The Thatcher government accelerated this trend with ambitions to create a property-owning democracy. Crucially, however, the property-owning democracy was not to apply in the countryside. Here Landowners with a capital 'L' hold sway. Their energies have been directed since time immemorial at preventing others sharing the cake. Their representative body, the Scottish Landowners' Federation, likes to portray itself as being representative of landowners (small 'l'). At the Justice Committee of the Scottish Parliament, the SLF recently claimed that 'we represent owners of one to several thousand acres of land' (Scottish Parliament 2002b).

They do not. Full membership of the SLF, with voting rights is open only to individuals who own ten acres of land or more. Due to the lack on any national inventory of landownership in Scotland, we do not know how many people this represents but it is likely to be in the region of 20,000 or so. The SLF currently has around 3,500 full members owning between them around 40 per cent of Scotland. Clearly, they have scope to expand their membership; but were they to reduce the acreage threshold and provide voting rights to all those who own land and property in Scotland, they would face the prospect of being dominated by owners of more modest parcels of land. This would not be acceptable because the rationale of the SLF is to protect the interests of its members. In addition to the restricted membership, the SLF applies a scaled fee system whereby the largest landowners pay more dues than the smaller ones thus conferring greater political clout on the largest (Scottish Landowners' Federation 2002). But the strength of landowning as an institution is also its greatest weakness – lack of numbers. Paradoxically, one powerful argument for land reform is that it can dramatically increase the number of landowners (and thus potentially boost the membership of bodies such as the SLF).

Perhaps in recognition of this, new organisations have emerged which suggest that, for the largest landowners, the SLF is no longer the most effective means of representation. The very largest landowners in the UK recently formed themselves into an organisation called Landowners' Group (no definite article in the name). Landowners' Group represents 22 major private landowners in the UK, a third of whom own land in Scotland totalling over half a million acres. Even more recently, their interests in Scotland appear to have been taken over by the Scottish Estates Business Group, chaired by the factor of Seafield Estates, Alexander Lewis (and whose secretary is Richard Williamson of Buccleuch Estates).

Landowners (capital 'L') obviously still feel the need to discriminate between themselves and landowners (small 'l') and, in addition, to discriminate within themselves as between the very largest and the rest. All of which suggests that landowners are struggling with the emerging agenda on land reform because for centuries their power and influence has been channelled through elite social and political structures which have permitted them to continue with a worldview increasingly divorced from that of the ordinary citizen. It is no coincidence that with the establishment of the Scottish Parliament they have been forced to adopt the same means of influencing public debate as the rest of society, namely, putting their case openly and in public.

This has not always been comfortable for landowners for reasons already alluded to. It is even less comfortable for those landowners who have traditionally been the focus for particular enmity – the absentees. Whilst resident landowners are increasingly gaining the skills to take an active part in public debate in defence of their interests, those based in London and elsewhere are becoming increasingly restless precisely because their interests were well served by their proximity to Westminster and the House of Lords. Now they feel isolated and misunderstood. Unfamiliar and ill at ease with devolution, their reactions are sometimes hyperbolic. Max Hasting writing in *The Field*, for example, claimed that:

> The delusion is widely held in Scotland . . . that the Highlands are a paradise in a state of natural grace, which might more properly be held in public ownership. The Scots must be told again and again until they start to believe it, that their hills are in reality intensively and expensively managed by private landowners, almost all of whom incur huge financial

cost in doing so, which would have to be made good from the public
purse if they were not there. (Hastings 1995)

Such sentiments are not untypical. Much of the response of the landed
establishment to the prospect of land reform can be characterised as complacent,
naive, unsophisticated, reactionary, amateurish and confused. Lacking any grasp
of the issue, why it has sprung to prominence, or how to respond to it, huddles
of inarticulate, bemused lairds have been gathering together in meetings to try
and make sense of a political landscape changed out of all recognition to the
cosy, well-ordered and predictable world they knew before. The more
intelligent, progressive and smart landowners and agents, however, are being
rather more circumspect in their approach, realising perhaps that keeping quiet
and keeping their heads down is a strategy which has served them well in the
past. The rhetorical zeal for land reform, it is assumed, will fizzle out once the
Parliament encounters the formidable difficulties associated with reform.

But land reform is now a mainstream political project which, despite the
relative modesty of current proposals, will not disappear. Whatever legislative
programme is embarked upon by the Parliament, there will be a growing level
of scrutiny, analysis and debate over time which will deepen and broaden
people's understanding of the real nature of the land problem. Landed interests
are faced, therefore, with a choice: they can go with the flow or they can resist.
Never before has the importance of making the right choice been so acute.

A prominent example of how this choice might need to be made lies in the
brief mention of a topic in recent parliamentary discussions which will, if
followed through, pose a fundamental challenge to centuries of landed
hegemony, namely, succession law. Throughout most of Europe, the laws
governing how land is inherited are very different from those pertaining in
Scotland and provide legal rights for children to inherit land. As a consequence,
the pattern of landownership in most European countries is pluralistic. In
Scotland, by contrast, children enjoy no such rights despite major reforms under
the Succession (Scotland) Act of 1964. The cultural practice whereby the eldest
son inherits the land continues all too frequently at the expense of women in
general and other children in particular. Succession law has thus been probably
the most important non-feudal element of property law in perpetuating the
concentrated pattern of private landownership in Scotland.

The reform of succession law also bears on fundamental questions relating to
aristocratic titles and, ultimately, to the monarchy. Titles tied to land which can
only pass through a male heir would no longer have the same status. Giving
women equal rights under the law will also ultimately result in the abolition of
primogeniture in monarchical succession (whereby Prince Andrew's daughters
Beatrice and Eugenie precede Princess Anne in line of succession for no better
reason than that they are daughters of a male heir). On 20 March 2002, in the
Stage One debate on the Land Reform Bill, a number of MSPs made direct

reference to inheritance. Were reforms to be enacted giving legal rights to spouses and children, the persistent pattern of large-scale landownership would slowly be eroded.

How the landed classes react to such a move will reveal much of the philosophy and politics which governs their approach to public affairs. Currently, they make little distinction between a worldview constructed out of the impacts reforms might have on their vested interests as landowners and a worldview shaped by what is best for a system of property law in a democracy.

The history of landed power in Scotland is a history of a class whose authority and hegemony has never been effectively challenged, whose possession of disproportionate property holdings has never been broken and whose influence on debates on landownership and use has been conspicuous by its formidable extent and discrete application. This careful and assiduous process of consolidation and entrenchment now faces its sternest test. Democratic scrutiny is exposing the validity or otherwise of traditional modes of thought and argument. New laws will, whatever their shortcomings, inevitably contribute to an ongoing process of change. The next time an anatomy of Scotland comes to be written, will there be any cause for an anatomy of the landed class? Or will the long association between land and power have eventually been broken?

# 26

# THE ROLE OF RELIGION AND THE CHURCHES

*Graham Walker*

In 1999, the new Scottish Parliament took up temporary residence in a Presbyterian building. Even within the narrow confines of the history of devolution in the United Kingdom, there was a precedent for this. In 1921, the then newly established Parliament of Northern Ireland met in the Presbyterian Theological College in Belfast, and continued to sit there until 1932. The religious symbolism was obvious and highly fitting: Northern Ireland's first devolution experiment was characterised by a political culture centred on religious identification. Moreover, sectarianism has left a political legacy which the Province's current legislators require to address in the context of the different devolved structures put in place by the Belfast Agreement of 1998.

The symbolism of the Church of Scotland's General Assembly building being home to the Scottish Parliament is also not inappropriate. The Church's contribution to post-war campaigns for the restoration of a Parliament, within the context of the UK, was substantial, and the proceedings of the General Assembly itself were widely regarded as a kind of surrogate, particularly in view of the increasingly political nature of some submissions and debates through the 1980s and 1990s. Although an agnostic, the late Donald Dewar, First Minister from the Parliament's inception until his death in October 2000, once described himself as a 'conspicuously cultural Presbyterian', and took a scholarly interest in the lives of Scottish divines such as Thomas Chalmers.

Furthermore, and notwithstanding the unique intensity of the Northern Ireland conflict in the context of these islands, any assessment of the role of religion in the development of Scottish politics and society in the age of devolution must involve wrestling with sectarian controversies. These are not as played-out as many commentators assumed until recently, and are the product of Irish influences in the shaping of modern Scotland.

# THE SECULARISATION OF SCOTLAND

As representatives of the country's churches and faiths are well aware, the cultural context of contemporary Scotland is resolutely secular. Where once a leadership role for the churches in terms of moral and social guidance was guaranteed (Brown 1997), the present reality is one of struggle to appear relevant to the mass of the country's unchurched population. The national Kirk, the Church of Scotland, has seen its membership cut in half in the last 40 years, although it should not be forgotten that it could muster some 1.3 million members in 1961. Similarly, the Roman Catholic Church, the second-largest denomination, has suffered plummeting Mass attendance figures and a collapse of recruitment to the priesthood. Press commentary on the 'dying flames' of Protestantism, and speculation about the further withering of Catholicism in the wake of the death in 2001 of the populist figure of Cardinal Thomas Winning, have reinforced the impression of inexorable institutional decline and the final triumph of secular values and behavioural norms. Clearly, the new devolutionary order poses a challenge to organised religion to stake its claim to be heard; it may also represent the last chance for the churches in their present form to refashion their role in society and review their message.

The difficulties involved should not be underestimated. For the Church of Scotland, there is the unmarketability of Calvinism as a theological doctrine, besides the unfashionability of theological dispute in general. At the advent of the Scottish Parliament, a Kirk commentator wrote in his introduction to a volume of essays on Scottish Presbyterianism: 'The problem in Scotland is that the mood for political change inevitably creates a crisis of identity and that at this critical moment in Scottish history the single most important element in the country's religious identity will not only be under-emphasised but misunderstood, disparaged, and caricatured' (Kernohan 1999: 9).

What was being signalled here was the facile use of the 'dour' and 'joyless' Calvinist stereotype in Scottish culture, and the sense in which the momentous influence of Presbyterianism in Scotland's historical development has been so widely reduced to crude notions of the Knoxian 'bogeyman'. And it would be largely true to say that the dominant impression of Presbyterianism in contemporary Scotland is derived from comedian Rikki Fulton's skit on the stereotypical kirk minister, 'the Reverend I.M. Jolly'. In some ways, the Church of Scotland has suffered a similar fate to the Roman Catholic Church in Ireland during the last decade: a once magisterial presence in society has been satirised into cultural retreat on account of its authoritarian past. Media and general public interest in Presbyterian matters in recent years has tended to focus on the pronouncements, activities and schisms of the small fundamentalist churches concentrated in the western Highlands and Islands. This has tended to result, simultaneously, in the reduction of the Presbyterian tradition to 'Wee Free' dogmatism, and the expression of cosmopolitan secular condescension towards the Highland communities.

There have been recent scholarly re-evaluations of Calvinism's intellectual legacy in Scotland (Beveridge and Turnbull 1989; 1997), however, which have transcended the caricature so fondly indulged by many literary, artistic and radical Nationalist figures in twentieth-century Scotland, most notably Hugh MacDiarmid and Tom Nairn. As Will Storrar, a notable Presbyterian thinker, has observed, such reassessments, albeit emanating from secular quarters, have underscored the key role played by Calvinist theology in 'Scotland's intellectual internationalism' (Storrar 1999). Storrar himself has detected a 'civic' Calvinist influence in the recent mobilisation of Scottish society in support of self-government, and argues the case for extending this to the creation of a democratic culture of active citizenship in civil society as the proper context for the new Scottish Parliament. Certainly, the religious dimension to the distinctive Scottish notion of sovereignty, which played such a part in the construction of the case for a Scottish Parliament, and which found such eloquent expression through the Constitutional Convention of the late 1980s and early 1990s, are indications of life beyond the popular stereotype. Nevertheless, as another leading Church of Scotland commentator has argued, the Church will only be likely to make an impact on the new Parliament if its submissions are of high quality and if it is properly led. It will not be enough to depend on its status as the 'national' church, which in any case is a highly dubious proposition in the context of a secularised society in which Presbyterianism is just one of several minority faiths (McKay 1999).

The question of leadership is indeed crucial. The Church of Scotland is disadvantaged by its otherwise admirable tradition of internal democracy. Moderators change every year, and the 'recognition factor' has thus proved more of a problem, in a visual media age, than for the Roman Catholic Church or even the small Episcopal Church. Both Cardinal Winning and the Episcopal bishop Richard Holloway made a deeper impact on recent public and political controversies than Church of Scotland ministers. Moreover, in the case of Cardinal Winning, there was also an outspokenness and a taste for dispute which was almost of Presbyterian vintage, and many ordinary Church of Scotland members and laypersons seem to feel that the Kirk has lost its way and is failing to pronounce clearly on the matters of the day (Wright 1999). Such criticism is often too glib, and does not weigh sufficiently the possible damage resulting from excessive judgementalism: Cardinal Winning's outbursts in the debate on the teaching of homosexuality in schools may have, in the long run, weakened the faith of many Catholics, and discredited the Church in the estimation of outsiders. Nevertheless, the impression persists of a Kirk which is too complacent about a range of social and moral issues, and too politically artless and timid.

# THE SECTARIAN DIVIDE AND SCOTTISH SOCIETY

The minefield of sectarianism has certainly been one area the Church of Scotland has recently tiptoed around, notwithstanding the readiness of the Church's magazine, *Life and Work*, to open its pages to leading Orangemen and Catholic controversialists. The issue is certainly a complex one, not always easily defined, and in the current climate possibly even distinguishable from religion itself. As one scholar has indeed asked: 'What precisely does "religion" contribute to "religious identity"?' (Brown 2000: 281). The answers to that may be as many as the people involved, yet the readiness of large numbers to proclaim a 'religious identity' and to act in a tribal fashion on the basis of it is reason enough for the churches to engage with the debate, and in so doing evaluate their own role in the evolution of the problem.

Where once the issue of sectarian division was largely left undiscussed, the context of devolved government appears to have brought many matters into clearer political focus. For many years the religious tensions epitomised by the 'Old Firm' football rivalry between Rangers and Celtic were obscured by the wider context of British politics in which the concerns of those parties aspiring to govern could not afford to be anchored in local phenomena. There had nonetheless been warnings: the Monklands Council affair of the early 1990s involved Protestant allegations of discrimination by Catholic councillors, and a sectarian taint to the by-election campaign in the area in 1994. Such developments suggested that the political significance of sectarianism had not been exhausted, at least not in west-central Scotland. Neither should it be forgotten that evidence of a strong correlation between religion and voting behaviour in Scotland until the mid-1960s was plentiful (Budge and Unwin 1966: 60–65, 68–71), and that the SNP's disproportionately Protestant vote in the early 1970s was not unconnected to Catholic fears of a Scottish Parliament becoming another Stormont.

The Labour Party's capacity to draw substantial support in Scotland from both Protestant and Catholic working classes arguably disguised the extent to which sectarian attitudes and dispositions persisted, co-existed, and in some ways even reinforced class-consciousness, providing a vital collectivist sense of belonging in often economically deprived and socially harsh circumstances. The success of 'machine politics' in areas like Lanarkshire contributed to a context in which sectarianism, to an outsider, seemed ritualised and compartmentalised, manifesting itself in the colourful set-pieces of Old Firm games and Orange Order, Ancient Order of Hibernians, and Republican parades. All Scottish political parties, from the 1960s onwards, shied away from confronting issues which might exacerbate sectarian tensions and return Scotland to more religiously-influenced habits. Thus, the question of Northern Ireland, from the outbreak of the 'troubles' in 1969, was kept at a distance for fear of similar antagonisms engulfing Scotland. Scottish society remained, relative to Ulster, stable and calm, but at the cost of the suppression of debate about religious divisions and how to tackle them. Also missing was a much-needed distinctive contribution to the ongoing problems in Northern Ireland and the proper context for their resolution. Throughout the period between the outbreak of the Northern Ireland troubles and the advent of devolution in Scotland, sporadic bursts of violence at Old Firm matches and the strength of the 12 July Orange demonstrations in Scotland in particular served as awkward reminders that Scotland possessed a profoundly Irish popular cultural make-up, and that Protestant–Catholic relations would not simply be secularised into insignificance.

## BREAKING TABOOS

In the space of several months in 1999 the conventions of the past in which the subject was hushed up were decisively broken. There were bouts of public soul-searching and media analysis occasioned by the Donald Findlay affair, and the intervention of Scottish Catholic composer James MacMillan. The latter's view, that anti-Catholic bigotry was 'endemic' in Scottish society, provoked a substantial response, both supportive and critical (Devine 2000). Since then there has been the well-publicised 'Nil by Mouth' campaign against the use of sectarian language and abuse, and the proposal by Liberal Democrat Scottish Parliament member Donald Gorrie to make sectarianism a criminal offence. Gorrie's intervention, as well as the affair of the Irish Famine Memorial at Carfin, which caused serious damage to diplomatic relations with the Republic of Ireland (*Sunday Herald*, 11 February 2001), highlighted what was referred to as 'the cosy and incestuous' relationship between the Scottish Labour Party and the Catholic Church, and the party's links to the Ancient Order of Hibernians (AOH) (*Scotland on Sunday*, 11 March 2001). It was unusual for the latter organisation to be given prominence; in contrast to the Orange Order, whose numbers are much greater, the AOH has long been discounted as a force in Scottish society. However, it may be the case that its links with the Labour Party in certain regions of Scotland have been of similar significance to the influence exerted by the Orange Order on the Conservatives (or 'the Unionists') in the late-nineteenth and first half of the twentieth centuries, limited as that influence in general was (McFarland 1991; Walker and Officer 1998). The Orange Institution has, in effect, been politically marginalised since then.

These recent developments and examples of more open discussion of religious divisions have reflected the extent to which questions of identity politics have become more prominent in Scottish discourse. There has, in particular, been growing comment and scholarly deliberation on the topic of Catholic identity and its Irish dimensions in contemporary Scotland (Boyle and Lynch 1998). Against the background of constitutional changes in the UK and the peace process in Northern Ireland, it is perhaps not so surprising that this is so; new possibilities appear to be opening up for a refashioning and restructuring of relationships within these islands, perhaps especially those between Scotland and both parts of Ireland (Devine and McMillan 1999: Dickson 2001). In addition, there is the question of other ethnic minorities and identities in Scotland, and the challenge to a new Scotland to respond justly to the politics of identity and of difference beyond those of Protestants and Catholics.

As such, concepts such as 'sectarianism' will require more rigorous definition and careful use. As is the case with racism, of which many would contend sectarianism is a form, political correctness sets dubious boundaries to discussion. Sectarianism, like racism, is always what 'other people do'. Easy targets, such as crudely offensive songs, are held up as evidence; more difficult issues, such as the Catholic Church's inflexible position on mixed marriages for the greater part of the twentieth century, are sidestepped. Indeed, following James MacMillan's intervention in 1999, anyone questioning the broader benefits for society of state-subsidised Catholic schools was liable to be charged with sectarianism. The campaigns by 'Nil by Mouth' and Donald Gorrie, while laudably motivated, seem to assume that sectarianism is a concept whose meaning is obvious and generally agreed, and that its perpetrators can be somehow distinguished from their surrounding communities and wider cultural and environmental influences. Should we, moreover, distinguish 'sectarianism' from 'tribalism'? Arguably, in contemporary Scotland, perceptions of the latter breed the former.

Scottish political and religious leaders, and opinion-formers of all kinds, must also ask themselves how far traditional understandings of sectarian tensions fit them to appreciate the greater range of identities – some religion-based – which look likely to make a political impact in the future. For instance, it might be said that a fixation on the Protestant–Catholic factor in relation to education inhibits the kind of dialogue required in today's multi-cultural and multi-faith society. Remarks such as that of the late Cardinal Winning that Catholicism was set to become Scotland's sole faith sometime this century (*The Scotsman*, 16 January 1999), are also revealing of old bitternesses which pay little heed to changing social and cultural patterns. As Will Storrar complained of James MacMillan, a pluralist goal is still obstructed by recourse to the 'binary madness of the green and the orange' (*Sunday Herald*, 26 December 1999). In short, it will be necessary to open up the category of 'sectarianism' and not restrict it, as arguably James MacMillan and certain scholars have done (MacMillan 2000), to one meaning, namely, perceived anti-Catholic prejudice.

The Carfin affair also seemed to suggest that the Protestant dimension to the Irish story in Scotland requires more attention, and that Protestantism in Scotland has lost the will or the capacity to make itself heard at such moments beyond the extremist fringe. It may be the case that the Kirk is all too aware of the dark currents running through its own past in relation to the anti-Irish

Catholic interventions of the inter-war years, the years when, in Storrar's words, it was a 'bully pulpit for an ethnic Protestant Unionism' (Storrar 1999: 124). Such awareness may have led to inhibitions about entering such controversies today. However, there are those for whom this sends out a message of abandonment. One factor driving the continuing anti-Catholic sectarianism still to be found in Scotland might be the embittered mentality of a people who feel alienated by the mainstream of their own cultural background and tradition. Indeed, the recent observations by Rev. Ian Meredith, Chaplin of the Orange Order in Scotland, attest to a picture of working-class church members treated disdainfully by a middle-class church establishment (*The Herald*, 30 September 1998). Among the Protestant working class such alienation has been compounded by perceptions of political favouritism towards the Catholic community by the Labour Party for many years, and by the SNP more recently in their attempts to make inroads into what remains a formidable 'block vote'. Certain Protestant perceptions of the relative cohesiveness of the Catholic community fuel suspiciousness and an edginess manifest in such matters as educational controversy. Besides the heterogeneity of Protestant Scotland, politically and, to an extent, religiously, the Catholic community still appears much more 'tribal'. Certainly, it is generally insufficiently appreciated how defensive, rather than triumphalist, the mindset of populist Protestantism is in contemporary Scotland, although, as one scholar has suggested, there is still much 'cheap mileage' left in denouncing a Protestant sectarianism which has 'shot its political bolt' (Edwards 2001: 12).

In sum, religious institutions and leaders in today's Scotland face many challenges. They operate in a largely secular environment which is sensitive to what is often viewed as the 'intrusion' of religion into political life, yet there is also a weight of expectation on churches to take up positions on the issues of the day, and prove they have a contribution to make to civic society in the widest sense. They are obliged to adapt to the media and information age while preserving a sense of venerable continuity and status. In the case of the Protestant and Catholic churches, they are under severe moral pressure to help combat the sectarianism which is a feature of certain parts of the country, while simultaneously responding to the disaffections felt by many in their ranks and the needs of many for a sense of belonging in an era of 'identity politics'. As the new devolved Scotland ponders questions of its changing identity as a nation, the churches face the task of redefining theirs in ways which will prove compatible with a highly diverse and unpredictable society.

# 27

# Countryside Alliances: Rural Scotland

## Torcuil Crichton

By definition, historians read the past better than they predict the future. In *Age Of Extremes*, Eric Hobsbawm claimed that what would distinguish the twentieth century from any other would be that by its end there would be more people living in urban areas than in the countryside. We would, he wrote, witness the death of the peasantry in our lifetimes, fewer people would work in agriculture and a human connection with the soil, a bond across centuries, would be broken (Hobsbawm 1994).

In many ways, Hobsbawm was right. Immigrants to most of the great cities in the Western world – whether they be Latinos heading north to Los Angeles or Highland students drinking in Glasgow's Park Bar – are likely to have some memory, if not actual experience, of agrarian life – but those who follow the human tide to the metropolis in a decade's time will not. The people they leave behind Hobsbawm would see as the last vestige of peasant society. In Scotland, the majority of rural-dwellers are unlikely to milk a cow, plough a field, or cast a net for fish for a living.

Yet, in defiance of Hobsbawm, more people live in rural Scotland at the beginning of the twenty-first century than did at the end of the last one. The demographics and nature of Scotland's rural areas are changing dramatically, a transformation best caught in a sarcastic passage in an island-hopping guidebook published a few years ago. Despairing that every bed-and-breakfast establishment on the Isle of Skye appeared to be run by people with southern accents (they are not), the author suggested that any tourist wishing to encounter a native islander should head to their natural habitat – the Co-op supermarket on the outskirts of Portree. It may be a truism, but rural-dwellers are more likely to contemplate a 40-mile round trip to a supermarket than they are to consider planting a potato.

# THE REVIVAL OF RURAL SCOTLAND

The population of rural Scotland increased by 35,000 between 1991 and 1995 – what has been called 'counterstream migration' (Jedrej and Nuttall 1995: 112). Every subsequent study suggests that the high quality of life in rural areas, strong communities and Scotland's natural heritage will continue to attract migrants from urban Scotland and further afield. The census data also shows that out-migration, while continuing to be a feature of demographic change, is less than the overall gain, although there are still pockets of population loss connected with lack of work and economic decline, particularly in the Western Isles, parts of the Shetland Islands, Kintyre and Cumnock and Doon Valley, where the figures for depopulation and an ageing population are alarming. Overall, the more remote areas are projected to see a decline in population, whereas rural communities in the urban hinterland, such as Stirling, are projected to see an increase.

If the patterns of migration continue as projected, by 2006 the population of rural Scotland is expected to increase to 1,558,000 people, a rise of over 6 per cent in ten years. The 1991 census data showed that young people in the 16–29 age group formed 36 per cent of those moving to rural areas, and that only 7 per cent of migrants in the areas were over 65. Migrants are usually younger, highly educated and economically active, which may suggest a potential for prosperity that runs counter to the perception of a low-wage, declining economy, with its familiar story of young people leaving behind an elderly and dependant population – even this is not borne out by the statistics. In 1998, 20 per cent of the Scottish population were aged over 60 compared to 21 per cent in rural Scotland. This similarity also applies to other age groups.

Such changes, both demographic and economic, make 'rural Scotland' difficult to define. Does it mean simply the countryside, the absence of pavements and streetlights, now common and much-resented features of many villages? Is it defined by distance from urban centres, by scarcity of population or by the kind of work people are engaged in? Does the spread of supermarkets represent the erosion of a distinctively rural way of life, the village shop, or does it reflect how rural residents choose to use services? Definitions of remoteness are difficult too. The late Donald Dewar, when Secretary of State for Scotland, made an informal visit to the district of Uig on the west coast of Lewis. 'You're very remote here,' he commented as an opening gambit over the obligatory scone and tea. 'Remote from where?' came the avuncular reply from his host, who had lived there most of her life and clearly felt at the centre of her own universe.

Still, large parts of Scotland are unquestionably remote and sparsely populated. As a country, Scotland has a sparse population – especially within the European context. Average EU population density is 1.1 people per hectare, almost double the Scottish average of 0.66. This scarcity is even greater in places like the Western Isles where Donald Dewar scoffed on scones. Using a geographical definition, rural Scotland represents a significant component of the Scottish nation. It accounts for 89 per cent of Scotland's land mass, 29 per cent of the population and 27 per cent of employment. However, considerable variation exists between remote rural areas and those close to the central belt, some of which have become city dormitories, a sprawling rur-urbia of repeat-pattern private housing built with commuters in mind.

## RURAL SCOTLAND AND DEVOLUTION

Attention to the needs of rural Scotland has moved up the political agenda since the advent of the Scottish Parliament (Fairley 2001). This may be in no small part due to the fact that it is in rural constituencies that there is the most intense competition between the political parties at elections. In the 2001 general election, the only seat to change hands in Scotland – from the SNP to the Tories – was Galloway and Upper Nithsdale, while the SNP came close to losing Perth as well. Late in the 2001 campaign, Labour strategists detected that they might have more than a fighting chance in seats like Argyll and Bute and Caithness and Sutherland, where the incumbent MPs were standing down, and so put in a last-minute push. In the event, the realisation came too late and the governing party's rural representation remained the outposts of the Western Isles, Inverness East in the Highlands, and Dumfries. Only those with long political memories can recall the Conservative dominance of rural Scotland. Now they hardly figure on the map, which is under an SNP banner in the north-east and covered by the Liberal Democrats in the rest of rural Scotland.

Fitting, then, that the Scottish Executive's dedicated Rural Affairs Minister should be a Liberal Democrat. Ross Finnie, whose influence in the former Liberal Party secured Jim Wallace the inheritance of Jo Grimond's Orkney and Shetland Westminster seat, found himself amply rewarded years later with a seat in the first Scottish Executive. Finnie and Wallace, the Lib Dem members of the coalition cabinet, are now the only ministers to have held the same posts since the Parliament came into being in 1999. The Executive's dedicated Rural Affairs Minister is complemented in the Parliament by a powerful Rural Affairs Committee and a number of list MSPs from all parties who jostle for the attention of rural voters. A fair proportion of parliamentary legislation has been devoted to rural issues, too. One of the first private member's bills banned the rural pursuit of hunting with hounds. The most distinctive piece of legislation passed by the Parliament has been the Land Reform Act, a bill (at the time of writing) which formalises access to the countryside and – most importantly – enables communities to bid for the land they live on.

The increased attention of the Scottish Parliament on rural affairs may be at the expense of other democratic institutions. For example, the Highlands and

Islands Convention, a round-table forum of local authorities, development agencies and politicians set up by the last Conservative Scottish Secretary, Michael Forsyth, and adopted by the Labour Scottish Office, now only meets once a year. Other rural groupings have also fallen by the wayside.

The jealousy felt by the Borders and Galloway regions over the special attention paid to the Highlands before devolution has, however, in some way been offset by the Parliament. The foot-and-mouth crisis and the dramatic decline of the Borders textile and electronics industries have played a part in shifting the focus southwards to the extent that there is a palpable fear in the Highlands and Islands that an Edinburgh administration could be less sensitive to its needs than a Westminster one. Although there is no empirical evidence for the downgrading of the area in the government's eyes, the perception is borne out by the shuffling of responsibility for the Highlands and Islands and Gaelic on to junior ministers in the Executive who have no connections with the area or the language. Partly this is a result of the success of the Highlands now selling itself as something of an economic miracle. Jim Hunter, chair of Highlands and Islands Enterprise, complains that there is now a shortage of skilled labour in the area and that unemployment has fallen from twice the Scottish average to the current position where it is marginally lower than the Scottish figure. There remain, he accepts, parts of the Highlands where the population could fall as much as 17 per cent in the next 15 years, which could have critical consequences for some island and mainland communities but areas like Inverness and Skye and Lochalsh are booming (Cameron 1996).

## THE RURAL ECONOMY

Most people living in rural areas are not involved in what we would consider rural employment. Fewer than 8 per cent are employed in agriculture, forestry and fishing, compared to 11 per cent in tourism. Only in four districts does the proportion involved in agriculture rise above 15 per cent, with Orkney the highest at 17.3 per cent.

The service sector is overwhelmingly important in rural Scotland, making up over two-thirds of all jobs, and its dominance is growing. Most of these service jobs are provided by the public sector in the form of local authorities, health boards and development agencies.

Of the 32 local authorities in Scotland, three serve the island groupings of Orkney, Shetland and the Western Isles, which are regarded as being entirely rural, while a further 11 councils are predominantly rural. These 14 local authorities employ more than 58,000 staff, spending nearly £2 billion on revenue expenditure and £279 million on capital expenditure in 1996/7. The local authorities provide a wide range of essential services, such as primary and secondary schools, social work services, local roads and ferries, refuse collection, street cleaning and lighting, and through planning powers have a significant impact on decisions taken by individuals, commerce and business.

In that sense, local authorities wield enormous social and economic influence in rural areas, with populations having a high dependence on the councils for employment and service provision. However, politically, their power is disparate. If municipal politics in Scotland are characterised by the dominance of the Labour Party then the politics of local government in rural Scotland can be typified by independent politics. Few rural authorities are run by political groupings, although all have representatives of the major political parties aboard. Instead, they rely on informal coalitions of individual interests and the personalities of their council leaders for driving policy forward. As a result, the political focus tends to be parochial and strategic planning and forward direction of the local authority sector is left largely in the hands of key officials and a handful of senior councillors.

Much of their thunder has been stolen, however, by the network of local development agencies set up more than a decade ago under the Conservative administration. Initially resented by local authorities, the Local Enterprise Company network, under the auspices of Highlands and Islands Enterprise and Scottish Enterprise, now takes the bulk of responsibility for promoting economic development in rural Scotland. Both organisations – HIE based in Inverness and Scottish Enterprise in Glasgow – operate through a network of local enterprise companies (LECs), whose boards are representative of local business communities.

LECs have wide discretion to establish their own priorities for investment in the light of their own assessment of local needs, and many LECs – not just in the Highlands and Islands but also in areas such as the Borders and Dumfries and Galloway – are wholly concerned with rural areas. They are therefore able to take account of the particular difficulties of stimulating economic development in rural areas. The track record of the LECs, according to their own analysis, is good; but the failure of business start-ups in Scotland is not restricted to urban areas.

Nor is rural Scotland an Arcadia waiting to be discovered by fleeing urban migrants. Earnings in the countryside tend to be lower, prices higher, there is a shortage of affordable housing for rent and purchase and there are more homes below tolerable standard. Unemployment and rural poverty are still very real issues and, although levels of health are generally better in rural Scotland, this tends to be counterbalanced by an older age structure with higher illness rates.

## VISITING RURAL SCOTLAND

Tourism contributed around £4 billion to the Scottish economy in 2001, representing 5 per cent of GDP. It employs 193,000 people, or 8 per cent of the

Scottish workforce, and sustains many small businesses and rural communities. In the Highlands and Islands, the value of tourism per head of population is four times greater than for Scotland as a whole, accounting for roughly 20 per cent of the gross domestic product of the area, and supporting 20,000 jobs, approximately 13 per cent of the workforce of the area. In some areas, Skye and Lochalsh for example, the seasonal tourist trade is the largest sector of the economy.

While it may be a huge economic lever, the importance of tourism is only just being realised by the Scottish Executive. A minister with specific responsibility for tourism has been created in the new devolutionary set-up but the incumbent does not sit in the cabinet. Of course, no Tourism Minister can guarantee the standard of care at every hotel. While most of the mass-market tourism in Scotland remains a rather indifferent experience, the focus on quality and high-end tourism, and a new attention to service and training by development agencies and government, has paid dividends for those companies prepared to invest money, time and training in providing the top-class service.

The industry itself, represented through area tourist boards and by the national promotion agency, visitscotland, has never exercised political muscle. Industry-wide development is left in the hands of individual operators. Quality businesses often feel assured they can survive and thrive without the work of the tourist boards, while smaller operations complain of being neglected in promotional and advertising drives. All that may change, however, after the convulsing experience of the foot-and-mouth epidemic. Tourism, more than agriculture, suffered from the crisis that swept through rural Britain in the spring of 2001. Although in Scotland only Dumfries and Galloway and parts of the Borders were affected, the precautionary closure of the entire countryside had a dramatic impact on the tourist trade.

The shock of the foot-and-mouth episode in the Dumfries and Galloway area, and the response to the crisis, provided a useful insight into devolutionary government in action. After some behind-the-scenes wrangling, control of the response to the disease was moved to the Dumfries and Galloway council headquarters at the epicentre of the Scottish outbreak. For once, the Edinburgh civil service devolved – physically, in the case of key staff – to the area most affected. There were also frequent visits by the Rural Affairs Minister and, on one occasion, the First Minister accompanied by the Secretary of State for Scotland.

During the outbreak, Scotland was fortunate that most animal movements – the prime cause of the disease spreading so rapidly – had been in a north-to-south direction. The farming community was also lucky that the devolved administration in Edinburgh was better able to coordinate action and proved to be more responsive to the industry's demands than those in the south. The Scottish National Farmers Union managed to turn the crisis to its political advantage through its close coordination with the Executive and in making the politicians reliant on its advice and support in all their actions. The close relationship the Scottish NFU fostered, particularly with government ministers, could prove instrumental as the UK agriculture sector prepares itself for a major shakedown.

As an industry, agriculture is by far the largest land-user and has been crucial in shaping much of Scotland's rural landscape. If upstream suppliers and downstream processors are included, some 150,000 people are employed full or part time in agriculture or related industries. Agriculture on its own contributes 2.2 per cent to Scottish GDP, with a far higher share in rural areas. Through agriculture, a considerable amount of public money is channelled into rural areas, some £400 million a year in direct payments alone.

Farming, albeit heavily supported from the public purse, remains an important factor in the economic structure of rural communities, although farmers through the ages always plead poverty. According to the NFU, the average farm income in 2000 was £3,800 per annum and the average net income for hill farmers just £300. It suits most farmers and their accountants not to show a profit on their business income but, as foot-and-mouth demonstrated, without agricultural activity and the spin-off benefits it creates in ancillary industries, the viability of some rural communities would be threatened, as would be the preservation of landscapes largely shaped by farming practices past and present. The trouble is that the agriculture industry is in danger of disappearing, at least in the form in which we recognise it now (O'Hagan 2001).

The expansion of the European Union eastwards and the inevitable reform of the discredited Common Agricultural Policy will eventually spell the end of agricultural subsidy, which in effect will mean an end to farming and the countryside as we know them. The medicine has already been administered in New Zealand, where farmers had the subsidy rug pulled from underneath them by a left-wing government more than a decade ago. It hurt – but before subsidies were removed, agriculture contributed 14.2 per cent of the country's GDP; 15 years later, that share has increased to 16.6 per cent. New Zealand's farmers are market-focused, holdings are bigger and more efficient, and the remaining farmers do not want to go back to the old, subsidy-reliant way of life.

There is no doubt at Westminster that the government is determined to push through these dramatic and far-reaching reforms but Scotland's farming representatives think the skirt of devolution will shield them from the more drastic changes planned for the rest of the UK. The Scottish Executive has already published *A Forward Strategy for Scottish Agriculture*, emphasising the social and economic importance of farming to the rural community and the need to continue supporting the industry (Scottish Executive 2001b). However, the Scottish NFU feels the industry is insulated from change for the time being thanks to the influence it has had in shaping policy in Scotland.

The present Scottish NFU president, Jim Walker, an articulate, bullish and eternally optimistic leader, earned the respect of Scottish Executive ministers with his calm handling of the foot-and-mouth crisis. He believes what most farmers accept in private: that most farming support will in the future be environmental and social. Like some, he feels ready for the challenge of the unprotected marketplace but he looks to the Scottish Executive to protect farmers and, by extension, protect consumers. 'If people are really interested in food safety and animal safety, then we need to have some food security in this country, and for that we need farmers,' says Walker. 'You can import all the foreign food you want, but that wouldn't do much to reassure consumers about food safety.'

## THE FUTURE OF FISHING

While the future of the agriculture industry may be uncertain, the fate of Scotland's fishing communities, who have wielded economic and political power in the north-east for generations, appears to be sealed. There are, quite simply, not enough fish left in the sea. The sea fishing industry is a significant aspect of the Scottish rural economy. The total value of landings into Scotland was some £300 million in 2000. There are some 7,300 fishermen in Scotland, with a further 8,600 engaged in fish processing, located mainly in north-east Scotland. The catching sector is concentrated in the north-east and the west Highlands. Sea fishing is also a major contributor to the economics of Shetland and Orkney. The value of landings in the Highlands and Islands represents approximately 6 per cent of GDP for that area.

In their hearts, the fishermen know they are much to blame for the crisis in which they find themselves; but during a temporary closure of the haddock fishery in 2001, fishermen succeeded in turning their own culture of denial into a fantastic projection of guilt onto the government. In conjunction with John Swinney, the SNP leader, they accused the Executive of locking fishermen into a choice between bankruptcy in port or savaging stocks at sea. With local MP and former SNP leader Alex Salmond sailing as admiral of a political armada, the north-east fishing fleet positioned itself under the Forth Bridge during the enforced tie-up, providing picture power that could only be matched by Greenpeace on a good day.

There was no political stomach or acumen within the Labour ranks to respond by asking who exactly had plundered the oceans over the past 20 years – politicians or trawlermen? Successive governments, Tory and Labour, have gone into successive Common Fisheries Policy negotiations arguing against scientific advice to reduce the catch to save stocks. Faced by the power of science and the evidence of their own dwindling catches, more and more fishermen now accept that stocks are all but gone and, despite the rhetoric, they are voting with their feet. The Executive's £25-million decommissioning programme, which aimed to permanently take out of service 20 per cent of Scotland's 600 or so white fish boats, was oversubscribed almost immediately after it was announced, according to ministers. Fishermen look at the paltry haul in their nets, at their discarded small fish, and they know it is a way of life their sons will not share with them. Modern fishing is a business in which the winner will not be conservation or fish stocks or fishing communities.

Into this sinking industry a lifeline has been thrown from a very unlikely source. The World Wildlife Fund (WWF) has produced one of the most progressive documents on the fishing industry for many years. The WWF has found common cause with Scottish fishermen to save the ocean ecosystem, arguing that government money has to be invested in the fleet and in recovery programmes now so that there will still be fishermen to take advantage of stocks when (or if) they recover. 'We can avoid a biological catastrophe and pointless human misery,' says Malcolm MacGarvin, one of the report's authors. 'We either spend the money on a recovery programme or pay the social security bills, the unemployment benefit and the job creation schemes that will be the consequence of failure to act. It's a simple choice.'

Along with the Scottish Fishermen's Federation, the WWF has put the case for reforming the EU's Common Fisheries Policy so that planning is devolved to a local level in which fishermen have a stake. They want to get away from the annual crisis negotiations, set long-term recovery goals and secure funds to scrap vessels and pay for lay-up schemes. Such alliances of environmentalists and industry are a rare occurrence in rural Scotland. More often than not, the environmental lobby is at odds with the economic interests of rural communities, whether that be in marine fish-farming or, more recently, moves to exploit clean, natural energy through wind-farming. While organisations such as the WWF and the Royal Society for the Protection of Birds probably boast a larger membership than most trade unions and political parties in Scotland, support for the environmental lobby in rural Scotland remains slim. Fishermen, farmers and crofters believe they are the best stewards of their own environment and remain suspicious of the activities of agencies like Scottish Natural Heritage, obliged by statute to enforce UK and European environmental regulations.

The end of agriculture, as Hobsbawm predicted, the end of fishing, perhaps the end of the countryside? The rural Scotland we have in our heads will not disappear overnight but it is due for some drastic changes. More people will move in, fewer will be reliant on traditional industries, the nature of the countryside will change, sometimes enhanced by environmental protection, sometimes sterilised by environmental regulation. Study after study suggests that the dynamic population turnaround and in-migration is bringing prosperity to rural Scotland. The high levels of self-employment amongst migrant households have made a valuable contribution to the rural economy and, overall, migration appears to have had a positive impact on job creation, which is good news for the areas that are experiencing the boom.

Despite more than three decades of programmed development assistance, there are still parts of rural Scotland, particularly in the Highlands, that have not found the remedy for depopulation. The Executive's Initiative on the Edge campaign – coordinating the activities of key development agencies in such areas – may bring some hope of change. The one measure which has been a positive boon in building community self-confidence in rural Scotland has been the series of community land buy-outs which have taken place in recent years.

Setting aside the politics of land reform (which are dealt with in Chapter 25), it is worth considering the potential in unlocking the self-confidence of rural communities and empowering them to take a stake in their own lives. The early examples of community buy-outs demonstrate that, ultimately, economic, social and political power in rural Scotland lies with communities, if they are given access to the means of development themselves. More often than not, this means access to land for housing, community developments and public services. The dramatic turnaround in the fortunes of the island of Eigg, one of the first buy-outs in the current phase of community land purchases, is an example of this in action. Backed by Highland Council and the Scottish Wildlife Trust, the island is, in contrast to a decade ago, a hive of industry and activity. It has been rescued from stagnant decay by a community which now feels it has a real sense of going somewhere. Empowering rural communities, it seems, is the key to rural transformation – although, of course, there may be several different communities of interest even in a single rural area.

The reverberations of the foot-and-mouth crisis may have led to the one change in the political landscape in the 2001 general election, when the Conservatives gained Galloway and Upper Nithsdale at the expense of the SNP. The successful candidate, Peter Duncan, worked hard at reviving the traditional Conservative vote by community campaigning and attributed victory to his ability to tap into the different concerns of the electorate, rather than to foot-and-mouth. 'We have rediscovered the art of community politics in Galloway and Upper Nithsdale,' he said afterwards. 'It is a very disparate rural constituency. There are many different communities with different problems and we worked hard at identifying these different needs.' By accident or design, it appears Peter Duncan came across the key to rural politics – addressing the disparate needs of a large number of interest groups and individuals who find themselves part of the rural community.

# 28

# THE GAELIC COMMUNITIES

## *Joni Buchanan*

A few years ago, I was asked by a woman who wanted to speak Gaelic whether the language was difficult to learn. My response was unwittingly glib. Of course not. It is no more difficult than any other language. Speaking Gaelic is, for me, like drawing breath, part of my being and my soul. How could I judge its complexity to the learner's ear? I had not intended to be unkind but merely to state a matter of fact. On more considered reflection, however, there was so much more that I could have added in order to emphasise how welcome it would be if she and others like her would take the trouble to acquire the language.

For while this precious thing is indeed integral to my very being, my life is not as saturated in it as my father's was, or his as his mother's before him. With each succeeding generation, the richness of the language diminishes, and I fear that when I draw my last sweet Gaidhlig breath, my children cannot possibly know it even as I did. And will their children know it at all? Above all, I should have said to my friend: 'Please go and learn it because Gaelic's natural community lost, long ago, the ability to produce succeeding generations of native speakers in sufficient numbers to ensure its future. We need you and many like you.'

Yet it is difficult to communicate adequately about something that is so close to you. It is wearing to read and hear so often about the 'death' of your language, often from people who you suspect would really quite like to help it on its way. But Gaelic is not going to die, certainly not in the present century and probably not well into the next one. Something as complex as a language does not obligingly 'die' within a given day or decade. The real question is what level of life it will be sustained at.

# THE DECLINE OF THE GAELIC NATION
# AND HOW TO REVERSE IT

As each decade passes, census figures show fewer and fewer Gaelic-speakers. At the last estimate, 65,000 people or 1.35 per cent of the Scottish population spoke Gaelic (13.5 per cent in the Highlands and Islands) (McLeod 1998: 61); early indications from the 2001 census suggest continuing decline. There is nothing remotely surprising about that. It is merely an inevitable reflection of the age profile among Gaelic-speakers. Nobody can prevent death at the upper end of the age range. The only question is whether, at any stage, it can be balanced by the influx of new speakers, either through the school system or by the expansion of adult learning. If that can be done, then the census figures a decade or two from now will start to turn around. If not, they will continue to decline.

The concentration of Gaelic-speakers within what might still loosely be termed the Gaidhealtachd has also been heavily diluted, mainly by out-migration for economic reasons. By 1991, only 37 per cent of Scotland's Gaelic-speakers resided in the language heartlands, while 40 per cent lived and worked in the Scottish lowlands (MacKinnon 1993). The outwards drift of Gaelic-speakers from their native areas throughout most of the twentieth-century has resulted not just in the straightforward loss of native speakers – only one in three people speak Gaelic now in these 'heartland' areas as a whole – but in a social class imbalance amongst Gaelic-speakers. For example, in the Western Isles Gaelic-speakers are underrepresented in the higher occupational groups and overrepresented in the manual categories. Professional positions have tended to draw in non-Gaelic-speakers who are thus overrepresented in the higher managerial and administrative groups. Meanwhile, there continues to be a strong correlation between the maintenance of the language and the primary occupations of agriculture, weaving and fishing (MacKinnon 1993).

Each decade takes its toll on the numbers of Gaelic-speakers, the maintenance of the language in the areas where it is still relatively strong becomes more critical. Language cannot be separated from the wider economic and social context and there is a lot of validity in the maxim: 'No jobs means no people and no people means no language.' While there are significant headline successes for economic development policies in the Highlands and Islands over the past 40 years, they have tended to disguise the fact that population loss has continued to afflict the peripheral areas of the region, including those where Gaelic is strongest. Acknowledgement of this reality has underpinned recent economic initiatives like Iomairt aig an Oir, which aims to prioritise the needs of peripheral communities and bring new thinking to their regeneration. But it is late in the day and the relentless decline of these places has weakened the Gaelic base in a way that is disproportionate to the numbers involved. My own native area, Uig in Lewis, has seen its population fall from 600 to 417 since 1961, in spite of some welcome inward migration.

Yet all is not gloom and the education system offers the best hope for growth. It should not be beyond its capabilities to replace the natural annual loss of Gaelic-speakers by guaranteeing a thousand new recruits to the language each year. A strategy of stimulating parental demand, ensuring the availability of teachers and setting realistically achievable targets for each local authority area would allow the number of potential speakers to stabilise, and perhaps at some future time even to grow. If, on the other hand, the current piecemeal approach to language development is maintained then no such targets will be set or attained and this generation of politicians, administrators and parents will be responsible for driving another nail into the Gaelic coffin. The language won't be 'dead' but it will have passed the point of no return.

The creation of a devolved administration in Edinburgh offers unparalleled opportunities for ancient and ongoing difficulties to be remedied and for Gaelic to become normalised in the cultural life of Scotland (MacKinnon 1992; 2001). There is, on the surface, a good deal of sympathy for Gaelic amongst politicians across the spectrum. Mike Watson, the current minister with responsibility for Gaelic, affirmed his support for the extension of bilingualism throughout Scotland when he said at a recent conference on Gaelic education: 'It is very important for me that we see Gaelic as part of all our culture' and pledged to do 'whatever we can to stem the loss and to strengthen and bolster Gaelic as a living language for generations to come'. Support for Gaelic is also one of the founding pledges in the Scottish Parliament's *Partnership for Scotland* (Scottish Executive 1999a).

But words are cheap and actions cost money. It need not, in the case of Gaelic, be a lot of money by the standards of public expenditures. But the point has to be made, without ambiguity, that unless an adequate level of resources is willed to the needs of the language, then the fine words and founding pledges are not worth the breath they are spoken with or the paper they are written on. Equally, it must be said that there is little evidence in the day-to-day behaviour of the Scottish civil service that it has ever heard of these pledges and principles. To obtain from them as much as a few bilingual road-signs still involves as much obstructionism and negativity as it did a generation ago.

Tremendous work has been done in recent years to develop Gaelic-medium education. The wheel is not in need of reinvention – only of wider use. In the current year, £2.8 million is being spent by the Scottish Executive on specific grants to education authorities throughout Scotland to support Gaelic education. As a benchmark against which to measure that amount, one education authority might receive a similar sum for the development of its modern language provision. Nevertheless, within modest parameters there has been progress in Gaelic education, especially in the primary sector, where almost 2,000 children are now taught through the medium of the language in 60 locations, both in the Gaelic-speaking areas and also in the rest of Scotland. Successful units in places with minimal Gaelic tradition, like Cumbernauld and

Kilmarnock, are interesting examples of what is possible if Gaelic was treated seriously as a national asset. Very little of the growth in the primary sector is evident in secondary schools, with only 352 pupils being taught one or two subjects through the language, though around 200 are taught it as a subject (Scottish Executive 2000b). At the tertiary level, the Gaelic-medium further education college Sabhal Mór Ostaig continues to be a remarkable success story and is now extending its operations to the island of Islay. Gaelic is also well represented in some of the Scottish universities.

## THE RISE OF GAELIC BROADCASTING

Specific government support for Gaelic, apart from broadcasting, is now close to £4 million per annum. Since 1990, Comataidh Craolaidh Gaidhlig has been funded by government to support 150 hours of Gaelic television, while a further 100 hours is provided by the television companies. The fund has been critical to the growth of independent Gaelic production companies and has stimulated new Gaelic writing and a variety of other creative skills. Gaelic radio, provided by BBC Scotland, has extremely high listener loyalty among those who understand the language and does a remarkable job in providing a wide range of good-quality programmes in spite of the small, and diminishing, speech base by which it is constrained. The major demand within broadcasting at present is for a Gaelic-based channel, comparable to Telefios na Gaelige in Ireland, but using a digital transmission system.

In purely economic terms, the case for a television channel may be difficult to justify. But in terms of the language's future prospects, it is vital. This points to the wider truth that it is over-simplistic to reduce the demand for an adequate response to Gaelic's needs to one of money alone. Realistic levels of spending will only happen if and when more fundamental philosophical decisions have been taken by Scotland's politicians. Do they, in their heart of hearts, want Gaelic to survive? Do they have a vision of Scottish identity which embodies the Gaelic dimension? Do they feel any sense of responsibility for its status and well-being, both within Gaelic-speaking communities and within Scotland as a whole? Do they have any comprehension of what is in imminent danger of being lost? Perhaps most basically of all, do they have any feeling for the potential of Gaelic as opposed to the problem of Gaelic?

There are proposals in front of the Parliament which will draw out answers to these questions. Quite simply, we are currently facing the best and possibly the last opportunity to alter the course of decline and to secure Gaelic's place within a modern, tolerant, multi-cultural Scotland. The MacPherson report has called for £10 million per annum non-broadcasting expenditure in support of the language, a small Gaelic-speaking department within the Scottish Executive and a Gaelic development agency responsible to it (Scottish Executive 2000c).

The Scottish Executive is committed, in principle but not yet in practice, to granting secure status to the language; a legal underpinning which would create vital enforceable rights, particularly in the field of education. Then there is the Milne report, which presents the case for a dedicated Gaelic television channel (Scottish Executive 2000b).

Before any of these specific demands are confronted, I strongly recommend that the Scottish Parliament first seeks to establish a philosophical consensus on its approach to Gaelic and how it wants its attitude towards Gaelic to go down in history. Because it is only within such a framework that rational or meaningful decisions can be taken.

## PRESERVING THE LANGUAGE

The miracle is, of course, that Gaelic survives at all. It has been in retreat since the fourteenth century, although it lingered even beyond the Highland boundaries for several centuries thereafter. As one model study of Gaelic's retreat has reminded us, the Gaidhealtachd in the last decades of the eighteenth century included the areas around Loch Lomondside, the Lake of Menteith, Strathyre, Callander and Aberfoyle. But by then it was not the natural language of youth. Proximity to growing urban and predominantly English-speaking centres came in the way of the natural inter-generational passing on of the language (Newton 1999). Scots- and English-speaking ministers and educators replaced Gaelic-speakers, and with them came an anglicised education and way of life. Almost without exception, by the middle years of the nineteenth century, Gaelic had become the language of the generation of people who had reached the last decades of life. Area by area, that has been the story of Gaelic's retreat.

It was abetted, of course, by the political will of those who held power. Even before Culloden, the combined might of Church and the embryonic education system saw it as their business to root out the native tongue and, in establishment eyes, the decidedly subversive culture that went with it. The mission of the Scottish Presbyterian Church and that stern-sounding body, the Society in Scotland for the Propagation of Christian Knowledge (SSPCK), was to proscribe Roman Catholicism, Episcopalianism and the Gaelic language. But conscious of its dual function – to spread Presbyterianism as well as rooting-out Gaelic – the Society had to allow the use of Gaelic (or Irish) in spiritual instruction. However, no corner of Scotland was to be immune from this cultural cleansing. Even the schoolmaster on St Kilda was instructed to 'be diligent not just to teach them to read English but also to write'. No encouragement was to be given to 'the teaching of Irish books in the Society's schools or to the printing of them for their use'. Their aim was 'not to continue the Irish language but to wear it out, and Learn the people the English tongue' (Withers 1984: 71).

When, a century later, the progress of spirituality within the Gaidhealtachd was taking longer than expected, another educational movement – the Gaelic Society schools – was set up to preserve Gaelic, but only as a means by which to improve comprehension of the English language and consequently of the scriptures. Quite apart from the obvious damage inflicted on Gaelic by such strategies, the more pernicious one was the subordination of the language to English in the minds of the Gael. English had become the language of education, of scholars and of progress. And the anglicised way of life was constantly identified as the only road out of poverty. These attitudes were deeply ingrained and have persisted in the attitudes of many teachers and parents who were themselves Gaelic-speakers.

A similar linguistic policy was pursued by the Presbyterian churches. Gaelic was fine for communicating with God and devouring the scriptures. But the learning of English alone brought worldly advantage. Even that great Highland institution, the Free Church, recommended as late as 1876 that 'Gaelic should not be hunted to extinction but should be permitted to decay gradually' (Withers 1984). Ministers, educators and administrators were all of a similar disposition: Gaelic was a waste of time, an unnecessary burden in a world where it held no currency. It is not so surprising, then, that Gaelic people themselves began to regard their language, culture and way of life as inferior and superfluous.

All of this took place, of course, against a backdrop of desperate poverty, eviction and dispossession, when every other aspect of life was being torn asunder and much of the Highland population driven to the four corners of the earth, taking their language and culture with them. Clearances in the literal sense were followed by generations of out-migration, as Gaelic-speakers left their impoverished homelands either to fight in wars or to seek work wherever it could be found – the fishing ports of Britain, as they followed the herring; the factories of the Industrial Revolution; the construction sites of the new Dominions; the ranches and pampas of the Americas. By the beginning of the twentieth century, there were almost certainly more Gaelic-speakers outside Scotland than the 250,000 who remained within it.

Gaelic's fight-back can be dated to 1872, when the language's supporters rallied in response to its exclusion from the terms of the Education Act, which introduced compulsory schooling. The Gaelic Societies of Inverness and Glasgow, An Comunn Gaidhealach and other Gaelic groups spearheaded the resistance. They were joined by great Land League figures like John Murdoch of the *Highlander*, Charles Fraser Macintosh, Donald MacFarlane, J.S. Blackie and Mairi Mhor nan Oran. The movement was influential. When the Napier Commission presented its recommendations to the government in 1884, it included a strong statement in favour of the language: 'We think it desirable that all children whose mother tongue is Gaelic should be taught to read that language . . . we think that the discouragement and neglect of the native language in the education of Gaelic-speaking children, which has hitherto so largely influenced the system practised in the Highlands, ought to cease.'

In 1885, the Scottish Education Department gave way, but only to a very limited extent. They agreed to have Gaelic taught in Scottish schools as a specific subject and to employ Gaelic-speaking teachers for Gaelic-speaking infants. It took another 30 years for it to concede the right of every Gaelic-speaking child to be taught to read and write in the language. For many years thereafter, and (although the progress of Gaelic-medium education has been immense) arguably up to the present day, the level of educational provision has depended very much on the attitude of each local authority and, more specifically, on individual headteachers and directors of education.

Gaelic has defied the hostility of the centuries by continuing to survive and often to flourish. Its resilience is reflected in the strength of the Gaelic arts where it has continued to produce a flow of fine singers, musicians, poets and writers out of all proportion to the size of the linguistic community. Gaelic can still produce academics of high quality to study and teach it. But none of this can last indefinitely if, relentlessly, the number of speakers continues to decline. That is the point, above all others, at which action is required. And it is the absence of any sense of urgency in addressing it which, above all others, exposes Scotland's ambivalence towards the language.

Gaelic has suffered the oppression and disadvantages common to many minority languages. It has been marginalised by both church and state. It has seen its natural population base eroded by war, clearance, emigration and economic neglect. It has endured ridicule, denigration and prejudice within its own land. It has been patronised and paid lip-service to in a manner that has never been matched by the commitment of necessary resources. And through it all, Gaelic has survived as a living, breathing language of antiquity, relevance and richness. That is the basis on which it confronts its new political masters at the start of a century that, by all the natural laws, Gaelic should never even have seen.

The coming years will demonstrate whether the new political order in Scotland has anything more to offer Gaelic than supportive words. No rocket science is involved – just a series of measures, backed by serious resources, which would allow any minority language to survive in the global village of the twenty-first century. Anyone with the power to deliver that outcome, and who chooses not to, is really no better than those who were at least honest enough to articulate the view that 'Gaelic should not be hunted to extinction but allowed to decay gradually'. Surely we have moved beyond that. Surely Scotland is capable of valuing something which is unique to itself.

# 29

# A Slow Revolution?: Gender Relations in Contemporary Scotland

*Fiona Mackay*

I expected the Parliament to look different, but it doesn't. It looks like the rest of life, where women and men are present in roughly equal numbers except when gender segregation is imposed – openly or otherwise – for a special reason. (Innes 2001: 249)

Women have a high profile in the new political landscape of Scotland. They make up 37 per cent of members of the Scottish Parliament – one of the highest proportions in the world – and hold a number of key ministerial posts. As Sue Innes notes in the quotation above, in some respects, these developments are a reflection of what can already be observed in other areas of 'ordinary life'. As such, they may be only the most visible signs of a slow and ongoing process of transformation in the balance of power between men and women.

The roles of women and men in society – and the relations between the genders – have been undergoing fundamental change in Scotland as elsewhere. Social attitudes about 'a woman's place' have changed considerably and legislative and economic developments have opened up new opportunities. Women have increasingly entered the labour market, including mothers with dependent children. Girls have been outperforming boys in Scottish schools for decades (Scottish Executive 2002: 56). We can also see young women moving forward: they now consist of about half of new undergraduates in Scottish universities, including medical students. Women have made significant inroads into many professions. For example, they account for 41 per cent of medical consultants aged under 35; one in three new police officers is female, as is one in every two newly qualified solicitors. In law, journalism, academia, the arts and business, there are some prominent – albeit still rather few – women (Mackay and Bilton 2000; Scottish Executive 2002). However, despite these changes, disadvantage, segregation and stereotyping on the basis of gender persist. These may be exacerbated or ameliorated by other social divisions such as class, race/ethnicity and sexual orientation.

This chapter provides a brief overview of some aspects of gender relations in contemporary Scotland, particularly the current state of play with regard to paid and unpaid work. It also considers what implications the gender dynamics of the Scottish Parliament might have for gender relations in wider Scottish society.


## GENDER AND WORKING LIVES

The workplace has changed beyond recognition in the past half-century or so, with the massive growth in female employment. Women now make up around a half of the Scottish workforce. The most significant rise in female economic activity rates over the last ten years has been amongst women with dependent children: the proportion of working mothers with children aged under five increased by 10 per cent between 1988 and 1998. Most employed women work full time (56 per cent), although a large proportion (44 per cent) work part time. Around one-third of women with disabilities are economically active compared with around three-quarters of non-disabled women. Black and minority ethnic women are nearly twice as likely to be unemployed as white women in Scotland.

Recent figures show that the gap between employment rates for working-age women and men has narrowed considerably over the last 40 years, from about 50 per cent in 1960 to about 10 per cent in 2001. The female employment rate has increased from 44.7 per cent of working-age women in 1960 to 66.9 per cent in 2001. In contrast, male employment rates fell over the same period from 96.5 per cent in 1960 to 77.2 per cent in 2001, reflecting the impact of economic restructuring on traditional male industries such as manufacturing and the growth of service industries. These trends have challenged traditional gender relations and the male 'breadwinner'/female 'homemaker' model which underpins the Welfare State, tax-benefit systems and social organisation more generally.

However, as noted earlier, gender stereotypes still result in segregation and disadvantage – or what McIvor (1996) has described as 'gender apartheid' – in patterns of employment, paid and unpaid, and income. We see continuing horizontal segregation, with female workers concentrated in a relatively small number of areas of the Scottish economy – shops, hotels, restaurants, financial and business services, education, health and social work. These employment sectors are sometimes called 'pink collar' because they are seen to be 'women's jobs' and to relate to women's traditional caring responsibilities in the home. Women still experience relative exclusion and discrimination in other sectors. For example, men make up 91 per cent of construction workers, 85 per cent of employees in water and energy industries and 76 per cent of those working in transport and communication.

We also see vertical segregation, with women typically concentrated in lower occupational grades than men. This trend can be found in manual, skilled and professional sectors. For example, a recent study of women and men in the professions in Scotland found that there is a larger proportion of women in lower grades than higher grades across all professions (Kay 2000). This trend applies not only in those jobs and professions sectors that have traditionally been seen as 'men's jobs' but also in areas where women have predominated, such as primary education. So, for example, although men are less than one in ten primary school teachers they comprise one in every five primary head teachers.

Unequal pay is currently a high-profile public issue: women earn around £0.80 for every £1.00 their male counterparts earn, despite 30 years of equal pay legislation. Awareness of the gender pay gap in Scotland has been raised through the 'Close the Gap' campaign led by the Equal Opportunities Commission and the Scottish Executive. The reasons for the pay gap are complex, but they relate in most part to gender stereotyping and the gendered division of labour. Gendered assumptions about 'women's work' and 'men's work' are deeply rooted: women face both outright and indirect discrimination when attempting to make inroads into non-traditional sectors, such as engineering, which are seen as 'unsuitable' jobs for women. Meanwhile, traditional women's jobs tend to be lower-status and less well paid, reflecting the low value placed on caring work. Furthermore, where women have tipped the balance in an employment sector, such as banking and financial services, the 'feminisation' of the sector has been accompanied by a loss of status and a depression of salary levels. Of course, gender stereotypes can also work to disadvantage men who seek to enter traditionally feminine jobs, such as nursing or primary school teaching. However Kay's (2000) survey illustrates the way in which gender stereotypes may also benefit men in such atypical employment through accelerated promotion, a managerial position being seen as a more suitable job for a man.

Across working lifetimes, women's overall economic activity rates are lower than those of men. A major explanatory factor which affects women's ability to take on paid work is their family responsibilities. As noted earlier, a substantial proportion of women in employment are part-time workers, and part-time workers, both men and women, are particularly vulnerable to low pay (although improvements are likely as a result of the implementation of European Commission directives). However, more than half of women in full-time work are also low paid. Female full-time workers are also disadvantaged by the long-hours culture which operates in many jobs and professions, and the assumptions of many employers that their workers do not have to juggle working lives with caring responsibilities.

Research commissioned by the UK Cabinet Office Women's Unit (now the Women and Equality Unit) dramatically exposed the 'cost of being a woman' (Rake 2000). The study estimated that the average unskilled woman forfeits nearly £200,000 over a lifetime, a woman with mid-level qualifications £250,000, and a highly skilled women loses £143,000 as a result of the gender pay gap. Over and above the 'female forfeit', the research found that women also lost out through the mother gap – that is, the impact on lifetime earnings of having children. The projected loss in earnings for mothers with two children is £285,000 for an unskilled woman, £140,000 for a woman with mid-level skills, and £19,000 for a highly skilled woman. Highly skilled mothers are projected to lose considerably less income than their less-skilled sisters, as they are most likely to retain their place in the labour market. However, as the research points out, these women may also incur very high childcare costs.

## RENEGOTIATING GENDER RELATIONS?

Whilst the shift by women into the labour market and public life has been marked, there is less evidence to suggest that this has signalled a significant renegotiation of gender roles in terms of domestic and caring responsibilities being taken on by men. In a recent survey (Scottish Executive 2001a) only one in three couples reported that they equally shared childcare; about a quarter of couples reported that they shared cleaning and cooking duties; and about a third equally shared responsibility for grocery shopping. The 'double-shift' involving both paid and unpaid work characterises the daily life of many women in Scotland. This unequally gendered division of labour underscores the continuity of unequal relations of power between women and men.

In response to the need to juggle work and family responsibilities, women have lobbied for flexible working practices and have pioneered innovative solutions such as job-sharing: in spring of 2001, 82 per cent of Scottish job-sharers were women. On the negative side, it must also be noted that women are also more vulnerable to exploitative job 'flexibility', such as zero-hours contracts, and job insecurity. Many women who work part time would prefer to work longer hours but are stymied by the lack of high-quality, affordable childcare.

Gender stereotyping plays out in the way that work–life balance is still seen as a predominantly 'women's issue'. Traditional attitudes also present barriers to those men who want to play greater domestic and parenting roles. Men in the UK work the longest hours in Europe. In Scotland, 22 per cent of men do 46 hours or more of paid work per week, compared with 5 per cent of women. More than a third of men would like to work fewer hours and would be prepared to earn less. However, research (Scottish Executive 2002) suggests that powerful cultural stereotypes relating to masculinity and work mean that part-time jobs and job-sharing remain socially unacceptable to many men who expect and are expected to work full time.

Social data about men's and women's changing attitudes and behaviour in respect of gender relations in relationships and families in Scotland are few. As

McIvor notes, 'the internal life of the Scottish family remains relatively mysterious' (McIvor 1996: 163) and under-researched, although our knowledge should improve with new social surveys such as the Scottish Household Survey and the Scottish Social Attitudes survey, and through the work of the newly established Centre for Research on Families and Relationships in Scotland. In the short term, it is hard not to concur with McIvor's view that gender relations in the Scottish family lag behind changes in the public world of work.

Gender relations are in flux but change in some areas has been slower and more uneven than might be expected. Family responsibilities continue to shape women's working lives, their opportunities and their income. In general, women are still more vulnerable to poverty than are men. Women in Scotland experience poverty through unemployment, as lone parents, and as pensioners. Households headed by a female are less likely than those headed by a male to have a bank account, savings and investments or home contents insurance, and are more likely to be dependent on state benefits. Meanwhile, many women's lives – across all classes – continue to be restricted or brutalised by the fear or reality of male violence, predominantly (although not exclusively) at the hands of known men, including partners and ex-partners.

Breitenbach notes in her recent assessment of gender relations in Scotland that, whilst there has undoubtedly been change in some individual men's lives, '. . . the extent to which men are re-examining their attitudes and behaviour, and their conceptions of masculinity, remains limited' (Breitenbach 1999: 231). In this context, it is interesting to note that men may be beginning to reflect upon gender roles in that most traditionally macho of arenas, that of politics.

## WOMEN AND MEN IN THE SCOTTISH PARLIAMENT

Scottish political culture has been commonly characterised as macho and hostile to women – dominated by those Kelly (1995) memorably described as 'wee hard men from the Rust Belt'. Although women make up around half the population, they have found it hard to gain an equal place in Scottish political elites and institutions, even though their lives are equally regulated by politics. The achievement of a Scottish Parliament with 37 per cent of women and with equal opportunities as a key principle was, therefore, significant. It serves as both an indicator of the progress women have made within political parties to positions of influence and also as a sign of the recognition that they have far to go. As has been charted elsewhere, pressure was exerted by women campaigners from within political parties and from the wider women's movement for gender concerns to be integrated into the design of the new Parliament. The drive for gender balance and the blueprint of a less adversarial structure with 'family friendly' working hours became a powerful shorthand for the aspiration for a different sort of politics (Brown 1998, Brown et al. 2002) that might be more amenable to women and that, it might be argued, women would be better equipped to practise (Mackay 2001). The desire was to create a Parliament which was more responsive to women's concerns and more likely to tackle structural discrimination.

It is not within the scope of this chapter to provide a detailed assessment of the gender impact of the Scottish Parliament and Executive. However, gender concerns have been institutionalised in a number of ways. These include the four key principles of the Parliament – sharing of power, accountability, access and participation and equal opportunities; the observation of family-friendly working hours; the establishment of a cross-cutting Equal Opportunities Committee in the Parliament; and the setting up of an Equality Unit within the Scottish Executive. The Executive has adopted a 'mainstreaming' approach, endorsed by the Parliament, whereby equalities considerations, including gender, are integrated into the everyday work of government, including policy development. Opportunities to feed in the views of women in the community or from different groups and organisations have been greatly enhanced by the consultative channels and mechanisms which operate for the parliamentary committees and the pre-legislative process, and through the establishment of the Civic Forum. These new arrangements represent the potential for a shift in the gender balance of power in terms of political voice, and the increased substantive representation of women and their interests.

Turning now to the relatively large proportion – or 'critical mass' – of women MSPs, contemporary research (Mackay et al. 2001) suggests that there is a broad consensus that the presence of women has made at least some 'difference' to political practices and the political agenda in the Parliament, although this impact is highly conditioned by political conditions and contexts. Women backbenchers have been seen to raise issues and ensure they have stayed on the mainstream political agenda. This is best illustrated by the high profile given to domestic abuse and sexual violence by both the Parliament and the Scottish Executive. For example, the first committee-initiated legislation (The Protection from Abuse Act) is concerned with strengthening the police and judicial safeguards for women who have been abused by partners or ex-partners. The presence of women is felt to have increased both the priority or 'weight' accorded to certain issues, for example concerns relating to children and childcare; and also to have introduced a fresh perspective in areas which have traditionally lacked a gender analysis, for example rural development. Women in the Parliament were prominent in the move to abolish warrant sales and to press for the provision of free care for the elderly. In the early days of the Parliament, women backbenchers provided crucial support for the then Communities Minister Wendy Alexander in face of powerful resistance to the abolition of Section 28; and for the then Health Minister Susan Deacon when she and her teenagers' sexual health education strategy were condemned by the Catholic Church. In the Executive, women ministers have been seen to have championed a high-profile equality strategy, work on equality mainstreaming and on domestic abuse, and the introduction of gender perspectives in social justice, health and transport policy areas.

On the one hand, there appear to be gender differences between female and male politicians. Women appear to have different views of power and of the political process to those of their male counterparts, and use different indicators of political efficacy. They perceive that they conduct themselves in different ways to men: in particular, they suggest that they work in a low-profile, 'solution-orientated' way. Male MSPs are more ambivalent about whether there are gendered differences in style but they do feel that the high proportion of women had an impact on the culture and atmosphere of the Parliament, particularly in terms of 'normalising' the idea of female politicians. Moreover, those male MSPs who have served at Westminster see stark contrasts between the two institutions. There is an apparent difference in terms of policy priorities that can result in an impact on political agendas and policy outcomes. These differences are most obvious in respect of gender issues.

On the other hand, the research also suggests that differences between female and male politicians in terms of political practices are not large and that we may be observing convergence. If that is the case, we might ask if women are becoming more like men? Or are men becoming more like women? The short answer is probably both. Despite self-conscious attempts by the Parliament to promote 'new politics', the pull of traditional adversarial political behaviour and the constraints of party discipline are strong. Political performance is still largely judged by traditional 'male' criteria. All these factors pressurise women to behave 'like men'. However, that is not the full story: the interviews suggest that, in many respects, men, rather than women, are on a learning curve, in part prompted by women pointing out inappropriate behaviour or attitudes. Some male politicians perceive that the strong presence of women has enabled them to reflect upon their own political practices and to think and act in less traditional or adversarial ways. The 'family friendly' hours of the Parliament and the lessening of opportunities for all-male cliques to develop were also seen by men to have had an impact on conduct. Some male MSPs feel that they are able to raise or contribute to new issues and a broader agenda. As such, the presence of women may have provoked a reconsideration of the masculine norms, values and behaviours traditionally played out in power politics (Mackay, Myers and Brown 2001).

It is important, however, not to overplay these changes in political life and culture, nor to underestimate the 'pull' of 'politics as usual'. Indeed, a recent audit of the Parliament demonstrates that Holyrood is not as different from Westminster as some would like to think it is (Winetrobe 2001). Nevertheless, preliminary observations suggest the presence of a substantial proportion of women politicians in a new political institution shaped, in part, by women and feminist ideas, has contributed to a more 'feminised' Parliament. Within this new institution there is a wider range of political possibilities for both women and men in terms of practice, norms and values and priorities. The 'normalising' of women politicians and their concerns is an important part of a new – more balanced – political culture and a broadening of the mainstream political agenda.

## CONCLUSIONS

> Change in gender relations is ultimately about change in the balance of power, both within the sphere of family relationships and within the public sphere of work, civil society and political life. (Breitenbach, 1999: 237-8)

Gender relations are undergoing a long and slow revolution. Undoubtedly, progress has been made and continues to be made in both public and private spheres: occasionally in leaps, such as the representation of women in the Scottish Parliament, more often in the form of two steps forward and one step back. Change is contested and traditional stereotypes and behaviours have proved remarkably resilient to challenge. Put simply, whether you are a woman or a man still significantly shapes the pattern and nature of your working week and your working life, your share of social and economic resources, and your power and influence over your own life and those of others. Life chances are also shaped by other social divisions, such as class, race/ethnicity and sexual orientation. The presence of women MSPs – and the concerns of ordinary women – as a normal and unremarkable part of the polity presents a significant challenge to cultural stereotypes which still constrain and disadvantage, and to the traditional imbalance of political power and influence. The new gender settlement in the Scottish Parliament stands as both a sign of how far we have come and a reminder of how far we still have to go.

# 30

# THE 'OTHER' SCOTLAND: SEXUAL CITIZENSHIP AND LESBIGAY IDENTITIES

## David T. Evans

In 1993, Scottish gay social historian Bob Cant observed that:

> Lesbians and gay men are, for the most part, invisible in modern Scotland. The few public references to us – by teachers, by preachers, by politicians, by pundits – imply that we are Other, that we are 'these people', that we do not belong. (Cant 1993: 1)

Nearly ten years on – and despite some positive but much negative media coverage, the continuing, often high-profile growth of the commercial gay scenes of Edinburgh and Glasgow, and the 'repeal' of Section 28 – little has changed. We 'belong' as lawyers, actors, teachers, shop assistants, traffic wardens, and recipients of unemployment benefit; we 'belong' as neighbours, sons, daughters, uncles and aunts, even parents; we 'belong' as voters, consumers and producers – but only if we deny who we are. For as soon as we reveal ourselves, we cease to be lawyers, teachers, unemployed, uncles or mothers or fathers, but acquire the prefix 'gay', 'lesbian', 'bi' or some other more colourful and offensive epithet which proclaims our 'Otherness'.

## THE CONSTRUCTION OF THE 'OTHER' SCOTLAND

The choice is apparently simple, between concealing or revealing this 'Otherness' and to whom, but resolving this choice – in practice, a never-ending series of choices depending upon the constituencies with whom we are dealing – is always problematic. Not only because of the unpredictable risks of revelation, but because we have to be sure who we are sexually in the first place. We have to negotiate with the 'Otherness' we are said to be, and integrate the results into our composite beings. To tell people we are gay is to become identified first and foremost by our 'deviant' sexualities, our 'Otherness'. To conceal from people we are gay is to apparently be a fully rounded normal person, assumed to be 'straight' but for whom sexual identity and lifestyle is not the primary or sole reason for being. Small wonder that most gay men and women conceal their sexual status from the great majority of their day-to-day contacts.

Yes, there are exceptions, individuals who insistently present themselves to all their social contacts as Scottish citizens who just happen to be homosexual, but I can guarantee that all of them would have numerous tales to tell of everyday, commonplace harassment and discrimination, especially at work, often barely masked behind 'we are so tolerant' humour. After 30 years in my job as a lecturer in Sociology at Glasgow University, alongside many colleagues of as many years' service, I still have to smile weakly (aided by face muscles petrified from too much past laughter), indeed weekly, as they entertain each other with jibes about my assumed interest in make-up, leather or post-midnight rambles in Kelvingrove Park.

Atypical? Over-sensitive? I do not think so. These often well-meant 'we embrace you' comments, which are certainly preferable to a kick in the teeth (and I have come close to many of those), implicitly say 'because you are different', 'because you are "Other"'. The irony is that, being 'Other', our sexual orientations and lifestyles are constantly the focus of heterosexual and heterosexist attention, whilst not being 'Other', i.e. 'normal', invites no comparable comments whatsoever. I do not hear any 'amusing' anecdotes or off-the-cuff remarks about my (allegedly) straight male colleagues' use of pornography, or their night-time circular drives around Finnieston; nor do I hear 'we don't really mean it' jibes at parents about their sexual, physical or emotional abuse of their children. That would be such bad taste. Oddly, I do not even hear any satirical comments about married feminist colleagues who have not only got married but who, without any apparent sense of contradiction, have willingly adopted their husbands' names and identities. Being 'normal' means 'no comment': no wonder so many gay men and lesbians conceal their 'Otherness'. One is reminded of Joe Orton's *Loot*, in which one male character observes to another: 'We wouldn't have been nicked if you had kept your mouth shut. Making us look ridiculous by telling the truth. Why can't you lie like a normal man?'

## THE INVISIBILITY OF GAY SCOTLAND

Being gay or lesbian – despite the now regular anodyne media exploitation, especially of 'lesbian chic' – remains in the real world a disadvantage in all aspects of life. How many high-profile gay or lesbian Scots can you name?

MSPs? Lawyers? Doctors? Political pundits? Actors? Footballers? Athletes? Arts administrators? Well, we do actually have one out and proud MSP: Iain Smith, Lib Dem MSP for North East Fife. And Chris Smith – well, he is from Dundee.

There are rumours, fairly well-founded suspicions, as well as in some cases incontrovertible evidence (though one is loath to mention any names in print for fear of causing offence or litigious reactions), but how many notable Scots individuals are publicly 'out' as proof that being gay or lesbian in contemporary Scotland is harmless or irrelevant? There are admittedly some predominantly middle-class areas of employment and residence which are, in all probability, now less prejudiced about homosexual employees and neighbours than they were a decade ago. But, as I have hinted, the obliterating tolerance of political correctness carries with it its own stigma, and Cant's jaundiced 'for the most part' view still pertains, as recent political events such as the 'repeal' of Section 28 have demonstrated.

Elements of the middle-class professional state – further and higher education, arts and culture organisations, certain, often privileged, parts of the legal establishment (the Advocates' Library in Edinburgh, for example) – have in Scotland, as elsewhere in the world, provided niches into which gay men and lesbians are drawn, can congregate and sometimes be 'out'. But this does not amount to a sizeable portion of Scotland's lesbians, gay men and bisexuals, and nor does it remotely outweigh the majority of lesbians and gays who remain resolutely not 'out' and invisible.

Representing this 'Other' Scotland in one appropriately discrete brief separate chapter is, as a result, fraught with difficulties. It has to serve as a reminder that a goodly minority of Scots are gay, lesbian, bisexual, and transgendered, but we should not sustain the lie that we are confined to and by this chapter: we are a hidden 'Other' presence in every word and deed of this anatomy.

It would be wrong, however, to conclude that, unlike 10 or especially 20 years ago, there is now anything distinctly Scottish about this 'Otherness'. The political and moral institutionalisation and visible presence of male and female homosexualities in Scotland, along with the sexual attitudes and values of the Scottish population, are now largely consistent with those of the rest of the United Kingdom, which are in turn increasingly at one with global first-world trends. Scotland may have its own legal system, but Scots sex laws diverge in only modest ways from those of England and Wales. Past major changes south of the border, such as the qualified legalisation of adult male homosexuality in 1967, took until 1980 to be legally replicated north of the border. Such Anglo-Scots legal time-lags were generally explained in the past as due to Scotland being 'a backward, repressed and socially conservative country' in the words of Tim Luckhurst, former editor of *The Scotsman* (*The Sunday Times*, 24 June 2001). However, as far as the sexual values of its population are concerned,

ıld now appear to be very similar to England, in large measure no
⁄the dramatic decline in religious affiliation and observance over the
three decades.

ng to the Scottish Social Attitudes Survey 2000, compared with 1983,
wheiı ⌐⌐ per cent of Scots believed that homosexuality was 'always wrong', by
2000 the proportion had fallen to 39 per cent. In England during the same period
the proportion fell from 48 per cent to 36 per cent (Park 2002: 102). In 1983, 32
per cent and 29 per cent respectively of English and Scottish populations
professed no religious affiliation. By 2000, the figures were 40 per cent and 41 per
cent. In the year 2000, 33 per cent of English respondents claimed to be Church
of England and 9 per cent Catholic, whereas in Scotland 35 per cent claimed to
be Church of Scotland (a fall from 45 per cent in 1983) and 12 per cent Catholic
(a fall from 22 per cent in the same year) (Parks 2002: 95–97). As these latter
figures imply, over sexual matters – whether of deep or superficial doctrinal
significance – such as abortion, contraception, homosexuality and premarital
sexual relations, religious affiliation and practice is now far less likely to have a
distinctive 'backward, repressed and socially conservative' Scottish dimension
than 20 years ago. Within Scotland, all the expected social correlates emerge: the
more politically conservative, less educationally formally qualified, religiously
active males remain the most illiberal. These optimistic conclusions are, however,
questionable, being based on ambiguous snapshot 'facts' which hardly tapped into
the complexities of popular attitudes and behavioural trends that were to some
extent revealed in the campaigning for and against repeal of Section 28,
incidentally taking place at the same time that these 'facts' were being assembled.

## SECTION 28 AS MORAL CRUSADE AND CULTURAL BATTLEGROUND

The Scottish Parliament's repeal of the infamous Section 28 in 2000 could be
taken as providing further evidence of 'Scotland's liberal shift' on matters
sexual, and that homosexuals and homosexuality have a legitimate place in
contemporary Scottish life (*The Sunday Times*, 24 June 2001). However, the
highly successful and widely supported populist, but to its critics illiberal,
'Keep the Clause' campaign powerfully suggested that any movement towards
and even beyond English sexual standards, where Section 28 has still to be
repealed, has neither been a simple drift towards standards which are simply
more liberal, nor has it meant the complete abandonment of the core
traditional heterosexist values of monogamous, lifelong, marital, reproductive,
stable sexual and emotional relationships as the ideal to which all should
aspire.

The debate and battle over Section 28 was like nothing Scotland had ever
previously seen. For a start, it brought the subject of homosexuality and the

rights of lesbians and gay men into the public domain in a way which was unprecedented. The Scottish political and polite circles had previously avoided having any public discussion on homosexuality, the 1967 partial decriminalisation being in England and Wales, and the 1980 Scottish reform was passed by a Tory government fearful of European action and facing an embarrassed Labour Party and, generally, silent gay and equality opinion. But now politics as 'moral crusade' and 'cultural war' was brought right into the heart of the Scottish body politic. This was an Americanised version of politics, where moral conservatives and liberals fight over key social issues (abortion, homosexuality, teenage pregnancy), the big issues of class and economy no longer being seen as part of the mainstream political discussion. And it proved a very uneven fight. The new institutions of devolved Scotland, the Parliament and the Executive, were wrong-footed and put on the defensive by a multi-million-pound aggressive campaign shaped by the press. The Keep the Clause campaign found its voice and a language it could address to a ready audience via the Scottish tabloids, and the *Scottish Daily Mail* and *Daily Record* in particular (Otton 2001). The equality campaign, despite the notional support of the Parliament, Executive, trade unions and voluntary groups, never found the confidence to argue its case and take on the opposition.

There is no question that in Scotland as in England and Wales the dominant regime of truth is that 'Heterosexuality [remains] institutionalised as a particular form of practice and relationships, of family structure and identity. It is constructed as a coherent natural, fixed and stable category as universal and monolithic' (Richardson 1996: 2). Implicitly, the continuing 'Otherness' of homosexuality could not be more succinctly or unflinchingly expressed. Nor could the steady disintegration of these idealised family values, indeed the family itself, be more effectively concealed, and this is in part why we will always be needed as the 'Other': we distract attention from the lie that is 'normal' and are taken to potently represent the powers of subversion. Indeed, in many organisations the 'gay lobby' is identified as the 'enemy within', and we prevent society focusing on the inherent and inevitable demise of 'the family', as conventionally defined.

'Rising divorce rates, one-parent families, abortion, homosexuality, pornography – all have been cited as indices of a nation facing social (and moral) collapse' (Durham 1991: 3), to which may be added 'paedophiles in the community', global sex tourism and teenage and child prostitution. Not only are the forces of sexual subversion and decline encircling the city of morality's walls, neither is all well with the family within. Divorce in Britain has increased five-fold since the 1960s (Lees 1993). Sixty-nine out of every thousand pregnancies in Britain occurs amongst females aged between 16 and 19, compared with nine in every thousand in the Netherlands. According to research by the International Planned Parenthood Federation, 87 per cent of British adolescent births occur out of wedlock, the highest proportion in the world. Twenty per cent of children in Britain now live in one-parent families, and 'less than half live in "traditional" families in which marriage is the core component' (Williams 1999: 12). Simultaneously, 'the family' and 'marriage' are being redefined controversially in more inclusive ways. Belgium, in 2001, joined the Netherlands in legally recognising same-sex marriages, whilst (informally, as well as formally) alternative methods and means of same-sex parenting through surrogacy, IVF treatments or adoption have become, to varying degrees, legally and economically feasible, if not widely affordable, or morally acceptable.

As one would expect, Scotland, as a small and relatively parochial society, manifests these general concerns, developments and debates found in all late-modern societies, but on a more modest and conservative scale. This was recently crystallised in the ultimately 'successful' 'repeal' of Section 28 by the fledgling Scottish Executive. Section 28 (in truth Section 2a in Scotland, where it remains forever Section 28 in political myth) was an anachronistic piece of legislation, widely ridiculed as bad law, but a most powerful rallying standard for those concerned about what they perceive as the rapid sexual and moral decline of contemporary Britain (Evans 2001). The Scottish battle over Section 28's repeal tells us much about the contemporary state of Scotland and our emphatic 'Otherness' within.

On 21 June 2000 the Scottish Parliament voted by 99 to 17 to repeal Section 28, which disappeared from the statute books following royal assent six weeks later. However, from an initial position of abolition without condition or replacement, ministers moved several times to try to placate public opinion as the scale of opposition became clear, the last concession being the inclusion of the word 'marriage' in the statutory guidelines for schools on sex education lessons. But ministers insisted that marriage would not be placed above any other form of relationship. The *Scottish Daily Mail* mourned, 'The law which prevented the promotion of homosexuality in schools, abolished despite impassioned pleas by church leaders, family values campaigners and parents groups' (*Scottish Daily Mail*, 22 June 2000). A spokesman for arch-opponent of repeal, the late Cardinal Winning, stated, 'We are totally unconvinced of the need for repeal. We have some reassurance but that could have been given months ago and spared . . . the Church, the Executive, but also the whole country from this damaging battle' (ibid.). Brian Souter, the Stagecoach millionaire and underwriter of the Keep the Clause campaign, observed 'the fight had been worthwhile'. He was pleased the Executive had agreed to endorse the position of marriage in the guidance issued to teachers which will replace Section 28, saying, 'It is good to see marriage placed at the centre of statutory guidance for future generations of Scots' (ibid.).

The McCabe Committee set up to review sex education in schools recommended that marriage should be promoted as an important part of a 'stable family life and the responsibilities of parenthood. Section 28 will be repealed but marriage will not be ignored'. The *Scottish Daily Mail* called repeal a 'A Pyrrhic Victory for Scotland's Parliament', on the grounds that it demonstrated the moral and political disjunction between population and Parliament, and because it followed a totally unnecessary eight-month demonstration of this disjunction during the Parliament's first year (*Scottish Daily Mail*, 22 June 2000). On 22 March 2001 the new guidelines for the teaching of sex education in schools were published, at the heart of which was the directive that: 'children should be encouraged to appreciate the value of commitment in relationships and partnerships including the value placed on marriage by religious groups and others in society' (*The Scotsman*, 23 March 2001). Cardinal Winning concluded that, 'This statement will go some way towards allaying the concerns of many parents who were alarmed at the repeal of Section 28.' The statement also went some considerable way towards the formal political recognition that no matter how 'equal' before the law homosexuals and homosexuality become, the fundamental immorality of what Winning called 'this perversion' was resolutely reaffirmed.

The evidence of the Keep the Clause campaign and outcome therefore strongly suggests that, despite the efforts of the Scottish Executive, Scotland remains as far as homosexuality is concerned 'a backward, repressed and socially conservative country' in which religious institutions and the populist media, with the financial backing of wealthy defenders of moral faith, have more power than the nation's legally elected assembly. However, the publication of the Scottish Attitudes Survey 2000 referred to earlier was based on research carried out in the immediate aftermath of the Keep the Clause campaign. Surely this provided a quite different view of Scottish sexual mores? The broadsheet media certainly believed so. Referring back to the Keep the Clause campaign, *The Sunday Times* (24 June 2001) reminded its readers of the Scottish moral majority on the march behind Brian Souter, 'which had supposedly had the Scottish government on the run' and greeted what it described as 'this landmark' survey as 'scotching the myth that Keep the Clause was a telling symptom of a deep moral conservatism in the new Scotland' because it provided evidence that Scotland is 'abandoning its hard attitudes to homosexuality . . . at a rate that has amazed the academics involved in the study'.

Certainly the findings of the Scottish Social Attitudes Survey 2000 hardly tallied with the popular support for the Keep the Clause campaign – but was *The Sunday Times* right to give greater weight to the former, when the Keep the Clause campaign had mobilised over one million Scots to vote in the referendum to keep Section 28? It quoted a John Deighan, parliamentary officer for the Catholic Church, who hardly explained the discrepancy by claiming it was due to 'a great deal of moral confusion out there'. Tim Hopkins of the Equality Network put the mass Keep the Clause support down to misinformation and tabloid-directed moral panic: 'I never really believed Scotland was more backward and more homophobic than England.' He cited as further counter evidence the Scottish Executive's 'equality strategy', which has declared war on all discrimination, including that of sexual preference. *The Sunday Times* concluded, 'The time may yet come when Keep the Clause seems less like a portent and more like an aberration.'

The Scottish Social Attitudes Survey 2000 and Keep the Clause evidence are not necessarily discrepant, however. Nor are the two bodies of evidence necessarily indicative of the public's 'misinformation' over Section 28 or its wider 'moral confusion' over sexual matters. Rather, there are ample well-reasoned grounds for concluding that, in their own very different terms, both bodies of evidence accurately indicate the distinction now made between legality and morality in the general popular consciousness, and in the main key political, religious and economic institutions of the land. It is now far more likely than in the past for populations to recognise the right of consensual adult gay men and lesbians to *legally* exist and pursue alternative lifestyles. This, however, is only insofar as our 'out' 'existence' is confined to some form of 'private' or discretely distinct socio-cultural urban territories, and does not therefore cause 'public' offence to the moral majority which has the greater legal, and moral, right not to be so offended. The growing liberalisation of attitudes to the legal status of minority sexual behaviours and rights should, in other words, be set against a majority commitment, notwithstanding, to uphold clear conventional moral standards, especially in the protection of the sexually innocent and vulnerable child, as evidenced by the following:

> In providing programmes of sex education, local authorities should also take account of Section 35 of the Ethical Standards in Public Life etc. (Scotland) Act 2000 which puts a duty on councils to have regard to:
> The value of a stable family life to a child's development;
> And the need to ensure that the content of instruction provided by authorities is appropriate having regard to each child's understanding and stage of development. (Standards in Scotland's Schools etc. Act (2000): Conduct of Sex Education in Scottish Schools: www.Scotland.Gov.UK)

As Conservative MSP Phil Gallie observed: 'I've no problem with people who live within their own premises and do their own thing quietly and in the background but there's far too much of a promotion aspect in things today and this clause refers to the promotion of homosexuality' (Phil Gallie MP, *Scotland Today*, 10 February 2000). Possibly the most significant but ironic implication within the combined recent evidence of Keep the Clause and the Scottish Social Attitudes Survey 2000 is that within the complex sexual post-devolution climate, Scotland is now indistinguishable from England. In both countries, gay men's and lesbians' legal rights of existence are increasingly recognised, but only within specifically circumscribed and monitored contexts so that the 'moral community' is not offended, contexts which emphasise our moral and sexual 'Otherness' and which pay due respect to the heterosexist norm.

# THE LIMITS OF 'GAY COMMUNITY'

It is out of these contemporary developments that a further ideological fable of our 'Otherness' is born: that we belong to a discrete and unified collective called 'the gay community'. This is descriptively a fallacious label for what is, in practice, a loose constituency of various sexual minorities who consequently only have in common their relative exclusion from 'normal' society. However, ideologically 'the gay community' is a potent means of imposing moral order by setting all sexual dissidents apart and together and by underlining the boundaries between 'us' and 'them'. Inevitably, in Scotland as everywhere else, sufficient numbers amongst these minorities fall into line and an ersatz 'gay community' develops, which appears to consist of a fully rounded collection of minority interest groups, political organisations and support networks, but which is in practice little more than a niche market for gay leisure and lifestyle consumption.

Most obviously this 'Other' Scotland is geographically associated with the commercial gay 'scenes' of the two largest cities, Glasgow and Edinburgh, as mapped out in the likes of the listings at the back of the monthly magazine *Scots Gay* and other guides. In both cities, what was originally dispersed and discrete has become increasingly concentrated – in Broughton Street and Merchant City areas, respectively – giving rise to the adoption in both cities of another fallacious sobriquet, the use of which is sadly devoid of much-needed camp irony: the 'gay village'. These 'villages' consist of virtually identical bars and clubs not even owned by 'village' members.

In practice, the majority of gays, lesbians and bisexuals make at most only occasional use of these specifically gay social territories, and even fewer support the various specialist representative political and support groups organised around improving gay rights which underline the homosexual 'Otherness'. The addresses, contact and other details of the latter, which range from lesbigay student and youth groups, bereavement groups, organisations for homosexual Christians, atheists/humanists, and older gays, to rape and sexual abuse helplines, and various trade union groups may be found in magazines such as *Scots Gay*; however, the scale of resources available to such enterprises can be measured by the fact that *Gay Scotland*, a well-produced bi-monthly (and then monthly) could not find the revenue in sales and advertising to be viable.

Mention should also be made of the following national organisations: Outright Scotland, which describes itself as 'Scotland's oldest gay, lesbian, bisexual and transgender organisation . . . currently focusing on work around the Scottish Parliament, Scottish Executive and the Scottish public institutions such as the NHS, police and justice system' (convener@outright-scotland.org); Beyond Barriers, 'a National Lottery funded project challenging prejudice and homophobia whilst linking minority and majority groups within Scotland' (info@beyondbarriers.org.uk); Equality Network, 'working for lesbian, gay, bisexual and transgender equality within Scotland' (en@equality-network.org); Pride Scotland, which organises the annual 'Gay, Lesbian, Bisexual and Transpeople' Pride Rally (info@pridescotland.org); and Stonewall Scotland (scotland@stonewall.org.uk). Useful facilities include the Lesbian Archive and Information Centre in the Glasgow Women's Library (gwl@womens-library.org.uk) and the Glasgow LGBT Centre (lgbt.glasgow@gglc.org.uk), which hosts a number of subsidiary organisations such as Lesbian Inclusion Co-ordination (AliJarvis@unify.freeserve.co.uk). In addition, there are relatively developed support and fund-raising groups and activities organised around the specific issue of HIV/AIDS, with Body Positive groups in most cities and regions: Strathclyde (bpstrathclyde@enterprise.net), Fife (bodypositive@care4free.net), Tayside (admin@bptayside.sol.co.uk).

In contemporary Scotland there is, therefore, this overt 'Other' presence, just as in this anatomy of Scotland there is this comparable, neatly compart-mentalised chapter in recognition of Scots lesbigay citizens. But do not be misled into believing that we are so constrained and that this is where we may be found because, to return to Cant's opening judgement, 'for the most part lesbians and gay men are invisible in modern Scotland'. To put this another way, 'these people' are present in all areas of contemporary Scottish life and throughout the different sections and chapters of this anatomy, but their 'Otherness' imposes at least caution and, in most instances, secrecy and silence.

# 31

# ASIANS IN SCOTLAND: THE FORMATION OF AN ELITE?

*Elinor Kelly*

It is an intriguing challenge to analyse the formation of an 'Asian' elite when we do not have essential data that will emerge in the very near future. For years analysts of 'race' and ethnic issues have been pointing towards the urgent need for systematic ethnic monitoring in official data and public reports (Cant and Kelly 1995a). The situation is serious enough in England and Wales, where ethnic monitoring has been occasional and erratic; it is even more serious in Scotland, though, because either Scotland was simply not included in 'national' surveys, or was submerged as a region. Scottish political analysts such as Bochel (1998) have, accordingly, not taken an interest in 'race' and ethnic issues.

But the results of the Census for 2001 are imminent and the battle to ensure that Scotland adopted the same ethnic and religious categories as England and Wales was won (Kelly 2000a: 130). As a result of the Race Relations Amendment Act 2000, all public bodies and many employers will be required to release 'ethnic' data. In addition, in Holyrood, serious research into the facts of life for black and minority ethnic communities has been commissioned by Scottish ministers. Within a year, we should know far more about the ways in which new Scots have, or have not, entered the systems and structures of civic Scotland. And yet, how could an anatomy of the new Scotland be published in 2002 without reference to the migrants, refugees and Scottish-born black and minority ethnic communities who live and work in all our cities, towns and villages; who are displaying both an extraordinary amount of entrepreneurial courage and flair, and a growing impatience with the barriers that are hemming them in in isolation from the mainstream of civic life?

Political will, interest in ethnicity and the flow of essential data are closely linked. Scotland's black and minority ethnic communities are missing from the corridors of power: 28 out of 32 councils have no black and minority ethnic councillors at all, there are no black or Chinese councillors, there are only six

Asian councillors, four of whom are in Glasgow (Vestri and Fitzpatrick 2000). There is just one Asian Member of Parliament, Mohammed Sarwar, and he has been tainted by accusations of bribery that were made immediately after his election in 1997. There was widespread shock and deep anger when the Scottish Parliament was elected without a single member from among New Scots, especially because all political parties had been warned repeatedly that their selection procedures were exclusionary and would lead to this outcome. Scotland is diversifying faster than ever before and there is urgent need for recognition of the contributions being made by New Scots to our economy and culture – but where is that recognition to be found?

'Asians' as a term is a misnomer, part of the problem of research inequality. When first adopted in Britain it was with reference to the immigration status that dominates political and administrative thinking. 'Asian' is not an accurate description of geographical origin, but a substitute for 'Indian', the term that was used when British India was the jewel in the crown of Empire. Three independent states – India, Pakistan and Bangladesh – were to emerge out of the former India. 'Asian' became the composite term to encompass all three 'nationalities', to be differentiated from 'Chinese', 'Black' and 'White'. This four-fold distinction was adopted by the 1991 Census and structured public data for the next decade, giving spurious legitimacy to analysis that became specialised and disconnected from the mainstream of economic and social inquiry – class analysis usually stops the moment that ethnic categories are inserted. The crudities of 'ethnic' analysis are such that Scotland is usually omitted, left aside because there were insufficient numbers of Asians, blacks and Chinese to 'merit consideration' (Kelly 2000b). Numerically, 'Asians' are the most prominent of the New Scots, and they have also become the most visible in the fragments of data that are available to us at present. This chapter is therefore an exercise in partiality, taking advantage of what can be extracted in the current situation, an antecedent to wider-ranging research in which fragments must be sewn together, as minorities that are even more neglected than the 'Asians' emerge into research reality.

Why is it that Scottish Asians have so little part in the mainstream of political process? What are the consequences of Asian absence from the corridors of power where key decisions are made? What are the barriers that lie in the way of the formation of a South Asian elite within the Scottish establishment? Has the success of the few eased the loneliness and vulnerability of the many who are making their living among people who are as poor as themselves?

## ASIAN MIGRATIONS TO SCOTLAND

In his book, *The New Scots: The Story of Asians in Scotland*, Bashir Maan traces the origins of the Asian settlement in Scotland back to 1916, when Noor Muhammad Tanda left Bombay and found work in a Greenock shipyard, stayed for two years during which time he was joined by some compatriots, travelled extensively, but then returned to share a business in the Gorbals that traded under the name of Tanda, Ashrif and Company (Maan 1992: 98). Tanda's biography is an archetype for what was to be repeated many times over. Migrants from British India, and later from partitioned India, travelled the routes pioneered by men from their region, especially Punjab. The Indians of the time worked as seamen (lascars) but also as street hawkers, traders and itinerant peddlers (see, for instance, the story of Nathoo Mohammed in Maan: 108-118), in other words, turning their hand to any niche that they could identify within the local economy. Maan estimates that in the 1920s there were only about 40 Asians in the whole of Scotland, mostly poor migrant peasant farmers from Punjab. By 1991, there were 21,000 Pakistanis, 10,000 Indians and 1,000 Bangladeshis. In each of the communities, 45 per cent or more were British-born (Dalton and Hampton 1995: 5).

Making a living selling small items to people as poor as themselves was a struggle, exacerbated by the hostility they frequently experienced at the hands of their neighbours and customers. Maan refers to the 'race riot' that took place in Glasgow in 1919 when sailors' unions in every British port launched their campaign against the employment of black seamen (Maan 1992: 98–9); he also describes an assault on Nathoo and his friends, which led to the death of young Noor Mohammed (ibid.; 111–114). Nonetheless, Nathoo, realising that there was real economic potential in peddling, called over relatives and friends, thus initiating the 'chain migration' that was to bring increasing numbers of Indian men to Glasgow, and, as competition between them increased, to their dispersal across Scotland. As the farmer-peddlers spread they encountered other Indians who had migrated as students, some of whom, such as Jainti Dass Saggar, decided to stay in Scotland. Having qualified at the University of St Andrews, Saggar practised medicine in Dundee for many years, joined the Labour Party and was elected as Scotland's first Asian councillor in 1936, serving for 18 years (Maan 1992: 127; Cant and Kelly 1995b: 17).

In the 1930s the first Indian wholesale textile and drapery warehouses were opened in Glasgow, managed by men who spoke the same language as their customers and who were willing to extend credit. Maan traces the first grocery/general stores to that period:

> The tradition of Indo-Pakistanis going into the textile/drapery and grocery businesses thus started in the mid-'30s . . . Life was a lot easier now for those who were living in Glasgow. They had easy access to their merchandise which they could obtain any time they desired. The traditional ingredients for their food and all the spices were readily available from the shops owned by their countrymen. These shops, and

especially the warehouses, also served as meeting places for those lonely
men . . . It appears that the community in those days was very close-knit.
(Maan 1992: 137-9)

The migration chain was disrupted by the Second World War and the religious
hatred unleashed during Indian partition, resulting in the forced migration of
Muslims out of India, and of Hindus and Sikhs out of Pakistan. After the lull
of the 1940s, the numbers of migrants from India and Pakistan rose, including
many 'twice migrants' who were displaced across the new borders, then moved
overseas. For instance, Yaqub Ali, who was to become a millionaire and one of
the most prominent of New Scots, migrated twice, first from India into
Pakistan, then four years later, to join his brother in Scotland (Maan 1992: 159;
Kelly 1998: 9–12). The growing number of newcomers found that peddling and
trading was becoming more difficult in the post-war economy, and looked for
other forms of work, preferably self-employed but, when necessary, in factories,
mills and transport. From 1955 onwards, peddling declined as the lead
occupation for Scottish Asians as shopkeeping and trading grew in significance
(Maan 1992: 161–4).

The Scottish Asian community not only grew but also dispersed and
diversified whenever there was a local labour shortage. In the 1960s, compatriots
moved north from the Midlands and Yorkshire in order to work the shifts in
Dundee mills. When 'Asians' in the newly independent states of East Africa –
Kenya, Uganda, Malawi – experienced harassment and persecution, many fled,
like the Okhai family. Ibrahim Okhai hurriedly left Malawi, started a painting
and decorating business in Dundee, moved into property, and in 1981 bought
James Keiller's Confectionery and Preserves Factory and three other substantial
businesses:

> Thus this one family, which arrived in Scotland as penniless refugees, has
> so far provided work and brought prosperity to about 700 Scottish
> families directly, and many hundreds more indirectly. Their astounding
> success is due mainly to their hard work, their determination and their
> entrepreneurial skills. (Maan 1992: 168)

## ASIANS IN SCOTLAND TODAY

The story of the remarkable few is no substitute for evidence about the many. In
the various small-scale studies that have been carried out, there are indicators
that there have been many casualties of the risks that are run by entrepreneurs
(Deakins et al. 1995; 1997). There are also clues about the continuing barriers
that surround even the wealthiest of Asians, slowing their formation into an
elite with presence in wide-ranging areas of Scottish civic life. But, again, it must

be reiterated that we lack the robust statistical data, coded by ethnicity, that could form the context within which to analyse the significance of the Scottish Asians who have emerged into prominence (as featured in *Eastern Eye*'s 2002 listing of Britain's Richest Asians).

In its interim analytical report, *Ethnic Minorities and the Labour Market* (Cabinet Office 2002), the Cabinet Office in Westminster has reviewed data, coded by ethnicity, that can be extrapolated from the Labour Force Survey and other mass data. Their findings suggest that 'trends in education, employment and unemployment, health and housing are shaped not only by ethnicity but also by gender, and possibly by class' (2002: 15). In other words, minority ethnic communities, aggregated and obscured by the crudities of existing forms of data, are diverse and various, and income differentials among Asians are great, straddling extremes of wealth and success as well as poverty. Occupational distribution differs markedly between Asian, Black and White, and, among Asians, between Bangladeshis, Indians and Pakistanis. For instance, twice as high a proportion of Indians are in professional and managerial posts; more Asians than either Black or White, are small employers and own account workers (12 per cent as compared with 4 per cent and 8 per cent, respectively). The conditions under which small businesses function, especially those located in areas of poverty, suggest many experience a form of ethnic lock – encapsulated sectors within which a living can be gained, but at the price of long hours and precarious income, and from which it is difficult to escape.

## Key findings summarised from the Cabinet Office Report 2002

- In the Labour Force Survey marked differences in occupational distribution have been detected between Asian, Black and White: 42 per cent of Indians, 22 per cent of Pakistanis and 8 per cent of Bangladeshis are in professional and managerial posts; 12 per cent of Asians are small employers and own account workers, compared with 4 per cent of Black and 8 per cent of White.
- While many British South Asians are self-employed, there are significant differences in the performances of the ethnic groups that are self-employed.
- Within the private sector, ethnic minorities seem to be over-represented in small business and under-represented in large companies.
- Small ethnic minority businesses tend not to recruit across ethnic lines, or even outside the family group, excluding other minorities and the white population. This reduces demand for other ethnic groups in highly diverse areas where different ethnic minority communities live together.
- Ethnic minority businesses have less capital to expand or to pay salaries.

In the review commissioned by the Scottish Executive, *Audit of Research on Minority Ethnic Issues in Scotland from a 'Race' Perspective* (Netto et al. 2001), there is a chapter dealing with Employment and Enterprise, and one on Poverty. Below, I summarise some key findings.

### Key findings summarised from the Scottish Executive Report 2001

- Self-employment is five times higher among the minority ethnic population than for the population as a whole; indeed, the rates of self-employment in Scotland may be higher than for Britain as a whole.
- Minority ethnic businesses and enterprises face competitive threat; are concentrated in a limited number of sectors; have restricted access to business training, support and advice; rely heavily on personal networks for finance; and face racial discrimination.
- There are differences within and between minority ethnic groups in their experiences of poverty.

It seems that Scotland's black and minority ethnic communities experience the same barriers and prospects as their peers in England and Wales. There is a Scottish equivalent of ethnic lock that ties down the poorest.

## FROM RAGS TO RICHES? SCOTLAND'S ASIAN MILLIONAIRES

Once a year, in March, lists of Britain's richest Asians are published, and a lavish Asian Business Dinner is held in London. The lists are headed by Lakshmi Mittal, steel magnate, and the Hinduja brothers, international traders, who have created vast fortunes, and include two men who have been made members of the House of Lords (Lord Bagri, chair of the London Metal Exchange, and Lord Paul, steel magnate). Also included are 11 millionaires in Scotland (see Table 1 below). *Eastern Eye* indicates that three of Scotland's millionaires (Rasul, Ali and Sarwar) are migrants who started with little or nothing and Maan tells us that the Sher empire was initiated by Sher Mohammed and his brothers, who initially worked as peddlers (Maan 1992: 176). Hayat, the Khushis, Ali, Ramzan, Sarwar, the Mobariks and the Kohlis are all leading import–export and wholesale warehouse businesses; Rasul leads Global Video, Gill owns the Harlequin Leisure Group, the Tulis created the chain of The Jean Scene shops. Glasgow dominates in the list – Sandhu started business in Hong Kong but has invested heavily in Glasgow since 1985, while House of Sher, AA Brothers, United Wholesalers and Clyde Importers are all prominent features on the Glasgow retail landscape. Global Video and The Jean Scene are located in most shopping centres and high streets, and the Harlequin Group owns some very popular, trendy restaurants often featured in the Scottish press. The millionaires span two, if not three, generations from Yaqub Ali, aged 69, to Sunny Tuli, aged only 30.

Although some arrived in Glasgow literally penniless, we do not, at this time, have sufficient information to judge the class origins of these entrepreneurs. Yaqub Ali was educated to primary school level in India, arrived in Scotland without any money, studied English in evening classes in Glasgow while his brother worked as a conductor on the buses, and kick-started his fortune through cut-price trading in liquor (Maan 1992: 177–8), but Tuli was able to borrow £3,000 from his mother. If, indeed, it can be proven that most of the Asian millionaires started from nothing, then this is a remarkable feat unprecedented in Scotland's business history.

## ETHNIC LOCK OR BUSINESS RESOURCE?

In their studies of the Tobacco Lords of the eighteenth century and Scottish business leaders 1860–1960, Devine (1975) and Slaven and Kim (1994) describe the enclaves in which entrepreneurs could thrive, raising the credit they required and reducing, as far as possible, the risks of expansion in trade. The Tobacco Lords led Glasgow and its satellite ports into a position of dominance in transatlantic trade with the British colonies in North America. They invested the capital required to turn Glasgow into an entrepôt of international standing, with a sophisticated financial and commercial system and a vigorous urban culture; they also won the backing of American planters by providing them with investment capital on long-term credit. Slaven and Kim (1994) studied business leaders a century later, both in longer-established trades and industry and in the rapidly expanding trades in shipbuilding, metals, vehicles and construction supply.

The tobacco merchants formed a small, tightly knit group linked by partnership connection, marriage alliance and kinship loyalties; yet the merchants were not a self-perpetuating caste. Insolvency among established families and the very considerable rate of expansion in the colonial trades combined to loosen the bonds of any enduring monopoly and to offer openings to the ambitious. On the other hand, existing contacts within the community and a measure of wealth were normally vital; most were the offspring of merchants, lairds and professional families; the majority had reached a commendable level of educational achievement and most had access to sources of credit and capital among their kin. The Glasgow men evolved commercial methods well adapted to the needs of both clients in America and customers in Europe. The reward for the successful was wealth on a scale never before imagined in Scotland (Devine 1975: 171–3).

In the study by Slaven and Kim, four out of five of Scottish business leaders

301

were either founders or inheritors of the business, not professional managers. He found that family background and family influence were more significant than formal education in the success of the businessmen. Family ownership and family were the major influence in almost all the main sectors of the economy and the fathers of more than a third of the founders, and four-fifths of the inheritors, were upper middle class. The nature of the Scottish economy 'propelled the businessman into a kind of mutually supportive, yet competitive community. The regional economy was small in scale, concentrated in location and characterised by a complex interdependence of supply and demand linking the great staple industries. Their entrepreneurs were likewise enshrined in coterie networks, within which emerged a number of leading coteries who essentially formed Scotland's business aristocracy . . . such patterns of interaction were frequently reinforced by marriage' (Slaven and Kim 1994: 156–168).

In its *Update Scotland*, the Royal Bank of Scotland isolates the reasons why the Scottish economy is 'underperforming', that is to say, growing at a rate below trend, lagging behind that of the rest of the UK. While the consumer sector is relatively healthy, the manufacturing sector is in recession; the Scottish economy is more trade-exposed than the UK overall and therefore vulnerable to the shock of the slowing global economy. It is also more dependent upon 'traditional' manufacturing sectors in long-term decline, and on factory-based electronics industries that are more vulnerable to closure. Especially, it emphasises:

> New business start-ups in Scotland – an important source of growth for the economy – are poor compared to the UK. Scotland has a business birth rate of 28 per 10,000 population compared with 38 in England. The greater dependence upon large, traditional manufacturing industries and the role of the public sector as an important employer may have created an 'employment culture' rather than an entrepreneurial one. (Royal Bank of Scotland 2001)

Asian migrants started many businesses, but will their descendants – Scottish-born Asians – choose to emulate their parents? If the businesses are small, low-paid and unrewarding, the evidence points towards young Asians seeking to escape via educational attainment and entry to salaried posts. If the businesses are successful, then Asian youth, such as the daughters of Charan Gill (*Scotland on Sunday*, 1 April 2001), may decide to stay within the dynasties that are now taking shape. However, at both ends of the scale of prosperity, there are constraints unlike those faced by Scots in the past. Scottish education has been celebrated as a significant path out of poverty, especially in families of Irish Catholic descent disadvantaged by widespread sectarian prejudice and discrimination (Paterson 2000c). Asian youth who step beyond the confines of its ethnic enclave experience racist discrimination (Hampton and Bain 1995; Hampton 1998).

Malini Mehri, director and founder of the Centre for Social Markets, argues that the time has come for Asian businesses to show leadership in the arena of corporate social and environmental responsibility. Nowadays, the status and reputations of businesses are probed because people want to know how the wealth was won and the uses to which it is being put. Asian business is estimated to contribute more than £5 billion to the British economy, but one in five British children lives in poverty. 'Are Asian businesses investing in Britain's poorest communities (often their own)?' (Mehri 2002).

Wealthy Asians seeking to emulate the industrial barons and great traders of the past must, according to *Eastern Eye*, expect to pay a disproportionate price in modern forms of media scrutiny:

> It has been an eventful year for Asian businesses. The top two from our list – Lakshmi Mittal and the Hindujas – have rarely been out of the news, sadly for all the wrong reasons . . . the huge publicity surrounding them [has] not been helpful for Asian businesses in the UK. There was an unpleasant racist undertone to much of the publicity in both cases. And in the long term it will be very damaging if political leaders now create a distance between themselves and Asian-owned businesses for fear of being accused of accepting donations in return for access to the corridors of power . . . We hope that our list, now in its sixth year, helps to correct some of the false perceptions created by the media frenzy during the past 12 months. (Mehri 2002: 3)

Bashir Maan, the author of the only book to have been written about Asians in Scotland, migrated in 1953 and was formerly business partner of Yaqub Ali. In addition he has a remarkable record of public service. He is currently a Glasgow City councillor and Convener of the Strathclyde Joint Police Board, having first been elected as a councillor in Glasgow Corporation in 1970 – the first muslim in Britain. For many years he chaired Strathclyde Community Relations Council, and served as Deputy Chair of the UK Commission for Racial Equality. He is a leading member of many Pakistani and muslim organisations, President of the National Association of British Pakistanis, Scottish representative of the Executive Committee of the Muslim Council of Britain. In 2001, he was invited by the President of Pakistan, General Musharraf, to serve as a member of his Task Force on Human Development in Pakistan.

Is appreciation of Yaqub Ali, and acknowledgement of years of public service by Bashir Maan any real substitute for the formation of an elite and its expansion into Scotland's polity? Do we not need more diverse political representation now that Scotland's ethnic map is changing faster than ever (Kelly 2002)? Within the community of Tobacco Lords, there was an inner elite whose friends and relations provided the provosts, councillors and baillies who ruled in Edinburgh during the late eighteenth century. Will Asians ever achieve such prominence in the Scotland of the twenty-first century?

## Table 1: Wealthy Asians in Scotland 2002

Profiles, extracted from *Eastern Eye* 2002

*1. Munawar Hayat and Family*
Hayat (56) is managing director of Sher Brothers (Glasgow) Bonnypack and House of Sher, family-owned companies in Glasgow dealing in import, export, wholesale and retail of clothing, hardware, family goods, electrical equipment, toys and foodstuffs. Sher Brothers alone is worth about £10 million, as is Bonnypack. The group recently invested £5 million in a goods wholesale business and has created another company dissociated from the rest in order to manage the vast land bank. Future plans are to develop the land for residential purposes. With other assets, the family will be worth perhaps £35.5 million and their value is set to keep rising.

*2. Maq Rasul*
It was reported last year that Rasul (48) is continuing his 'multi-million-pound expansion' of Global Video into England, with plans to have 290 shops and one million members. In 1964, Maq moved from Pakistan to a Glasgow tenement as an 11-year-old child. In 1976, he graduated from Paisley College of Technology with a degree in civil engineering and scraped together the money to buy a grocery shop. From that base, he moved into video rentals. In 1998, profits rose to £3 million on sales of £31.2 million. The Rasul family retains more than 75 per cent of the shares.

*3. Afzal and Akmal Khushi*
Brothers Afzal (56) and Akmal (46) own all the shares in Jacobs and Turner, a Glasgow-based ski and sportswear clothing manufacturer and wholesaler. The business, incorporated in 1970, made £670,000 profit on sales of £17.4 million in the year to June 2000, but gross profit stood at £12 million. The brothers are estimated to be worth £25 million.

*4. Amarjit Sandhu*
In 1972, Amarjit (65) started business in Hong Kong but has invested heavily in Glasgow since 1985. He has two Scottish companies, ABS (Scotland) and Saraki (UK) plus a Hong Kong business, IPJ Agencies. He divides his time between Scotland and Hong Kong. ABS (Scotland) made a profit in the year to December 2000. His businesses are worth £25 million.

*5. Yaqub and Taj Ali*
Yaqub (69) left Pakistan after Partition with less than £5 in his pocket and worked as a door-to-door salesman in Glasgow. With his brother Taj, he built up a large cash-and-carry operation called AA Brothers, which was sold and the

site redeveloped as a retail park. The Ali family assets are worth £18 million.

### 6. Mohammed Ramzan
Mohammed Ramzan (44) is the business partner of Mohammed Sarwar, the Labour MP for Glasgow Govan. Between them they own United Wholesale Grocers, a huge cash-and-carry company. In the year to 2000, profits were £900,000 from a turnover of £88 million. Ramzan's stake in the company, plus other assets, take him to £13 million.

### 7. Mohammed Sarwar MP
Mohammed Sarwar (50) came to Britain from Pakistan in 1978 and settled in Glasgow. A year later he launched United Wholesale Grocers, a cash-and-carry operation which has since grown into a huge business. Sarwar was elected as Labour MP for Glasgow Govan in May 1997. United Wholesale is estimated to be worth £20 million, with sales of £88 million and profits of £900,000. Sarwar's personal wealth is estimated at £12.4 million.

### 8. Shokat and Riaz Mobarik
Shokat (40) and Riaz (66) are directors of LTC Distributors, a family-owned wholesaler based in Glasgow. In 2000, LTC made £1.3 million profit on sales of £19 million. With a strong balance sheet showing assets of £5.4 million, the Mobariks are worth around £12 million.

### 9. Charan Gill
Charan (47) is managing director of Glasgow-based Harlequin Leisure Group. The pubs-to-restaurants and frozen foods group was founded in 1987 and is owned by Gill and his family. His business is worth £10.7 million, with profits of £260,000 on sales of £1.3 million in the year to October 2000.

### 10. Harvinder and Bhupinder Kohli
Kohli Harvinder (59) and Bhupinder (51) own Clyde Importers, an electrical goods wholesale business in Glasgow. The Kohlis and their family own all the shares in the business founded in 1974 and worth £10 million, with profits of £311,000 on sales of £9 million.

### 11. Raju and Sunny Tuli
In 1983 Raju (39) borrowed £3,000 from his mother to buy some branded jeans, which he sold in markets around his Scottish home. From these beginnings, he has created The Jean Scene, one of Scotland's fastest-growing retailers. With his brother Sunny (29), the company is now diversifying into other areas. In the year up to January 2001, sales were up by £1 million, gross profit up by £500,000, and net profit was £62,000 due to the costs of company growth. The company is valued at £10 million.

# References

Adonis, A. and Pollard, S. (1997), *A Class Act: The Myth of Britain's Classless Society*, London: Hamish Hamilton.

Aitken, K. (1992) 'The Economy', in M. Linklater and R. Denniston (eds.), *Anatomy of Scotland*, Edinburgh: Chambers.

Aitken, K. (1997), *The Bairns o' Adam: The Story of the STUC*, Edinburgh: Polygon.

Alexander, W. (1999), 'Tackling Poverty and Social Inclusion', in G. Hassan and C. Warhurst (eds.) *A Different Future: A Modernisers' Guide to Scotland*, Edinburgh: Centre for Scottish Public Policy/*The Big Issue in Scotland*.

Bailey, N., Turok, I. and Docherty, I. (1999), *Edinburgh and Glasgow: Contrasts in Competitiveness and Cohesion*, Glasgow: University of Glasgow.

Bain, R. (1968), *The Clans and Tartans of Scotland*, Glasgow: Collins.

Baird G. (2001), 'The Myth of the "Creative Industries"', in A. Peacock, G. Baird, G. Elliot, G. Havergal, D. Macdonald, A. Massie and A. Murray-Watson, *Calling the Tune: A Critique of Arts Funding in Scotland*, Edinburgh: Policy Institute.

Barker, C.R., Ford, P.J., Moody, S.R. and Elliot, R.C. (eds.) (1996), *Charity Law in Scotland*, Edinburgh: Green/Sweet and Maxwell.

Barnett, C. (2001), *The Verdict of Peace: Britain Between her Yesterday and the Future*, London: Macmillan.

Bennie, D. (1995), *Not Playing for Celtic: Another Paradise Lost*, Edinburgh: Mainstream.

Bentley, T. et al. (2001), *What Learning Needs: The Challenge for a Creative Nation*, London: DEMOS/Design Council.

Benzeval, M., Judge, K. and Whitehead, M. (eds.) (1995), *Tackling Inequalities in Health: An Agenda for Action*, London: King's Fund.

Beveridge, C. and Turnbull. R. (1989), *The Eclipse of Scottish Culture*, Edinburgh: Polygon.

Beveridge, C. and Turnbull, R. (1997), *Scotland After Enlightenment*, Edinburgh: Polygon.

Black, D. (2001), *All The First Minister's Men: The Truth Behind Holyrood*, Edinburgh: Birlinn.

Bloomer, K. (1999), 'The Local Governance of Education: An Operational Perspective', in T.G.K. Bryce and W.H. Humes (eds.), *Scottish Education*, Edinburgh: Edinburgh University Press.

Bloomer, K. (2001a), *Learning to Change: Scottish Education in the Early 21st Century*, Edinburgh: Scottish Council Foundation.

Bloomer, K. (2001b), Speech to Chartered Institute of Public Finance and Accountancy Conference, 6 April 2001.

Bochel, C. and Bochel, H. M. (1998), 'Scotland's Councillors 1974–1995', *Scottish Affairs*, Summer 1998, No. 24.

Bolger, D. and Pease, B. (1998), *Reinventing Management*, Edinburgh: Eglinton Management Centre.

Boyle, L., Davies, M., Elrick, D., Leicester, G., Lyon, A. and McCormick, J. (2001), *Out of the Ordinary: The Power of Ambition in an Uncertain World*, Edinburgh: Scottish Council Foundation.

Boyle, R. and Lynch P. (eds.) (1998), *Out of the Ghetto?: The Catholic Community in Modern Scotland*, Edinburgh: John Donald.

Boyle, S., Burns, M., Danson, M., Foster, J., Harrison, D. and Woolfson, C. (1989), *Scotland's Economy: Claiming the Future*, London: Verso in conjunction with the Scottish Trades Union Congress.

Bradley, J. (1995), *Ethnic and Religious Identity in Modern Scotland: Culture, Politics and Football*, Aldershot: Avebury.

Breitenbach, E. (1999), 'Changing Gender Relations in Contemporary Scotland' in G. Hassan and C. Warhurst (eds.) *A Different Future: A Modernisers' Guide to Scotland*, Edinburgh: Centre for Scottish Public Policy/*The Big Issue in Scotland*.

Brooks, D. (2000), *Bobos in Paradise: The New Upper Class and How They Got There*, London: Simon and Schuster.

Brooksbank, D. (2002), 'Self-employment and Small Firms', in S. Carter and D. Jones-Evans (eds.) *Enterprise and Small Business: Principles, Practice and Policy*, London: Financial Times/Prentice Hall.

Brown, A., Barnett Donaghy, T., Mackay, F. and Meehan, E. (2002) 'Women and Constitutional Change in Scotland and Northern Ireland', in K. Ross (ed.) *Women, Politics and Change*, Oxford: Oxford University Press.

Brown, A. (1998) 'Deepening Democracy: Women and the Scottish Parliament', Regional and Federal Studies, Vol. 8 No. 1, reprinted in E. Breitenbach and F. Mackay (eds.) *Women and Contemporary Scottish Politics*, Edinburgh: Polygon.

Brown, A. P. (2001), *The Voluntary Sector and the Scottish Parliament: Opportunities and Challenges*, York: Joseph Rowntree Foundation.

Brown, C.G. (1997), *Religion and Society in Scotland since 1707*, Edinburgh:

Edinburgh University Press.

Brown, C.G. (2000), Review of R. Boyle and P. Lynch (eds.), *Out of the Ghetto?*, *Scottish Historical Review*, October 2000, Vol. 79.

Bruce, A. and Forbes, T. (2001), 'From Competition to Collaboration in the Delivery of Health Care: Implementing Change in Scotland', *Scottish Affairs*, Winter 2001, No. 34.

Budge, I. and Unwin D. (1966), *Scottish Political Behaviour*, London: Longman.

Burt, E. (1998), 'Charities and Political Activity: Time to Re-think the Rules', *Political Quarterly*, Vol. 69 No. 1.

Burt, E. and Taylor, J.A. (2001), 'Giving Greater "Political Voice" to Charities in Scotland?', *Public Money and Management*, Vol. 21 No. 4.

Cabinet Office (2002) *Ethnic Minorities and the Labour Market*, London: The Stationery Office.

Cahill, K. (2001), *Who Owns Britain?*, Edinburgh: Canongate.

Callaghan, G. (1997), 'Stakeholding and the Scottish Parliament', *Renewal: A Journal of Labour Politics*, Vol. 5, No. 3/4.

Callander, R.F. (1986), 'The Law of the Land', in J. Hulbert (ed.) *Land: Ownership and Use*, Dundee: Fletcher Society.

Cameron, A. (1993), 'Theatre in Scotland: 1294 to the Present', in P. H. Scott (ed.), *Scotland: A Concise Cultural History*, Edinburgh: Mainstream.

Cameron, E.A. (1996), 'The Scottish Highlands: From Congested District to Objective One', in T.M. Devine and R.J. Finlay (eds.), *Scotland in the 20th Century*, Edinburgh: Edinburgh University Press.

Cannadine, D. (1990), *The Decline and Fall of the British Aristocracy*, New Haven and London: Yale University Press.

Cant, B. (1993), *Footsteps and Witnesses: Lesbian and Gay Lifestories from Scotland*, Edinburgh: Polygon.

Cant, B. and Kelly, E. (1995a), *The Roads to Racial Equality: Challenging Racism and Developing Positive Action in the Scottish Voluntary Sector*, Edinburgh: Council for Voluntary Service.

Cant, B. and Kelly, E. (1995b), 'Why is There a Need for Racial Equality Activity in Scotland?', *Scottish Affairs*, Summer 1995, No. 12.

Caughie, J. (1982), 'Scottish Television: What Would It Look Like?', in C. McArthur (ed.), *Scottish Reels: Scotland in Cinema and Television*, London: British Film Institute.

Checkland, S. and O. (1984), *Industry and Ethos: Scotland 1832–1918*, London: Edward Arnold.

Clay, N. and Cowling, M. (1996), 'Small Firms and Bank Relations: A Study of Cultural Differences between English and Scottish Banks', *Omega*, Vol. 24 No. 1.

Commission on Local Government and the Scottish Parliament (1999), *Moving On: Local Government and the Scottish Parliament*, Edinburgh: The Stationery Office.

Committee on Standards and Privileges (2000), *Complaint against Mr John Maxton and Dr John Reid*, London: The Stationery Office.

Consultative Steering Group (1999), *Shaping Scotland's Parliament: Report of the Consultative Steering Group*, Edinburgh: The Stationery Office.

Cowling, M., Sugden, R. and Samuels, L. (1991), 'Small Firms and Scottish Clearing Banks', *Fraser of Allander Quarterly Economic Commentary*.

Crouch, C. (2000), *Coping with Post-Democracy*, London: Fabian Society.

Dalton and Hampton, K. (1995), *Scotland's Ethnic Minority Community 1991: A Census Summary*, Glasgow: Scottish Ethnic Minorities Research Unit, Glasgow Caledonian University.

Danson, M. and Gilmore, K. (2000), 'Devolution and the Political Economy of Scotland', in A. Wright (ed.), *Scotland: The Challenge of Devolution*, Aldershot: Ashgate.

Davie, G. (1961), *The Democratic Intellect: Scotland and her Universities in the Nineteenth Century*, Edinburgh: Edinburgh University Press.

Davies, H.T.O., Nutley, S.M. and Smith, P.C. (eds.) (2000), *What Works?: Evidence-based Policy and Practice in Public Services*, Bristol: Policy Press.

Deakins, D., Majmudar, M. and Paddison, A. (1995), *Ethnic Minority Enterprise Development in the West of Scotland*, Paisley: University of Paisley.

Deakins, D., Majmudar, M. and Paddison. A. (1997), 'Developing success strategies for ethnic minorities in business: evidence from Scotland', *New Community*, Vol. 23 No. 3.

Denver, D. and MacAllister, I. (1999), 'The Scottish Parliament Elections 1999: An Analysis of the Results', *Scottish Affairs*, Summer 1999, No. 28.

Department for Culture, Media and Sport (2001), *Creative Industries Mapping Document*, London: Department for Culture, Media and Sport.

Devine, T.M. (1975), *The Tobacco Lords: A Study of the Tobacco Merchants of Glasgow and their Trading Activities c. 1740–90*, Edinburgh: John Donald Publishers.

Devine, T.M. (1999), *The Scottish Nation 1700–2000*, London: Allen Lane.

Devine, T.M. (ed.) (2000), *Scotland's Shame: Bigotry and Sectarianism in Modern Scotland*, Edinburgh: Mainstream.

Devine, T.M. and McMillan J.F. (eds.) (1999), *Celebrating Columba: Irish-Scottish Connections 597–1997*, Edinburgh: John Donald.

Dickson, D. et al. (eds.) (2001), *Ireland and Scotland: Nation, Religion, Identity*, Dublin: Centre for Irish–Scottish Studies.

Dinan, W., Miller, D., and Schlesinger, P. (2000), Submission to Standards Committee Consultation on Lobbying the Scottish Parliament, Stirling Media Research Institute, December 2000. http://staff.stir.ac.uk/david.miller/Standards-submission.html.

Drucker, H. (ed.) (1982), *John P. Mackintosh on Scotland*, London: Longman.

Dunbar, R. (2001), 'Legislating for Diversity: Minorities in the New Scotland', in L. Farmer and S. Veitch (eds.), *The State of Scots Law: Law and Government after the Devolution Settlement*, Edinburgh: Butterworths.

Durham, M. (1991), *Sex and Politics: The Family Morality of the Thatcher Years*, London: Macmillan.

Edwards, O.D. (2001), 'Ireland and the Liddell Reconquest of Scotland', *Scottish Affairs*, Spring 2001, No. 35.

Enterprise and Lifelong Learning Committee (2002), *Interim Report of the Lifelong Learning Inquiry*, Scottish Parliament, March 2002.

Evans, D.T. (2001), 'Keep the Clause: Section 28 and the Politics of Sexuality in Scotland and the UK', *Soundings*, Summer/Autumn 2001, No. 18.

Exworthy, M. and Berney, L. (2000), 'What Counts and What Works?: Evaluating Policies to Tackle Health Inequalities', *Renewal: A Journal of Labour Politics*, Vol. 8, No. 4.

Fairley, J. (2001), 'Scotland's New Democracy: Opportunities for Rural Scotland', *Scottish Affairs*, Winter 2001, No. 34.

Farmer, L. (2001), 'Under the Shadow over Parliament House: The Strange Case of Legal Nationalism', in L. Farmer and S. Veitch (eds.), *The State of Scots Law: Law and Government after the Devolution Settlement*, Edinburgh: Butterworths.

Ford, P.J. (2000), 'Public Benefit Versus Charity: A Scottish Perspective', in C. Mitchell and S. Moody (eds.), *Foundations of Charity*, Oxford: Hart.

Fraser of Allander Institute (2001), *Promoting Business Start-ups: A New Strategic Formula*, Glasgow: Fraser of Allander Institute, University of Strathclyde.

Fry, M. (1987), *Patronage and Principle: A Political History of Modern Scotland*, Aberdeen: Aberdeen University Press.

Galbraith, R. (1995), *Without Quarter: A Biography of Tom Johnston*, Edinburgh: Mainstream.

Galloway, L. and Levie, J. (2002), *Global Entrepreneurship Monitor: Scotland 2001*, Glasgow: University of Strathclyde.

Genn, H. and Paterson A. (2001), *Paths to Justice Scotland*, Oxford: Hart.

Glendinning, M., MacInnes, R. and Mackechnie, A. (1996), *A History of Scottish Architecture: From the Renaissance to the Present Day*, Edinburgh: Edinburgh University Press.

Goss, S. (2000), 'Public Services: Can New Labour Make A Difference?', *Renewal: A Journal of Labour Politics*, Vol. 8, No. 4.

Grant, J. (1976), 'Introduction', in J. Grant (ed.), *Independence and Devolution: The Legal Implications for Scotland*, Edinburgh: W. Green and Sons.

Hampton, K. (1998), *Youth and Racism: Perceptions and Experiences of Young People in Glasgow*, Glasgow: Scottish Ethnic Minorities Research Unit, Glasgow Caledonian University.

Hampton, K. and Bain, J. (1995), *Poverty and Ethnic Minorities in Scotland: A Review of the Literature*, Glasgow: Scottish Ethnic Minorities Research Unit, Glasgow Caledonian University.

Hanham, H. J. (1969), *Scottish Nationalism*, London: Faber and Faber.

Harvie, C. (1977), *Scotland and Nationalism: Scottish Society and Politics 1707 to 1977*, London: Allen and Unwin.

Hassan, G. (2002), 'The Paradoxes of Scottish Labour: Devolution, Change and Conservatism', in G. Hassan and C. Warhurst (eds.), *Tomorrow's Scotland*, London: Lawrence and Wishart.

Hassan, G. and Warhurst, C. (eds.) (1999), *A Different Future: A Modernisers' Guide to Scotland*, Edinburgh: Centre for Scottish Public Policy/*The Big Issue in Scotland*.

Hassan, G. and Warhurst, C. (eds.) (2000), *The New Scottish Politics: The First Year of the Scottish Parliament and Beyond*, Edinburgh: The Stationery Office.

Hassan, G. and Warhurst, C. (eds.) (2002a), *Tomorrow's Scotland*, London: Lawrence and Wishart.

Hassan, G. and Warhurst, C. (2002b), 'Future Scotland: The Making of the New Social Democracy', in G. Hassan and C. Warhurst (eds.), *Tomorrow's Scotland*, London: Lawrence and Wishart.

Hastings, M. 1995, 'Animal Rights and Wrongs', *The Field*, June 1995.

Hawkins, J. (2001), *The Creative Economy*, London: Penguin Press.

Healey, J. et al. (2001), 'Public Services: Second Term, Last Chance', *Renewal: A Journal of Labour Politics*, Vol. 9, No. 2/3.

Hennessy, P. (2002), *The Secret State: Whitehall and the Cold War*, London: Allen Lane.

Herman, A. (2002), *The Scottish Enlightenment: The Scots Invention of the Modern World*, London: Fourth Estate.

Hobsbawm, E. (1994), *Age of Extremes: The Short Twentieth Century*, London: Michael Joseph.

Holland, P. (1995), *The Hunting of the Quango*, London: Adam Smith Institute.

Howson, A. (1993), 'No Gods and Precious Few Women: Gender and Cultural Identity in Scotland', *Scottish Affairs*, Winter 1993, No. 2.

Hutchison, D. (ed.) (1978), *Headlines: The Media in Scotland*, Edinburgh: Edinburgh University Student Publications Board.

Independent Committee of Inquiry into Scottish Funding (1999), *Student Finance: Fairness for the Future*, Edinburgh: The Stationery Office.

Innes, S. (2001), '"Quietly Thrilling": Women in the New Parliament', in E. Breitenbach and F. Mackay (eds.), *Women and Contemporary Scottish Politics*, Edinburgh: Polygon.

Jedrej, M.C. and Nuttall, M. (1995), 'Incomers and Locals: Metaphors and Reality in the Repopulation of Rural Scotland', *Scottish Affairs*, Winter 1995, No. 10.

Johnston, T. (1909), *Our Scots Noble Families*, reprinted Glendaruel: Argyll Publishing.

Jones, P. (1997), 'Scotland's Next Step', *Prospect*, April 1997.

Jones, P. (2001), 'The Euro Debate Goes On', *Scottish Banker*, December 2001.

Kay, H. (2000), *Women and Men in the Professions in Scotland*, Edinburgh:

Scottish Executive Central Research Unit.

Keep, E. (2000), *Upskilling Scotland*, Edinburgh: Centre for Scottish Public Policy in conjunction with Scottish Enterprise.

Kellas, J. (1989), *The Scottish Political System*, Cambridge: Cambridge University Press 4th edn.

Kelly, E. (1995), 'Sweeties from the Boys' Poke?': *An Examination of Women's Committees in Scottish Local Government*, unpublished MSc dissertation, University of Strathclyde.

Kelly, E. (1998), 'A New Dawn Shared by Scotland and Pakistan: Reflections on August 1997', *Scottish Affairs*, Spring 1998, No. 23.

Kelly, E. (1999), 'Stands Scotland Where It Did?: An Essay in Ethnicity and Internationalism', *Scottish Affairs*, Winter 1999, No. 26.

Kelly, E. (2000a), 'Racism and the Scottish Parliament', in G. Hassan and C. Warhurst (eds.), *The New Scottish Politics: The First Year of the Scottish Parliament and Beyond*, Edinburgh: The Stationery Office.

Kelly, E. (2000b), 'A Future for Multi-ethnic Scotland?: Evaluating the Parekh Report', *Multicultural Teaching*, Vol. 19, No. 1.

Kelly, E. (2002), 'Asylum Seekers and Politics in Scotland: August 2001', *Scottish Affairs*, Winter 2002, No. 38.

Kelman, J. (1989), *A Disaffection*, London: Secker and Warburg.

Kemp Commission (1997), *Head and Heart: The Report of the Commission on the Future of the Voluntary Sector in Scotland*, Edinburgh: SCVO.

Kendall, J. and Knapp, M. (1995), 'A Loose and Baggy Monster: Boundaries, Definitions, and Typologies', in J.D. Smith, C. Rochester, and R. Hedley (eds.), *An Introduction to the Voluntary Sector*, London: Routledge.

Kerevan, G. (2000) 'Glasgow: The Sick City', *Sunday Herald*, 12 March 2000.

Kerevan, G. (2001) 'The Power Game Threat to Glasgow', *The Scotsman*, 8 May 2001.

Kerevan, G. (2002) 'Into the West: The Challenges Ahead for Scotland's Largest City', *The Scotsman* Supplement, 30 April 2002.

Kerley Committee (2000), *Report of the Renewing Local Democracy Working Group*, Edinburgh: Scottish Executive.

Kernohan, R.D. (1999), 'Introduction: Questions of Identity', in R.D. Kernohan (ed.), *The Realm of Reform*, Edinburgh: Handsel Press.

Kirkpatrick, J. (2001), 'Change and Creative Futures', in M. Ivey (ed.), *Exploring the Interface between Education and the Creative Industries*, Dundee: University of Dundee.

Lally, P. and Baxter, N. (2000), *Lazarus Only Done It Once: The Story of My Lives*, London: HarperCollins.

Landry, Charles (2000), *The Creative City, A Toolkit for Urban Innovators*, London: Comedia/Earthscan.

Law, A. (1995), 'Wither the Armourers?: The Rise and Fall of Military Industry in Scotland', *Scottish Affairs*, Autumn 1995, No. 13.

Leadbeater, C. (1997), *The Rise of the Social Entrepreneur*, London: Demos.

Leadbeater, C. (1999), *Living On Thin Air: The New Economy*, London: Penguin.

Leech, M. (1999), 'Further Education: Further Education in Post-incorporation', in T.K. Bryce, G. and W.H. Humes (eds.), *Scottish Education*, Edinburgh: Edinburgh University Press.

Lees, S. (1993), *Sugar and Spice: Sexuality and Adolescent Girls*, Harmondsworth: Penguin.

Leicester, G. and Mackay, P. (1998), *Holistic Government: Options for a Devolved Scotland*, Edinburgh: Scottish Council Foundation.

Lenman, B. (1977), *An Economic History of Modern Scotland*, London: Batsford.

Levie, J., Brown, W. and Steele, L. (2002) *How Entrepreneurial are Strathcylde Alumni? An International Comparison*, paper to Fourth McGill Conference on International Entrepreneurship, University of Strathclyde.

Linklater, M. (1992), 'Foreword', in M. Linklater and R. Denniston (eds.), *Anatomy of Scotland*, Edinburgh: Chambers.

Lynch, M. (ed.) (2001), *The Oxford Companion to Scottish History*, Oxford: Oxford University Press.

Maan, B. (1992), *The New Scots: The Story of Asians in Scotland*, Edinburgh: John Donald.

MacDonald, K. (1994), *Scottish Football Quotations*, Edinburgh: Mainstream.

MacDuff, R. (2001), 'Legislating for Lobbyists', *Holyrood Magazine*, 2 July 2001.

MacInnes, J. (1992), 'The Press in Scotland', *Scottish Affairs*, Autumn 1992, No. 1.

MacInnes, J. (1993), 'The Broadcast Media in Scotland', *Scottish Affairs*, Winter 1993, No. 2.

MacKay, D., Cuthbert, J., Cuthbert, M., Dowds, G. and Balfour, A. (2001), *Scotland's Enterprise Deficit: What It Is and What Can Be Done*, Edinburgh: Policy Institute.

Mackay, F. (2001), *Love and Politics: Women Politicians and the Ethics of Care*, London: Continuum.

Mackay, F. and Bilton K. (eds.) (2000), *The Gender Audit 2000*, Edinburgh: Engender and Governance of Scotland Forum.

Mackay, F., Myers, F. and Brown, A. (2001), *Making a Difference? Women and the Scottish Parliament – A Preliminary Analysis*, paper presented at the Women and Parliaments seminar, Centre for the Advancement of Women in Politics, Queen's University Belfast, 26 October 2001.

MacKinnon, K. (1992), *An Aghaidh nan Creag/Despite Adversity: Gaelic's Twentieth Century Survival and Potential*, Inverness: Comun na Gaidhlig.

MacKinnon, K. (1993), *Occupational Class, Age and Gender in the Gaelic Speech-community*, Fifth International Conference on Minority Languages.

MacKinnon, K. (2001), 'Fàs no Bàs (Prosper or Perish): Prospects of Survival for Scottish Gaelic', in J. Kirk and D. O'Baoill (eds.), *Linguistic Politics: Language Politics for Northern Ireland, The Republic of Ireland and Scotland*, Belfast: Clo

Ollscoil na Banriona/Queen's University Press.

Mackintosh Commission (1999), *Commission on Local Government and the Scottish Parliament: Moving Forward: Local Government and the Scottish Parliament*, Edinburgh: The Stationery Office.

MacMillan, J. (2000), 'Scotland's Shame', in T.M. Devine (ed.), *Scotland's Shame?: Bigotry and Sectarianism in Modern Scotland*, Edinburgh: Mainstream.

MacPherson, M. (1985), 'Crofters and the Crofters Commission', in I. Evans and J. Hendry (eds.), *The Land for the People*, Blackford: Scottish Socialist Society.

Macwhirter, I. (2000), 'Scotland Year Zero: The First Year at Holyrood', in G. Hassan and C. Warhurst (eds.), *The New Scottish Politics: The First Year of the Scottish Parliament and Beyond*, Edinburgh: The Stationery Office.

McCrone, D. (1992), *Understanding Scotland: The Sociology of a Stateless Nation*, London: Routledge.

McCrone, D. (1996), 'We're A' Jock Tamson's Bairns: Social Class in Twentieth Century Scotland', in T.M. Devine and R.J. Finlay (eds.), *Scotland in the 20th Century*, Edinburgh: Edinburgh University Press.

McDowell, W.H. (1992), *The History of BBC Broadcasting 1923–1983*, Edinburgh: Edinburgh University Press.

McFarland, E. (1991), *Protestants First!*, Edinburgh: Edinburgh University Press.

McIvor, A. (1996) 'Gender Apartheid? Women in Scottish Society', in T.M. Devine and R.J. Findlay (eds.), *Scotland in the 20th Century*, Edinburgh: Edinburgh University Press.

McKay, J.R. (1999), 'Is the Kirk still Relevant?', in R.D. Kernohan (ed.), *Realm of Reform*, Edinburgh: Handsel Press.

McLeod, W. (1998), 'Scotland's Languages in Scotland's Parliament', *Scottish Affairs*, Summer 1998, No. 24.

McMillan, J. (1969), *Anatomy of Scotland*, London: Leslie Frewin.

McQuaid, R. (1999), 'The Local Economic Impact of the Scottish Parliament', in J. McCarthy and D. Newlands (eds.), *Governing Scotland: Problems and Prospects: The Economic Prospects of the Scottish Parliament*, Aldershot: Ashgate.

McQuaid, R.W. (2000), 'Edinburgh and Its Hinterland', unpublished paper.

McTernan, L. (2000), 'Beyond the Blethering Classes: Consulting and Involving Wider Society', in G. Hassan and C. Warhurst (eds.), *The New Scottish Politics: The First Year of the Scottish Parliament and Beyond*, Edinburgh: The Stationery Office.

Mehri, M. (2002), 'It Ain't What You Do, But The Way That You Do It', *Eastern Eye*, March 2002.

Miller, D., Dinan, W. and Schlesinger, P. (2001), Response to the Standards Committee Consultation Paper: Statutory Registration of Commercial

Lobbyists: June 2001, Stirling: Stirling Media Research Institute.

Mitchell, J. (1990), *Conservatives and the Union*, Edinburgh: Edinburgh University Press.

Mitchell, J. (2000), 'The Challenge to the Parties: Institutions, Ideas and Strategies', in G. Hassan and C. Warhurst (eds.), *The New Scottish Politics: The First Year of the Scottish Parliament and Beyond*, Edinburgh: The Stationery Office.

Mitchell, R. and Dorling, D. (2002), 'Poverty, Inequality and Social Inclusion in the New Scotland', in G. Hassan and C. Warhurst (eds.), *Tomorrow's Scotland*, London: Lawrence and Wishart.

Moore, C. and Booth, S. (1989), *Managing Competition: Meso-corporatism, Pluralism and the Negotiated Order in Scotland*, Oxford: Clarendon Press.

Moorhouse, B. (1989), '"We're Off to Wembley"': The History of a Scottish Event and the Sociology of Football Hooliganism', in D. McCrone, S. Kendrick and P. Straw (eds.), *The Making of Scotland: Nation, Culture and Social Change*, Edinburgh: Edinburgh University Press.

Mulgan, G. and Landry, L. (1995), *The Other Invisible Hand: Remaking Charity for the 21st Century*, London: Demos/Comedia.

Munro, C. (1999), 'The Parental Dimension in Scottish Education', in T.K.G. Bryce and W.H. Humes (eds.), *Scottish Education*, Edinburgh: Edinburgh University Press.

Munro, N. (2002), Interview with Jane W. Denholm and Deirdre Macleod, Edinburgh, 20 January 2002.

Murray, B. (1998), *The Old Firm in the New Age: Celtic and Rangers since the Souness Revolution*, Edinburgh: Mainstream.

Nairn, T. (1970), 'The Three Dreams of Scottish Nationalism', in K. Miller (ed.), *Memories of Modern Scotland*, London: Faber and Faber.

Nairn, T. (2000), *After Britain: New Labour and the Return of Scotland*, London: Granta.

Nairn, T. (2002), *Pariah: Misfortunes of the British Kingdom*, London: Verso.

NCVO (1998), 'Blurred Vision – Public Trust in Charities', *NCVO Research Quarterly*, No. 1.

Nelson, F. (2001), 'Is This Devolution or Just Duplication?', *The Times*, 26 June 2001.

Netto, G., Arshad, R., de Lima, P., Almeida Diniz, F., MacEwan, M., Patel, V., and Syed, R. (2001), *Audit of Research on Minority Ethnic Issues in Scotland from a 'Race' Perspective*, Edinburgh: Scottish Executive Central Research Unit.

Newton, M. (1999), *Bho Chluaidh gu Calasraid (From the Clyde to Callander)*, Stornoway: Acair.

O'Hagan, A. (2001), *The End of British Farming*, London: Profile/London Review of Books.

O'Neill, A. (2000), 'The European Convention and the Independence of the

Judiciary: The Scottish Experience', *Modern Law Review*, No. 63.

Otton, G. (2001), *Sexual Fascism: Sex in the Scottish Media*, Edinburgh: Ganymede Books.

Park, A. (2002), 'Scotland's Morals', in J. Curtice, D. McCrone, A. Park and L. Paterson (eds.), *New Scotland, New Society?*, Edinburgh: Polygon.

Parry, R. (1999), 'Quangos and the Structure of the Public Sector in Scotland', *Scottish Affairs*, Autumn 1999, No. 29.

Parry, R. (2000), 'The Civil Service and the Scottish Executive's Structure and Style', in G. Hassan, and C. Warhurst, (eds.), *The New Scottish Politics: The First Year of the Scottish Parliament and Beyond*, Edinburgh: The Stationery Office.

Parry, R. (2002), 'Leadership and the Scottish Governing Classes', in G. Hassan and C. Warhurst (eds.), *Tomorrow's Scotland*, London: Lawrence and Wishart.

Paterson, A., St J.N. Bates, T. and Poustie, M. (1999), *The Legal System of Scotland*, Edinburgh: W. Green and Sons, 4th edn.

Paterson, L. (1994), *The Autonomy of Modern Scotland*, Edinburgh: Edinburgh University Press.

Paterson, L. (1999), 'Why Should We Respect Civic Scotland?', in G. Hassan and C. Warhurst (eds.), *A Different Future: A Modernisers' Guide to Scotland*, Edinburgh: Centre for Scottish Public Policy/*The Big Issue in Scotland*.

Paterson, L. (2000a), 'Scottish Democracy and Scottish Utopias: The First Year of the Scottish Parliament', *Scottish Affairs*, Autumn 2000, No. 33.

Paterson, L. (2000b), *Crisis in the Classroom: The Exam Debacle and the Way Ahead for Scottish Education*, Edinburgh: Mainstream.

Paterson, L. (2000c), 'Salvation Through Education: The Changing Social Status of Scotland's Catholics', in T.M. Devine (ed.), *Scotland's Shame?: Bigotry and Sectarianism in Modern Scotland*, Edinburgh: Mainstream.

Paterson, L. (2002), 'Social capital and constitutional reform', in J. Curtice, D. McCrone, A. Park and L. Paterson (eds.), *New Scotland, New Society?*, Edinburgh: Edinburgh University Press.

Paterson, L., Brown, A., Curtice, J., Hinds, K., McCrone, D., Park, A., Sproston, K. and Surridge, P. (2001), *New Scotland, New Politics?*, Edinburgh: Polygon.

Paxman, J. (1990), *Friends in High Places: Who Runs Britain?*, London: Michael Joseph.

Peacock, A., Baird, G., Elliot, G., Havergal, G., Macdonald, D., Massie, A. and Murray-Watson, A. (2001), *Calling the Tune: A Critique of Arts Funding in Scotland*, Edinburgh: Policy Institute.

Pearson, K. (1999), 'The Independent Sector', in T.K.G. Bryce and W.H. Humes (eds.), *Scottish Education*, Edinburgh: Edinburgh University Press.

Peat, J. and Boyle, S. (1999), *An Illustrated Guide to the Scottish Economy*, London: Duckworth.

Perman, R. (2001), 'Regulation Rules OK', *Scottish Banker*, October 2001.

Pickard, W. (1999), 'The History of Scottish Education: 1980 to the Present

Day', in T.K.G. Bryce and W.H. Humes (eds.), *Scottish Education*, Edinburgh: Edinburgh University Press.

Putnam, R.D. (2001), *Bowling Alone: The Collapse and Revival of American Community*, New York: Simon and Schuster.

Quirk, B. (1999), 'Progress from Inertia: Forces of Conservatism in the Public Sector', in M. Taylor and J. Godfrey (eds.), *Forces of Conservatism*, London: Institute for Public Policy Research.

Rake, K. (2000), *Women's Incomes over the Lifetime*, London: Cabinet Office Women's Unit.

Renewing Local Democracy Working Group (2000), *Report of the Renewing Local Democracy Working Group*, Edinburgh: The Stationery Office.

Rice, G. and Johnstone, I. (2000), *Scotland's Global Opportunity: Seizing It or Losing It?*, Glasgow: University of Glasgow Business School.

Richardson, D. (1996), *Theorising Heterosexuality*, Milton Keynes: Open University.

Ritchie, I. (2001), Speech to Scottish Financial Enterprise, October 2001.

Royal Bank of Scotland (2001), *Update Scotland*, August 2001 www.royalbankofscotland.co.uk

Royle, T. (1992), 'Defence', in M. Linklater and R. Denniston (eds.), *Anatomy of Scotland*, Edinburgh: Chambers.

Sampson, A. (1962), *The Anatomy of Britain*, London: Hodder and Stoughton.

Sampson, A. (1982), *The Changing Anatomy of Britain*, London: Hodder and Stoughton.

Saville, R. (1996), Bank of Scotland: A History 1695–1995, Edinburgh: Edinburgh University Press.

Saxton, J. and Game, S. (2001), *Virtual Promise: Are Charities Making the Most of the Internet Revolution?*, London: Third Sector.

Schlesinger, P., Miller, D. and Dinan, W. (2001), *Open Scotland?: Journalists, Spin Doctors and Lobbyists*, Edinburgh: Polygon.

Scott, J. and Hughes, M. (1980), *The Anatomy of Scottish Capital*, London: Croom Helm.

Scottish Charity Law Review Commission (2001), *Charity Scotland: The Report of The Scottish Charity Law Review Commission*, Edinburgh: The Stationery Office.

Scottish Enterprise (2001), *Smart, Successful Scotland: Ambitions for the Enterprise Networks*, Edinburgh: The Stationery Office.

Scottish Enterprise (2002), *Generating Entrepreneurial Dynamism*, Edinburgh: The Stationery Office.

Scottish Executive (1999a), *Partnership for Scotland*, Edinburgh: The Stationery Office.

Scottish Executive (1999b), *The Development of a Policy on Architecture for Scotland*, Edinburgh: The Stationery Office.

Scottish Executive (2000a), *National Cultural Strategy*, Edinburgh: The

Stationery Office.

Scottish Executive (2000b), *Gaelic in Scotland Factsheet*, Edinburgh: The Stationery Office.

Scottish Executive (2000c), *Gaelic Television: A Dedicated Channel: Gaelic Broadcasting Task Force Report*, Edinburgh: The Stationery Office.

Scottish Executive (2000d), *Revitalising Gaelic/Ag Ath-Bheothachadh Gaidhlig*, Edinburgh: The Stationery Office.

Scottish Executive (2001a), *Men and Women in Scotland: A Statistical Profile*, Edinburgh: Scottish Executive National Statistics Publication.

Scottish Executive (2001b), *A Forward Strategy for Scottish Agriculture*, Edinburgh: The Stationery Office.

Scottish Executive (2001c), *Public Bodies: Proposals for Change*, Edinburgh: The Stationery Office.

Scottish Executive (2001d), *A Policy on Architecture for Scotland*, Edinburgh: The Stationery Office.

Scottish Executive (2001e), *Designing Places: Blueprint for Scotland*, Edinburgh: The Stationery Office.

Scottish Executive (2002), *Social Focus on Women and Men*, Edinburgh: Scottish Executive National Statistics Publication.

Scottish Landowners' Federation (2002), http://www.slf.org.uk/slf/join_ info.asp

Scottish Office (1997), *Scotland's Parliament*, Edinburgh: The Scottish Office, Cmnd. 3658.

Scottish Office (1998), *The Scottish Compact*, Edinburgh: HMSO, Cmnd. 4083.

Scottish Office Education and Industry Department (1992), *Upper Secondary Education in Scotland*, Edinburgh: HMSO.

Scottish Parliament (2002a), *Official Report*, 20 March 2002, Cols. 10413 and 10404.

Scottish Parliament (2002b), *Official Report of Justice 2 Committee*, 9 January 2002, Col. 840.

Scottish Trades Union Congress (1989), *Standing Commission on the Scottish Economy Final Report*, Glasgow: Scottish Trades Union Congress.

SCVO (2001a), *The Voluntary Sector and Devolution: Funding the Voluntary Sector*, York: Joseph Rowntree Foundation.

SCVO (2001b), *Factsheet*, 27 October 2001.

Shaw, E., Shaw, J. and Wilson, M. (2002), *Unsung Entrepreneurs: Entrepreneurship for Social Gain*, Durham: University of Durham.

Shaw, M., Dorling, D., Gordon, D. and Smith, G.D. (1999), *The Widening Gap: Health Inequalities and Policy in Britain*, Bristol: Policy Press.

Sillars, J. (1975), 'Land Ownership and Land Nationalisation', in G. Brown (ed.), *The Red Paper on Scotland*, Edinburgh: Edinburgh University Student Publications Board.

Slaven, A. with Kim, D.W. (1994), 'The Origins and Economic and Social Roles of Scottish Business Leaders, 1860–1960' in T.M. Devine (ed.), *Scottish*

*Elites*, Edinburgh: John Donald.

Smith, A. (1813), *Inquiry into the Nature and Causes of the Wealth of Nations*, Edinburgh: Ross and Co.

Smith, M. (1994), *Paper Lions: The Scottish Press and National Identity*, Edinburgh: Polygon.

Spaven, M. (1983), *Fortress Scotland: A Guide to the Military Presence*, London: Pluto.

Standards Committee (1999), *Official Report*, 10 November, Col. 233.

Standards Committee (2000), *Official Report*, 12 September, http://www.scottish. parliament.uk/official_report/cttee/stan-00/stp00-13.pdf.

Standards Committee (2001a), *Official Report*, 28 February, Col. 712.

Standards Committee (2001b), *Official Report*, 14 March, Col. 769.

Standards in Scotland's Schools etc. Act (2000): *Conduct of Sex Education in Scottish Schools*: www.scotland.gov.uk

Stewart, S. (ed.) (1998), *The Possible Scot: Making Healthy Public Policy*, Edinburgh: Scottish Council Foundation.

Stirling Media Research Institute (2001), *Evidence to the Standards Committee of the Scottish Parliament: February 28th 2001*, Stirling: Stirling Media Research Institute, http://www.scottish.parliament.uk/official_report/cttee/stan-01/stp01-03.pdf.

Storrar, W. (1999), 'Three Portraits of Scottish Calvinism', in R.D. Kernohan (ed.), *Realm of Reform*, Edinburgh: Handsel Press.

Surridge, P. (2002), 'Society and Democracy: The New Scotland', in J. Curtice, D. McCrone, A. Park and L. Paterson (eds.), *New Scotland, New Society?*, Edinburgh: Polygon.

Tawney, R. (1931), *Equality*, London: Allen and Unwin.

Thomas, H. (ed.) (1959), *The Establishment*, London: Anthony Blond.

Universities Scotland (2001), *Response to Departmental Review of Scottish Higher Education*, Edinburgh: Universities Scotland.

Vestri, P. and Fitzpatrick, S. (2000) 'Scotland's Councillors', *Scottish Affairs*, Autumn 2000, No.33.

Walden, G. (2000), *The New Elites: Making A Career in the Masses*, London: Faber and Faber.

Walker, G. (1990), '"There's not a team like the Glasgow Rangers": Football and Religious Identity in Scotland', in G. Walker and T. Gallacher (eds.), *Sermons and Battle Hymns: Protestant Popular Culture in Modern Scotland*, Edinburgh: Edinburgh University Press.

Walker, G. and Officer D. (1998), 'Scottish Unionism and the Ulster Question', in C.M. MacDonald (ed.), *Unionist Scotland 1800–1997*, Edinburgh: John Donald.

Walker, W.M. (1979), *Juteopolis: Dundee and Its Textile Workers 1885–1923*, Edinburgh: John Donald.

Wanless, D. (2002), *Securing Our Future Health: Taking a Long-Term View*,

London: HM Treasury.

Warhurst, C. and Thompson, P. (1999), 'Knowledge, Skills and Work in the Scottish Economy', in G. Hassan and C. Warhurst (eds.), *A Different Future: A Modernisers' Guide to Scotland*, Edinburgh: Centre for Scottish Public Policy/*The Big Issue in Scotland*.

Weir, S. and Beetham, D. (1998), *Political Power and Democratic Control in Britain*, London: Routledge.

Wightman, A. (1996), *Who Owns Scotland?*, Edinburgh: Canongate Books.

Wightman, A. (1999), *Scotland: Land and Power : The Agenda for Land Reform*, Edinburgh: Luath Press.

Wightman, A. (2002), unpublished data.

Williams, J. (1999), 'The Family and Gender Identities', *Sociology Review*, Vol. 8, No. 3.

Wilson, A. (2001), 'Statutory registration of commercial lobbyists', Letter to Dr Sam Jones, Standards Committee Clerk, The Scottish Parliament, 9 August 2001.

Winetrobe, B. (2001), *Realising the Vision: A Parliament with a Purpose: An Audit of the First Year of the Scottish Parliament*, London: Constitution Unit.

Withers, C.W.J. (1984), *Gaelic in Scotland: The Geographical History of a Language 1698–1984*, Edinburgh: John Donald.

Wright, D.F. (1999), 'The Kirk: National or Christian?', in R.D. Kernohan (ed.), *Realm of Reform*, Edinburgh: Handsel Press.

Wylie, A. (ed.) (1999), *Dynamic Security: Skills and Employability in Scotland*, Edinburgh: Scottish Council Foundation.

Young. A. (1999), 'Beyond Kvaerner: The Scottish Economy in a Globalising Age', in G. Hassan and C. Warhurst (eds.), *A Different Future: A Modernisers' Guide to Scotland*, Edinburgh: Centre for Scottish Public Policy/*The Big Issue in Scotland*.

Young, A. (2002), 'The Scottish Establishment: Old and New Elites', in G. Hassan and C. Warhurst (eds.), *Tomorrow's Scotland*, London: Lawrence and Wishart.

Young, M. (1958), *The Rise of the Meritocracy 1870–2033: An Essay on Education and Equality*, London: Thames and Hudson.

# CONTRIBUTORS

Keith Aitken is an award-winning journalist and broadcaster. His early career was on *The Scotsman*, where he was variously parliamentary correspondent, industrial editor, economics editor and chief leader-writer. Freelance since 1995, he is currently a columnist for *Scotland on Sunday* and the *Scottish Daily Express*, and has worked extensively as a radio writer and presenter. He is author of the history of the STUC, *The Bairns o' Adam*, published in 1997 by Polygon.

Neil Baxter is director and founder of Neil Baxter Associates, which he established in 1988 as a specialist marketing, architectural, design and interpretation consultancy. He has devised and coordinated exhibitions, arts and architectural events, as well as writing for *The Herald*, *Homes and Interiors Scotland* and the *Architects' Journal*. He was co-author with Pat Lally of Lazarus *Only Done It Once: The Story of My Lives* (HarperCollins 2000).

Joni Buchanan is a native Gaelic-speaker from Mangurstadh in the Uig area of Lewis. A history graduate of the University of Strathclyde, she wrote *Na Gaisgeach: the Lewis Land Struggle* and is working on a book about Hebridean women in the twentieth century. She has contributed extensively, in both English and Gaelic, to the *West Highland Free Press*.

Eleanor Burt is a lecturer in management and associate member of the Centre for Public and Policy and Management, University of St Andrews. Her research interests include voluntary sector policy and management, the role of voluntary organisations in the democratic arena, and new technologies and organisational innovation.

Angus Calder is a poet and historian working in Edinburgh and previously worked for 14 years as staff tutor in arts for the Open University in Scotland.

He is author of *Scotlands of the Mind* (2002), *Revolving Culture: Notes from the Scottish Republic* (1994), *The Myth of the Blitz* (1991), *Revolutionary Empire: The Rise of the English Speaking Empires* (1981) and *The People's War: Britain 1939–1945* (1969).

Peter Casebow is a director of Good Practice, the online publisher. He has worked in banking and technology and has particular research interests in government processes and communications.

Andrew Collier is a writer and broadcaster. His work covers a wide range of subjects, although he specialises in business, finance and technology. He contributes to a variety of publications including, *Business a.m.* and *Scottish Business Insider*, and also provides corporate writing services to blue chip companies.

Torcuil Crichton is Westminster Editor for the *Sunday Herald*. His journalism has taken him to all corners of Scotland and across continents, from Africa to Asia. A Gaelic-speaker from Lewis, he started writing with the *West Highland Free Press* and has worked for *The Herald* and *Scotland on Sunday*. He also spent five years with the BBC as a television director.

Andrew Cubie is a senior partner of Fyfe Ireland WS and a non-executive director of a number of public and private companies. He is chairman of the Court of Napier University, the Scottish Credit and Qualifications Framework, Quality Scotland Foundation, the WS Society Education Programme and a range of other bodies. He was chair of the Independent Committee of Inquiry into Student Finance.

Jane W. Denholm is a founding partner in the public policy practice Critical Thinking – a consultancy which specialises in UK education and training policy. She was formerly a deputy director of the Scottish Higher Education Funding Council and deputy director of the organisation now known as Universities Scotland. She was a policy adviser to the National Committee of Inquiry into Higher Education, and secretary to the Garrick Committee, drafting the report which became the basis of higher education policy in Scotland.

William Dinan is a research fellow at the Stirling Media Research Institute. His research interests include political communication, public opinion, interest-representation and public policy. He is currently engaged in an ESRC-funded project examining public relations in multinational corporations.

David T. Evans is a senior lecturer in the Department of Sociology, University of Glasgow. His teaching and research interests concern all aspects of human sexualities and all forms of music. Publications include *Sexual Citizenship: The Material Construction of Sexualities* (Routledge 1993) and *Phantasmagoria: A Sociology of Opera* (Ashgate 1999).

Margaret Ford is the chief executive of Good Practice, an online publisher, and is the chair of English Partnerships. A former chair of Lothian Health Board, she is also a non-executive director of Ofgem. She was active in the Scottish devolution campaign and served as a member of the Financial Issues Advisory Group (FIAG), the group that drew up the financial blueprint for the Scottish Parliament.

Juliette Garside is arts and media correspondent for the *Sunday Herald* and has been learning and writing about the Scottish media for two years. She moved to Scotland to join the paper after working for over three years as a writer for the London media trade press.

Gerry Hassan is director of Big Thinking. He has produced a range of books and publications in the last few years, including *Tomorrow's Scotland* (Lawrence and Wishart 2002), *The Almanac of Scottish Politics* (Politico's 2001), *The New Scottish Politics* (the Stationery Office 2000) and *A Different Future: A Modernisers' Guide to Scotland* (Centre for Scottish Public Policy/*The Big Issue in Scotland* 1999).

Christopher Hope joined *The Herald* in London as City Editor in January 2002, after spending three years in Scotland writing about business for *The Scotsman* and, latterly, for *Business a.m.* as chief business writer. Before that, he worked in trade magazines for *Construction News* and *PrintWeek*. He is married to Sarah with a son, Barnaby.

Elinor Kelly has published many articles about race and the criminal justice system, asylum, sectarianism and Pakistan. She is a member of research teams investigating the experience of minority ethnic pupils in Scottish schools, Strathclyde racist incidents and racism and justice in Europe.

George Kerevan is associate editor of *The Scotsman*. He was an elected member of Edinburgh District Council from 1984 till 1996, where he was convener of the Economic Development Committee and represented the council on COSLA. He was previously an academic at Napier University and is also a documentary television-maker.

Jonathan Levie is director of the Hunter Centre for Entrepreneurship at the University of Strathclyde, Glasgow, Scotland. He was formerly research fellow at the London Business School, visiting research fellow and part-time lecturer in management at Babson College, EC research fellow at INSEAD, France, and college lecturer at University College, Cork, Ireland. He has been researching and teaching entrepreneurship for 20 years and has managed both new and growing firms.

Stuart MacDonald is director of the Lighthouse, Scotland's Centre for Architecture, Design and the City – the largest private facility of its kind in Europe – since its inception in 1998. He was previously director of Glasgow's International Design Festival 1996, Glasgow UK City of Architecture and Design 1999 and senior education adviser for Strathclyde Region 1991–6. He is a teaching fellow at the University of Dundee, and visiting lecturer at Glasgow School of Art and the University of Glasgow 1997–2001. He is president of the Reseau European Art Nouveau Network and vice-chair of the Charles Rennie Mackintosh Society.

Fiona Mackay is a lecturer in politics at the University of Edinburgh. She teaches and writes in the broad area of women and politics, and gender and public policy. She is author of *Love and Politics: Women Politicians and the Ethics of Care* (Continuum 2001) and co-editor of *Women and Contemporary Scottish Politics* (Polygon 2001) and *The Changing Politics of Gender Equality in Britain* (Palgrave 2002).

Deirdre Macleod is a founding partner in the public policy practice Critical Thinking – a consultancy which specialises in UK education and training policy. Prior to that, for eight years she worked for the Scottish Higher Education Funding Council, where she was head of academic policy, and the Further Education Funding Council for England where she was principal policy analyst and head of longer-term strategy.

Joyce Macmillan is chief theatre critic of *The Scotsman*. She has also been a political and arts columnist for *The Herald*, theatre critic for *Scotland on Sunday* and Scottish theatre critic for *The Guardian*. She was chair of the Scottish Constitutional Commission, a member of the Consultative Steering Group on the procedures for the Scottish Parliament and is an executive member of the Helsinki Citizens' Assembly.

Iain Macwhirter is chief political correspondent of the *Sunday Herald*, Scottish political commentator for BBC Scotland and presenter of BBC Scotland's Holyrood programme. He has been a political correspondent for *The Scotsman*, *Scotland on Sunday*, *The Observer* and BBC Radio Scotland. He has contributed widely to the debate on Scottish devolution and UK politics and contributed to *The Scottish Government Yearbook* and *Scottish Affairs*.

Roddy Martine lives in Edinburgh and has written over 20 books on Scottish-interest subjects. He is a contributing editor to *Scotland Magazine*, writes for a wide range of UK newspapers and periodicals, and is a regular radio and occasional television broadcaster on Scottish social and current affairs topics.

David Miller is a member of the Stirling Media Research Institute. His most recent books are *Market Killing: What the Free Market Does and What Social Scientists Can Do About It* (Longman 2001, with Greg Philo) and *Open Scotland? Journalists, Spin Doctors and Lobbyists* (Polygon 2001, with Philip Schlesinger and Will Dinan).

Jonathan Northcroft has been a football writer for *The Sunday Times* since 1998, having previously worked for *Scotland on Sunday* and *The Herald*. He is married to Alice and has only recently started using the calendar to chart his age (31) rather than the years when World Cups occur.

Lindsay Paterson is professor of educational policy at Edinburgh University. He has written widely on Scottish politics, Scottish education and Scottish culture and is author of *Crisis in the Classroom: The Exam Debacle and the Way Ahead for Scottish Education* (Mainstream 2000), *A Diverse Assembly: The Debate on A Scottish Parliament* (Edinburgh University Press 1998) and *The Autonomy of Modern Scotland* (Polygon 1994).

George Rosie is a writer and broadcaster who has been editor of *The Observer* Scotland, a correspondent with *The Sunday Times* and a reporter for *Scottish Eye* and Channel 4. He has made a range of award-winning programmes, including *After Lockerbie* (1999), *Our Friends in the South* (1998), *Secret Scotland* (1997–8), *Independence Day* (1996), *Losing the Heid* (1991), *Scotching the Myth* (1990), *Selling Scotland* (1989) and *The Englishing of Scotland* (1988). He is author of a number of books and stage plays, including *It Had To Be You* (1994) and *Carlucco and the Queen of Hearts* (1991), winner of a Fringe First.

Trevor Royle is a well-known author and broadcaster specialising in the history of war and empire. As a journalist, he is associate editor of the *Sunday Herald* and is a regular commentator on defence matters and international affairs for the BBC. His most recent book is *Crimea: The Great Crimean War 1854–1856* (Little, Brown).

Philip Schlesinger is professor of film and media studies at the University of Stirling and director of Stirling Media Research Institute. He is also a visiting professor of media and communication at the University of Oslo. He has written widely on European and national identities, the media and politics, and his most recent book (with David Miller and William Dinan) is *Open Scotland? Journalists, Spin Doctors and Lobbyists* (Polygon 2001). He is a fellow of the Royal Society of Edinburgh.

Eleanor Shaw lectures at the Department of Marketing, University of Strathclyde, and was formerly director of the MA in Entrepreneurship at the Centre for Entrepreneurship, University of Durham Business School. She is a researcher in entrepreneurship and marketing and has published in both the UK and the USA. She has undertaken a variety of freelance research and consultancy projects for a number of support organisations throughout Scotland and the north-east of England.

Chris Spry was an NHS chief executive for nearly 25 years, in Glasgow (1996–2001), the South Thames region, Newcastle and Nottingham. He is a visiting professor at Glasgow University and was awarded the CBE in 2002. He is now a director of OD Partnerships, a network of NHS organisations.

John Taylor is dean of Caledonian Business School and a professor at Glasgow Caledonian University. His research focuses on the adoption and diffusion of new technologies by organisations and on their impact. His work is mainly on the public and voluntary sectors, where the use of new technologies has governance, organisational and democratic implications. He has published widely in both book and article form and is frequently invited as a conference speaker.

Graham Walker is a reader in politics at Queen's University, Belfast. He was born in Glasgow and has written on the history and contemporary politics of both Scotland and Northern Ireland. Among his books are a biography of *Thomas Johnston* (Manchester University Press 1988) and *Intimate Strangers: Political and Cultural Interaction Between Scotland and Ulster in Modern Times* (John Donald 1995).

Chris Warhurst is director of the Scottish Centre for Employment Research at the University of Strathclyde. His publications include *Tomorrow's Scotland* (Lawrence and Wishart 2002), *The New Scottish Politics* (The Stationery Office 2000), *A Different Future: A Modernisers' Guide to Scotland* (Centre for Scottish Public Policy/*The Big Issue in Scotland* 1999) and *Workplaces of the Future* (Macmillan 1998).

Andy Wightman is a writer and researcher specialising in landownership and land reform. A leading advocate of land reform, he is an honorary research fellow at the University of Aberdeen and research associate at the University of Edinburgh. He is the author of *Who Owns Scotland* (Canongate 1996) and *Scotland: Land and Power: The Agenda for Land Reform* (Luath 1999).

# INDEX

# INDEX